RIOT DIET

RIOT DIET

ONE MAN'S RADICAL RIDE THROUGH AMERICA IN CHAOS

RICHIE MCGINNISS

PIGEON PRESS
ISBN: 979-8-9917749-0-1
ISBN (eBook): 979-8-9917749-2-5

Cover Photo: E. Mackey @emackeycreates
Cover Design: Rodger Roundy, Karolina Matsiuk, and Richie McGinniss
Editorial Advisor: Anthony Swofford
Editorial Director: K.D. Sullivan
Copyeditors: Ginni Smith and Devin Murphy
Interior Designer: Maria Johnson
Title Page: Photo by Shelby Talcott, design by Rodger Roundy/Richie McGinniss
Illustrations: Richie McGinniss

This book, as well as any other Pigeon Press publications, may be purchased in bulk quantities at a discounted rate. Contact pigeon@pigeonpress.com for more information.

All people, locations, events, and situations are written to the best of the author's memory and according to thousands of videos recorded on his phone. The events described are true, although some names have been changed to protect the privacy of the people involved.

Pigeon Press
New York
pigeonpress.com

Published in the United States of America 1 2 3 4 5 6 7 8 9 10

CONTENTS

AUTHOR'S NOTE.

If you favor a political tribe at this particular moment in the third decade of the third millennium after Christ, that's your prerogative. That's not my cup of tea, because I'm here to toss it all into the Atlantic like those boys did in '73. 1773, that is.

Call me a fence-sitter, a Bernie Bro, Trumper, shitlib, or right-winger, whatever makes you feel better. But I was there, and the videos I recorded and then transcribed are gonna tell a tale.

You will find yourself shoulder to shoulder with the people that the press labeled as heroes or white supremacists, martyrs or pedos, nazis or terrorists, and plenty of goofy freaks too. My role was to roll the camera and ask questions rather than pass judgment on their actions, many of which were hilariously stupid or heroic or evil and reprehensible beyond comprehension. Oh wait, that's my judgement talking. My inner dialogue will be written for your understanding of why I aimed my camera where I did, why I asked this and that, why I laughed and definitely never cried, why I mostly ran but occasionally stood my ground. So let's call it opinion—that will be more fun. I will venture an odd opinion or jab. Mostly, I will give my perspective on the people desperate enough to take to the streets, and let you decide for yourself. I will give you personal background because it is impossible to separate my own tragedies from the American ones I saw up close.

I set out to write this book with a goal in mind. Rather than replaying a celebratory assertion of "here's why my side is right and yours is wrong," typical of the Trump era, this account will chronicle experience from on the ground, then relay to the reader how our little riot squad's recordings were interpreted and cannibalized by the greater media. The whole point of the exercise is to show what it was like to witness a reality that was distinctly different from the dueling narratives everyone watched and read. We were on the field. The armchair quarterbacks were not.

You might wonder where my coworkers were at times; the answer is, if they're not included while I was in the shit, it's because one can't locate much of anything wearing a gas mask or with pepper spray in your eyes, or several beers and hard seltzers deep with the umbrella gang, especially when you throw in some tobaccy or a doob.

The history I added for context won't fit on a Twitter timeline or a Facebook post. It's not in vogue to look in the rearview in this young country. I think it's important to survey our past from a bird's-eye view before we can map the road ahead. I studied history and a few languages, enough to know America may not be perfect, but she's the best we got.

I published this book meself with the help of a messenger Pigeon. The flightless Peacocks and Penguins are the ones who can't do much other than squawk about how Americans must choose a side, which is what got us into this mess in the first place. Besides, they think a screw got knocked loose around the time of my 69th pepper spray and 17th concussion on January 6. Fact check: False! The screw has been loose since I was born in 1989!

Working in a pickle is all I knew my whole life—in the middle between an older and younger brother, as a DC-media professional working on both sides of an increasingly hardened left and right, behind the bar between drunkards and the booze they wanted me to serve, testifying in the internationally prominent homicide trial that pitted my objective observations against the prosecution and defense, and as a video guy placing myself between the rioters/demonstrators and the cops. If you have a helmet that is accessible, I would advise you put it on before reading further. If not, proceed at your own peril.

We will at times speed to well over a hundred miles an hour, then jam on the brakes, and slow down to a crawl. This book is mine, and it will be yours, too. Let's ride.

PROLOGUE.

The rioters and cops volleyed munitions back and forth. One side threw pieces of brick and shot fireworks. The other blasted off 40 mm shells of tear gas and CO_2-propelled plastic balls. The police hid behind plexi-glass shields and armored vehicles on the broad boulevard in front of the courthouse. The rock-throwers attacked from makeshift barriers of black umbrellas and repurposed road signs in the middle of the town square. I strolled between the two groups in no-man's-land, wearing a gas mask, my hands in the air.

I kneeled while primitive and modern projectiles crossed above my hockey helmet. I scooped up fragments of rock from the ruined asphalt. I held each one in front of my cell phone camera so the viewers could get a sense of their size and weight. A particularly heavy apple-sized stone rolled past my running shoe through the overgrown grass on the edge of the park. It clanged off the historic trolley tracks that once ferried well-paid factory workers and municipal clerks to their jobs in downtown Kenosha.

I panned the camera to the police line. The street before them was strewn with trash: plastic bottles, shattered glass, expended shells, and fragments of building materials that came up short of their intended target.

A man ventured from behind the umbrellas and stepped into the frame. He wore a leather apron and green welding goggles, football

1

shoulder pads and a black bandana on his face. With leather motorcycle gloves, he gripped a wicker broom, the bottom engulfed in flames. I saw in him every American struggling to make it paycheck to paycheck, sweeping their swelling debt continuously down the road. With the vast field of rubbish scattered about, he gingerly brushed a few pieces of plastic to the curb. Each swing of the broom fanned the fire that burned its straw bristles. The more he swept, the more the wicker disintegrated into ash, until little was left but the burning tip of a spear.

The police halted the onslaught, and the rioters stopped their counterattack while everyone watched the surreal, fire-sweeping welder man in his fruitless effort to clean things up. A summer breeze drifted the thick cloud of tear gas and gunpowder away from the old courthouse, like a curtain revealing graffiti from the previous night of unrest.

Kenosha had come undone the night prior because of the police-involved shooting of Jacob Blake during a domestic violence call. According to police, Blake was armed with a knife. But minor details didn't matter much in the summer of 2020. The community knew a young black man had been shot by a cop, and the young man was likely to be paralyzed. The grisly video was right there on the internet for the whole world to see. It was time to paint the town.

Someone behind the camera interrupted the silence when they shouted, "That's metal as fuck!" On the white wall next to the boarded-up entrance, a hastily spray-painted message declared in black letters, "BE WATER, SPREAD FIRE."

I have been puzzled by the meaning behind this graffiti ever since. But I do know that over the next two nights, the fire spread. Among burning cars a few blocks from the courthouse, I interviewed a baby-faced young man. He wore a fanny pack med kit, and around his shoulders was slung an AR-15. That was thirteen minutes before the shooting. I was steps behind Baby Face when he was chased by a man who came directly from a mental hospital to the protest-turned-riot. He screamed, "Fuck you!" and lunged for the weapon.

During that summer society suffered a trauma, but one that was endured while eating delivery food watching HD television at home. This was absurd. How can one gather meaning from it? More technology only brought more stupidity to the discourse. It went like this:

POTUS-tweet. Newsman mad because Orange Man bad. Black-on-black crime in DC's Anacostia neighborhood? Eh. Political violence in DC? Click!

We all tuned in because there was a story to tell. Two narratives to be exact. Both were partially true.

⋮

The complete reality was a combination, plus some intergenerational tragedy that no one cared to discuss. In order to tell that story, I start from the only place I know, back when I had a broom that wasn't aflame, but one I thought was good and sturdy and could clean some things up. This book is not quite so tidy. It is a true story, linked by anecdotes from one perspective. It is not a final answer, but a window that may give you a glimpse into these crazy times.

How I ended up in that fiery but once majestic city called Kenosha began with what I guess you could call a career in DC media. This "career" could more accurately be described as a series of mundane tasks: serving Reverend Al Sharpton his Tea and Toast, lugging cameras and tripods and lights to the Capitol to record lengthy interviews with senators and congressmen, answering phones, making thousands of big videos small. But through these toils, I saw behind the veil of the billion-dollar algorithms and cable news scripts that determine how we think and see the world today. Spoiler alert: the tech companies and their news partners are making us all dumber and more divided. Put the phone down, pick the book up.

I am Sisyphus. We are all Sisyphus. America is the rock. Or is it the hill?

1. THE MOST RIOTOUS NEWSROOM IN DC

Trump and the "Fake News"

December 12, 2012, Morning: NBC Washington Bureau, Washington, DC

The state of a king shuts him from the world, yet the business of a king requires him to know it thoroughly.
—Thomas Paine, *Common Sense*

It was my third day working at NBC News' Washington Bureau. Hundreds of employees gathered in the newsroom to hear the president and CEO of NBC Universal at the time, Jeff Zucker, speak. He traveled from his fifty-first-floor Rockefeller Center office in NYC to address the NBC Network News employees in DC. Like most of the other recent college grads who worked at the network, I attained the job based more on nepotistic connections than requisite skills. When I was asked during my job interview what qualified me to work in the news biz, I responded, "I have always loved history, and it's basically history, but more recent." I would come to learn that the victors may be the authors of history, but a few big companies are the ones who master the news.

I sat next to the production assistant who was training me on how to run the phone at the crew desk. This was a bank of phones at the epicenter of the newsroom next to the assignment editor, who directed NBC's Washington coverage, and the desk editor, who coordinated the nuts and bolts: which cameramen went where, their hours/rates, and when to call in additional resources for breaking coverage. As the de facto secretaries of the Washington Buro (this is how busy news folks abbreviate "bureau"), our job was to field calls from cameramen asking us to order lunch, relay information between the on-camera talent and the assignment editor, assist old codgers who couldn't get MSNBC to play on their TV sets (usually the cable box wasn't plugged in), and everything in between. My position at the center of the entire DC operation would provide me with an excellent vantage point to learn how a cable news network works.

Despite my position at the literal center of it all, I was at the absolute bottom of NBC News' towering hierarchy. Zucker was at the very top.

The CEO president began with a speech about how NBC was adjusting to the times. The internet was quickly taking over the lion's share of the discourse. Traditional staples like NBC's *Today Show*, *Nightly News*, and every MSNBC program were losing market share by the day. Zucker proclaimed that MSNBC was no longer in the business of "breaking news." He made his mark as a producer on NBC's *Today Show*, later took over NBC Entertainment, and finally became the boss of the whole thing—NBC Universal. He was never a hard news guy like most of the political junkies in DC. His vision of entertaining rather than spending resources on original reporting was met with confused looks and muffled whispers. To me, it sounded like a barber was telling his employees that they were no longer in the business of cutting hair.

Seemingly unaware of the consternation in the room, Zucker continued on a spiel about how *Rock Center* was going to become NBC's millennial version of CBS's long-running program *60 Minutes*. He repeatedly stated that the new show, hosted by legendary newsreader Brian Williams, would use what's "trending" to inform editorial decisions, as if his institutional news apparatus could suddenly copy and paste #*trendingtopics* onto a rigid corporate editorial structure that was, by design, removed from the rapidly changing internet trends of the American youth. On this cold December morning, despite landing my dream job at a prestigious news organization a half year out of college, my millennial mind grew more pissed off each time Zucker uttered the word "trending." It seemed he thought this one word would be the key to unlocking a gateway between overpaid NBC executives and the disenchanted youths they so desperately needed to save their bloated and failing news operation.

Even after taking a paid gig at NBC, I had to continue my second job as a bartender to supplement my twelve-dollar-per-hour wage. This supported what I had seen living in the New York metropolitan area and then DC: the bigshots were living large while our troops overseas were getting paid peanuts, many maimed or killed under false pretenses, and while my fellow millennials struggled to find a livable wage at home. Obama won reelection a month before I started. I canvased for his first campaign in northern Virginia in 2008, studying his policy proposals, his promises, his impassioned speeches, so I could properly articulate them to curious voters when I knocked on their door. I was an eighteen-year-old idealist, proud for playing my role in turning Virginia blue for the first presidential election since 1964. But after voting for him a second time, I was beginning to see that despite a second term, Obama was doing little to inspire "Hope" around the country, or "Change" anything about the way things were run in DC.

While campaigning to potential voters in Virginia on Obama's behalf, I recited the words from his July 2008 *Washington Post* op-ed that promised to pull the troops out of Iraq, "That is why, on my first day in office, I would give the military a new mission: ending this war." Yet by the end of 2012, his admin was still perpetuating the two forever wars in Iraq and Afghanistan that were initiated by Bush. Obama also bailed out the banks. The '08 financial cataclysm was due in part to Bill Clinton's repeal of the 1933 Glass-Steagall Act, a Democrat continuation of Republican deregulation that opened the flood gates to a complicated leveraged gambling spree known as Wall Street speculation. This ended disastrously at the end of Bush's second term when the entire global financial system staggered toward collapse.

While the American bourgeoise were defaulting on their predatory loans, kids my age were still dying every day in oil-rich faraway deserts. Obama was drone-striking brown people and then smooth talking through press conferences, with the press lapping it up like puppy dogs. Zucker seemed to be spouting the same abstract hogwash that Obama used to get elected, and my face was growing hot. Six months earlier, my dad had been diagnosed with melanoma, and I didn't know whether he would live to see 2013.

When Zucker opened the room to questions, perhaps what I did next had to do with a recklessness associated with the prospect of losing my dad, or anger from the realization that the country I grew up in was far more corrupt than I was led to believe. Either way, as with other consequential moments in my life, I do not recall a thought process. It was as if an electric shock caused my brain circuitry to shoot my hand in the air. Zucker called on me. My memory is cloudy on exactly how my question was worded—obscured by the tear-in-the-eye embarrassment I experienced when I saw hundreds of NBC employees staring angrily in my direction—but here is an undoubtedly more eloquent version of what I asked. "You said that you will use what's trending to inform the stories on *Rock Center*. According to Twitter, the current trending topics are cats flying through the air and Instagram removing image forwarding. If NBC has long been a bastion of editorial judgment, how will you use topics like this to tell Americans the important stories they need to hear?"

I recall Zucker's answer repeatedly used the term "trending" and other ambiguous C-suite buzzwords that were about as clear as mud. I barely registered the nonanswer, because the glares and mutters of my colleagues were now directed toward me. A wave of self-consciousness washed over me as it sank in. They were probably grumbling about how I was a cocky and insolent newbie trying to rock their boat. The only guy who came up to me after and said he thought my question was hilarious was a chill media traffic controller named Ralph. He confirmed that most of my new colleagues thought I was a piece of shit after that; they were not wrong. The testosterone coursing through my young veins provided a misplaced idea that I actually knew something, which I did not. But time would prove that the instincts behind my challenging question were right too.

I got back to the dingy row house that I shared with four other room-mates and immediately called my parents for an update on my first week. "Yeah, well, I think I'm gonna get fired."

Luckily, I avoided getting axed, although I sensed a general dislike from my coworkers over the following months. During this same time period, Jeff Zucker took a new job as the president of CNN. General Electric completed the sale of 100 percent of NBC Universal to the massive telecom provider, Comcast. *Rock Center* was canceled due to terrible ratings. The newsman Brian Williams, an idol of mine, had a direct legacy from his mentor Tom Brokaw back to Brokaw's close friend Walter Cronkite, widely regarded as the greatest anchor of all time. When Cronkite was the face of network television, there were only three channels. Ninety percent of Americans tuned into the nightly news for information on the events of the day. As the information age superseded the television era, the overwhelming majority of Americans began consuming their news online. Zucker was right about that.

August 25, 2015, 5:30 PM PST: Baja, Mexico

> The more men have to lose, the less
> willing they are to venture.
> —Thomas Paine, *Common Sense*

The *federales* refused to accept the fact that I drank all of the empty Tecates. They counted each one before tossing the empties onto the side of the dusty highway along with most of our other belongings—the wetsuit I'd borrowed from my older brother, surfboards also borrowed from my brother, my dad's antiseizure meds, even some leftover tacos from our favorite spot, El Flamazo. With each additional can they discovered crumpled under the back seat, El Sargento looked at me with increasing incredulity, "*Once...doce...trece...catorce?*"

The *policia* were known for shaking down gringos in this stretch of Carretera Federal 3. We took the inland route to bypass the much busier port of entry at Tijuana, but this turned out to be a mistake. These were not the *policia*—they were the big boys—and I made the even more grave mistake of trying to offer them dinero using the gutter Spanish I'd picked up surfing in every country in Central America except Honduras and Belize, and working with a bunch of Guatemalans behind the bar of a Mexican joint in Dupont Circle in DC. My side job of bartending became my primary source of income, and I ripped through Tecates as easily as an eighteen-wheel-truck driver burned diesel.

My dad was the one driving, and they were convinced that he was drunk too. He told them that he was a doctor and he was totally sober. The language he was using usually came out as a combination of French, which he spoke fluently, English, and a sprinkle of Spanish, which he did not speak beyond about fifty words. What he did not include was that he *used to be* a doctor but could no longer perform his duties because of his medical condition. That would have explained why one of his eyelids was drooping, but he had neither the vocabulary nor the amenability to admit it. A fiercely independent man, my dad refused to give up his driver's license and rode plenty of waves that morning. Even if he could no longer operate with a scalpel, he was still the best driver I knew and surfed well enough to enjoy the glide.

My frayed khaki pant-shorts were filthy, and my salty mop for hair certainly didn't help our case. I looked like one of those dirty California hippies who regularly ran dope, over-the-counter benzos, and whatever else they could get their hands on through this less-traveled path. They finally let us off in spite of my failed bribe because my dad walked in a perfectly straight line.

Bumping along the rugged landscape with the sun dipped behind the Sierra Juarez Mountains, I was on the downhill side of my beer buzz and had the distinct feeling that my life was in a rut. I was imminently crossing the border into harsh reality rather than to the land of opportunity.

My only solace was the memory of the reeling cobalt waves we'd surfed with my older brother at a high-speed right-hander known as San Miguel, sixty miles south of the border. My older brother drove his own truck home so he could leave early for work at a medical clinic. My dad and I relished the last waves before my month-long sojourn came to a close.

I had been sleeping on my brother's couch for three weeks. Before our daily surfs each morning, my dad would come over from the nearby Econo Lodge with stale mini bagels as his way of helping me without giving me money outright. Before our Baja trip, my brother's girlfriend finally broke the news that I had overstayed my welcome and it was time to head home.

I was one year out from finishing up at NBC as a contracted employee. Toward the end of my time there, I passed up an eighty-thousand-dollar salary plus equity as an Arabic translator for an NYC startup company that sold its breaking-news data to hedge funds and large banks. They wanted me to run their new Middle East division with my former Georgetown Arabic classmate. She was a straight-A student. I was not. When I turned down the offer, the head of the news division told me I was making "the biggest mistake of your life."

"You don't know me," I replied, the stubborn Mick Wop that I am. Then I walked through the immaculate open floor plan of the office. The neoindustrial design raised the ceiling to expose Chinese-manufactured light fixtures and air ducts, whose cheapness was made a mockery by the well-paid employees below. I felt good about telling that hoity-toity news guy to kick rocks.

I walked a different and rockier path after my contract ran out at NBC. I left with no job and started from scratch as a freelance video producer. I wanted to learn how to pound nails before I claimed to know how to architect a house. Every month was a race to find an extra bar shift or a new gig to make rent—producing videos for private schools or private clubs, shitty little montages for the sons and daughters of Beltway bigwigs. The most tangible by-product of my toils was the vomit that our customers would spew on the front door of the bar where I worked.

When we got back to Encinitas, my dad and I walked into a fish restaurant lit by blue LED light strips and yellow electric candles that flickered artificially. Before I sat in a dark plastic chair that made a poor effort at mimicking a mahogany antique, I dusted off my pant-shorts.

I'd purchased the shorts—khaki pants before the previous owner cut them at the knee—from a thrift store in Austin, Texas. My surfing buddy Jeff and I stopped there on our drive from the east coast to the west coast to visit my younger brother, who was in graduate school for mechanical engineering at University of Texas. I also needed the cheap shorts because, during the first night of the cross-country trip, I had less than $500 in my bank account and the bag with all my belongings flew out of the truck bed somewhere between West Virginia and Richmond. Fortunately, the expensive drone I spent my savings on and the decent laptop where I could edit my footage were stored inside the cab.

My brothers were on their way to illustrious careers, one as a doctor and the other an engineer, while I was effectively an unemployed bum who owned one half of a pair of pants. But I did have the gear with which I could produce a stunning reel, in search of a more stable video-editing job.

My dad thankfully offered to pay the check. As he signed the bill, I pushed his generosity a bit further and asked for some extra cash to pay rent on the open room in a house with four former roommates in Northwest DC.

"Go kick rocks, kid."

I felt like a fucking idiot for passing up that cushy job.

My dad's rejection distilled to desperation for a living wage; the next day I created a dazzling combination of aerials I filmed with my drone zooming across the diverse landscape of the United States. I received an email requesting an interview for a job at a new digital news show in northern Virginia forty-five miles from DC. My return to the city of feds brought some hope that my stalled career was about to kick back into high gear.

The video editor job I was applying for would nearly triple the $26,000 I made working at NBC. All I knew about the host of the show that I was applying to work for was that he was an unnamed, but well-known news personality.

I toured the palatial studio in northern Virginia. The show would be anchored behind an exact replica of the oak and mahogany Resolute Desk, which had sat in the Oval Office of the White House since 1880. The program was apparently all online, though the production quality—from the nine-foot jib crane camera to the oil paintings of the Founding Fathers on the wall—was more sophisticated than the plexiglass desks and digital backgrounds that characterized prime-time cable news sets. I sat down with the showrunner, David Padrusch, and the show's executive producer, Doug Goodstein, who'd previously run the operation for Howard Stern's TV show. I was familiar with Howard Stern because my preteen friends and I would turn it on after the parents had gone to bed. This was during the time before the uncensored internet ended up in almost every American home, and the show was our only place to learn about the world of boobs. When the bosses finally told me the host of the show was Mark Levin, I had no clue who he was. But I was desperate for the job, so I reacted with reverence and awe.

I looked up Levin after the interview and realized that my sheltered coastal upbringing kept me from knowing who "The Great One" was. I knew the details of the fall of the Ottoman Empire and the Balfour Declaration, the intricacies of how a White House Daily Briefing was conducted, but I never heard of this hero of the political right. He was directly behind Rush Limbaugh and tied with Sean Hannity as the second biggest radio personality in the U S of A. Mark Levin was well known among the people living in the small towns I drove through across the country. This revelation made clear that I was a privileged young man-child who traveled across five continents but had no clue how the other half of America thought.

I got the job. The shameful truth was I was most relieved by the fact that I wouldn't have to move back home, where I would be forced to watch my dad wither away.

December 2016, 8:30 AM EST: *Daily Caller* HQ, 17th and K Streets, NW Washington, DC

Immediate necessities make many things convenient,
which if continued would grow into oppressions.
Expedience and right are different things.
—Thomas Paine, *Common Sense*

Three different cuts and twenty-eight fresh stitches were still bleeding on my face as I entered the *Daily Caller* offices for the first time. The desks were scattered with various talismans: football helmets, Hillary Clinton dolls, cutouts of Trump, and a signed copy of the Jerry Sandusky book *Touched*. TVs played MSNBC, CNN, and Fox News, all running breathless coverage of Trump's shocking victory with the volume turned off. The reporters in the *Caller* newsroom, mostly in their twenties and far younger than the team at the show where I previously worked, *LevinTV*, were screaming across their desks. They were engrossed in some debate

I was not privy to because they ceased their chatter when I came close enough for them to see my face, gawking with amusement at my wounds as I walked through to the CEO's office.

I had sustained the injury during a men's league hockey game the night before. A heavyset man from the opposing team smashed his shoulder into my face in a chaotic scrum in front of the net. I didn't leave the hospital until 3:00 a.m.

I was here now inside of a ragtag proto-conservative media outlet because I wanted to become the architect of a video operation rather than a pounder of nails. I had been working as a video editor at one of the first all-online news programs hosted by conservative fire-breather Mark Levin. It was a well-paying, easy gig, but I served as nothing more than a cog in a machine; I was a cutter of promos and a creator of Monty Python–style animated cold-open intros to the show. The job I was applying for would pay 30 percent less and required at least twice as much work, but I wanted an opportunity to build something from the ground up.

My old bartending buddy Christian Datoc worked at *Daily Caller*. In the months before Donald Trump's 2016 win, I'd watched Christian's "Locker Room Toc" Facebook show garner hundreds of thousands of views, which meant many things to many people; to me, those numbers meant the possibility of monetizing a skill I'd developed—creating news videos for an internet audience rather than the captive cable news viewer. *Daily Caller* videos were poorly produced from a technical standpoint, and I knew my expertise could improve the quality of their content. My time at Levin gave me the blueprint on how to produce a professional show and a catchy promo for social media. Christian arranged an interview for me with Vince Coglianese, then the editor-in-chief of the website, as well as Neil Patel, the CEO and founder of *Daily Caller*. When I contacted Christian at 12:00 a.m. from the hospital, he insisted I still come in for the interview despite my wounds. "They're gonna love it," he said. The interview was supposed to be for a reporter position, but I knew what I really wanted.

Heavily concussed and running on a few hours of sleep, with blood still dripping from my face, I told the CEO that I didn't want a reporter job. Instead, I wanted to leapfrog the popular front page of the website and Facebook presence into a video news network.

May 8, 2017, 8:45 AM EST: 17th and K Streets, NW Washington, DC

There is something noble and generous in
an instant of clamor and confusion.
—Thomas Paine, *Common Sense*

When I showed up to my first day at work for the new company, I decided on a shirt and tie. Typically, I was the most underdressed person everywhere I went. But I figured that my proposal to create a news network for my future employer was so ambitious that I had to look the part. The moment I showed up to *Daily Caller*, I realized this was not like NBC or Levin. Rather than focusing on my facial wounds this time, every eye in the newsroom fixated on the purple paisley tie, which suggested that I had violated some sacred credo. Most of the men were wearing a variety of casual golf polos that were as comfortable as a pajama shirt, but still had a collar. The women were a mixed bag of jeans and T-shirts with a few dresses that looked even more comfortable than pajamas. This was not the buttoned-up conservative outlet that I'd expected.

I walked into my new office overlooking 17th Street just north of the White House. There was a man sitting down, perhaps a few years my junior but emanating the jovial innocence of a college kid. He asked me immediately, "Hey, are you my new boss?"

I will call him Bunker. The first thing he did after I sat down was head to the office kitchen and return with a beverage that looked like cola. When he sat at the only other desk stationed in our small offshoot of the newsroom, I was overcome with the scent of vodka. The smell rushed me back to when I spent weekends knocking on doors as a volunteer for Barack Obama's 2008 campaign then slugging Burnett's blueberry vodka in my dorm with my hockey buddies. We guzzled the cheap swill to get a proper buzz before we paid an exorbitant rate for more booze out on the town. The confusion after the 2008 financial crisis bore resemblance to the languishing that characterized the early months of the Trump presidency, as if the whole of America's alleged leaders were not the steady rocks we'd thought.

What turned out to be Bunker's drink of choice, Stoli Blueberry, was slightly classier than our favorite college vodka. But it had the same cheap fake smell that masked the terrible taste of reality, which was too hard to swallow for anyone who hoped for a sweeter world than the one in which we lived.

As I navigated through my first day in the newsroom, I met various colleagues who came into our small office for introductions while I filled out the paperwork for the company's health insurance. I was psyched about the variety of nutty characters I met, as well as the health insurance, because I had been without it for over two years. My only doctor visits were for stitches or staples, which usually cost less than the deductible on any affordable insurance anyway. Bunker stepped out to refill his glass two more times, then took a lunch break that lasted from 1:00 to 2:30 p.m.

My friend Christian ran in. He was a politics reporter, and he looked perturbed by the empty seat next to me. "Where's Bunker?" Bunker staggered back in.

"Dude, are you running the White House briefing? Did you miss it again? This happens every day. Sean [Spicer] has been talking for ten minutes, and it's not streaming on Facebook yet!"

Bunker fumbled with his laptop to get the briefing up as I sat there absorbing the scene. Bunker had the thousand-yard stare of a man who wasn't going to remember what he was looking at the next day. The entire Washington press corps was freaking out over the antics of Trump's early administration and, for different reasons, so was I.

My dad's fight with cancer lasted five years even though the docs only gave him five months. Being an ER doctor himself, my dad knew that there was no waking up from this nightmare. On my third day at *Daily Caller*, my dad's sixty-eighth birthday, I received a call from my younger brother at around 1:00 p.m. "Richie, I just took Dad to the hospital. He had another seizure. This time he was even more confused than normal."

October 13, 1928, Afternoon: Quantico, Virginia

The general and his men sat on recycled railroad steel atop concrete that they had poured when they carved the stadium out of the valley wall in the forest. After World War I, the Marines returned from the ashes of the Old World. A grassroots effort employed everyone from private on up to the youngest major general in the armed forces named Smedley Butler. They rolled up their sleeves to convert Quantico, Virginia, from a frontier camp to a permanent home for the Marines. Butler was the commander of the base and an integral part of his vision for the conditioning of a modern fighting force included building a stadium for the Quantico football team. In Butler's "Old Gimlet Eyes," as he was nicknamed by his men, the brutal nature of the uniquely American sport of football was the perfect way to keep the Jarheads disciplined, relatively sober, and in good physical shape. He knew a thing or two about war readiness. At this time, Butler was the most decorated US Marine in history, having earned two medals of honor while fighting overseas wars on behalf of the blooming American empire.

On this particular Saturday in the fall of 1928, his men looked anything but ready for battle. The Quantico squad was getting routed in a practice game against Navy's eleven men. At the sound of the halftime whistle, the score was 42-0. Butler had just returned from fighting alongside the China Marines during the bloody chaos of the Communist Revolution that began in 1927 and lasted until 1949. He was more than upset by the spiritless effort his men were displaying on the field. According to Leatherneck lore, the Navy band was playing "Anchors Aweigh" when their drummer kicked the Marine mascot, a bulldog named Jiggs. General Butler, who'd signed the dog's enlistment papers, sounded a battle cry that rang out across the concrete and iron stands, "Chaaaarge!"

The Marines stormed the field, and a proper riot broke out. As shirts were torn and a few jaws were broken in the melee, the general himself ended up with a split lip. The playing of "The Star-Spangled Banner" was the only thing that finally brought the rabble-rousing football fighters to attention. It took sixteen choruses before the melee finally calmed down.

A telegram from the War Department commanded, "General Smedley Butler, you are hereby requested to institute an immediate de-emphasization of football and similar body contact sports." The general took the reprimand in stride, penning a letter to a friend, "It was almost worth it, watching a charging squad of Marines in action."

After his departure from the Corps, Smedley Butler evolved into a populist public figure. In May of 1932, the country was in the throes of the Great Depression. Seventeen thousand veterans traveled to DC for an occupied protest called "The Bonus March." They settled into ramshackle huts and tents in Southeast DC and refused to leave until they received early delivery of cash bonuses that the federal government had promised to those who served in World War I but did not agree to pay until 1945. Many of the picketing vets had no home to return to anyway. Two months later, the occupied protest still had no resolution on Capitol Hill.

Smedley Butler visited this "Bonus Army," at their camp in Southeast DC. The headline of *The New York Times* on July 20, 1932, read "Gen. Butler Urges Bonus Army to Stick/Ex-Marine Officer Makes Fiery Address to Veterans in Camp at Anacostia." The article went on, "With a 'damn' or a 'hell' in every few words, General Butler evoked tremendous applause when he mounted an improvised stand on the wide and now arid Anacostia flats, where about sixteen thousand bonus marchers are quartered.

"'If you want to go home and haven't the courage to stick it out here, then go on home,' he shouted. 'But the rest of you hang on. As soon as you pull up your camp flag this thing will evaporate into thin air.'"

Days later, the Senate rejected the bill that would have awarded the veterans their much-needed cash. A military force led by General MacArthur assembled on the ellipse beneath the Washington Monument. His aide, future President Dwight Eisenhower, relayed orders as they began their march to the Bonus Army's camp. Two hundred cavalrymen led the charge under the command of the soon-to-be-legendary General George Patton while four hundred infantry, tanks, and armored trucks followed in their wake. They launched tear gas and clubbed those who stood their ground, then burned the camp to the

cinders. The Bonus Army was no more. It was as if it evaporated into thin air.

Once the tear gas and flames settled, reports of the brutal
crackdown appalled the American public. Republican President
Herbert Hoover was smoked in his reelection bid against Franklin
Delano Roosevelt, which signaled that America's lower classes
were suffering and voted accordingly.

Butler wrote in his book *War Is a Racket*:

A racket is best described, I believe, as something that is
not what it seems to the majority of people. Only a small
"inside" group knows what it is about. It is conducted
for the benefit of the very few, at the expense of the very
many. Out of war a few people make huge fortunes.

March 28, 2018, 6:00 AM EST: Quantico, Virginia

Perhaps the sentiments contained in the following
pages, are not yet sufficiently fashionable to procure
them general Favor; a long Habit of not thinking
a Thing wrong, gives it a superficial appearance
of being right, and raises at first a formidable
outcry in defence of Custom. But the Tumult soon
subsides. Time makes more Converts than Reason.
                    —Thomas Paine, *Common Sense*

We drove out of Washington, DC, toward Marine Corps Base Quantico,
through the hollow between moonlight and sunrise. The low clouds lingering from a passing storm seemed to dim everything further, including
our moods. I was with Ford, the unfortunate host of the new show. We
were groggy and a bit apprehensive, unlike our Marine boss, Geoff, in
the car behind us. It was just as well he'd ridden in a separate vehicle,
presumably full of piss and vinegar, as he tended to be during the earliest
hours in the newsroom of the company where we worked, *Daily Caller*.
The youngster staff would slink into the office hours after he arrived,
unable to escape his denim-blue-eyed gaze served up with a spicy quip

about how he lifted heavy weights, biked eight miles to the office, edited four stories, and had two meetings before they even bothered to show up. As the boss who commanded the entire news operation, his early-bird chirps were a projection of the discipline he picked up during his days in the Corps. In fact, Geoff was on his second tour in Iraq while the sheepish new hires were still crapping in their hands and rubbing it on their noses.

My relationship with Geoff was that of a scrappy younger brother who had never been to war. When I received the email informing the staff that Geoff was moving from running *Daily Caller* News Foundation to leading *Daily Caller* for profit, I had no thought process—less than six months out from losing my father, sandwiched in between two brothers, especially when battling an older, more seasoned, bigger, and stronger opponent. After I finished reading the staff-wide announcement, I snuck up behind Geoff's chair at the head of the DCNF newsroom and put him in a surprise attack chokehold. To the horror of the recently graduated news fellows, Geoff refused to go down quietly. He fell out of his chair and wrestled me to the floor, at which point, Geoff's inner Jarhead or inner Pennsylvania redneck—or a combination of both—kicked in. He started prying my fingers in a direction that might cause them to snap. I finally relinquished my hold because I needed the full function of my fingers to edit video all day. The entire News Foundation was appalled, but I had succeeded in showing Geoff that if he would oversee my little video operation, he should know we were not normal folks. When Geoff took over as the editor-in-chief of *Daily Caller* proper, he was sure to take a desk that allowed him to sit with his back to the wall.

We were up early to film a few episodes of a new series, *Reporter vs Marine*, which was created with a simple concept in mind: Reporters try to perform tasks required of the average Marine and fail miserably because they are about as battle-hardened as the silk ties that DC's professional class wear to work every day. The footage of their spectacular failure would center-stage the white-collared reporters' inability to succeed in the old-fashioned world, where physical strength was valued as an essential attribute for any man who wanted to put food on the table for his family.

During the meeting where we brainstormed the show's premise, both our CEO Neil and Geoff were gleefully confident that the website's blue-collar audience would knock back *Reporter vs Marine* episodes like a cold beer on a hot day. The premise of the program was seeded in the growing schism between rural and urban America. In the all-online world where nearly every citizen carried a smartphone, the population was more connected than ever. And yet it was also more isolated, driven further apart by digital algorithms that indulged viewers with bias-confirming news, and rewarded clickbait headlines with follows and clicks.

The most viral clips produced by our conservative-leaning site, founded by Tucker Carlson and his college roommate Neil Patel, usually came from "rage clicks," which supplied evidence that radical liberals were destroying the modern society built atop the foundation of the old world. For the progressive-leaning side of the media, the equivalent would be videos and headlines demonstrating that Bible-thumping Trump dummies were taking us back to the time before women or minorities had rights.

Though Trump did not rise to political prominence until after I left NBC, I saw firsthand how DC's elite media looked down their noses at the same flyover hillbillies and Christians who had put Trump in office in 2016. "Flyover" referred to the states that the coastal elite would fly over when traveling between New York or DC and L.A. Across the ideological spectrum, the business was the same. Any news outlet that wanted to keep their employees paid in the age of so-called social media needed to find favor with the almighty algorithms on the platforms where everyone now consumed their news.

The word *news* at one time could have been described as an acronym for information about the happenings across all four corners of the country and the globe—north, east, west, and south. Yet as American history progressed, the information increasingly became what the eastern and western edges of the country deemed important. It was those in the skyscrapers that rose up in power centers along the coasts where the national news leviathans swallowed up local outlets and determined what the masses saw and listened to on their phones. The rest were forgotten.

The followers of our nascent, antiestablishment website largely resided in these forgotten towns and cities. Trump won by securing their vote. This ridiculous form of low-budget reality TV would provide our flyover audience with an affirmation that DC was filled with an atrophied press who, instead of holding truth to power and standing up for voiceless Americans, had become softened by the profits bestowed by the moneyed special interests that both the government and the entrenched media favored over the little guy.

Two years into his presidency, it was not yet clear if Trump could fulfill his campaign promise to "drain the swamp," which was still looking pretty swampy as we navigated the wet road along the Potomac River south of the nation's capital. Even still, most of our audience was convinced that Trump's moniker for the "fake news" was the real reason why flyover country was getting screwed by the city-slicking elite. They weren't entirely wrong either.

⋮⋮⋮

We approached the security checkpoint that led to the tarmac where Ford, who was driving, would fight a simulated airplane fire, then throw on a gas mask, and rescue a human-size dummy from the smoky furnace of a fuselage. I turned the lens of my cell phone toward me for an intro to a day of many challenges, all of which Ford was destined to fail. My blond mustache was barely visible despite six months of growth. "All right the sun is barely up. We're gonna go see an airframe light on fire. This is normally when I go to bed, but we'll see how it goes. How you feeling?"

I turned the camera to Ford, drowsily hunched over the steering wheel, peering through the gray haze toward a security checkpoint flanked by a razor-wire fence. Ford was strong-jawed, with the tempered and deliberate confidence of a man older than 25. His five o'clock shadow at 6:00 a.m. was further evidence that he had been a man for longer than most his age. Ford glanced at the camera and delivered his reply in an accent that combined a Southern drawl with the twang of Appalachia, rounded smooth by the flat-talking northerners who were slowly invading his home city of Raleigh, North Carolina. "Still waking up a lil bit. Let's light it up, though."

The skeleton of an airplane, devoid of the engines that once lifted it to the skies, sat in the middle of a circle of fire trucks and government SUVs. We watched the Marines fight a simulated fire that engulfed the middle portion of the hobbled plane. The tarmac was wet, which was no problem because the fire would be ignited by man-made propane gas. The episode's challenge required Ford to run into the airframe and recover a 125-pound dummy faster than his Marine counterpart.

The man who would go up against him was about the same height, though it was difficult to size up his bulk beneath the fire suit. When I started the camera and the clock, Ford's challenger strode to the airframe, cranked open the latch on the door, located the mannequin, and then pulled the dummy back down the ramp at the back of the fuselage. The Marine crossed the finish line in under a minute.

Ford was up next. He appeared completely out of place strapping the gear over his delicate micropuff Patagonia windbreaker. Though he had a broad, athletic frame, Ford appeared handicapped under the burden of the air tank, a self-contained breathing apparatus that looked like a gas mask but was connected to a twenty-nine-pound hunk of metal housing oxygen on his back.

Geoff started the clock, "Set...go!" Ford stomped toward the plane as if someone had poured concrete into his sneakers, although perhaps he was slowed by his jean pants. Or the gut he'd earned through countless beers at the end of a day in what *Daily Caller* newsroom jokingly referred to as "the Ol' Facebook Mines." Facebook was where our videos and website garnered most of its traffic, and therefore the most cash.

Geoff barked impatiently, following with his hands in the muff of his hoodie, "Walk with urgency, Ford!"

Ford wrenched the door open without too much difficulty, but within moments of grabbing the armpit area, Ford's oxygen hose wrapped around the dummy's neck. Mimicking the Marine's under-the-armpit method proved too hard, so Ford resorted to grabbing the lifeless hands and dragging the plastic doll across the floor. When the mannequin arrived at the ramp exiting from the back of the plane, it stubbornly slid down the corrugated steel. I imagined that a real human victim would be in dire straits. "Come on, Ford. He's dying!"

Ford's muffled groans behind the mask signaled exhaustion. He dropped the dummy flat on its back as he regained some strength. "This thing is not a hundred twenty-five pounds." The beleaguered pair crossed the finish line with a time of two forty-five. Ford looked deader than the dummy that was lying on the cold ground. Ford was back in good spirits within a few minutes, but he did not realize the day held far more daunting challenges ahead.

⁙

We stood in front of a crimson sign that read, "USMC/Military Working Dogs/Quantico, VA." I hit Record and asked Ford to do an intro to the next episode. As a humble reporter rather than a seasoned TV guy, he continued staring blankly at the lens.

"Do you need me to say anything or…?"

I replied nonchalantly. "Yeah, my name's Ford. I'm about to get bit by a dog."

The realization that he was about to get mauled by a military dog betrayed a grim demeanor, though he feigned a smile for the audience, then delivered his intro.

We proceeded to a fenced park spotted with various obstacles for the training of some of the world's most dogged dogs. A Marine wearing a thick protective jacket stood in the center of the grass for a demonstration.

Staff Sergeant Andrew Kwowtko wore the kind of cap that servicemen wear, with the small brim pulled down to shade his eyes. He explained why the dog is trained to target the arms. "If you have a sixty-seventy-pound dog tearing at your flesh and your bone, probably breaking bone, you only have one arm you can do anything with. The guy runs. The dog runs. The guy gets bit."

Ford watched with concern as a heavily jacketed Marine ran away and the dog took off after him. The Marine observed the quick movements over his shoulder and was prepared when the animal caught hold of his arm. He lifted the writhing dog in the air as a sportsman would hoist trophy fish for a photo to be displayed in his office; evidence that the person sitting at the desk was still manly when he wasn't sitting in a comfy chair during the week.

Ford took his turn with the protective jacket, also adding a pair of padded pants in case the dog decided it wanted a taste of his lower extremities. The Marines brought out a slightly smaller but more vicious-looking Belgian Malinois named Mo. The contrast between Mo's spunk and Ford's sluggishness was apparent as Ford slogged into the middle of the field like the Tin Man stranded and in need of oil. The sergeant gave Ford some final words of encouragement. "Just take off running and then the pain train is on its way, all right?"

Ford seemed unaware of the sergeant's friendly pat on his padded back. "The pain train?"

The sergeant ordered Ford to flee. "Go ahead. Run! Just run!"

Geoff joined the screaming chorus from behind the camera, "Run, Ford! Run, Ford! Run!" His movements would be more accurately described as a slow amble than a run.

Mo took off next, covering 10 feet to Ford's 1. When Mo latched onto Ford's left arm, the dog's momentum continued forward, while Ford was basically stationary at the moment of impact. The force of the 65 pounds attached to Ford's upper body yanked him forward with enough energy to fling his sneakers above his head. Ford's dome, the only part of his body that was not protected, hit the ground first. When I ran over with the camera, Ford lifted his face from the grass with a smile, though it rapidly faded as the dog violently thrashed his arm. The sergeant implored Ford to stand still, except that was impossible because Ford was sitting on his ass and the dog wouldn't stop thrashing. The trainer had to choke Mo with his own collar before Mo finally gave up.

I asked Staff Sergeant Kwowtko what he thought of Ford's performance. The sergeant replied with a sarcastic response that typified the Jarhead's no pain, no gain worldview. "He's gonna have to learn to stay on his feet if he wants to join us."

We all laughed, although when I panned the camera to Ford, he had an understandably meeker smirk than the rest of us.

"Who do you think won, Ford or the Marine dog?"

"Easily Mo. The dog always wins."

⋮ ⋮ ⋮

With an hour to kill before the final *Reporter vs Marine* challenge, we stopped for lunch in downtown Quantico. Ford had earned himself more than a few beers. Geoff and I assured him that the company card would expense as many as he liked—the more he drank, the more entertaining and spectacular his final failure would be.

I narrated for the camera while Ford washed down the last bite of a fried chicken sandwich and plate of fries with a Pilsner. "One beer down!

Oh, he's got another beer! Don't you have to do some kind of training course after this?"

Ford downed the last of the first 24-ounce glass and held a new pint up, saying cheers to the camera before he took a huge gulp. "I don't need no water."

∴ ∴

We walked into Butler Stadium, named for the irascible General Smedley Butler. What was once a frontier stadium was dwarfed by the unprecedented explosion of defense spending following WWII, the Cold War, and the War on Terror. Standing on the field with a cheap little camcorder ninety years later, it was obvious that this time the Marines had the upper hand.

Ford's opponent in the combat fitness test, Corporal Odum, was a head taller and twice as wide. The unit of a man looked like he had less fat on his entire body than what Ford had consumed in the fried chicken sandwich and fries twenty minutes prior. While there was a new opponent for each challenge, Ford was on his third challenge, and he appeared the worse for wear.

I. I asked a question I knew the answer to, for the sake of entertainment. "How many performance-enhancing beers did you have at lunch?"

"Zero, sir. Just H-2-0," said the man who looked more like Hercules than a Marine.

Odum appeared in his element while stretching his fridge-sized quads in the end zone with the Butler colosseum in the background.

Ford looked like he was anything but in his element, though he had the strangely calm demeanor of a man who had accepted his fate. "I had two beers. I feel great."

Ford actually consumed one 24-ounce and one 16-ounce beer, which amounted to around 3½ beers, by American standards. The combat fitness test required active Marines to complete timed tasks that simulated what they might have to do while performing their duties on the battlefield:

I. 2 laps around the 440-yard track wearing camos and standard-issue boots, 30-pound ammo-can deadlift max reps in under 2 minutes

II.   Timed, 300-yard "maneuver under fire," including:
- a.   30-yard sprint
- b.   60-yard agility course
- c.   10-yard crawl (low then high crawl)
- d.   75-yard fireman carry through cones
- e.   22.5-yard grenade toss into marked circle
- f.   5 pushups

III. 75-yard ammo-can carry to finish line

The test began with the running stage. Odum's standard-issue boots, which were not ideal for running, were still much less of a handicap than Ford's denim pants and decadent lunch. Odum's swiftness off the starting line was impressive given his size, arriving at the finish line in 2 minutes and 34 seconds. Ford came in at 3 minutes and 14 seconds, which was an impressive 20 seconds under the maximum time for male Marines. Ford was breathing heavily but remained in surprisingly good spirits. That was about to change.

They both executed the timed ammo-can deadlift simultaneously. It looked like Odum was lofting a block of Styrofoam, while Ford appeared to be lifting a boat anchor. For every 2 reps that Odum completed, Ford was able to do 1. At the end of the 2 minutes, Odum had 127 reps. Ford had 68, which was 1 above the minimum required for an enlisted male. Our show host mustered the only comment he could provide between gasps for air, "Fuck."

Fortunately, our reporter got a rest while Cpl. Odum went first for the final "maneuver under fire" section. Odum breezed through the sprint, navigated the agility and crawls with ease, then picked up Ford, and carried him 75 yards as a frat boy would sprightly carry a 30 rack of Keystone Light. Odum barely even broke a sweat by the time he scooped up the 32-pound ammo cans and ran them across the finish line with a total time of just over 2 minutes.

Ford took off at a decent pace. I was amazed that he was able to put the giant Marine onto his back for the fireman carry, and even more surprised when he carried Odum the full 75 yards. Out of breath, Ford picked up the fake grenade and shouted, "Tom Brady!" I chuckled at his tired joke from behind the camera. Odum's dead weight had taken the wind out of Ford's sails, and the ammo-can sprint was more of an ammo-can walk. Ford finished at 3 minutes and 28 seconds, only 4 seconds over the maximum time.

Before we could film the ending of the episode, Ford collapsed onto his back with the only words he could utter, "Oh shit." Geoff, luxuriating in his retirement from the Corps, casually sipped a cup of coffee when he asked Ford how he was feeling, though he knew that his exhausted and mauled reporter was in no condition to provide a response.

When Ford staggered into the newsroom in downtown DC, he was a limping testament to what happens when a keyboard warrior reporter gets thrown into wartime conditions.

March 12, 2020, 4:07 PM EST: 1920 L Street NW, DC

Government is not reason, it is not eloquence. It is force.
Like fire, it is a dangerous servant and a fearful master.
—Thomas Paine, *Common Sense*

We all got up out of our office chairs in the newsroom as Trump walked out of the West Wing into the Rose Garden on a cold but not freezing day typical of a DC winter. Spring may have been just around the corner, but it was a gray and desperate time in the nation's capital. The coronavirus was nearly a full-blown pandemic, and the way forward was yet unclear. In any event, we were celebrating our last days in the office with Centers for Disease Control approved beers.

The White House Press Corps sat in neatly assembled chairs as Trump took the podium with a row of doctors and cabinet members behind him. From his seat at the Resolute Desk the night before, Trump declared an international travel ban that included European countries. The ban was set to take effect at midnight. I was nervous that the president may take the ban a step further and ground all domestic travel. I had just bought dirt-cheap tickets to Hawaii. There were waves on the way, and I figured I could work remotely while also scoring epic waves. I had no clue how bad things were about to get.

We all knew this was our last time assembling in the newsroom before the company went remote. Things were especially rowdy, a last hurrah before we were all shut down in our homes. I screamed at the television, "No travel ban! Hawaii, here I come!"

I was glad that I had this trip ahead of me, a light at the end of the tunnel of uncertainty and fear. We were in a city that was supposed to have all the answers, but at the present moment appeared more confused and afraid than the rest of the nation.

A cold drizzle fell on the attic room of my house in Georgetown as I packed my bags for Kauai: four pairs of boardshorts, three T-shirts, two tank tops, my laptop, headphones, my little quadcopter drone, and five rolls of toilet paper as a gift for my host. This was my idea of a joke because TP was a hot commodity after news of an unknown disease caused a shortage in supermarkets across the globe. I packed a cloth mask just in case, although they were not yet required to travel on planes in the United States. The items that I packed reflected just how unprepared I was for what was about to come. Rather than running away from my dad's sickness to DC, this time I was running away from DC and the yet-unknown sickness we all faced. As with other tough times in my life, I hoped that the waves would bring me calm while the rest of my world hysterically spiraled out of control.

Mom, Dad and I in the NBC Washington newsroom (summer 2013). Dad should have been the newsman. I'm wearing his blue polo shirt, and it meant a lot that I would wear his same shirt on TV after the shooting seven years later. *Photo by Ralph.*

Dad at age 60, shredding way south of the border.

Dad walking the lot at San Miguel before grabbing his board from the back of the Tacoma for a final session.

Somewhere in the Sierra Juarez mountains.

View from the truck bed from which my bag disappeared somewhere in West Virginia.

The cross-country crew—me wearing my thrift store pant shorts and clutching the drone that I drained my savings for—but got me a job.

Somewhere between DC and California—one of the drone shots that helped me land the gig at *LevinTV*.

Set of *LevinTV* at time of launch—Resolute Desk on the left, with Founding Fathers in the background (2015).

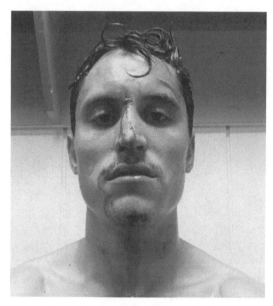

Pre-stitches, approximately 10 hours before *Daily Caller* job interview (December 2016).

24 hours after the 28 stitches—still clearly concussed.

Daily Caller newsroom (summer 2017).

On set at the original *Daily Caller* studio (summer 2017)—with co-director Sean Moody behind the camera.

On set at the new *Daily Caller* studio I built with me own hands on a $2K budget (spring 2018). *Photo by Sagnik Basu.*

Unsuccessful rescue attempt.

Mo biting Ford's arm.

Mo won't let go.

Much deserved beer(s) before the combat fitness test.

Hercules, aka Corporal Odum—zero beers, just H20.

2. THE APOCALYPSE IS NIGH IN KAUAI

The COVID-19 Pandemic Hits America's Shores

June 4, 2017, 5:00 PM EST: New Canaan, Connecticut

So someday you will depart, but till
that distant day Sing, and dance.
—Sippar Tablet, *The Epic of Gilgamesh*

The night my dad chose to die, my brothers and Mom and I huddled around the bed. By this point in his fight against cancer, my father's tumor-addled brain could barely signal his lungs to inflate with air. We sobbed beneath the sound of his struggle to breathe, all terrified but thankful that we had gotten him home.

After nearly a month in the hospital, we won our battle with the bureaucracy to transport my dad home in an ambulance. The health administrators told us that he would likely die in transit because his condition was so frail. Our dad, a fiercely independent man, stated many times that he did not want to die in a hospital, most especially the same one where he had been head of surgery for over a decade. My two brothers and I kindly informed the administrators that they could either help us get our dad home or prepare for court.

Four days after we got him home, Dad embraced his passing when he heard the hospice nurse leave the room. Now that he was alone with his wife and three boys, he opened one of his eyes for the first time in days. His eye darted between us, and his breathing became quicker. We suspected the end was close.

My younger brother, the affectionate one, composed himself enough to recount his favorite story from a surf trip to Costa Rica when he was twelve years old. He held onto an old film photo taken from the journey. It showed both of them sunburned but smiling in front of the remote surf spot named Witch's Rock. Their four blue eyes and the blue sky shone on the faded image in the dimly lit bedroom.

My older brother, the stable, quiet one, was still in medical school. He rose to retrieve a stethoscope and placed it atop our dad's laboring heart. His hand held the receiver steady while he listened to the last beats with tears in his eyes.

I was between both of them. The extroverted one prone to emotional outbursts, I poured tears as silently as I could. We all hugged each other while I watched my father's blue eye slowly disappear behind an impenetrably dark and expanding pupil.

The sound of his failing lungs finally turned to silence as they collapsed. My older brother gently lowered his eyelid for the last time after the life left his body. It was tragic but beautiful, like a majestic wave of energy expiring onto the sand.

Though my dad's condition meant we could not make it with him to a destination as remote as Indonesia again, my brothers and I traveled there when the world opened back up after the pandemic in May 2023. Riding a wave together, we scattered his ashes into the pristine crashing wave off a remote island where the antics of the monkeys were out of earshot, though my oldest brother abruptly cut back and clipped my youngest brother's legs at the end of our ash-laden ride.

February 14, 1779: Kealakekua Bay, Hawaii

A violent winter storm destroyed the foremast of Captain James Cook's ship, *Resolution*, as it sailed away from the Hawaiian Islands. Mother Nature's wrath had interrupted his transglobal exploration in the name of the British Crown. The explorers returned to Kealakekua Bay on Hawaii's Big Island to mend the wounded vessel. The crewmen brought the mast to one of the Hawaiians' sacred ancient burial grounds, known as a *heiau*, for repair. They knew it to be a good source for timber; they had already taken fencing and statues, thinking that the wood would serve as excellent kindling to burn in the ship's furnaces, and the statues would make fine souvenirs.

When Cook and his men first arrived in Hawaii in January of 1778, the captain from humble, working-class origins was accepted as a god. This time, he and his crew were seen as offenders. After the native population received news of the Europeans' disregard for the effigies of their departed ancestors, then saw that the men they thought gods couldn't even keep their vessel shipshape, the Hawaiians rose up in protest. In the middle of the night, the natives stole one of Cook's most valuable cutter boats, which he needed to continue his navigation of Alaska's uncharted shores.

The friendship that had existed between the Hawaiians and the Brits turned to hostility overnight. Sensing a revolt on the horizon, Captain Cook assembled an armed gang of Royal Marines capable of quelling the insurrection. They oared a launch boat from the *Resolution*'s moor in the bay, landed on the beach, then marched into the village, and captured the natives' leader, King Kalaniopuu. The aging tribal leader was highly respected by his people for his strength and surfing abilities. Back then, surfing the dangerous waves that crashed onto Hawaii's unforgiving shores was a pastime reserved for nobility, rather than the embodiment of the counterculture lifestyle that emerged from Southern California after WWII.

Cook himself seized the king and headed back to the launch boat with his new political prisoner. As the extraction team neared the beach, an old kahuna medicine man heard the commotion. He blocked the Europeans' path while he conspicuously chanted a traditional Hawaiian song. The band of white men became preoccupied by the old shaman, unaware that an angry mob of native warriors were gathering near the shore. By the time the small troop of explorers realized they were surrounded, the Hawaiian horde attacked. Cook's men fired their weapons to fend off the revolt but were quickly overwhelmed.

Despite their technological disadvantages, the indigenous Hawaiians were able to free their king and push Cook to the sand. Amid the crashing surf, they stabbed him to death with a steel blade, one which was originally fashioned on the British Isles. The world-famous explorer's third trip around the world ended as his blood washed away with the white foamy waves into the immense Pacific Ocean.

Four other Royal Marines were killed in the melee. The rest of the group escaped in their launch boat and returned to the safety of the *Resolution*. The Englishmen aboard the *Resolution* watched with horror through a looking glass and fired their cannons at the village in retaliation. Many natives perished in the barrage.

Meanwhile, the Hawaiians carried Cook's corpse back to the village. As the captain of the white men, Cook's remains were prepared in a funerary ritual normally reserved for kings; they disemboweled the body, baked his flesh, and then cleaned his bones so they could be preserved.

Cook's successor, Captain James King, secured the recovery of what was left of Cook and buried him at sea. King recorded an account of the natives' surfing exploits in the very same sacred bay where Cook was killed. For the native Hawaiians, surfing was the sport of kings. For British colonials like Captain King, it was a bizarre exercise of freedom and skill in the midst of the chaos of the sea. He recorded the following in his ship log:

Whenever, from stormy weather, or any extraordinary swell at sea, the impetuosity of the surf is increased to its utmost height, they choose that time for this amusement.

The first wave they meet, they plunge under, and suffering it to roll over them, rise again beyond it, and make the best of their way…out into the sea.

The second wave is encountered in the same manner with the first; the great difficulty consisting in seizing the proper moment of diving under it, which, if missed, the person is caught by the surf, and driven back again with great violence; and all his dexterity is then required to prevent himself from being dashed against the rocks.

March 17, 2020, 4:15 AM HST: Kauai, Hawaii

My friend, the mountain which you
saw in the dream is Humbaba.
—Tablet IV, *The Epic of Giglamesh*

The Hanalei Bay valley lay in darkness when I awoke at 4:00 a.m. for the start of the workday on East Coast time. A deluge of rain beat down on the bungalow's roof while I sent emails and reviewed videos in the dark. The announcement of a global pandemic brought our roaring American economy—and our company's revenue—to a screeching halt.

The CEO was already asking how I planned on keeping everyone paid. I assured him that ViD SqUAd saved a rainy-day fund sizable enough to figure things out. But if the sunken revenue couldn't be salvaged, I would soon be forced to confront my worst fear, laying off a number of my ViD SqUAders. The ViD SqUAd was *Daily Caller's* video team that I managed with my co-director Sean Moody. It was a ragtag band of eight-to-ten twenty-somethings who I considered the most creative and renegade folks in the news biz. Sean and I had built this team from scratch, laboring seven days a week for three years to get to this point.

A video news outlet at *Daily Caller* looked like a sad delusion where I sat on a remote island in the Pacific. I was half a world away from home and with no idea how to save the team that we'd built. If I'd known that we were heading for a full-blown economic and immunological cataclysm, I might not have gone to visit my childhood friend on Kauai.

The trip to surf with my friend "Bodhi" was intended as a warmup before my two brothers and I embarked on an Indonesian boat trip scheduled for the end of the spring, a quest to surf perfect, empty waves then spread my dad's ashes into the sea on his seventy-first birthday, May 10, 2020.

Our plan all but evaporated with the arrival of the global pandemic on America's shores. By the time May rolled around it appeared I'd be more likely to scatter the ashes of my career instead.

I considered my uncertain future beneath the unyielding rain pummeling the roof of Bodhi's bungalow on the steep mountainside overlooking Hanalei Bay, on the northern reaches of Kauai. It had been pouring for three days straight. Later that morning, I read a *Washington Post* article, "Tuesday's tornado warnings—the first issued in the Aloha State since 2008—were no mistake. The first came at 1:22 a.m. local time, when strong rotation was detected just southeast of the island of Niihau. A more intense circulation barreled ashore in Kauai, the northwestern-most populated island in the chain, at around 5:55 a.m." I was so enthralled by news about an invisible virus, I didn't notice that half of the four tornado warnings (since recording began in 1986) were declared on the island where I sat working all morning.

Bodhi, a tall, dark-skinned, heavyset, and heavily bearded man, stumbled sleepily into the kitchen. The rising sun barely made it through the storm clouds, casting the kitchen in a dull, warm light. We ate a breakfast of eggs, fresh fruit, and black coffee on his lanai overlooking the green jungle. In the subset of the English vernacular known as "surf pidgin," Bodhi asked how my morning went. "How goes dem DC news grinds?"

I raised my voice to communicate my professional woes over the sound of the falling rain beading off thousands of waxy leaves of the koa trees, which were common on Kauai. The word "koa" means "strong warrior," and was used to name these trees because of the iron-like strength of their wood.

Kauai was the only island that had not been conquered by the Hawaiian kingdom that killed Captain Cook. Cook died on the Big

Island during his third trip around the globe, but on his first trip landed on Waimea Bay, a huge volcanic canyon on the southern belly of Kauai. Buzzing around the steep mountain roads on Bodhi's moped, I saw many bumper stickers that said, "Unconquered," because the Kauai locals were extremely proud of this heritage. In fact, Kauai was finally conquered in 1898 when it was annexed by the swelling American empire.

Bodhi and I decided to celebrate the end of the workday by taking a bunch of hallucinogenic mushrooms then going for a stormy surf. My office would be clocking out early to celebrate the St. Patrick's Day holiday. Except this year they would not be drinking free Guinness from an open tab at DC's best Irish pub, Dubliner, as the tradition went. All the restaurants in our nation's capital were shuttered due to government mandates. I hoped that the mushrooms would show me a way out of my present predicament, and that St. Patrick's Day would bring luck to my McGinniss name.

The tires of Bodhi's Toyota Tacoma spun in the slippery mud as we pulled into the empty lot at the top of the cliffs. Due to excessive flooding, the bridge to Hanalei Bay was closed, so we opted instead to drive to a spot with parking on higher ground. Raindrops beat down on the roof of the truck, which nearly drowned out the tunes we blared to get energized. Future Islands' "Light House" played as I sent a last email from my phone. I eyeballed a sizable dose of powdered hallucinogenic mushrooms.

I dumped it in my mouth and washed it down with cold, bitter Hawaiian black coffee. The ground-up mycelium was mostly powder with some larger chunks. The gray substance resembled my dad's ashes, and the stems were like the fragments of bone that had survived the embalming flames.

Bodhi looked at me with a grin from behind a zinc-oxide-caked face. He handed me the tube of sunblock and I traded him for the bag of shrooms. He took a notably smaller scoop, maybe one-fifth my dose. I estimated I had just eaten about 3.5 grams of magic shroomies, also known as a "hero's dose." Given that consuming the powdered variety hit your bloodstream more quickly than eating the whole mushroom, we were both going to be feeling the effects shortly. I spread some sunblock on my face as if applying war paint before a battle.

We jumped out of the cab into the maelstrom. The rain came crashing down on my back. I looked around at the lush landscape. But all I saw was my entire business model, along with most of the American economy, washing away as quickly as the streams of water that flowed down the jagged volcanic cliffs on Kauai's shores. The silver streams on the steep mountainsides that surrounded the bay looked like liquid ladders rising into the heavy, low-hanging clouds. The song was interrupted by an email notification on my phone. I dipped my head back into the truck and briefly returned to the doldrums of the digital world.

Bodhi yelled, "Get your cleats ready, bruddha! You gonna need 'em today."

He looked at me, awaiting an eager reply, but I was engrossed in the email I just received from my CEO. The boss was worried about how we could keep the team afloat. He wanted a daily list of projects completed by our staff along with new ideas on how to keep the team productive remotely. My soaking hair dripped onto the screen. It was impossible to type with water pooling on my phone.

Bodhi could tell I was brooding over something unsavory because he asked, "You good, broski?"

"Yeah." I dried my device and quickly replied to the CEO, "Understood."

I jumped back outside and flashed Bodhi a grin. It was the elated expression that surfers wear when they know they're about to be phoneless in the salt water for the next few hours. Time to turn off the tunes and engross ourselves in the sounds of our surroundings.

Bodhi killed the engine. We were left with nothing but the roar of the waves and the clang of metal smacked with key lime–sized tropical rain. I placed worn-in soccer cleats from a thrift store in northern Virginia onto my bare feet. Bodhi had told me they would be required to descend the slick red clay famous on Kauai.

I decided to surf shirtless because the ocean was bath warm and the clouds would block the sun from scorching my back, which was vulnerable and pale after a long winter. Bodhi signaled with his head to the truck bed. Time to grab our surfboards. I rubbed wax on the board, a ritual surfers perform to provide extra grip before they attempt to ride the powerful waves generated by Mother Nature. Almost every time I grabbed the bar of wax, I would remember how my dad would use this final opportunity to ruminate on the deeper philosophical trajectory of our lives. He learned how to surf along with his three sons when I was eight years old. He was the ripe age of forty-eight but was determined to learn because it would be his excuse to take us around the globe on surf trips; his own way of showing us the broader world beyond the insulated bubble where we grew up, in an affluent neighborhood just outside New York City.

May 30, 2012, Morning: Bali, Indonesia

The dream was marvelous but the terror was great;
we must treasure the dream whatever the terror.
— The Dream Tablet, *The Epic of Gilgamesh*

My dad and I met my brother for a surf trip as a graduation gift the week after I finished college. He collapsed onto the reef in seizure next to my brother as they followed me out for a surf. At that moment, the stable world helmed by my father would be capsized into the depths of the unknown. But it would also imbue in my brothers and me the greatest lesson a father could give his sons: how one can rise above the horrible shade of the unknown, and face death with fortitude.

I picked out my steps carefully as I clambered along the 50-yard stretch of sharp reef leading to the main peak at Uluwatu.

We traveled to the remote location to the world-class surfing spot, which jutted out into the wide-open Indian Ocean in the shadow of the famous eleventh-century Hindu temple called Uluwatu. The crystal-clear breaking waves peeled perfectly for nearly a mile on the better days, like a machine made by God with the specific intent of providing surfers evidence of the universe's eternal glory. My dad always insisted that we get a healthy dose of "culture" on every surf trip, so we visited the temple the day before he fell.

As my older brother, Dad, and I walked around the complex, I recall my dad joking that the monkeys harassing us for food were just like his boys when we ran out of money. We got to the edge of the temple and watched the groomed waves corduroyed all the way to the horizon. The temple looked down at the waves like a beacon guiding the organized and powerful curls into their final destruction as they washed over the reef below. I liked to think of surfing as an artistic endeavor, which was especially evident upon realizing that once men decided to surf these waves, their final moments were transformed into a creative human experience.

The drumming of the waves that existed before surfers and commercialism crowded the lineups, overpowered even the sound of rambunctious monkeys howling above. Walking back to the hotel, we noticed my dad had a bit of a limp. I told my brother that I'd seen him stumble during our layover in Frankfurt. And he did sideswipe the left side of the rental car when he was parking that day—and Dad had never crashed his car before. But he seemed to be surfing perfectly well that morning. My brother and I wrongly assumed that he was just a jet-lagged old man.

Behind me, my dad and brother emerged from the keyhole in the sheer cliffs to begin the long walk. Since my brother was taking his turn to slowly walk Dad out, I impatiently scurried along the spiky coral to immerse myself amid the dreamlike waves as quickly as possible. Our dad wore reef booties, but we preferred to grip the board with bare feet. My brother and I relied on our callouses, which we'd developed through practice. People would laugh at us when we showed up to Georgetown college parties without shoes. If the preppily dressed partygoers asked why we were barefoot, my older brother or I would explain we were hardening our feet for the very crab walk I was enduring to surf the heavenly waves in front of me.

In just one of these rides, I could get as much surfing time as in an entire week at the far shorter, local wind swell waves that I surfed back on the East Coast. While those waves lasted only a few seconds after traveling a few hundred miles from the heavy wind and rain that generated their power, the waves here in Indonesia came from massive storms thousands of miles away near the Antarctic. These waves could last minutes rather than seconds.

"Yewww!" I exclaimed at the best conditions since we arrived.

But my dad and my brother never made it out beyond the breakers. I searched for a wave in to see what went wrong. I waited for nearly 30 minutes, paddling furiously against the outgoing tide that sucked up the point and out to sea. Finally, the current moved the crowded group of surfers beyond my position, and a swell approached me from the horizon. The massive hunk of water was nearly too fast for me to paddle in on my tiny board. Despite being undergunned, I popped to my feet at the peak and, as I free-fell down the face, I hoped for the best.

After 15 years of trials, my blind drop into the wide-open trough of the wave was well-rehearsed. Thousands of pounds of water folded over itself then detonated on the shelf at the tip of the Bali peninsula, beneath the temple of priests of the past. I made it through the momentary free fall of the initial takeoff. The rest was easy.

I carved broad strokes across the unsullied face of the wave. Approaching the section known as "racetracks," I knew to pick up my speed from countless videos I'd watched of the famous wave. When I pumped down the line, my leisurely turns became a sprint to avoid calamity on the shallow shelf of coral. Charging along the edge of cataclysm, the shimmering tunnel of water spun around me. For a moment, fears about my dad's safety were lost in the deep sound of exploding ocean behind me. I ducked in front of the lip of the wave just before it closed out. I rode into the shallows on the final remnants of the once majestic wave, the smooth face transformed to a frothy foam. When I dismounted the board, my feet hit jagged reef, and anxiety of reality replaced the adrenaline from the wave's energy.

I hastily scurried across the stretch of sun-bleached coral exposed by the drained tide.

Explanations for why my dad and brother disappeared raced through my brain as I ascended the steep stone staircase that snaked through Uluwatu's sheer cliffs. My feet were bleeding with scratches and burned on the hot pavement where I discovered the car was gone from where we parked. I jogged nearly an hour back to the hotel, where at the front desk, they told me that my dad was sick, and my brother had taken him to the hospital. I rented a scooter and rushed through the most jumbled and confused traffic that someone who grew up outside New York City had ever seen.

My brother met me at the automatic doors of the Balinese ER, though his stoic demeanor gave no indication of dad's condition. Unlike me, my older brother was a man of few words, though he read more than anyone I knew. When he did speak, he did so with the truncated precision of a scalpel.

"He had a seizure. It's not looking good."

We sat down in the waiting room among gnarly motorbike injuries, and he told me the docs took a CT scan after he was admitted to the hospital. The swelling they saw indicated a stroke. They showed us the scan of his brain in which the entire right side showed a big blob of white.

Feeling terrible about missing the nightmare of getting my dad's writhing body off the reef and into the ambulance, I spent the afternoon helping him shower and go to the bathroom. Meanwhile, my brother remained on the phone with American Express, trying to find a way to get dad back to the States for whatever lifesaving surgery he might need. After hours of fitfully moaning and moving his mouth in an attempt to talk, his bright blue eyes glowing with frustration, my dad finally gave up and went to sleep. Nearly the entire left side of his body was paralyzed.

My older brother and I used his nap as an opportunity to go out to dinner and discuss what the next steps would be. We weaved through the heavy traffic on the small scooter, seemingly underpowered amid the sea of noisy motorcycles and trucks on the Indonesian roadway, buzzing wildly around us in some kind of semiorganized fashion I did not understand.

We stopped the bike in front of a beachside restaurant. Though it was May, there were strings of Christmas lights that cast my older brother's tanned skin in a pale light as he ran through our family's finances. Too drained to take it in, I focused instead on the palm fronds that made up the roof, fluttering above in the hot trade wind of the East Indies, while he identified all the towering family costs that we would not be able to afford without my dad's income. At the time, I had graduated less than a week prior, and my brother was using his Chinese language skills to lead the misbehaved kids of wealthy Westerners on adventurous sojourns through the Chinese countryside for only a few thousand bucks a pop. This was not even enough to afford taxes and utilities on our home.

Given that our dad couldn't even wipe his own ass on that given day, my brother who would go on to become an ER doctor grimly assessed that Dad might die shortly or remain a vegetable. He unenthusiastically poked at the fresh tropical fish with his wooden chopsticks, "If Dad dies, we are basically fucked. We might have to sell everything." While I was paralyzed by fear of losing our dad, my brother was always the practical one. Like my dad, he barely showed any emotion even when speaking about such a somber topic.

I was actually extremely hungry after the whole ordeal. I didn't even care that tears fell onto the sushi while I sobbed as quietly as I could and listened to my brother's gloomy predictions. I couldn't stop thinking about the fear in Dad's eyes as he fruitlessly tried to speak from the hospital bed. I could tell that as a doctor he knew exactly what was happening to him. His frustration seemed to confirm that the outlook was not good.

Thanks to a lengthy dialogue with American Express, we finally secured a medical escort and tickets to bring him back to the United States. Dad always stated that he loved Amex because they could save your ass whenever you got into trouble abroad. Not only did this prove true for me when I ran into money trouble in Egypt in December of 2010, it turned out to save his life after Amex paid the exorbitant cost incurred from the Indonesian hospital and the arrangements to get home safe. He received brain surgery immediately after landing. We found out that he had not suffered a stroke but had a golf-ball-sized tumor in his brain that swelled from the stress of traveling halfway around the world from the US to Indonesia. The tumor metastasized from a melanoma known more commonly as skin cancer.

After removing the tumor, the neurosurgeon and colleague of my dad stated that he was the only patient he'd ever seen emerge from brain surgery, then immediately demand the nurse discharge him from the hospital. The docs gave him five months to live even after the apparent success of the surgery. He ended up living five years because he refused passage before he prepared the family and our finances. He would go in for his checkups and ask the medical staff as if he was opening a standup routine, "What are you gonna do to my potato field today?" A "potato field" was an Irish dark-humor name for his brain, which they continually zapped with radiation and cut with a scalpel in an effort to defeat the cancer that kept coming back. When a meek doc tried to prick his arm for blood, he quipped, "What is it—your third year of residency? Give me a real doctor!" The nurses did not laugh at this bit, but they confirmed that his assessment was right.

Despite the severity of his sentence, my dad, my brothers and I surfed hundreds of waves around the world together during the numbered years he had left to live. When he finished renovating our house to make it a rentable asset rather than a burden that we could not afford, he simply said, with one of the final twinkles in his blue eyes, "I quit."

March 17, 2020, 1:37 PM HST: Kauai, Hawaii

> Ever the river has risen and brought us the
> flood, the mayfly floating on the water. On
> the face of the sun its countenance gazes,
> then all of a sudden nothing is there!
> —Utanapishtim Tablet, *The Epic of Gilgamesh*

Bodhi and I walked through dense vegetation before the cliff's edge. When we arrived at the overlook, it was impossible to tell the size of the waves because of limited visibility of the reef a few hundred yards offshore. I looked down at my potato chip board and suddenly felt inadequate.

"Brah, am I gonna have enough foam to paddle into these? Sounds like the surf is big as hell." Bigger boards afford the surfer more paddle speed, which is essential for larger, faster-moving waves.

"It's double overhead-ish, so you should be fine?"

The cartoon-voice question mark at the end of his sentence told me he had no confidence that I would be fine. But surfing had to be about risk, or it wasn't worth it. Nothing would peel me away from the break today, and we both knew it. I raised my eyebrows. Bodhi laughed. It was a nervous laugh. My mainland sensibilities were reasonably intimidated by the size and power of these Hawaiian waves that had been raging from the storms over the last few days. Bodhi's tan skin was testament that he'd lived on Kauai for the last eight years and he thought the massive surf was fun. But even for him the conditions were pretty gnarly.

We slipped down the cliffside, clinging to muddy ropes and halfway-intact metal guard rails. The mushrooms had entered my veins. The roots of the tropical fauna, guard rails, and ropes looked like snakes. The red mud streaming down the cliff resembled thick blood. I focused on one cleat in front of another. When they squelched in the muck it sounded like stepping on guts.

I calmed when we reached the firm, wet sand. The waves breaking at the beach were neither big nor intimidating. Their power had already been unleashed on the outer reef where we intended to surf. But the volcanic rocks that met us on the water's edge were sharp and alive. I had the cuts from previous sessions to prove it (I fell at the end of a wave the previous day and scraped my entire back on the reef). I followed Bodhi through a soft spit of sand that zigzagged in between the barbed rocks until it was deep enough to start paddling. Anxiety about my professional life disappeared into the waves roaring beyond the fog. I abandoned my expertise in Arabic after college to pursue a career in media because I believed that I could change the destructive nature of our government from a newsroom in DC. Now, the newsrooms were empty, and the business I spent years building was imploding faster than the waves collapsing to sea level on the reef.

I looked back toward dry land longingly. But after traversing the "snakes" and the blood, I had come too far to turn back. Bodhi looked back at me and chuckled when he saw my wide eyes.

"You good? Them mushrooms are bumpin', aren't they?"

"You don't feel them?" I asked.

"I'm just feeling a little tickle," he replied. At least one of us still had their perceptions under control. If only I could stick with Bodhi, my surf shaman, I would be fine.

But surfing is an individual sport, and once we duck-dived under our first wave, it would be every man for himself. I looked back over my shoulder toward the serpentine jungle and the rusty red clay before I paddled after him.

I needed to maintain the calm breaths required to make it through the marathon paddle. Unlike the perfect waves at the flooded bay up the coast, this spot did not have a deep channel where you could escape the constant pounding between you and the lineup beyond. I sliced my board beneath the surface and fought against bus-size mounds of water. For a moment, it would be peaceful and silent down below. Then I returned to the surface and the constant grumbling of oncoming waves.

My troubled mind turned to the stable spirit of my departed dad. After he passed away, I logged my dreams into a journal. Dreams were rare for me at the time. I smoked weed precisely to avoid them because I regularly had nightmares in which something bad was taking place, and my dad would be there standing silent, stoic, and unphased. I would be terrified. I would try to scream out all of the things I wish I'd said to him, but remained paralyzed and unable to speak. When the mushies kicked in, the dreamlike state would induce more active communication with the spirits, whom I loved but could no longer interact with in the normal world. To the soundtrack of the crashing waves, I envisioned a recurring dream that I had written into the journal at my bedside immediately after I woke up one morning:

11/1/2017

Dad and I saw a lighthouse over the dunes through the fog and
toward the ocean. But when I climbed the dune I realized all but
the top of the lighthouse was submerged and being washed in
a circle by the sea.

All I could see in front of me was a seemingly insurmountable wall of fog and froth. I had been out in bigger surf, but never while on a hero's dose of mushrooms. Bodhi caught the riptide perfectly and was swiftly paddling out with the current at his back. I could barely see him 50 to 60 yards out and to my left. When I started paddling, I took deep gulps of air after I emerged from diving under each wave, preserving my energy as best I could. The mushrooms did not help.

With no horizon in sight, my fearful mind drifted to my dad's twin brother who'd drowned at age forty. I was too young to remember him, but according to my dad, his brother Gary was never the same after the car accident he'd suffered in high school. My uncle's arm was pinned under the oversized engine of his own capsized muscle car. His arm was maimed beyond repair. My family and I believed our uncle Gary's accident was the main reason why Dad decided to become an orthopedic surgeon. After the crash, my uncle struggled with drugs, which eventually caused his untimely death. Authorities found his body drowned in a river near one of the bars he frequented.

Gary was the charismatic and outgoing twin. While my older brother practiced the calm, quiet demeanor of my father, I think my dad saw a lot of Gary in me. As I paddled furiously through the angry sea, I shuddered at the thought of suffering the same fate as Uncle Gary.

With my mind distracted, rather than sneaking under the next slab of a wave, the lip landed right on the small of my back. The impact separated me from my board and drove me down toward the bottom.

The surfboard bobbed alone at the surface of the churning ocean. The leash that kept me tethered to the tail of the board pulled downward toward the reef, which also pointed the nose of the surfboard to the sky. Known as "tombstoning," the front of the board sticking up above the surface both resembled a tombstone and also indicated that the surfer was in grave danger down below.

I was running out of air, but I held onto the rocks. Waiting calmly for my chance to swim up would give me a better chance than battling the mayhem before it calmed down. When a second wave crashed above me, I gripped the reef harder, despite its sharpness. The entire world seemed to be swirling out of control. I tried to calm my mind, but I couldn't stop the terrified visions of drowning on drugs just like my uncle.

Consumed by hopelessness and the self-pity of dying before living a life fulfilled, the turbulence finally calmed down enough for my escape. I grabbed onto my board leash and pulled myself toward the light.

As my head broke the surface, I inflated my lungs with desperate gulps for air while I scrambled back onto my board. I was unaware of what loomed beyond the next wall of white water, though after traveling such a great distance I had to be close. With my last burst of energy, I scratched over the next wave. When I crested its peak, instead of more whitewater, I saw Bodhi solitary in the fog.

"Yyyyyyyeeeew!" he shouted through the haze.

After trading waves for an hour, Bodhi was the first to notice the change in the weather. He pointed toward the sun that peeked through the dark clouds. As the heat of the rays emerged from behind the storm front and reached sea level, the smoky atmosphere began to clear. We looked at each other in awe at the scene before us. Bodhi winked, implying that it was not just the mushrooms—this was real.

Before the squall fully cleared, a flash of lightning was followed by a boom of thunder. It reverberated off the mountains that surrounded the nearby bay like an amphitheater, careening down the steep mountain peaks. When it arrived at the bottom of the cliffs, the final crack sounded like an exploding gas tank of a burning car, a gunshot, or perhaps a firework. After the thunder's echoes through the valley subsided, Mother Nature became quiet. The remaining sound of the breaking waves was peaceful and harmonic.

I looked toward the beach where the clouds still masked the tops of the mountains, and I wondered if the thunder and lightning were gone for good. I couldn't see what was beyond the peaks—nor could I predict the extent of the misfortune that lay ahead for our country.

As the weather cleared, the wind switched and groomed the waves from sloppy storm surf to perfectly peeling curls. It was entropy-turned-order, right before our eyes.

The unyielding rhythm of the crashing waves had commenced long before me and Bodhi, before Captain Cook and the Hawaiian natives, and they would continue on long after all of us. At the same time, each individual breaker exploded dramatically before it expired and returned to the depths of the sea. Their magnificent form was both momentary and eternal.

I sat alone in the lineup, peering hopefully toward the horizon. Bodhi had paddled into an epic wave and was now making the long journey hundreds of yards back up the reef. A swell approached that traveled across the ocean before it was about to unleash on America's outermost shores.

I scratched my way farther out to sea to greet the approaching swell. I sat up, spun my board around, and sunk it entirely underwater, timing its corklike exit from the ocean with the arrival of the forming curl. I gave two hard strokes, syncing myself with the speed of the roller, then stood up. The lip of the wave spiraled over me. All of the bullshit—the worries about my failing business, the tragedy of death, the collapse of the world as we knew it—crashed down behind me onto the shallow reef. The roar of a spinning cavern of water was cathartic. From my liquid cathedral, I was surrounded by the inherent order of the universe. The destructive power of the torrential rain and wind made this salty dream possible. The vision gave me faith that disarray ultimately manifests into harmony.

As I exited the glass temple, I wore my revelation like a shield that could protect me. I glided effortlessly toward the shoulder of the wave, but my momentum felt everlasting.

With the energy of the wave dissipating before it finally terminated on the sand, I leaned on my toes and angled the board back toward the horizon. My motion across the surface of the sea slowed. The board began to sink beneath the ocean. As the water washed over my legs and torso, I looked to the sky and saw my father, his bright blue eyes even more vibrant than the lucid Hawaiian sky.

The enveloping water felt like my newfound suit of armor. Much like the eternal waves that would not have been possible without the stormy turmoil, the suffering from my father's death instilled in me a strength that would protect me from the perils that lay ahead. My head finally sank beneath the surface, and the water washed over my face.

Trump press conference from *Daily Caller* newsroom—surf trip a greenlight. *Photo by Henry Rodgers.*

The totality of my luggage for escape from DC (laptop backpack not included).

Relaxing on the first morning in Bodhi's bungalow—with no clue that the apocalypse was nigh.

Calm before the storm on our first day in Kauai—empty waves for da boys.

Pasty but ready for first surf—heart rate monitor secured with duct tape.
Photo by Bodhi.

Flooding near Hanalei Bay, as a massive storm hit Kauai.

Barreled in Indonesia the day before we scattered my dad's ashes on a remote island (spring 2023). *Photo by @mentawisurfco.*

Palm trees where the bros and I finally scattered Dad's ashes after a heavy storm in Indonesia (spring 2023).

Uluwatu, with temple perched atop the cliffs (spring 2012).

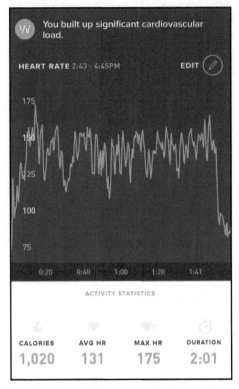

Heart rate monitor during mushroom surf—first spike when I thought I
was gonna die; final spike during epic wave to the beach. *Screenshot from
WHOOP app.*

Flooding receded near Hanalei Bay.

18
Total waves surfed

16.3
Top speed (mph)

291
Longest wave (yds)

3.9 mi
Paddled

01:52
Surf time

4.7 mi
Distance

Our final session in Kauai at Hanalei Bay. The last ride was 291 yards long–
Yewwww! *Screenshot from Rip Curl SearchGPS app.*

3. BAPTISM BY PEPPER SPRAY

George Floyd Protests/Riots and Trump's Bible Photo at St. John's Church

March 4, 1829: Washington, DC

President Andrew Jackson divided the country between two camps: his supporters thought he was a champion of the average American, and his detractors viewed him as a crude scalawag. A crowd of over twenty thousand Jackson supporters descended on the nation's capital in March 1829 for the first populist president's inauguration into the White House. Never before had a man from the frontier been elected president. Every other former president, including the incumbent whom Jackson unseated, Harvard graduate John Quincy Adams, was from either Virginia or Massachusetts and had retained a job in Washington prior to their election. Jackson, who grew up on the western frontier of the Carolinas and never attended a formal college, was a political outsider.

During the race of 1828, the American press leveled unprecedented personal attacks on both Jackson and his incumbent opponent, John Quincy Adams. One wild rumor alleged that during Adams' time as US ambassador to Russia, he procured one of his chambermaids for the sexual service of the Czar. On the other side, Jackson's wife, Rachel, was attacked as an adulterous whore because she married Jackson while she was betrothed to another man. Humiliated by the allegations, a deeply religious Rachel died weeks after Jackson's election. After his victory, this further incentivized the president-elect to dismantle the political establishment that had so viciously attacked his wife.

On March 4, 1829, his inaugural address was delivered from the Capitol for the first time in American history. Jackson gave a short speech in which he touched on his plan for the issue of Native Americans on the frontier: "It will be my sincere and constant desire to observe toward the Indian tribes within our limits a just and liberal policy, and to give that human and considerate attention to their rights and to their wants which is consistent with the habits of our Government and the feelings of our people." Jackson's Indian removal policy would turn out to be anything but humane. The forced displacement of tens of thousands of Native Americans was spearheaded under Jackson's two terms as president. What became known as the "Trail of Tears" would haunt Native Americans for generations and tarnish Jackson's legacy forever.

After he was sworn into office, Jackson rode his horse the short distance from the Capitol to a celebration at the White House. Thousands of his supporters followed the procession, much to the surprise of the Washington elites, who enjoyed an elegant reception on the southern veranda. Upon seeing ice cream, cakes, and whiskey-spiked orange punch, the celebratory crowd turned quickly into an unruly mob. They stormed the presidential mansion, smashing fine China and soiling the carpets with muddy boots and tobacco spit while they clambered for their own taste of high society.

Jackson, popularly nicknamed "Old Hickory," was pinned against the wall inside his new home. The president was forced to evacuate the White House out a side door. The anti-Jackson *Washington City Chronicle* reported, "Many were admitted... [who] certainly ought not to have been there." The more Jackson-friendly *Washington Daily Intelligencer* wrote, "The whole day and night of the Inauguration passed off without the slightest interruption of the public peace and order. ... At the mansion of the president, the Sovereign People were a little uproarious, indeed, but it was in anything but a malicious spirit."

The press was divided into two camps, impressing on the American people two completely different versions of the same event.

May 26, 2020, 10:30 AM EST: *Daily Caller* HQ, Washington, DC

O generation of vipers, who hath warned
you to flee from the wrath to come?
—Matthew 3:7

The day after George Floyd was killed in Minneapolis, I drove into downtown DC to meet Jorge Ventura at our company's empty new building. At this point, most Americans had never heard the name George Floyd. To those who had, his name sounded like just another in a long roll call of black men killed in grotesque ways while interacting with law enforcement. The widespread civil unrest stemming from Floyd's death would not begin for a few days.

I had no trouble finding parking because DC had been all but boarded up since the start of the pandemic. But once the protests of the summer of 2020 cast the nation's capital into chaos, the empty buildings downtown would be fortified with plywood over the windows, as if preparing for a once-in-a-generation storm.

Jorge shook my hand and said, "I'm a crazy motherfucker, and if you need me to go to Venezuela, I'll go."

I laughed and replied, "I like that. I like that."

I could tell from that moment that Jorge was a guy who I could call on when the going got tough. He originally joined the team as an unpaid intern, moving to the right coast from the left coast that week.

Jorge first contacted me while he was laboring through his second year of a journalism program at a community college near his home in Palmdale, California. Jorge was a big fan of my former coworker, Saagar Enjeti, who hosted a popular daily news program on YouTube. Knowing that I was always hungry for young kids with a work ethic, Saagar gave Jorge my information after Jorge tagged him in a tweet asking for career advice.

In early April, I talked on the phone with Jorge about a possible internship with *Daily Caller*. He clearly had the two qualities that I was looking for in a potential candidate: passion for the craft and a penchant for hard work. He also kept insisting that he could "be on a plane tomorrow" if I would give him a chance. I told him to slow his roll and submit a few samples while we figured out the whole pandemic thing.

I had a good feeling about Jorge because he was unabashedly ambitious, despite the fact that his video-editing and writing skills were very clearly rough around the edges. As a manager with a budget starved by the COVID-driven revenue downturn, an inexperienced intern who was hungry and eager was more desirable than a kid with skills who wanted a bigger paycheck and a good "work-life balance."

With the limitations that came from running a business that mostly relied upon revenue from the volatile algorithms of Facebook and YouTube, I always told our new members of the SqUAd, "I have no clue if you will be able to contribute. Come on as an intern or a very poorly paid fellow and as soon as I can justify paying what amounts to a semi-livable salary, I will get the greenlight from the CEO and get you paid."

As consolation for the meager pay, I told all my new employees I could get them a gig serving drinks if they still needed help paying the bills. I also assured them that they could either go to a larger outlet and double their salary in under a year or justify a large raise at our outlet if they performed well.

Even after hearing the grim outlook for his financial prospects in the near future, Jorge was enthusiastic about the position. After I met Jorge in person, it became clear that he would be a great asset for our team.

Jorge crashed on a mattress in his uncle's basement in Beltsville, Maryland, so he could save money. When the job required coverage in DC, Jorge spent countless nights snoring on the couches in my house. After the riots started, he spent most of his time on the road. Jorge's journey and meteoric rise from a dusty desert community college to nationally prominent field reporter was even more spectacular if you viewed it across generations.

Jorge's father served as a child soldier during the El Salvadoran civil war of the early 1980s. He arrived in the United States illegally but managed to support a family in Palmdale, California, on the wages of a long-haul truck driver. I think the fact that his dad could rise above this difficult past and make a comfortable life for his family gave Jorge a fearless drive; no assignment could be as daunting as his father's journey from El Salvadoran child soldier to middle-class American.

.:.

Shelby Talcott was another one of our young, fearless reporters who would become a member of the "Riot SqUAd." Shelby grew up in Long Island, New York, with an older sister, older brother, and two younger brothers. She was a former professional tennis player, which probably explained why she always maintained such a calm demeanor even in the most perilous situations. We got along when she started in 2019 because, as a fellow middle sibling and athlete, we could give each other shit and not take it personally. This kind of tough-love relationship would help us endure nine months together on the road.

I wasn't technically Shelby's boss because she was under Geoff's command, so she was basically the iron-nerved riot sister I never had. We constantly traded verbal jabs and treated Jorge as the younger brother of the bunch. He typically slept on the couch in the hotel room when we needed to save money and rolled in the back seat when we hopped in a rental car en route to the next peaceful, or not-so-peaceful, protest.

Though I believed we were in a self-perpetuating autocracy, Shelby was definitely the most politically liberal of the three of us. She regularly updated us on her mostly anti-Trump family's group texts. Let's just say that some of her family members approved of her work for a conservative-leaning news website more than others.

We jokingly observed these interfamily political debates as part of the territory working for a DC-based operation during such divisive times. Shelby, Jorge, and I constantly went back and forth about Trump's bull-in-a-china-shop style of running the country. Frequent debate about American politics and culture fostered a scrappy but compatible relationship among our little band of roving riot reporters.

Regardless of where we fell on the political spectrum, at the end of the evening we always saw eye to eye on our common goal: Show America the reality beyond where the prevailing institutional narratives focused their oversized, expensive cameras.

May 30, 2020, 7:30 PM EST: Long Island, New York

He shall baptize you with the Holy Ghost, and with fire.
—Matthew 3:11

I was with my family in New York when I received a message from Jorge. He was on his way downtown after hearing that protests erupted in front of the White House. Shelby texted she was on her way shortly after. The moment I logged onto Twitter, it was clear that Jorge and Shelby were in the middle of something serious, a level of anarchy that DC had not seen in decades. It was also immediately evident that Shelby and Jorge's ability to provide our audience with an unadulterated view of the mayhem was above and beyond the other journalists on the ground, who were framing their footage through a biased perspective that proved why their side was righteous and the other side was evil.

Shelby recorded the first viral clip of the evening. It showed a massive fire in the middle of H Street. The pit of my stomach churned with unease as I realized my coworker was filming a fire in front of America's seat of power. The caption stated, "American flag has been burned right in front of the White House." The video received over half a million views on Twitter that night. Minutes later, she filmed a building on fire adjacent to St. John's Church in Lafayette Park, located a block from the White House. The caption on this tweet read "Building on fire across from historic St. John's Church in DC!!" While many other reports conflated the facts by stating that St. John's Church itself was on fire, Shelby's caption got it right. Still, this was arson directly adjacent to a historic DC landmark. Every president for the last two hundred years had visited this church to pray after they had been inaugurated into office.

Just after midnight, Shelby captured the looting of a liquor store up the street from the fires. The video showed her enter the store through pulverized sidewalk-to-ceiling windows. Her sneakers crunched on shattered glass as dozens of masked individuals swiped top-shelf bottles of booze and then dashed out of the small business. It was not just the White House and the executive church that were under attack, the small businesses downtown were also being targeted by the lawless mob. Streams of looters ran past Shelby's steady camera clutching bougie booze.

In just a few videos, Shelby proved brave and in possession of a special ability to record content without confrontation without even a passing glance from the individuals who committed such brazen crimes.

At around the same time, Jorge filmed a heckling mob that chased Fox News correspondent Leland Vittert out of the plaza in front of the White House. In the clip, hundreds of people shouted obscenities while others pushed Vittert and threw trash on him. The terrified news correspondent clung to his cameraman, whose large camera was smashed. They stumbled two blocks to the exit of the plaza. One woman shouted at him, "Imagine what it's like to be a black man, feeling this every fucking day!"

According to Vittert, "It was the most scared I have been since being chased out of Tahrir Square by a group from the Muslim Brotherhood.... *Daily Caller* capturing it [the assault of Vittert and his cameraman in front of the White House] certainly helped."

During my trip to Tahrir Square a month before the Arab Spring in 2011, I'd seen the makings of an unemployed population simmering and ready to boil over. My time in the desert taught me that a tribal battle can turn into a violent mob in no time at all. But the chaos on Memorial Day weekend was not in Egypt or Jordan, it was at the president's house in DC.

The Fox News crew eventually made it to a police car at the edge of the park, thanks to the light from Jorge's cell phone camera, which deterred the mob from escalating violence further. Fox News contacted me and licensed the footage that Jorge and Shelby recorded, then played their work repeatedly over their weekend coverage of the riots in DC and around the country.

As Leland was chased and harassed, multiple Secret Service agents were injured by bricks thrown by protesters. When the Secret Service was outnumbered by hundreds of demonstrators and the risk was real that the mob might overrun the fence on the North Lawn, multiple unnamed White House officials confirmed that Trump evacuated into a bunker buried deep underneath the White House. This added gasoline to the press' coverage. The pro-Trump media used this as evidence of the barbarous violence that stemmed from Black Lives Matter demonstrations in DC, while the left-leaning media cited it as proof of Trump's cowardly nature. Regardless, the fact that the president of the United States was forced into retreat added to the historical nature of Shelby and Jorge's frontline coverage.

After millions of views on their first night, it was clear that Shelby and Jorge recorded pieces of media that we could monetize on our own platforms and also sell to other outlets. By maintaining low profiles with their cell phone cameras, Shelby and Jorge proved that they could capture historic American news events in a way that the greater media, with their large cameras and high profiles, could not.

By the time the fires were extinguished, and the store owners began sweeping up the shattered glass on Memorial Day weekend, 2020, there was a viable business model for our style of coverage of civil unrest. Shelby was our primary on-the-ground reporter who would give nightly summaries of the events on the ground. I would ensure that our videos were monetized properly as I worked with my editors to repurpose the footage on platforms like Facebook and YouTube. Jorge provided support for both me and Shelby, wrangling/conducting interviews, helping me carry camera gear, and giving us the lowdown of what the young Gen Z-ers like him were talking about online.

I headed back to DC a day early on Sunday, May 31, after DC's Mayor Bowser instituted a curfew that banned any unofficial movement throughout the city after 7:00 p.m. I had a strong suspicion that there would most likely be more protests, and more conflict ahead.

June 1, 2020, 6:30 PM EST: 16th and K Streets, Washington, DC

And now also the axe is laid unto the root of the
trees: therefore every tree which bringeth not forth
good fruit is hewn down, and cast into the fire.
—Matthew 3:10

The sun lingered above thousands of protesters gathered on Memorial Day in downtown DC. It was broad daylight, though in just over an hour, if anyone bothered to listen to Bowser, the city would shut down. I doubted many people would listen to Bowser.

As sweat beaded under my converted hockey helmet, I pondered whether we would be arrested when the 7:00 p.m. curfew rolled around. Hopefully my congressional press credentials would provide exemption, but I had never tried to report during a mandated curfew. My ride down to the protests and roommate/unofficial legal adviser "Harp" wasn't sure either.

My anxiety combined with the heat made me question my choice of a black Tamba Surf shirt that I purchased on Kauai. I selected the shirt because black would help me blend in with the black-bloc-clad hardcore protesters. "Black bloc" is a term describing the clothing utilized by dissenters who dressed from head to toe in dark, nondescript attire that masked their identities. The term originated when West Berlin protesters outfitted themselves in all black and masks to protest the police state in the dying days of the Cold War. I learned about black bloc firsthand when I covered extremist rallies and their counterprotests in DC years prior. I chose the Tamba brand so I could glide under the radar as a chill surfer brah.

I also wore a black hockey helmet because I saw Secret Service officers injured by flying rocks and other makeshift projectiles during the riots on Friday and Saturday. I had used it during men's league hockey, which was canceled because all rinks were temporarily shut down. A violent mob forcing Trump into a bunker was one thing, but shutting down my only source of respite from the canned, passionless existence in DC really pissed me off. I removed the metal cage mask that morning.

I also taped over the team logos with black duct tape to fit in with the black-bloc crowd.

Jorge and Shelby provided coverage at the corner of 15th and H streets, while I met up with two of our newest reporters, Kaylee Greenlee and Jordan Lancaster, a block away at the corner of 16th and H. Kaylee and Jordan began working at our outfit after the pandemic started; this was our first in-person meeting. They both laughed at my helmet, and I joked that my mom never let me leave my house without it. I asked about their level of experience in these kinds of situations. Kaylee admitted it was her first day. I thought twice about letting her dive headfirst into a potentially dangerous situation, but when I looked her in the eyes, they were fiercely blue and devoid of fear.

Unbeknownst to Jordan, Kaylee, and me, at the exact moment that we took down our masks and exchanged pleasantries from five feet apart, we were being broadcast live on CNN. The CNN commentator noted to her viewers our lack of masks or proper social distancing.

Apparently, conversing at arm's length in public without a mask was no longer permissible. The texts from my friends from back home in the northeast pinged my phone.

"I saw you on CNN. Put a mask on!" texted my childhood friend's mom.

"OMG what. Be careful," said one of my first girlfriends from high school. Then she sent another text. "But Richie works for this psycho right-wing news thing last I talked to him." Then one more message. "Oh wait I meant to send that to my friends hahaha everyone's flipping out on CNN. Sorry if this was a bad or psycho description [laughing emoji] I'm embarrassed."

I felt a pang of embarrassment. This was my high school girlfriend telling my other female friends that I worked for a "psycho" organization. This revealed how part of our country felt about the opposite side of the political landscape. My career trajectory—from intern at Al Jazeera Arabic to PA at the progressive MSNBC, then video editor of conservative Mark Levin, to finally running the video program at an antiestablishment news outlet—was something my mostly liberal friends would never understand.

When I took the job at *Daily Caller*, I did not realize how polarized our political discourse would become during the Trump presidency. It was early on in his term, and I saw the new gig as a once-in-a-lifetime opportunity. I could build a video team from the ground up, but also familiarize myself with a side of America that I had not been privy to growing up near New York City. This side of America felt overlooked by the coastal elite and saw Trump as a politician who finally understood their plight. On some of this, they were right.

Tucker Carlson, who'd founded *Daily Caller*, had just begun anchoring the coveted 8:00 p.m. slot on Fox News prime time. By 2020, he had the top show on cable news. Similar to Trump's role in the political realm, our audience welcomed Tucker as a hero, while the other half of America thought he was an evildoer.

The sounds of jeers in front of police shields interrupted the preoccupation with my reputation. I would learn later that, while we geared up and made introductions, we were a block away from the smoke grenades and pepper balls deployed on protesters ahead of Trump's now-infamous Bible photo op. I asked Kaylee and Jordan if they were keen on getting closer to the action. Jordan saw the street-wide line of cops minutes after the curfew expired. She politely refused and headed to a safer zone a few blocks up with one of our summer interns. Kaylee, on the other hand, was eager for action. We hustled toward the police line.

A CNN live shot showed me in the center of the screen, cell phone in hand. My eyes darted nervously between outraged protesters and a momentarily calm line of law enforcement who stood behind riot shields that said, "MILITARY POLICE."

At the bottom of the broadcast, the chyron, a technical term for the text that makes up the headline on news programs, read, "PROTESTERS NEAR WHITE HOUSE TEAR-GASSED, SHOT WITH RUBBER BULLETS SO TRUMP CAN HAVE CHURCH PHOTO OP."

According to CNN, Trump issued a direct order to tear gas the crowd in front of the White House so that he could take photos holding a Bible in front of St. John's Church. Trump was accused of performing the publicity stunt as a show of solidarity after the church was vandalized and nearly set on fire during the previous weekend of rioting.

$$\cdot\cdot\cdot$$

Over a year later, an inspector general investigation called this headline into question.

"The US Park Police did not clear racial injustice protesters from Lafayette Park to allow for then-President Donald Trump's march to St. John's Church last June, but instead did so to allow a contractor to install a fence safely around the White House, according to a new Inspector General Report," CNN itself wrote.

The "tear gas" canisters were actually smoke grenades, still unpleasant to inhale but a far stretch from the highly caustic chlorine-based compound known colloquially as "tear gas" and technically as "CS gas." Furthermore, "rubber bullets" were not used. Park Police officers used "pepper balls," which are fired from what is essentially a paintball gun, and shatter into a peppery powder on impact.

We would learn how much stronger the chlorine-based CS gas was when we traveled to Portland in less than two months. And as someone who has been shot by dozens of pepper balls and a handful of rubber bullets, I can also say that the difference is not a mere technicality. Pepper balls certainly sting and can lacerate the skin—even take out an eye though cops aren't supposed to aim for the face—but the rubber bullets pack a much stronger wallop by far. The Park Police definitely exercised excessive force in clearing what were by all accounts peaceful protesters in Lafeyette ahead of the curfew that afternoon, but the claim of "tear gas" and "rubber bullets" was a blatant exaggeration that mirrored Trump's tendency to lie through his porcelain teeth. CNN's reporting was akin to throwing stones inside of a glass house, and it set the stage for a long summer of journalism geared to make the Trump admin look as evil as possible, while details that equated to a more nuanced truth were tossed into the back seat.

As the incendiary headline that implied Trump was the mastermind behind the clearing of peaceful protesters blared across CNN's airwaves, tensions at our position intensified. I prepared a live video broadcast for our five million Facebook followers.

I pressed the red button and commenced the stream. The cops behind the shields wore camo and black bulletproof vests, not the typical Metro Police you'd normally see around these parts. Some of the demonstrators pulled down their masks and shouted insults at law enforcement. I crouched down between the shields and the agitators for a front-row seat.

Over twenty thousand people were watching my broadcast. From my crouched position, I panned over to a group of hecklers five feet to my left, yelling, "You trippin'!" repeatedly at the Military Police shields. I stood up for a moment to zoom in on the roof of the White House behind the camo cops, where two specks for Secret Service agents stood on the roof of the White House next to a tripod, presumably a sniper and his spotter that made up about ten pixels in the video on my phone.

Hundreds of Facebook users posted overwhelmingly negative opinions of the BLM demonstrators when the feed shut off abruptly. This was a common issue at large protests. It was possible that the thousands of phones overwhelmed the cell towers, or that law enforcement employed jamming devices, or perhaps a combination of both. After I lost the broadcast, I closed the Facebook app and saw the time. It was nearing an hour past the 7:00 p.m. curfew.

I tapped Kaylee on the shoulder, but she'd already noticed the troubling sight a half block up the road. Additional law enforcement mobilized with riot shields to our west. They fanned out into an unbroken line that spanned the entire width of the street. To our east, a similar line marched slowly in our direction. I feared that we were caught in the middle of a kettle (the word "kettle" was derived from a German military term for an army that is surrounded by a much larger and more powerful force).

The incoming tide of shields and batons filled every concrete corner between the buildings and the road. The buildings that housed offices of influential lobbyists and the cops that marched between them wielded far more influence than the protesters who sat like ducks in the street. Stuck in the middle, I feared that we were about to be arrested live on CNN.

We proceeded west, where the long shadows of the cops and their shields loomed on the pavement in the lowering sun. The silhouettes of these cops' uniforms were navy blue rather than camo and green. Their standard MPD (Metro Police Department) badges gleamed a sliver of hope for our escape from arrest. Over the last twelve years, MPD had pulled me over many times for what we will call minor traffic infractions, but thanks to a combination of extreme politeness and Irish-Italian white skin in a largely black city, I never received a ticket. I liked my chances of getting past the Metro cops in blue more than the Military Police who wore camo.

We approached the line of stern faces and prepared to plead our case. Kaylee clung to the canvas backpack that I considered lucky because it had accompanied me through countless reckless adventures while I lived in the Middle East.

"Officer, excuse me. Officer, I have credentials." I flashed the congressional press pass that had been issued to me by the House Radio TV Gallery—a government body that regulated which news orgs got legit press passes, and which did not. A small token of legitimacy in a town that considered our news company outside the realm of legitimate outlets.

The nearest officer had a baby face and nudged a more seasoned-looking tattooed cop to his left. The officer with the tats then summoned an officer of higher rank from behind the line of shields. This ranking officer did not have a shield or plastic visor on his helmet, unlike the rest of the grunts who looked ready for a riot. He walked in front of the still-advancing police line.

"Excuse me, sir! I have credentials. As a member of the pre—"

Clearly, the cop was not keen on small talk because he interrupted me abruptly. "Yeah, yeah, OK. Get outta here."

As I filed through the police line, thinking we were free, the officer stepped in between Kaylee and me. Kaylee was doing a good job of making herself an appendage of my backpack until the cop disconnected her and inquired, "Hold on, where are her creds?" Kaylee looked at me. Her courageous eyes looked fearful for the first time.

"Uhhh, please sir!" I stuttered.

"I just started. I don't have them yet," she said.

"Doesn't matter," the boss replied definitively.

"Sir! Please!" I screeched, as if I was begging a men's league hockey ref who had just given me an unwarranted penalty. "It's her first day. How could we possibly get her a credential in time?"

The officer looked irritated by my sorry excuse. "Well, why the *fuck* did you bring her out here on her first day?"

I looked at Kaylee, who remained speechless.

"Yes, sir, but she's tough—"

The ranking officer yanked me through the line by my backpack with Kaylee in tow.

"Whatever, get the hell outta here," he grumbled, then marched onto the next group of protesters who also contested arrest.

"Yes, sir! Yes, sir!" I replied happily. Kaylee looked at me with relief.

After our narrow escape, we called it a day. Harp sent me a message showing Kaylee and me sneaking through the other side of the police line. We agreed that our parents would not have been happy if we had been arrested on live national TV.

A few blocks away, President Trump had hoisted a Bible and posed for photos with the chairman of the Joint Chiefs of Staff Mark Milley, Attorney General Bill Barr, and Secretary of Defense Mark Esper. My phone dinged all night with concerned and enraged text messages from old friends.

June 2, 2020, 6:25 PM EST: 16th and H Streets, Washington, DC

> He was not that Light, but he was sent
> to bear witness of that Light.
>
> —John 1:8

The cable news networks ran frenzied coverage following Trump's Bible photo op, and the next day thousands returned to protest in front of St. John's Church. They lined up along the new non-scalable fence along H Street, which blocked access to Lafayette Park. Around thirty Park Police officers stood behind the fence, seemingly guarding the statue of Andrew Jackson atop a rearing horse at the center of the park. I utilized my belt as a strap like I was climbing a palm tree on a surf trip. Instead of coconuts I was going for a good angle as I hung from a light post and filmed the formation through the mesh in the fence, the White House in the background of the shot.

Shelby was the first to notice boos resounding throughout the crowd. I turned in the direction of their discontent and zoomed in on a man who scaled a traffic light directly across H Street in front of St. John's. He yanked at the 16th Street NW street sign while bottles of water flew past him in disapproval. By the time he finally broke the sign off the pole, a young black man was attempting to pull him down by his shoes. He handed the sign down, and when he reached street level, the surrounding crowd pushed him to the periphery with continued ridicule.

This area along 16th Street would be officially renamed BLM Plaza by Mayor Muriel Bowser three days later. "BLACK LIVES MATTER" would be painted in bright yellow letters that spanned two blocks from 16th and K streets down to St. John's Church at the corner of 16th and H. The street sign that was removed amid overwhelming disapproval of the BLM protesters would be replaced with official street signs that read "BLACK LIVES MATTER PLAZA." The new sign was black, rather than the normal street name signs in DC, which were green. Mayor Bowser's city-sponsored support of the BLM movement was put on prominent display, less than two blocks away from Trump's residence at the White House.

Thirty minutes after the curfew, a sizable crowd remained. This time the police did not attempt any arrests. The sun glowed orange as the demonstration mobilized into a slow march east. When they turned onto Pennsylvania Avenue, the Capitol dome radiated faintly in the distance. Absent the pre-COVID traffic of cars and eager tourists, the expansive avenue was scattered with the flashing blue lights atop Metro Police cars. As the march progressed and the Capitol loomed closer, I scaled a traffic light for another elevated perspective.

⋮⋮⋮

I had a tendency to climb up for a better view of historical events ever since I moved to DC for college. After news that Osama Bin Laden had been killed, my Georgetown hockey team packed twelve guys into a Ford Expedition, then drove to the White House for the impromptu celebration. The cabin of the vehicle was literally packed to the brim, so my buddy Johnny and I climbed up and clung to the roof rack during the three-mile journey downtown. Upon arrival, our revelry rose to new heights.

There, we climbed a tree next to the fence in front of the White House North Lawn. We waved an American flag and cheered as we marveled at the ecstatic crowd below. After nearly an hour, the Secret Service finally ordered me and the rest of the tree climbers to come down.

By this evening, the tree that I ascended nine years earlier was no longer accessible to the public; the Park Police had shut down the entire plaza after the St. John's Church debacle the day before. The White House fence was in the middle of a renovation that would expand its height six feet and six inches to a hulking fifteen-foot wall by 2022.

In the coastal flats between the Capitol and the White House, the traffic signal switched to stop, reddening both of my arms as they wrapped tightly around the top of the light for support. I carefully ventured my right finger to the Record button on the phone clutched in my left hand. From the height of twenty feet, my camera showed the full perspective of the march. Loosely spread out, the mass of signs and masks below spanned an entire city block. A string of white bikes ridden by a dozen MPD officers buffered each side of the mostly black-clad sea of protesters. The protestors chanted, "Black lives matter!"

The tower of the Trump Hotel, converted from the old Postal Museum in 2016, was the silhouette in the background of my shot. I panned the camera 180 degrees to show the entirety of the march. The end of the shot showed the dome of the Capitol, bathed in the disappearing light.

The protesters arrived at the Peace Monument, where Capitol Police placed metal barricades that blocked further advancement. I came down from my perch to follow the leaders of the protest up a 150-year-old 44-foot marble memorial. The stone structure was erected in honor of soldiers who died in naval engagements during the Civil War.

Four Capitol Police squad cars idled at the base. I wondered why they hadn't called us down yet as I reached the top level and took out my phone. I began a Facebook Live broadcast from behind the leadership of the march. Hundreds gathered at the end of Pennsylvania Avenue down below.

One of the leaders stepped forth with a megaphone. The black woman wore light acid-washed jeans in a stark contrast with the dark attire of the crowd below. She prepared the group for a moment of silence in honor of George Floyd. "Please don't say anything. I need a moment of silence in three seconds. One, two, three!"

The crowd continued to mutter among themselves.

The bright-jeaned woman with the megaphone elaborated, "If we argue with each other, then how the fuck are we going to stand against them?"

The crowd clapped and cheered as she continued, "So please, we need a moment of silence for all those black lives that are [inaudible]. If you have to stand or cannot get on your knees, we understand. Black people, white people, people who have disabilities but please, be quiet!"

During the diatribe, a tall black man wearing a black short-sleeved shirt, black ski mask, and red gloves raised his hand high in the air. In the shot that streamed live to our viewers at home, his hand extended across the center of the crowd. His wrist reached up to the horizon in the background, and his fist in the foreground hung low in the sky. His balled-up red glove looked like a fiery sun because the actual sun had already set behind the clouds.

The crowd was so quiet that the only audible sounds were the chirp of the birds and the distant whirr of automobiles. I panned the camera from hundreds of protesters kneeling below to the recently renovated golden dome of the Capitol up above.

The silence continued for over a minute. Meanwhile, the comments of our Facebook Live viewers were displayed at the bottom of my phone screen. Without the riot shields and confrontational subject matter, the viewership was less than one-tenth of what it had been during my live broadcast the day before. But the longer duration of the video allowed for thousands of commenters to share their thoughts.

One commenter named Mike with a profile picture of a portly bearded man in a bucket hat on the beach weighed in. "Say your message and remain peaceful and I support. But then go home."

The next one, Tammy, whose profile picture depicted a picturesque sunset, had a different view. "Vote RED ... remove every democrat. Then you will have change."

A third, named Ida, whose photo showed a gray-haired woman and two small children on a beach said, "What good is it to declare a curfew, if no one follows? How many will get sick and even some may dye. [sic] Remember pandemic!! At least it looks peaceful!!"

Jennifer had a profile photo of a middle-aged woman with a haircut that looked like it belonged in the 1990s and earrings big enough to appear visible even on the tiny image on my phone. She said something I had already seen hundreds of times in comments on our protest coverage.

"Bring in the military already! This has been going on for far too long ... we get it, you don't have jobs and are bored!"

Clearly, not everyone in the country viewed the actions of the protesters as sympathetically as the BLM-friendly progressive media. Four days prior, MSNBC host Ali Velshi turned into a meme after he stood in front of a burning building in Minneapolis and, despite the destruction and rising fires behind him, set the tone for downplaying the violent rioting and arson that cost an estimated $500 million in property damage as, "mostly a protest, and not generally speaking unruly." However, when our largely conservative Fox News–watching audience was actually exposed to raw footage of peaceful protests, they expressed a degree of tolerance as long as the demonstrations were not destructive.

The press had chosen their respective corners. One side was determined to prove that Trump was the ultimate bad guy, while the other was convinced he was the only man that could save the flailing American republic. Witnessing the reality on the ground, all I could see were thousands of desperate protesters, spurred by the same binary lens to defend their cause by any means necessary. For some, this meant attempting to tear the entire corrupt system to the ground by hurling rocks at cops tasked with defending the life of the president of the United States. For others, it required exercising the right to peacefully protest outlined in the First Amendment of the US Constitution. Although these were two distinctly different groups, it was immediately clear that one side of the press only wanted to show the nonviolent demonstrations, and the other highlighted only the most savage ones. Our role was to show the reality on the ground through unadulterated video, and let the audience come to their own conclusions. It was a strange feeling knowing that I was witnessing history, but was simultaneously powerless to change its course beyond helming our miniscule ViD SqUAd. Our content was but pieces of bait in an ocean of media, snatched up for purchase by larger companies, then selectively edited into short clips as blood in the water that pushed the divide beyond a mere political sport.

As we marched back toward the sun's vanishing light, it was, in fact, an entirely peaceful protest. I felt personally moved by the scene in front of the Capitol because I realized that the hundreds who demonstrated on this particular night came with good intentions. They were disillusioned by the same broken system that Trump railed against on a daily basis. But the cinematic scene before us would not appear on Fox's airwaves because it did not jive with the narrative that Shelby and Jorge's more violent clips portrayed. CNN and MSNBC were still preoccupied with Trump's bunker retreat followed by his dastardly Bible photo op.

My legs ached and the sky grew dark. I probably walked over twelve miles in the previous two days while carrying a heavy backpack filled with camera and audio equipment. Yet the larger cameras were too conspicuous, and I'd barely used them at all during the previous forty-eight hours of coverage. It had become obvious that the unassuming cell phone would become the ideal tool for our protest coverage.

Just a few blocks northeast of our destination, I heard a stern voice boom from the side of the street. "Yo! Richie boy!"

I was barely able to pinpoint an unmarked GMC pickup with the engine running 30 feet ahead. My first thought was the feds were somehow messing with me.

The man behind the steering wheel yelled again after he saw me peer sheepishly toward the vehicle, "Yoooo! Rich boy!"

As I tiptoed closer, the driver flicked on the interior light. He was the captain of my hockey team, who just so happened to be an agent for a federal law enforcement agency. "Utah" looked slightly different kitted up in tactical equipment instead of hockey gear.

Shelby and I approached the window. As we arrived, I realized Utah wore a *LevinTV* hat that I gave him almost five years earlier. Utah was the first person I gifted Levin swag when I first started the job.

···

I began working for Mark Levin as a video editor when Obama was still president. Utah and I had been hockey teammates for nearly a decade, ever since I'd graduated college and started my less than illustrious career as a men's league scrapper. Being a lifetime conservative himself, Utah loved the hat that bore Levin's name. He referred to the radio personality by the nickname popularized by his fans, "The Great One." Given that, at the time, I was a pot-smoking creative type who voted for Obama and volunteered for his campaign in Virginia in 2008,

Utah found it amusing when he heard Levin rail on Obama's executive power grabs on almost a daily basis.

Utah also took a curious interest when I won a fight with the men's league leadership over my selection of the jersey number 420, the universal numerical symbol for cannabis. In the political battle of my lifetime at that point, I engaged in a three-month email debate after the league leadership told me the number was not allowed because it was three digits. I was finally begrudgingly granted the number because I suggested using the number 42.0 and they could not come up with a good reason to continue the ban. Utah was amused by the fact that his own federal agency considered the drug illegal, though it was technically legal to grow in my home of DC.

I always had a good laugh when the refs issued a penalty or a rare goal and would have to say, "Number four-twenty," for the scorekeeper's records. Even more entertaining were the chirps that I got from opposing players, many of whom were federal employees like Utah and could not enjoy marijuana since their security clearances would be revoked if they were caught chiefing the green ganja. I guess you could say that my acquisition of the number was a bit of a troll to the straight-edged types, but for me, it made the game more fun and interesting. Utah would often joke with me in the locker room, "Rich I busted one of your buddies in [redacted city] today!"

I approached the window of Utah's GMC pickup. He said, "Nice helmet."

I replied, "Nice hat!"

He answered without hesitation in the same stern voice, "I always wear it when I bust bad guys."

I peered into the window and stole a glance into the back of the truck that was presumably packed with weapons and other hardware that could quell an uprising.

Utah's partner in the passenger seat looked at the hockey helmet on my head with a puzzled expression. Utah weighed in for some context, "Richie plays hockey. He blocks a lot of shots." His partner smiled and nodded.

"It's my disguise," I announced. I hoped to communicate that I wasn't one of the protesters they were there to observe, although my appearance was exactly the opposite.

His partner's stare progressed to my ever-growing pandemic mop, which wisped out from the sides of the helmet. I imagined he considered my head an overgrown planter hanging from some humanities graduate's fire escape in Brooklyn.

My long hair was a poorly kempt testament to my immersion in a culture that neither my hockey teammate nor his partner understood. As I stood on a bridge between two worlds, I changed the subject in an effort to present us as arbiters of truth rather than bringers of chaos.

"Shelby right here was a professional tennis player. She's a certifiable badass. But I can still beat her in a foot race."

Both Utah and his partner looked to Shelby with anticipation. She shook her head indignantly. I actually hadn't raced her yet.

"Nice to meet you," Shelby said.

I explained to Shelby that Utah had spent some time in the hockey equivalent of the pro tennis tour and they both nodded in acknowledgement of their respective athletic prowess. My athletic credentials, on the other hand, didn't go beyond DC men's hockey league leading shot blocker and weekend nonprofessional small-wave surfer.

The tail end of the march streamed past the truck and some of the protesters eyed us suspiciously as we conversed with the enemy. Shelby and I bid Utah and his partner farewell.

At the next crosswalk, I challenged Shelby to a footrace. She beat me off the line with her first few steps, but after ten yards, I caught up, beating her to the 40-yard mark by a body length.

She was quicker than I'd expected.

In a few months, Shelby would utilize her speed as she ran to my aid during a homicide. I would be the one who sprinted accidentally into harm's way, and Shelby would be the one who dashed toward the gunfire for fear that I had been shot.

June 22, 2020, 7:30 PM EST: NW Washington, DC

> From the days of John the Baptist until now
> the kingdom of heaven suffers violence,
> and violent men take it by force.
> —Matthew 11:12

Three weeks later, I sat on my couch enjoying an air-conditioned Saturday on yet another muggy day. I watched a classic western film, *A Fistful of Dollars*, as my buddies and I concluded a summer harvest of our hydroponic marijuana crops. My roommate, a med student who we will call "Roach," was a botanist of sorts. Roach used what we grew in the garage as a remedy for many of the ailments for which he was studying to prescribe pills. His definition of a doctor differed from conventional medicine in the same way that my idea of a journalist diverged from the corporate newsperson supported by big pharma.

The mist burned off from a late afternoon thunder shower typical of summertime in the bog. I logged onto Twitter on the odd chance that the improving weather might yield some protest activity downtown. I immediately came across a clip of a sizable crowd removing non-scalable fences and metal barriers around the Andrew Jackson statue in Lafayette Park. They appeared to be repurposing the fence that blocked access to the area surrounding the Jackson statue for their own defenses. The caption of the video read "BHAZ: Black House Autonomous Zone."

Given that countless statues of historical figures were torn down by lawless demolition crews in the weeks since the death of George Floyd, I sprung out of my lazy recline on the couch. I yelled to the kitchen where my former roommate of seven years, "Rosie," a hulking, bearded Texan man, prepared a Saturday feast.

"Yo, check this out! Can you drive me to the White House?" Rosie had been a Capitol Hill staffer for nearly a decade and understood the gravity of the video just posted from a few miles down the road.

A second cameraman would be advisable, so I shouted upstairs for my roommate and coworker, Sagnik. Sagnik was an Indian lad who was so talented in graphics production that we were able to get him a three-year "extraordinary persons" visa. Attaining his visa required the submission of a 150-page legal brief, part of my harebrained strategy to pluck the best talent right off the vine before their work became recognized and they demanded far more compensation than we could afford. He produced spiffy graphics on popular *Daily Caller* ViD SqUAd productions such as "How to Grow a Beard with Ted Cruz," "How to Dress for Court with Roger Stone," and "Walls Across America: Los Angeles Celebrities Edition."

Sagnik had only officially lived in the house for a few months, but because he came to America on a student visa and wasn't permitted to be paid during his first year of internship with our company, he spent about half the previous year sleeping on one couch or another. Sagnik, like me, worked seven days per week anyway, and heeded my call; within ninety seconds he ran down the stairs with a camera in hand.

I was already wearing my trusty Tamba shirt, though my footwear selection could have been more riot appropriate. As we ran out the door, I threw on the nearest pair of shoes, which just so happened to be my "Fake News" slides. They were my favorite flip-flops, purchased by my brother for my twenty-eighth birthday in 2017.

My younger brother gifted me the Fake News slides because, as he tells it, he heard that I was wearing flip-flops to work at my new job at the *Caller* and thought I should have some nicer shoes to replace them. But when he went shopping for classier shoes, the first thing he saw was a pair of hundred-dollar slides that said Fake News in the Old English font used in a popular "Thug Life" meme.

Prior to the office shutdown during the pandemic, I wore the slides to work at least two times per week. I mostly enjoyed the glares that DC straight edges would send my way on the bus ride downtown. I would watch their eyes as they went from the huge-fonted slides to my T-shirt to my wispy mustached face, perplexed by the fact that I did not fit the mold for a DC rush hour commuter. It was my way of displaying my core ideology: the institutions of our media and government had become too symbiotic, corporatized, and concerned with political correctness.

Unlike the rest of the city, I worked for a company that gave me the freedom to throw off the status quo as much as I pleased. At a time when independent voices were superseded by HR-approved messaging, our small outlet valued journalists for their individual contributions rather than their adherence to a monolithic orthodoxy. The rest of the media mostly viewed us as a garbage tabloid.

The Fake News flops became a physical embodiment of that ethos, and conservative suit-wearing professionals turned their nose up at the flops the same as the well-dressed lefty ones. I wore the flops to the party for Sebastian Gorka's book *Why We Fight* at the Trump Hotel in 2018. The Trumpers eyed the slides just as dubiously as the rest of DC's professional class.

Fifteen minutes later with the Fake News slides on my feet, Rosie slowed down while MPD, Park Police, and Secret Service vehicles sped past us in the same direction.

It was the second longest day of the year, and despite the hazy sky there was still light enough to see dozens of cop cars double-parked up ahead. I aimed my phone out the window and hit Record as we passed a group of twenty MPD officers in a rush to prepare their riot equipment. The ones who had already donned their helmets and armor briskly walked toward the action. I narrated next to a group of officers midjog, "All right, guys, we are approaching the White House and we got riot gear. They are gearing up, ladies and gentlemen. Stay tuned."

When we arrived at the corner of 17th and Pennsylvania, I quickly thanked Rosie for the ride while I jumped out of the car. Sagnik and I made the short run to Lafayette Park. We mounted a bench a few hundred feet from the Jackson statue where we gained an elevated perspective of the surreal sight. I steadied my cell phone camera and pressed Record.

Five ropes were wrapped around the statue, a life-size representation of Jackson in military uniform atop his rearing horse. A handful of men yanked in unison as if taming the former populist president and his steed. His legacy of racism toward black and indigenous people made his effigy a prime target during the BLM movement. With only two of the horse's feet attached to the marble base and Jackson waving his hat in the air, they appeared unprepared for the ambush.

But the historic fifteen-ton bronze statue did not move. A crowd of a hundred scrambled around the foundation as the ropers continued their strained effort. Those not tugging on the ropes held the fences and metal barriers in preparation for police. Others realized their disorganized efforts were doomed and evacuated the park.

A small contingent of Park Police officers, easily distinguishable from Metro and Secret Service because of their light blue helmets, arrived first on the scene. Two young men remained on top of the statue frantically rearranging the ropes for a last-ditch effort at tearing down Old Hickory.

A helicopter hovered low overhead. The roar of its gasoline-powered rotors overwhelmed the desperate calls for a last stand, save someone who shouted into a megaphone repeatedly, "Hold the line! Hold the line!"

I zoomed in; graffiti across the base read "KILLER/X/SCUM." This clip received 1.7 million views on Twitter alone. Members of the White House Press Corps zoomed their cameras, with far larger telephoto lenses, from the safety of their position at the White House North Lawn.

Sagnik and I were two of just a few who were recording from the middle of the action.

I stopped the clip and jogged to another bench for a closer angle. My next video began when a dozen more Park Police reinforcements arrived. The last remaining ropers had abandoned their posts. One of the police officers replaced them atop the statue. He endured a cannonade of half-full water bottles and trash from the vanquished below.

I panned the camera to the helicopter overhead while I narrated for the audience, "Oh my God. All right we have some officers who are removing the ropes. People are dispersing here, folks." I aimed the camera back down to the failed takedown and raised my voice over the rotors, which now hovered only a hundred feet over the chaos. "Some people look like they are still remaining here. Most of the crowd is dispersing, though."

I dismounted the park bench for a closer view. In the sprint across the park, my Fake News slides became slippery from the wet grass. I arrived at the walkway that ringed the statue, ditched my slides, and jammed them into the waistband of my shorts.

A woman entered the left side of my camera's frame and shouted toward the police, "No justice! No peace!" She wore a black hoodie with plastic goggles atop her head and wielded a two-by-four in her right hand, a gas mask respirator in her left.

I snapped my camera to a wide angle for a broader perspective. Just as I steadied the shot, she smashed the wood on the four-foot iron fence that encircled the statue. After it remained intact, she tried two more times. My bare feet gripped the slippery bricks and then stepped on a discarded sign that read "HUMAN RIGHTS NOT TRUMP RIGHTS."

On the third strike the wood shattered into pieces. One piece landed in the grass near the two vandalized artillery cannons that flanked Old Hickory and his steed. One of the old cannons was flipped upside down amid the deserted ropes. The spokes of all the old-fashioned wheels that supported them had been smashed to pieces, just like the two-by-four.

The woman continued around the fence until she came upon the Park Police who now formed a wall of riot shields on the east side of the monument. A second line of cops stood behind them. With the monument's marble base at their backs, the second row of cops were geared up with billy clubs and mace. As the police inched toward the crowd, they commanded, "Back up! Back up!"

The line of rioters who stood their ground was at least twenty strong. Someone rallied fellow comrades for the showdown, "Let's go! Let's go!"

One couple dressed like they were out for a weekend stroll held hands and decided they should walk away. A dainty handbag hung from the woman's shoulder as they leisurely exited the park.

A second couple stood tall at the front line dressed as if this was their Bonnie-and-Clyde moment. The guy wore blue jeans with bright white Air Force One sneakers, and the girl donned sweatpants with Converse shoes. Confounding their casual clothes, both wore goggles like you would see at a swim meet.

Next to them stood a tall man with a smart-looking red backpack and a bright blue Bell commuter bike helmet. Above a hospital-grade N95 mask, his eyes darted nervously back and forth behind goggles that would be more at home in a high school science lab.

Beyond this group was a more menacing-looking individual with a black long-sleeved shirt tight enough to reveal a large, muscled frame. With a neck gaiter pulled high on his face and a bucket hat hanging low, all of his skin was covered except small slits for eyes behind safety goggles you might see at a shooting range. He pointed his yellow-gloved hands at the police line and yelled, "Fuck you, pigs!"

Behind him was another strong guy wearing a short-sleeved shirt that read "I MISS BEING PROUD OF OUR PRESIDENT." He wore an Israeli-made M15 gas mask, but a thick neck gaiter was hiked up around his mouth, which broke the seal between the gas mask and the user's skin. This would be like closing a screen door in the hopes that it would keep out the cold—a total amateur move.

A handful of individuals wearing black bloc stood behind them. They lined up their umbrellas side by side, one of many forms of the agitators' equivalent of a riot shield.

In front of the umbrellas a large fat guy with long blond curls chanted defiantly, "Whose streets? Our streets!" I noticed his bare feet and wondered if he came with the wrong footwear like me. Despite his laid-back appearance, the barefoot belligerent galvanized the crowd. They organized into a tightly packed mass across from police and shouted in unison, "Whose streets? Our streets!"

As the chant continued, Metro Police reinforcements with navy blue helmets bolstered the line. Law enforcement officers finally outnumbered the mob. One of the billy club boys in the back row tapped a frontline officer on the shoulder and whispered something I couldn't hear. Moments later, cops banged their shields into the horde of hecklers and began pushing to the edge of Lafayette Park.

A shield banged into my right shoulder unexpectedly. I glanced around the blow as I would in a hockey game, but in doing so, I snuck through a gap in the shields and accidentally ended up on the police side of the line. Then a club jammed into my back so I raised my hands in the air in recognition. "I'm moving!"

Luckily, a rioter with a gas mask grabbed hold of a police shield, because when he pulled it off the line, I snuck back through the gap with ease. As I fell back onto the other side, I bounced off a cardboard shield that read "BLACK LIVES MATTER." Its owner wore a brightly colored African tribal robe, which stuck out among the other black-clad rioters at the front of the line.

He stepped past me, placed his cardboard shield horizontally along the police shields, and then pushed against them. The billy club coppers behind the shields swung their riot sticks at the hands that supported the cardboard. Incensed by the violence, someone behind shoved me toward the swinging wooden truncheons. I was caught in the middle of the rioters' last stand.

The push against police ended almost instantly once the cops broke out the bear mace, which is basically the same thing as pepper spray but in a bigger canister with a more powerful stream. The spray drenched the entire gang in a thick surge of spicy solution. There were garbled screams as they ran from the line in pain, "Argh!" "Wahhhh!" and a high-pitched "Owwww!"

I defensively turned my head downward so the brim of my hat could shield the spray. That was a bad idea. One of the streams of spray came from an unexpectedly low angle through a gap in the shields. Instead of protecting myself, I aimed my face directly into the blast.

I staggered out of the park away from the cops, who continued the push forward until they cleared the entire brick walkway on the northside of Lafayette Park. After I gagged and spit out spray that had pooled in my mouth, I turned the camera toward my face. The shot showed the results of their nonlethal force: I looked like a toddler who cried himself so ragged that it was no longer clear where the tears ended and where the snot began.

By the time police reset their line of shields, the entire park had been cleared. When I sat down on the sidewalk, I briefly stopped recording. My hands burned as I wiped the spray off my camera lens.

More frantic yells came from St. John's Church. At my new position the church was only fifty yards away. Through my blurred vision I saw black graffiti painted on large pillars that front the church. I tried opening my camera but could not punch in the code. The touch screen was not functioning. After a quick wipe on my Tamba shirt, I opened the camera app and pressed the red Record button.

Protesters in various states of disrepair milled about the stairs of the defaced church. As I zoomed in on the graffiti, which read "BHAZ," with one letter on each of the four pillars of the church, one individual yelled toward the police, "Fucking monsters!" Another screamed, "Evil!"

I stopped recording and immediately logged into Twitter. The footage I uploaded would get millions of views, one side of the media using it to showcase police brutality while the other emphasized the savagery of the rioters.

Rachel Maddow, host of the top show on MSNBC at the time (or her producers), took my footage without permission and ran it at the top of her program that night. Sean Hannity and Tucker Carlson ran footage from the Fox News camera position at the White House. From this angle, Sagnik and I could be seen sprinting toward mayhem, with my distinguishable duck-footed stride hindered slightly by my slides. My goofy run became the brunt of the joke in our *Daily Caller* group. Later in the week, my former employer, Mark Levin, would run the footage. At the moment when I turned my camera toward myself after being pepper-sprayed, Mark cued the producer, "Stop!" The freeze-frame of my teary eyes appeared in the box next to Levin who matter-of-factly stated, "That's our man Richie, cameraman."

Multiple individuals in my footage, including the big barefoot belligerent, would have their likenesses tweeted by Trump, "Numerous people arrested in DC for the disgraceful vandalism, in Lafayette Park, of the magnificent Statue of Andrew Jackson, in addition to the exterior defacing of St. John's Church across the street."

The aftermath proved that both sides of the media and politics paid attention to our reporting when we were the closest ones to the action. If we could place ourselves in the center of the most extreme political unrest, then America would rely on us to show what really went down. This was the first time I was baptized by pepper spray in front of St. John's Church, but it certainly would not be the last.

June 23, 2020, 11:30 PM EST: BLM Plaza, Washington, DC

Whoever believes and is baptized will be saved, but whoever does not believe will be condemned.
—Mark 16:16

The day after every American cable news outlet broadcast footage of the attempted takedown of the Jackson statue and the ensuing police crackdown, the crowd of protesters in front of the White House numbered a few hundred, although this time there were almost the same number of cops. A company of Metro Police formed a buffer one block north of St.

John's Church. Sagnik, Shelby, Jorge, and I spread out through the crowd and filmed various angles.

Standing atop the newly painted "BLACK LIVES MATTER" mural that spanned across the roadway inside the plaza, about a hundred people doused an American flag in lighter fluid and hoisted it onto a light post. It took a few moments, but once the flag ignited, it went up like a piece of tissue paper set alight in a windstorm. Hundreds of others gathered for the spectacle and cheered on the demonstration of anti-American sentiment. Fireworks exploded overhead.

As I filmed from an elevated position at a safe distance, I noticed a crowd form around one camera guy documenting what remained of the flag, a smoldering pile of melted polyester.

His camera made him stand out amongst the cheering activists who filmed with their cell phones. In just a few seconds, he was confronted by a dozen angry onlookers. I got down from my perch for a closer look. A few men shouted for him to leave. "You gotta roll out! You gotta roll out!"

The journalist lowered his camera to his side and stopped filming as twenty people surrounded him. Though he was backpedaling away from the flag, the encircled journo refused to concede and leave. As I ran closer, the crowd obscured my camera angle just as an individual outside of the stubborn cameraman's periphery connected a punch with the side of his head. The sound of fist hitting bone caused the rest of the crowd to gasp. A woman went to help the man up. "Like I said, you gotta get outta here, bro."

Sagnik's footage revealed the strike, which came from behind the man's field of vision, a total sucker punch directly to the vulnerable point where the base of the skull connects to the neck.

The Metro Police were a full block away. For the most part, they allowed this rowdy group to remain unsupervised within the protest area as long as they only burned a few flags and didn't set off too many fireworks.

As a result, no one responded or even noticed when all-too-common screams accompanied the man with the large camera staggering to the side of the road, clearly seeing stars. He stumbled onto the curb. He could barely walk. Two large men grabbed each arm and escorted the concussed photojournalist out of the plaza. I still do not know the identity of the clocked camera guy. Perhaps if he reads this, he can let me know how it felt. As a connoisseur of concussions myself, I can confidently estimate that he was feeling nauseous and foggy for at least a few days.

To our SqUAd, the assault was a somber lesson on how quickly a situation could devolve into savagery. Absent police, and filled to the brim with angry activists, innocent protesters, and anarchistic thugs, a small spark could bring swift violence to whomever was perceived as an adversary.

After June 5 when DC's Mayor Muriel Bowser painted a massive "BLACK LIVES MATTER" mural in Trump's front yard, the area became the focal point for protests in the nation's capital. Over the course of the election season, the discord in BLM Plaza would mirror the political divisions that consumed the entire country. With one side scurrilously opposed to Black Lives Matter and the other in vehement support, major cities would become the stage upon which these two factions would collide. When Americans finally broke out of quarantine and flooded the streets in protest, corporate media and Democratic leadership framed the BLM movement as a binary struggle between the two political parties, rather than one that sought the overthrow of the entire rotten system.

With his pro-police position, Trump was the obvious enemy for the protests, yet the BLM movement was so blinded by keeping him from office, it was rare for them to present the realities of who was running the show on the other side. All the Democrat-run cities we visited would pledge allegiance to BLM and its allies, while Trump threatened federal intervention and became the tyrant they knew he was.

Their alternative for president was Joe Biden, a six-term senator from Delaware who was famously generous to the Fortune 500 companies headquartered in his state because of its low taxes. The paradox of Biden's presiding over a #DefundthePolice movement, specifically his full-throated sponsorship of the iron-fisted Crime Bill in 1994, was lost in a constant hysteria that spilled beyond the digital realm and flooded the nation's streets.

Biden was a part of the Clintonian neoliberal machine that started the White House daily briefing, and began the quarter century love affair between DC's elite press and pro-big business Democrats working in tandem with corporatist Republicans to keep the gravy train chugging along. The arc from William Jennings Bryan to FDR where the Democrats transitioned from the party of the South to the party of the working class had progressed beyond representing the blue-collar, ever-eroding middle class. As more jobs got shipped overseas and working with your hands was less valuable than "learning to code," the poor whites and blacks were fucked with equal measure and consistency for over thirty years. Yet it was the very machine that screwed this working class over that was cranking out BLM initiatives to prove that they weren't the problem, surely everything was the fault of that bigot named Donald J. Trump.

By encouraging the protests despite a global pandemic and escalating destruction, America's politicians would amplify the polarization, all while the mandate-abiding public remained at home fixated on their screens. These state-sponsored lawless environments would prove that no amount of progressive idealism or technological advancement could elevate Americans above the primal nature that lurks in the recesses of our brains.

Chaos in front of the White House—Leland Vittert in white with his camera guys as they evacuated. *Screenshot from video by Jorge Ventura.*

Tahrir Square, Egypt (December 2010).

Preparing for a livestream a block up from St. John's Church—large camera not required. *Photo by Kaylee Greenlee.*

Right before Kaylee and I almost got arrested live on CNN. Note the hyperbolic chyron. *Screenshot from CNN OutFront.*

St. John's Church minutes after Trump's photo op, with Jackson's rearing horse, the White House, Secret Service overwatch and the Washington Monument in the background.

Hundreds of protesters gathered in front of St. John's Church the day after Trump's Bible photo op.

A man removed the 16th St sign amidst jeers and a cannondale of water bottles outside St. John's Church. The sign was later replaced with BLM Plaza instead of 16th St NW.

Hanging from a streetlight on the march from St. John's Church to the Capitol.

A moment of silence from atop the Civil War Peace Monument in front of the Capitol.

When I ran into my men's league teammate, Utah, wearing the *LevinTV* hat I gave him and donning tactical gear instead of hockey pads. I removed the mask from my hockey helmet the day before.

RIOT DIET

Protesters raised their fists outside a non-scalable fence at Lafayette Park after their march back from the Capitol—with a police line and the White House in the background.

Rioters tried to yank down the Jackson statue before police arrived.

Police arrived to disperse rioters and remove ropes from the Jackson statue.

Police cleared rioters from Lafayette Park after an attempted takedown of the Jackson statue.

Billy clubs and pepper spray after attempted takedown of the
Jackson statue.

Post pepper spray at the police line in Lafayette Park after attempted
takedown of the Jackson statue.

BHAZ (Black House Autonomous Zone) spray-painted on pillars in front of St. John's Church.

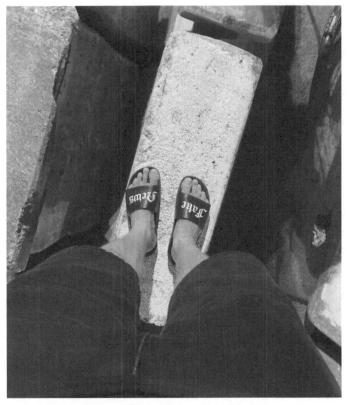

Fake News flops back on the feet, atop a concrete divider after baptism by pepper spray in front of St. John's Church.

Unnamed journalist after getting sucker punched for photographing the burning of an American flag—still clutching his camera, even though he had no clue what planet he was on.

4. LORD OF THE CHAZ

Seattle's Capitol Hill Autonomous Zone

July 17, 1897: Seattle, Washington

Reporting on the discovery of gold stirred up a national hysteria that was intensified because the gap between the richest and poorest Americans were at levels never before seen in American history. The SS *Portland* steamed into Seattle's harbor weighed down by over two tons of gold. On board the ship were sixty-eight lucky miners who'd discovered the mother lode in the remote Yukon-Klondike territory near the Alaskan border. This began Seattle's legacy as a quixotic hub of commercial power, though at the time it was just a small harbor in the American wilderness.

Newspapers across the country feverishly recounted the rags-to-riches story, spurring a westward stampede of prospectors known as the Klondike Gold Rush. In search of their own fortunes, thousands of dreamers rode the recently completed Great Northern Railway to the Pacific Northwest. One of the very first moving films in history showed a ship full of prospectors departing Seattle for the remote mining villages. As the nearest deepwater harbor to the mineral-rich frontier, the city prospered immensely from the discovery of gold. But the overwhelming majority of those who departed the docks in Seattle were unprepared for the brutal conditions. Even if they were fortunate enough to survive the grueling journey north, most would dig up only frozen dirt and return home with nothing more than dead dreams.

Beginning in 1870, the Second Industrial Revolution brought about corporate expansion that enriched the titans of industry, enabled by the policies of their corrupt political allies in the East. The term "Gilded Age," coined by American writer Mark Twain, connoted a gold-painted exterior of economic progress masking the harsh reality of America's interior, where the average farmer or laborer could barely make ends meet.

Such dire circumstances for the American worker presented an opportunity for a populist movement during the presidential election of 1896. At the Democratic convention, a thirty-six-year-old William Jennings Bryan delivered an address that highlighted America's unequal distribution of wealth. His now-famous "Cross of Gold" speech attributed this disparity to the gold standard, which provided a windfall for massive companies but did nothing to benefit the working class: "You shall not press down upon the brow of labor this crown of thorns; you shall not crucify mankind upon this cross of gold."

The speech so passionately captured the plight of the American worker that Bryan won the Democratic nomination for president of the United States. Though the dark horse nominee came up short of beating Republican establishment candidate William McKinley in the general election, Bryan's mere nomination demonstrated the power of his core message—economic progress should generate opportunities for the masses rather than just a small class of elites.

In the wake of Bryan's loss, America's industrial corporate machines continued on their path of continental domination. While the farmers, factory workers, and miners were the engines that drove this prosperity, they were not the ones who reaped its benefits. By 1900, the US Department of Labor stated, "The boom days of the Klondike are over, and the era of high prices and exorbitant wages are drawing to a close." But Seattle was entering a new era—from a remote enclave to a commercial powerhouse.

Seattle's native Duwamish tribe exemplified how this economic progress did not uplift the city's most vulnerable populations. Though the city was named after the tribe's Chief Seattle, his policy of reconciliation with the white settlers ultimately doomed his ancestral home to the machines of progress.

In the early 1900s, the burgeoning city funded a system of canals so that large vessels could dock in Seattle's inner harbor. Rivers were rerouted to create shipping lanes that opened trade routes to the Pacific Ocean. Hydroelectric generators illuminated the city.

But waterway diversions lowered the mighty Columbia River by nine feet, which dried up the estuaries that the indigenous peoples had lived off of for millennia. In 1893, after their population was reduced from thousands to just a few hundred, settlers burned the Duwamish tribe's longhouses so that their village could be cleared for new construction. With the natives decimated, entire hillsides were leveled in the building of Seattle's modern skyline.

Much like the native Duwamish and the stampeders of the Klondike Gold Rush, the people who took to the streets in 2020 had their dreams for a better world overtaken by the corporate machines—the real masters of America's future.

June 11, 2020, 9:01 PM PST: Outside City Limits, Seattle, Washington

In the middle of the scar he stood on his head and grinned at the reversed fat boy. "No grownups!"
—Ralph, *Lord of the Flies*

Jorge, Shelby, and I were packed in the back of our rideshare from Seattle airport while I marveled at the sight of the modern cityscape for the first time. I narrated while zooming the camera into the fog beyond the Seattle Seahawks stadium.

"Well, folks, somewhere over there there's a new country. And we're gonna see it."

After a week of protests and multiple riots on Seattle's Capitol Hill, on Friday, June 5, Mayor Jenny Durkan promised a thirty-day ban on the use of chemical irritants, pending an internal review. "This review should better emphasize de-escalation techniques." What ensued for the next two days was anything but "de-escalation" and was instead a continuation of the same shit show — rioters threw bricks and bottles, and shot fireworks at police. By Sunday, June 7, under a barrage of improvised projectiles, cops desperately discharged chlorine tear gas, the chemical irritant that the city's politicians pledged not to use.

I watched the escalation of progressive violence from a computer screen in DC. It concluded with a police evacuation as cops hastily loaded onto armored vehicles and drove away from Seattle's East Precinct. Hundreds of jubilant activists and agitators filled the void behind them. A trumpet man ushered in the occupying army of demonstrators. The boarded-up front of the station endured over a week of antipolice protests-turned-riots before they finally capitulated to the mob.

As night fell on Monday, the BLM demonstrators took control of the front of the station. By sunrise the next morning, they set up roadblocks and established checkpoints, expanding their inchoate dominion to a five-block area in the heart of Seattle's Capitol Hill. The ousters triumphantly named their new fiefdom "the CHAZ" (Capitol Hill Autonomous Zone).

Seattle Police Chief Carmen Best, the first black person to occupy the position, justified the boarding up of the station in a press conference after the establishment of CHAZ. "This is an exercise in trust and de-escalation." In reality, a major American city had ceded control of a multiblock area on their Capitol Hill, creating a Demilitarized Zone (DMZ) that would be ruled over by a bunch of young activists and whatever other malcontents decided to join. Among the demands from various protesters, one theme was consistent: reduce Seattle's law enforcement budget by at least 50 percent or institute the total abolition of the police force.

On Tuesday morning, Shelby sent me a video that showed the movement's self-proclaimed leader and local rapper, Raz Simone. With a rifle in his hands, Raz declared the area unequivocally off-limits to police. I convinced my bosses that we could recoup the costs of a trip, and Shelby, Jorge, and I flew out on the afternoon of Thursday, June 11. We splayed out across entire rows of the plane as we crossed the continent to the newly independent territory in the Pacific Northwest. With the coronavirus scare reaching a climax, airports in both DC and Seattle were as empty as the abandoned East Police Precinct.

On our ride to Capitol Hill beneath the slanting sun, we drove past Seattle's Pioneer District, where the city's founders had settled in 1852. At the center of the district rose the Smith Tower, which was the tallest building west of the Mississippi River at the time of its completion in 1914. The thirty-four-story building was one of the oldest monuments to corporate prospecting in Seattle. It was constructed in neoclassical architecture by New York typewriter and firearms tycoon Lyman Smith. In the background of my shot, the Smith Tower was dwarfed by larger skyscrapers that rose into the low clouds. They housed far larger and wealthier corporations.

Somewhere beneath the misty skyline was the CHAZ, the postmodern experiment without sanctioned businesses, or police, or posing politicians.

While videos of armed individuals patrolling the lawless zone at night had been widely broadcast on corners of the web, the prevailing institutional media narrative was that the occupied protest was very much a "partylike atmosphere." Cable newscasters parroted this line from their hits on location during broadcast hours, though none of them covered the situation late at night—after they returned to their luxury hotels for the evening.

The debate over CHAZ entered national politics the day before we arrived when President Trump tweeted, "Radical Left Governor @ JayInslee and the Mayor of Seattle are being taunted and played at a level our great Country has never seen before. Take back your city NOW. If you don't do it, I will. This is not a game. These ugly Anarchists must be stopped IMMEDIATELY. MOVE FAST!"

In tacit support of the protest, Democratic Governor Jay Inslee responded, "What we will not allow are threats of military violence against Washingtonians coming from the White House. The US military serves to protect Americans, not the fragility of an insecure president."

Then in another Tweet in the same thread the governor stated, "The Trump Administration knows what Washington needs right now—the resources to fight the COVID-19 pandemic."

The progressive Mayor of Seattle Jenny Durkan weighed in as well, with a reference to President Trump's retreat to the bunker under the White House on Memorial Day less than two weeks prior. "Make us all safer. Go back to your bunker. #BlackLivesMatter." The same day, Mayor Durkan was asked by CNN's Chris Cuomo how long her city's Capitol Hill would remain like this. Her response was, "I don't know. We could have the summer of love!"

June 11, 2020, 11:00 PM PST: Capitol Hill, Seattle, Washington

> This is our island. It's a good island. Until the grownups come to fetch us we'll have some fun.
> —Ralph, *Lord of the Flies*

At the entrance of the CHAZ, a sloppily spray-painted piece of plywood read "WELCOME TO THE CALZONE." Another, more formal sign painted white and cut in the shape of a house, said in neatly stenciled letters "YOU ARE NOW ENTERING FREE CAP HILL."

Can't be worse than that open-air drug market in San Juan, I thought. An amalgamation of city planters, road construction dividers, metal barricades, and plywood created a de facto wall that marked the border. The individuals who tended the checkpoint wore all black and carried walkie-talkies, but they appeared more interested in socializing than security.

The first thing we recorded as we stepped inside was a giant "BLACK LIVES MATTER" mural that spanned the width of East Pine Street, stretching eastward two blocks up the hill to the police precinct.

The purple letters of the mural were beautified with intricate decorations that embossed the political mantra into a work of art—much more creative than the neon yellow block letters in DC. With dozens of paint cans and brushes scattered on the roadway, the main drag looked more like an art studio than the center of a major American metropolis. To our left, new wave music blared from massive speakers on an astroturfed baseball diamond turned campsite.

At the intersection of East Pine Street and 11th Avenue next to the R in the "BLACK LIVES MATTER" stood a piece of plywood that read "DEFUND/NOT DECAF/COFFEE TEA COCOA." The neatly hand-painted sign featured a red-and-black color scheme and font that eerily resembled the antifa logo.

Antifa, short for "antifascist," represented a political movement that often employed violent tactics in its opposition to the 2016 election of President Donald Trump. Its black-and-red logo harkened back to the antifascist faction that opposed Hitler's rise to power in 1930s Nazi Germany. Though I'd heard much about "antifa" in American media, their decentralized organization and black-bloc attire made identification of its actual adherents difficult if not impossible. That is, unless they admitted to it or were literally flying its flag. By design, the core of the group lurked anonymously through the demi-world of the extremist left that sought the total overthrow of the capitalist system.

Directly in the center of the intersection, a set of couches were arranged in a circle. I narrated from behind the camera adding context for the viewers, "We got a lounge zone over here?" Two signs drawn on cardboard propped up by art easels with sharpie-drawn letters said "CONVERSATION CAFÉ/LET'S TALK ABOUT ANTIFASCISM."

The ground was covered in all forms of graffiti from chalk to spray and acrylic paints with messages like "FREE THE PROTESTERS" and "FUCK THE POLICE" written in elegantly scripted periwinkle letters. The patrons of the café sat forward in their relaxed furniture, seemingly engaged in some intense political discussion.

I panned the camera across the intersection lined with tables featuring donated food: bags of chips, granola bars, bottles of water, and toiletries. Shelby and I walked over to the main table of the "NO COP CO-OP," which was basically an open-air grocery store with a variety of selections, and plenty of choices for vegans. Behind the tables stood a guy who seemed like he oversaw the operation. He wore a black long-sleeved shirt with a generic blue mask, and he had a pierced right ear. He appeared friendly enough. I asked, "So what's going on here, can you tell us what's up?"

He seemed unfazed by the cell phone camera aimed in his direction and enthusiastically explained the origin story of the CO-OP, "The lady who set this up sent a tweet, 'Yeah can I get some tents,' then people brought tents and umbrellas, and she started bringing food from her own pantry. Then people started donating more food as we went. Yeah, so this is what we have now, free food; we also have other stuff that people dropped off like helmets, masks, all that cool stuff."

I zoomed in on the helmets and the plastic face shields on display, both of which would be helpful protection from pepper spray and other nonlethals in the event of a confrontation with police. "Yeah so, we're a market, we don't accept cash so if you guys have food in your pantry, come down to CHAZ and donate it!"

I pushed for more on how this market functioned. "So the form of payment is basically like a bartering system?"

He responded eagerly, "Yes, no government, nothing except—"

Someone outside the frame who perused the selection interrupted his shpiel, "Hey, can I grab this?"

The guy responded quickly, "Yes, please, whatever you like."

I continued my informal interview, "So it's like some people bring their goods and services and they exchange them for other goods and services?"

He nodded his head affirmatively, "Yeah."

I replied, "Gotcha."

Shelby picked up the interview where I left off, "So you guys are open twenty-four hours?"

He replied, this time with hesitation, "Uh, I said that earlier, and she kinda got mad at me, she's like, 'Are you staying?'" He gestured to an older woman, presumably the aforementioned founder of the NO COP CO-OP. With a nervous chuckle, he continued, "But, yeah, I'm staying here all night. I work the night shift as it is, so it's my day off."

Shelby had zeroed in on the disorganization of the whole operation with one question.

Now that she was onto something, she asked one more. "Is there always someone here? What happens when…"

He responded, "Yeah?" But the way he said it made it sound more like a question.

"I mean it's only been a few days, so whoever takes over takes over." It was clear to both of us that this guy had no clue what the long- or even short-term goals were for the operation.

Shelby and I looked at each other with raised eyebrows as if to say, "This ain't gonna last."

We continued through the Zone. A block ahead of the police precinct we encountered one guy on a ladder who used a large roller to paint bright yellow symbols over a green, black, and red background. The mural ran about seventy-five feet long, the entire length of the boarded-up storefront. He wore a USA hockey jersey with no name on the back and a heavy winter hat that was out of place given the warm summer weather.

"What do we got going on here?" I asked as I rolled up behind him.

"Just a backdrop for some beautiful words," he replied.

I was confused about his vision for the abstract mural, so I continued, "What does it say? I can't quite see the whole message here."

He replied but maintained focus on his work, "Oh, there's no words here. I'm just beginning the patch up."

"Oh, so you're just gonna paint over it?"

"Uh-huh, we will see if it makes it through the night. It's like an organic, the whole build and…everything is like a part of the art. You know, it's all part of the process." He chuckled as he stepped down from the ladder and dragged it farther down the work in progress. "Because you can't stop people, you know?"

I panned the camera from the artist, then back to the mural, and stopped the video.

As we walked up the hill to the abandoned police precinct, I contemplated this young artist's acceptance of the fact that hours of his labor could be painted over by the end of the night. Similarly, the hodgepodge plan for the NO COP CO-OP that supplied the budding community with essentials revealed the improvised nature of the entire undertaking.

Everyone danced and chatted giddily just like the kids in *Lord of the Flies*, who celebrated their newfound independence after they washed up on a deserted island and realized that there were no adults to speak of. But as time wore on, and intra-island power struggles developed, the young boys' tropical utopia descended into something far darker and more sinister. Jack and his hunting party took ultimate control of the island with their sticks sharpened into spears. Raz anointed himself leader of CHAZ with a rifle in his hands.

We reached the top of the hill, where the police precinct was surrounded by repurposed street barricades and chain-link fences. The giant silver sign above the door that previously read "SEATTLE POLICE DEPARTMENT EAST PRECINCT" now said "SEATTLE PEOPLE DEPARTMENT EAST PRECINCT," with the black "POLICE" lettering painted over with "PEOPLE" using black-and-gold spray paint. We noticed a solitary officer working under a desk light inside and wondered how he got in there with the entrance blockaded. We later found out that the station was still staffed by a few cops. They went out through an electronic garage door at the back during odd hours of the morning.

As the evening progressed, the live music performances, drum circles, and revelry reflected more of a quirky hippie summit than a protest zone. Luckily, we packed a few beers and hard seltzers just in case we needed to make friends. I figured that alcohol was a more appropriate vice for this occasion than the more street-legal cigarettes I brought out in DC. I was hankering for a drink given the long flight and the fact that airlines had stopped serving beer because of the coronavirus, or as we called it, Da 1-9.

A man in a full knight's suit of armor clanked down the middle of East Pine Street in front of the station. I took the spectacle as an opportunity to crack a White Claw and offer this guy a "Cheers." White Claws were by far the most novel and popular alcoholic beverage that summer, and I viewed it as the perfect drink to enjoy within the checkpoints of the CHAZ. "No laws, drink some Claws," I exclaimed.

The knight was occupied by a line of people who wanted selfie pictures with him. Realizing it would be difficult to wrangle an interview with this character, I grabbed a short video that captured the strange scene instead.

My camera panned up from the newly cracked spiked seltzer to the knight as he lowered the protective visor over his eyes. He clanked it shut with a hard slap to the metal helmet as I exclaimed from behind the camera, "Epic!"

I brought the phone over to Shelby and showed her what I thought was a hilarious piece of content. She appeared unamused by the fun and games. Shelby's primary goal on the trip was securing an interview with the warlord of CHAZ, the man named Raz. Realizing it was time to get back to business, I joined Shelby on her investigation of the security checkpoints that served as the CHAZ equivalent to ports of entry.

We walked a block beyond the precinct, and arrived at the intersection of Pine and 13th Avenue where an old Chevy Suburban was parked horizontally across the street. In front of that, providing additional roadblock was a Sprinter van covered in graffiti. I didn't know it at the time, but this was what would become the infamous "BLM Snack Van." A variety of barriers were stacked alongside the vehicle to reinforce the checkpoint that marked the easterly reaches of the dominion.

Three centurions manned the roadblock, smoking cigarettes and conversing amongst themselves. One man with a bright red beard and scraggly red hair flowing from a blue construction helmet sat on top of the nineties-era truck. I pulled out my phone and hit Record, aiming at the ground at first to avoid upsetting the security detail. The guy on the roof was in the middle of a diatribe about how to properly build a shield from PVC pipe, pool noodles, and duct tape.

"If the Zulu shields, which were just wood and leather, could stop a rifle round, duct tape can stop a rifle round. You just need enough of it!"

I injected myself into the conversation. "Yeah, the Zulus did beat the Brits that one time."

He brought a cigarette up to his mouth, raised the lighter, but then gestured with the cigarette instead of lighting it. "It was the only time that a technologically inferior group managed to whoop the ever-living *shit* out of the British!"

I chuckled. Now that we had him talking, Shelby went for a more relevant topic. "Do you think that the police—they came today right?"

He waved the unlit cigarette in her direction. "You know they might come back. They might be hiding in some bunker, gathering resources, waiting for one big-ass push against us. And I'd rather, when they show up with their goons with riot shields, we have our own going." He pulled both his hands up as if he held an imaginary shield in a defensive position with the cigarette protruding from his fist. "Ours look cooler!"

Shelby laughed nervously and sputtered, "Yeah."

The guard took the lighter and cigarette up to his mouth but abandoned it again. "I figured you were asking around people." Now he aimed the cig at me. "You seem like you're, you know, of some significance!"

I laughed from behind the camera, and Shelby chimed in, always eager to chirp me when given the opportunity. "Don't give him a big ego."

We all laughed, and the guard added gregariously, "Hey, we're all important. We're all just doing our part." He finally lit his cigarette.

Shelby used the silence for a shift in the topic of conversation. "How long have you been out here for?"

The didactic defender took a long huff on the cigarette before he replied. "I just got here today. I was at the [May] 30th protest." He coughed into his sleeve before he finished the story. "Got my ass beat by police. Healed up. Came back out!" He smoked the cigarette satisfactorily.

Shelby pressed. "It seems like there's no police out here tonight."

Exhaling the smoke and then inhaling air to inflate his chest, the guard growled, "Yeah, but you got the fuckin' alt-right retards threatenin', posturin', and just, like, all right, come out here. I am more Aryan than thou, motherfucker. Hitler loved him some blue-eyed gingers!"

I stifled a laugh, fearing his Hitler joke crossed the line and might attract negative attention from the other two guards loitering nearby.

Shelby ignored the joke and gently pressed him on his claim. "Have you seen a lot of alt-right people out here?"

The boisterous ginger looked around. "No I have not, not since I got out here. There was one Jeep that was circling around, and I was like, 'Why have you passed us multiple times? Are you friend or foe?'"

He hocked a loogie and spit in my direction. The large droplet of mucus splattered loudly on the pavement a few feet below my camera's microphone.

A shirtless, heavily tattooed man approached the checkpoint. The guy explained in slurred speech how he had been wronged during a fight earlier. He drunkenly appealed his case to the red-bearded security guy, seeking some kind of restitution.

We turned our attention to another border guard. The young man, who was maybe in his midtwenties, shifted anxiously from one foot to the other in front of the passenger door of the Suburban.

He wore black, top-of-the-line running shoes. He also sported an extremely expensive-looking black waterproof hiking bag and a windbreaker that probably cost more than many of the people inside the CHAZ had in their bank accounts. A needlepoint belt slung around his chest served as some kind of ill-fitting holster/sling for a large, silver .50 caliber Desert Eagle. The bright chrome of the gun was just barely visible from inside a black holster that had been looped through the belt. The firearm looked cartoonishly large alongside tight-fitting black clothing that clung to his scrawny torso.

Shelby and I moseyed over and made small talk. Shelby asked him where he got the needlepoint belt, and he said that his mom made it for him, and he thought it worked well.

In fact, it was not "working well," as the large caliber firearm swayed from side to side when the young man shifted on his feet. The firearm dangled between 20 degrees and 30 degrees shy of parallel to the ground, which meant it flagged anyone who crossed his path closely enough ("flagging" is when one unintentionally aims their firearm at another human). I caught myself thinking that Momma should have fed this guy more milk and protein and forced him into some manual labor instead of coddling him with homemade belts.

Convinced that the bony boy with the big gun was a hazard to our health, we approached a third guard, an Asian fellow who had a walkie-talkie with a large, silver antenna sticking up near his face. His equipment suggested he possessed some authority so we decided he might have insight on any semblance of a security protocol.

The sleeves of his gray flannel shirt were rolled up above the elbows, which rested on a repurposed plastic road divider. Large white stickers on the plastic barrier read "DEFUND SPD" in black letters with the symbol of a raised, closed fist that was synonymous with the BLM movement (and also closely resembled the logo for Maoist China's communist uprising).

He looked in our direction as we approached, holding a cigarette in his hand like a writer holds a pen. This time Shelby launched into her most pressing question right off the bat, "So is there anyone like running this? Or is it just like a whole group? Because I've seen news reports that claim there's a certain person running it?"

The guard clasped his free hand on the butt of the unlit cigarette and pondered the question before he replied, "I can really say with a lot of certainty that there is not a specific person running it."

He paused again. Shelby refrained from another question, instead waiting intently as he fumbled for the next thing he wanted to say.

"Um...are you talking about Raz?"

Both Shelby and I laughed and nodded. She exhaled. "Yeah, that's who I'm talking about."

The Asian man's walkie-talkie antenna waggled as he shook his head in disapproval.

Shelby explained herself further. "Because it seems that he himself has said that he is the leader?"

The guard responded quickly this time. "That guy self-declared himself sheriff." Then he fumbled for words while he delivered the cigarette to his mouth, unhinging his mask. "Do you mind if I smoke?"

"Yeah, no, we don't," I said.

He lit the cigarette, during which time the blue-helmeted red-beard climbed down from his throne on the Suburban's roof and stood on the back bumper like an up-and-coming politician preparing to deliver a soapbox speech.

Based on the level of his voice, it sounded like he was projecting to a crowd far larger than the three people that stood in front of him. "Like if you want to be a self-declared leader... No. Because you don't want to lead—you want to rule people." He said the word "rule" in a much deeper tone, implying that it was a perverse word around these parts.

The Asian guard chimed in approvingly, "Yeah!"

But the bearded ginger was on a roll now. "If you're going to be a leader, you're going to have people come up to you and go, 'You! You! What do I do?'"

Both of them paused and Shelby filled the silence with an unenthusiastic, "Yeah."

The beard-guy stood as tall as he could on the back of the old Suburban. "You have people who *don't* want to lead *lead*!" He said the word "lead" as he pushed out his chest, making it seem like he was auditioning for the leadership role himself.

The Asian guard took a rip of the cig and looked down exhaling the smoke, seemingly uninspired. Then he added his version in a much quieter tone, "Honestly, just speaking for myself, um…" He paused and leaned forward. "It really sucks to see the media focused on that guy [Raz], um …"

Shelby encouraged him with an inquisitive, "Yeah?"

He gestured with the hand that didn't hold the cigarette. The walkie-talkie antenna oscillated by his head with his growing animation, "Because specifically what I see my role as" —he placed his free hand on a tactical vest strapped on outside his flannel—"as a nonblack, person of color here, is basically to support the movement and make sure that they are able to basically do what they need to do to get their voices heard, um…"

He paused and looked down. Shelby and I remained silent, waiting for him to finish his thought.

"And a lot of the black leadership, pretty much all of the black leadership that isn't Raz, doesn't agree with him. But that's been something that like, in an autonomous situation here" —he gestured to the (mostly) abandoned police station and CHAZistani dominion down the hill behind him—"where no one is in charge." He turned back toward us, resting his elbows back onto the road divider as he finished his thought. "There's a lot of that sentiment but people haven't gone out and said anything yet."

Shelby looked satisfied by his answer so I requested a cigarette from the mutiny-minded checkpoint guard. I subtly slipped my phone into my pocket as he retrieved a smoke from his vest. I thanked him for the hoon and lit it up.

Shelby waved her head indicating that it was time to go. I took two more drags of the cig then ashed it prematurely. We thanked the guards and walked back toward the police station.

Save for the faint sound of a few partiers camped out in the baseball diamond, things were quiet. We reconvened with Jorge who confirmed that not much was going on. Shelby updated Jorge on the tenuous security situation at the border. After our first night, it was already apparent that this no-cop utopia had already developed infighting amongst the ranks of its so-called security force.

June 12, 2020, 11:45 AM PST: Luxury Apartment Complex Just Outside CHAZ, Seattle, Washington

He says the beastie came in the dark.
Littlun with the mulberry-colored birthmark
—*Lord of the Flies*

The next morning, we headed back to Seattle's Capitol Hill to inter-view a resident who lived in a nearby luxury apartment complex. We wanted interviews with not only those who participated in the protest, who viewed their demonstration as a means to curtail the power of the police, but also those who lived in the community near the area. When we entered the lobby of the apartment building, the spotless interior and vaulted angular ceilings contrasted starkly with the frumpy, grungy tents less than a hundred yards up the road.

This guy must be paying two grand a month to live next to a glorified home-less encampment, I thought.

The man we scheduled for the interview greeted us from a sleek armless leather couch in the lobby. Before we exchanged pleasantries, he glanced around furtively as he asked for assurance that his identity would remain anonymous; he feared retribution from hardcore support-ers of the protest.

Once we arrived inside his apartment, he let his guard down a bit, especially when he found out that we shared a mutual friend from his time living in Washington, DC. Our interviewee was part of the gay scene in DC with Ralph, who was one of my best work friends while I was a lowly production assistant at NBC News. Our timid interviewee decided he could trust us. While I set up the cameras next to a window that poured light into the spacious one bedroom despite the cloudy day, Shelby briefed him on what topics we would discuss so he could feel at ease. Typically, if a reporter wants authentic answers, they will ask the questions without much preamble. But this was a private citizen scared out of his wits, not a public figure like Hillary Clinton getting fed the questions ahead of a debate.

Shelby started by asking what life had been like since the establishment of the CHAZ.

"I haven't gotten a lot of sleep because for the first time in my life in Capitol Hill, I hear gunshots every single night and I've heard people screaming every single night outside. And they're not protest screams. I've heard protest screams. But I've also heard screams of terror out there."

Seattle police stated that 9-1-1 calls that reported robberies, rape, and other violent crimes had increased threefold, though police were not allowed entry to the zone to protect victims or to investigate complaints.

After he finished this anecdote, he choked up. Rather than jumping in with another question, Shelby just locked eyes with the guy and nodded silently. This was a tactic that she used, patiently waiting to see if the subject responded with more detail. I preferred a peace offering of cigarettes or alcoholic beverages in these instances, but to each their own.

Fighting back tears, he continued, "I called the governor. I called Governor Inslee, and I listened to a two-minute audio recording telling me about how to report nonessential businesses like hair salons for being opened and I'm just patiently listening through it, and I get through to a staffer."

His voice raised in subtle anger as he continued the story. "I told him that the police were going to lose the precinct tonight." He folded his hand over his knee, which was shaking nervously. "And this staffer in Governor Inslee's office, he gave me his customer service voice, and he said he would refer me to previous remarks the governor had made. And I said, 'Well, the governor made those remarks before what happened tonight,' and he said, 'All I can do is refer you to previous remarks."

Much like the protesters outside, the subject of our interview believed that the institutions designed to serve and protect had failed. He viewed the absence of police as treacherous, while the demonstrators outside thought the police were the problem.

After the interview, we returned to the hotel where I imported the footage into Adobe Premiere for the edit, which consisted of synching Shelby's audio, adding cuts, blurring our interviewee's face, and applying color correction. I masked the audio in his voice as if I was editing a sit-down with a defecting spy rather than a guy who just wanted to tell the world why he didn't like living in the neighborhood of an American city where cops were not allowed.

Once the editors back in DC approved the video, we published it on Facebook, YouTube, and Twitter. Shelby also embedded a YouTube link of the interview for an article that appeared on the front page of our website. Then we prepared for another long evening of coverage embedded in the protest, changing into our CHAZistani outfits.

June 12, 2020, 4:19 PM PST: Western Entrance to the CHAZ, Seattle, Washington

> We've got to have rules and obey them. After
> all, we're not savages. We're English, and
> the English are the best at everything.
> —Jack, *Lord of the Flies*

A light drizzle fell on the baseball diamond-turned-campground. A small crowd smoked weed from a bong and lounged by their tents while others threw frisbees and kicked soccer balls in the lingering mist.

We meandered to the top of the hill across from the police station where a hundred or so people gathered around a large PA system, surprisingly expensive equipment for a protest. As the CHAZistanis discussed what they wanted to achieve with their newfound social experiment, Shelby, Jorge, and I nodded to each other and fanned out into the crowd.

A black guy in his midforties, who seemed to be the MC of the event, pulled down a Seattle Seahawks mask and addressed the audience via wireless microphone. He wore jeans and a plastic poncho, resembling a dad at a rainy soccer game more than a hardcore anarchist with radical demands.

"We like to look at people who need help and help them. We need to look at people in need and be there for them. We need to make it a monument of social justice and reform. A monument of what we can do, and accomplish together as a people. So please let's remember why we are here. We came here to discuss things as a group and find solutions. We have been here all week. We do not have time to listen to everyone's story. I'm sorry. There are countless black lives that have been lost.

Countless! We do not have time for those who are just getting onboard and are just learning."

Based on this guy's speech, leaders of the movement were unsure who possessed the proverbial conch, the symbol for law and order that the young boys in *Lord of the Flies* used for the establishment of who would speak during their meetings. Much like the conch, whoever held the microphone was ordained with the power to shape what the aims of the protest should be.

This guy thought CHAZ could become an example of social justice for the rest of America. In his view, handing the conch to newbies who would share their personal stories might not be the best course of action to achieve those goals.

A short, slender individual with a purple mask securely over their nose and mouth stepped up to the microphone. The individual held a thickly bound Moleskine journal with a few papers on top of it, like an unofficial inspector clutching a clipboard.

"'Ello, I'm Benny. I use they/them pronouns. You can text me about any of the things that I'm going to say, after. So our group was the 'vibes' group, which from the get-go is a very large topic. We had a very hard time having real discussions about any one topic."

As Benny continued, I panned the camera around to show the congregation listening intently.

"So the overall thing from that was that, when that happens, we need to break into smaller groups. And we need a strategy for how to do that. One way I suggested to do that is to have everyone in your group go around, if they are comfortable saying their name, they may, um, the pronouns whatever other information is relevant, and three things they want to talk about in that one … or one thing they want to talk about in that topic, the 'vibes' topic, in three words. And then after that we can kind of see a shared…idea, and how to break into smaller groups from there. Because we weren't even able to talk about what 'vibes' even meant."

I peered over my phone to Shelby across the crowd, and we both gave each other puzzled, wide eyes.

"And larger ways to … talk about our vibes and how to connect that to larger groups as well because our vibe comes across in long-term goals and in short-term goals and in our night watch and our communication.

So, it's a very large topic, umm, ... and we need to be able to break out into smaller groups and maintain communication after that. So my suggestion is to include that way of breaking out at the beginning of conversations when you see the size of the group that you have."

Most of the crowd appeared equally perplexed by the speech. The MC next to Benny glanced around the audience uneasily, apparently unsure if the words registered with anyone.

Benny continued, seemingly unaware of the confusion. "Some of the topics that came up within vibes was holding space, having a conversation about holding space for different voices, people who may not be comfortable speaking in large groups, um, as well as facilitation and how to help facilitators and people who may not have as much experience facilitating and creating more facilitation, um creating some shared guidelines around how to facilitate. Uh, there was also a barrier group, talking specifically about the vibes that people get when they enter this area, what the barriers are like, and how we can make sure that they are continuously staffed. And then an extension of breakouts outside of these meetings and how to maintain those breakout groups beyond a 15-minute discussion. And that's...pretty much it."

Benny handed the microphone back to the MC. Uninterested in continuing the "vibes" discussion, the moderator segued away from the Black Lives Matter topic and went straight for a less confusing proposal. "Are you guys scared of Donald Trump?"

The audience replied emphatically, "*No!*"

Incensed by the screams of the crowd, he went on. "I love my city. We don't give a fuck about Donald Trump out here. I know that's right. Say it louder!"

The crowd replied again, "Fuck Donald Trump!"

The moderator encouraged another call and response. "Say it louder!"

The crowd screamed, "Fuck Donald Trump!" at the top of their lungs.

Hatred of Trump unified the CHAZ at that moment when nothing else seemed sufficient, even though Trump had no authority over state or city police or any measurable effect on the lives of Seattle residents. The tragedy that propelled the country into protest, the death of George Floyd at the hands of police, was due to problems with policing that existed long before Trump was elected. Yet this series of speeches solidified in our minds the one thing that everyone in CHAZ could agree on—any system that gave Donald Trump the presidency should be upended and replaced. The question of how concrete police reform could be achieved through protest was far less straightforward.

Like the kids in *Lord of the Flies*, determined that they could create their own society free of the onerous laws of the adults who previously ruled over them; the CHAZ represented a once-in-a-lifetime opportunity to show the world that society could turn a new page. That young people could lead us into a more compassionate and harmonious future than the one that had been established by our parents.

But Benny's "vibes" speech also showed that the final form of this new utopia was by no means clear to its builders, despite all of the apparent hallmarks of bureaucracy like clipboards and breakout sessions. Hypothetically, things like open dialogue and "facilitation" were methods through which the proper path could be discovered. But the demonstrators' idea of what was happening inside the CHAZ sounded completely at odds with the description provided by the resident we interviewed earlier. While he recounted nothing but tales of violence and chaos, Benny described only good "vibes" and productive efforts of "facilitation."

The truth was probably somewhere in between—a lot of positive dialogue took place inside of the Zone, but also instances where the lack of society's normal guardrails led to senseless brutality and destruction. All of the participants in this experiment unanimously stated, "Fuck Donald Trump," and yet they relied on what they referred to as "barriers" along their borders (god forbid they used Trump's favorite term "wall"), and stationed armed guards to monitor them. The barriers and firearms that protected the CHAZistanis were eerily similar to Trump's plan for a wall, which would, from some vantage points, place more security along America's border to ensure its sovereignty.

While the demonstrators at the CHAZ successfully forced the "fascist" police out of the area, they replaced them with their own armed patrol and security checkpoints. Whether or not this more idealistic police force was capable of securing a more harmonious society was still unclear. But we all had a creeping feeling that, sooner or later, someone was going to end up dead, just like Piggy in *Lord of the Flies*, who was smashed to death with a massive rock.

In the moment Piggy's body lay lifeless on the rocks amid the crashing waves, the boys of the island realized that their idealism could not overpower their animal natures. No matter how hard they tried to build a society better than what the adults created, they could not escape their innate tendency to descend into tribalism and violence.

June 13, 2020, 5:45 PM: Capitol Hill, Northern Border of the CHAZ, Seattle, Washington

> "I got the Conch," said Piggy, in a hurt
> voice. "I got a right to speak."
> —Piggy, *Lord of the Flies*

We received a tip that two individuals would take large American flags through the occupied protest. Jorge got the information from a controversial conservative commentator who worked for Blaze media, Elijah Schaffer.

Jorge ascertained the name of one flag bearer, Katy Daviscourt. Her reputation as a conservative activist made us curious whether these two would make it through the CHAZ unscathed.

They planned entry into the Zone from a grass park just north of the baseball field. Jorge, Shelby, and I awaited their arrival right next to some CHAZistanis who had hilariously raked over a thin layer of topsoil on top of cardboard boxes. Apparently, they were planting vegetables, which carried the ambitious assumption that the CHAZ would last long enough for the seeds to be harvested. I sparked a doob that I purchased at a dispensary to calm my nerves, and I couldn't help but laugh.

I ditched the joint the moment I saw individuals walk into the park carrying very large American flags. The first was Daviscourt, a blond woman with a Stars and Stripes bandana for a mask, camo pants, her flag supported by a 6-foot piece of PVC pipe. The other flag bearer was a black man standing about six feet tall, with no mask, his flag supported by a much longer, knobby pole about eleven feet long. Perhaps "log" would be a better description because it was at least five inches in diameter. Along with black boots, a denim vest, and matching jeans, he resembled a modern-day Daniel Boone, ready to conquer a new American frontier. The flag affixed to the log certainly provided a great aesthetic, but it would most certainly become cumbersome when they entered the bustling Saturday crowd at the center of the CHAZ.

The pair of flag bearers were flanked on one side by a stocky-looking guy with a camo gaiter hiked up above his ears and an American flag bandana folded and tied around his head. In an open-carry state like Washington, it was unclear whether his baggy Yankees jersey cloaked a firearm, but it certainly crossed my mind.

Another guy a few paces behind wore a Desert Storm–patterned camo hoodie with his hands hidden in the front muff of his jacket. His baseball cap was pulled low over his eyes, like a cowboy walking into town for a late afternoon showdown. The bill of his hat swiveled back and forth as he scanned for potential threats in the park before him.

They continued down East Pine Street toward the entrance to the Zone. Their flags waved in a temperate breeze that originated from the snow-capped mountains to our northeast. An indiscernible hip-hop beat played loudly through speakers in the baseball park. The laid-back vibe was incongruous with the indignant crowd that gathered as the flag bearers stopped twenty yards in front of the main entry point in front of the Black Lives Matter mural.

While they stood just outside the orange plastic road dividers that marked the border, the suspicious onlookers voiced their concern. The microphone of my camera picked up a security guy talking to his walkie-talkie. "Yeah, there are some people with a flag, and they're walking up here."

The flag folks, now accompanied by a few dozen onlookers and hecklers, proceeded to the main entrance on East Pine Street. When they passed through the barriers, the walkie-talkie security team allowed them to enter freely.

They marched over the huge Black Lives Matter mural while a black woman with a megaphone shouted disclaimers about the motivations of the intruders. "Understand that what they're doing with those flags is an act!"

Other less zealous spectators casually grabbed cups of Defund Not Decaf before they moseyed over and observed controversy. As more flocked to the spectacle, the flag flyers' pace slowed to a crawl.

A white male wearing a Cossack ushanka hat with a plastic hammer and sickle on the front stepped defiantly in their path. The male flag bearer stopped and planted the log at the intersection just beyond the BLM mural. The huge flag waved above both of them, brushing the comrade's fur hat as he staged his confrontation.

"How you gonna fly this fucking flag?" He gestured upward with his hand, which held a cardboard Starbucks cup. "That's like a Jew flying the fucking Nazi flag, man."

After he delivered his comparison, the comrade took a satisfied sip of the expensive beverage and stared down the black man with the flag. The irony of spewing radical communist rhetoric while enjoying a drink manufactured by a massive multinational corporation based in Seattle was lost on Cossack Ushanka. Based on the mood of the sea of masked faces with angry eyes still directed at the flag activists, I was the only one who got the joke. Maybe I was a little stoned.

A black man with a dark T-shirt emblazoned with a white "BLACK LIVES MATTER" logo ushered the guy with the Communist hat toward Katie Daviscourt, who was attempting to circumnavigate the quarrel when the two walked up by her side.

The furry Commie hat looked on intently while BLM Shirt inquired, "Don't you care about black lives?"

With the pole resting on her shoulder, the flag waving down her back, she replied, "Of course I do!"

The comrade who also loved Starbucks shot back, "Then don't fly the fucking flag!"

Out of the corner of the camera frame, a petite white woman who wore black jeans, a black jacket, black mask, and a black hat low over her eyebrows snuck up and snatched the flag from the preoccupied blonde. It yanked off the PVC flagpole with ease, but as the thief went for her escape, the flag folks' security guy with the camo hoodie bear-hugged her and the pilfered flag. The other security guy with the Yankees jersey joined in defense of the Ol' Glory.

The two men wrestled with the woman for a moment. Perhaps realizing that even if they could get the flag from the thief, they were now seriously outnumbered, the two men released the woman from their not-so-friendly embrace.

The flag snatcher ran down the street and around the corner. The comrade wearing the Commie hat exclaimed, "Yeah! Take that shit!"

Buoyed by the successful steal, the CHAZ defenders swelled with intensity. I was looking down at my phone, posting the video of the flag theft to Twitter, when a liquid splattered off the plastic surface of my hockey helmet and onto the last remaining flag, as well as its carrier. When it dripped onto my phone, I lifted it to my nose, did a smell test, and looked over to the flag bearer. We both flashed maskless grins and raised eyebrows in silent acknowledgment. "Yep, that's piss."

The security guy with the Yankees jersey, perhaps sensing the rising tide of excitement, signaled to the two flag activists who changed direction and pushed their way downhill toward the baseball diamond. Beyond the open space of the field, the walls of the park marked the northern reaches of the CHAZistani Empire.

As they trudged across the Astroturf, a swarm of hundreds of streamers (a term that refers to independent journalists who "stream" their coverage live on the web) and angry activists jockeyed along the fake grass for the last word. In the middle of the horde, the blonde's eyes flashed fearfully back and forth between the screaming activists and streamers. The last remaining flag bearer still appeared tranquil. He barely moved, save occasionally removing one hand's iron grip on the log to readjust the spectacles on his face.

I climbed a three-foot stone wall that marked the exit for a better perspective, spotting Shelby's salmon-colored athletic pants directly next to the scuffle. As Shelby put it afterward, when she played pro tennis, she was "really good at charging the net."

Meanwhile, Jorge backpedaled right below me. He hoisted his phone over his head for the climactic conclusion. Though the cell phone remained stable, his helmet was even more crooked than usual.

With the escape back to civilization looming only a few paces ahead, a handful of CHAZistanis made a last-ditch attempt to snatch the second flag. But the final bearer and his muscle with the Yankees jersey wrapped the flag around the log and hugged it for dear life. For a minute, the two groups yanked and fought over the knobby piece of wood swathed in the Stars and Stripes. The patriotic counterprotest devolved into a game of tug of war. The mob gave up after realizing their "flagversaries" would not relinquish the giant stick as long as they remained conscious.

Free from obstruction, the flag demonstrators jogged out of the CHAZ and into the streets of the sovereign United States. A few dozen CHAZistanis shouted profanities and continued past the border, unwilling to hand their adversaries an escape without giving them a piece of their mind.

The "flagitators" quickly piled into a nearby vehicle. They maneuvered out of the parking spot but were blocked by a gray Jeep Liberty in the middle of the road.

Is this the Jeep that the red-bearded centurion was referring to the other night? I thought.

Jorge ran to the window of the obstructing Liberty as the driver read the fleeing flag bearers' license plate number into a walkie-talkie.

The driver replied from behind a cloth mask and large sunglasses. "Hi! I'm the security on our side!"

"Why are you taking their license plate number?" Jorge asked.

The driver replied quickly, "They instigated! I'm from the John Brown Gun Club!"

Jorge walked to the rear of the vehicle. "What's your tag?" His cell phone camera revealed that the Jeep had no plate. Spooked by the inquiry, the driver sped out of sight. The flag bearers' vehicle departed in the opposite direction through screaming ridicule from both sides of the road.

Jorge holstered his phone and stepped in my and Shelby's direction. Perhaps the crooked helmet impaired his peripheral vision (it was angled in the direction of oncoming traffic), or perhaps he just didn't look, but as Jorge dashed across the street, a small sedan collided with his legs at about ten miles per hour. I looked on in horror as Jorge bounced off the hood and flew through the air. Upon landing, the plastic helmet smacked off the pavement and then popped off his head.

As Jorge lay there, my mind raced. How would I explain to my bosses that our new unpaid intern suffered a busted-up noggin — and worse — on my watch? With my stomach in my throat, I felt like Ralph after the other boys dropped the giant rock on his friend Piggy's head.

After a brief moment of dread, Jorge sprung back to his feet. I am definitely not a physics guy, but in my estimation, the fact that Jorge did not see the car initially was a godsend. Rather than tensing his muscles before impact, Jorge bounced off the grill of the car and the ground like Jell-O.

Jorge examined his superficial scrapes and deemed himself good-to-go. But our exit ordeal was not over yet. On our way back to the hotel, we noticed that there were a few black-clad characters on our tail about fifty yards back. Though there was no way to know their intentions, they carried walkie-talkies, a trademark of the CHAZ's border patrol.

We were surprised that they would pursue us even outside the Zone. Apparently, jurisdictional jurisprudence was not something that concerned the CHAZistani patrol. Jorge, Shelby, and I changed course to the opposite direction of both the Zone and our hotel.

After walking a few blocks at a brisk pace, the pair remained on our tail. We doubled back through an alleyway. They must have realized that we were onto them because the pair disappeared. I ordered a rideshare rendezvous about five blocks away. Around the next corner, we nearly bumped into a man with a hot pink respirator hung around his neck and safety goggles propped on his head. I recalled the distinctive colorful filters on the mask from inside the scuffle earlier.

I looked at Shelby and Jorge. It was time to boogie. We entered a dead sprint down another alleyway, and thankfully, our vehicle pulled up as we reached the next street. We jumped into the back of the car, and I set the destination for a riverside restaurant at the marina twenty minutes away.

The rain that Seattle was famous for began beating down on the roof of the car. We burst into laughter at the absurdity of the entire experience, with the timing of the rain adding to the drama.

Over beers and food, we reviewed the footage, which showed Shelby was nearly impaled in the tug of war over the log and the flag. From Shelby's video, we captured a screen grab of her non-phone hand pushing against the piece of wood as it swung toward her body. She swatted the wayward log like she might spike a lob shot on the tennis court.

When I asked how she did it, Shelby chirped about how I could never achieve reflexes like that because I wasn't a former professional athlete. She appeared completely unphased.

Between Jorge getting hit by the car and Shelby's close call with the log, I experienced the dreadful rock that lodged into the pit of my stomach when I faced a set of rogue waves, at the mercy of nature's fury and with nowhere to go but headlong into the froth.

June 13, 2020, 11:45 PM PST: East Precinct Police Station, Capitol Hill Autonomous Zone Seattle, Washington

> Ralph moved the lenses back and forth, this way
> and that, till a glossy white image of the declining
> sun lay on a piece of rotten wood. Almost at once a
> thin trickle of smoke rose up and made him cough.
> —*Lord of the Flies*

The top of the hill in front of the precinct very much resembled a "partylike atmosphere." This party line was the perfect descriptor for the CHAZ, at least on this particular Saturday night.

Instead of a backpack filled with cumbersome camera gear, I packed it with White Claws and craft West Coast IPAs. While I was on the clock covering the news for our website, I argued that the weekend revelry was part of properly blending in with the crowd. Most people would not tell the full truth to someone they perceived as an uppity reporter from DC.

We split up, and I bounced around what felt like an EDM (electronic dance music) festival, interviewing various characters. The most curious was a guy in a full wizard costume, complete with a twenty-five-pound crystal ball that he had somehow mounted on a wooden staff.

After further investigation, he admitted he found the staff in the woods while on a psychedelic mushroom trip. I told him about my experience paddling into a Hawaiian winter storm on mushrooms, and he rambled on about commonalities among all world religions.

A DJ behind him blasted the song "September" by Earth Wind & Fire. I asked if he could tell the audience more about the curious orb. Lights from the DJ booth refracted through the crystal ball into my recording phone camera.

"It lights things on fire, like a cigarette or a weed bowl. But, most importantly, I can draw artwork on wood with it. Burning etchings into wood. It just magnifies the sun's light."

I laughed loudly and thought he was joking. "You've etched wood with that thing?"

"Yeah," he replied matter-of-factly.

I was perplexed, partially because, by this point, I was rocking a serious White Claw buzz. "Wow!" Then I pivoted to the topic of the day. "And what do you think about the flag being grabbed and fought for?"

The orb went this way and that while he gestured an enthusiastic reply. "I think the only thing the flag should technically be used right now for is to have it upside down and flown in public. Upside-down flags mean they're in distress."

I concluded the interview after he launched into a long diatribe about the American empire and realized our audience probably wouldn't care for this content. My mind and my backpack grew lighter as I guzzled more White Claws and continued roaming.

By 2:00 a.m., I sat in the Conversation Café, where I found myself arguing with avowed communists about the values of critical thinking and free thought. I had somewhat diverged from my original aim of sitting down and learning more about the political philosophies of the CHAZistani people. Shelby thought that I had gone too far in revealing my own ideologies, while Jorge was more receptive to my claim that it was all in the name of immersing ourselves in the culture. Or maybe he just thought it was funny.

The Conversation Café was akin to the platform of granite where the boys passed the conch during their meetings in *Lord of the Flies*. It was a focal point for the search for common ground, a gateway to implement a brighter future. The café was, in theory, a place for culture to strive for a reinvention of the way we interact with the modern world. A world that was shaped by generations of our ancestors who carved some approximation of societal stability out of Mother Nature's chaos.

Shelby was a straight news reporter, which sometimes conflicted with my video-focused approach. I aimed for entertaining, eye-opening content with whoever might be willing to share their thoughts on camera. Shelby, on the other hand, told her stories through matter-of-fact articles that pieced together a broader picture. I provided a window into the madness, while she tried to explain what was going on in the entire madhouse. The more I peered through the window, the more I wanted to participate in what was going on inside.

It was admittedly difficult to make money off a late-night interview with a drunk guy explaining how to etch wood with a glass orb. But the mystical wizard and his staff struck me as significant; the staff was a symbol of how this young hippie made sense of the world around him. Like the sun's rays that could be focused on a marijuana bowl or piece of wood, the Wizard Man used this magical staff as a tool that could manifest order from the increasingly entropic universe in which we lived.

Much like Piggy's "specs" in *Lord of the Flies*, which were utilized by the boys on the island to make fire, we were all doing our best to focus on the important rays of light that shined into our cold-hearted realities. Or, the best of us were. The worst wanted the specs to create fire—fire meant not to feed or send signals for rescue but to burn down the entire isle.

Those who occupied the CHAZ, including myself, searched for meaning in the world and a way to turn it into something better. At the same time, absent any police, those with the strongest arms were the only ones with any tangible control.

But this particular night ended entirely peacefully, and we reported it as such.

June 14, 2020, 9:13 PM PST: Seattle West Precinct Police Station, Seattle, Washington

> He began to dance and his laughter
> became a bloodthirsty snarling.
> —*Lord of the Flies*

After we completed the mile-long march from CHAZ to the west police precinct in Seattle's commercial district, I recorded a clip of a man within the crowd of around sixty aiming the middle finger at the cops inside the station. I zoomed in on the officers who stood on the second floor above the entrance. They gazed at the lewd hand gesture through plate glass windows as if they were examining a fart in a jar.

A familiar voice shouted into a megaphone near the front doors. I recognized the speaker as the MC from the day before who sandwiched Benny's "vibes" speech. But the MC had changed. He no longer appeared as a soccer dad seeking unity. He was now clad in all black and took a more menacing tone.

"Does anybody understand what happened to the people who did not get onboard with the French Revolution?"

The audience responded, "Chopped!"

He continued. "That is the message we need to send. We are serious. This is not a joke."

The crowd supported his final statement with cheers. It is important to note that around this time, CHAZ attempted a rebrand to CHOP (Capitol Hill Occupied Protest), which sounded less like a bunch of armed nutter butters taking over a police precinct and more like the peaceful occupied protests of the past.

I'm gonna stick with the original name.

While the speeches were addressed solely at the police station, immediately to the south was the Seattle waterfront, which opened the floodgates for some of America's largest corporate enterprises. Within a mile of our location were the headquarters of some of the largest companies in the world.

A few blocks inland, at Pike Place Market, a young New Yorker opened the first location for what would become the world's largest coffee retailer, Starbucks.

Less than a mile to our north was Lake Union, where Boeing, the largest aerospace company in the world, launched its first seaplane flight in 1919.

To the west towered the Space Needle, the tallest building this side of the Mississippi when it was completed for the World's Fair in 1964. The 520-foot observation deck looks down on the Puget Sound, once the native habitat of the Duwamish.

Adjacent to the Space Needle was the headquarters for the Bill and Melinda Gates Foundation, the second largest nonprofit in the world, which was started by the founder of the Seattle software giant, Microsoft.

And just around the corner from the Seattle West Precinct loomed the 521-foot Day 1 Building, the largest of a three-tower complex that housed the global home base for Amazon, which was founded in Seattle in the midnineties by former Wall Street hedge fund manager Jeff Bezos.

The rank-and-file police were a far cry from the ruling elite in France, who gorged on cake while the masses starved in the streets. Why were the protesters focused on the little police precinct when one block to the west loomed the Amazon headquarters, whose annual income jumped from $11 billion to $21 billion in 2020? The little guys' businesses were shuttered by government mandate, and the protesters were targeting the precinct for a bunch of blue-collar cops while standing in the shadow of Amazon's massive HQ, whose founder became the richest man in the world thanks to the pandemic.

Looking back two decades, it was apparent why all the international conglomerates decided to get onboard with BLM and sway with the swing of monoculture's wings. In the final days of 1999, the same area of Seattle became the epicenter of a battle between globalization and its opponents—one that would come to characterize the primary political battle of the twenty-first century. Under the banner of the World Trade Organization, the world's top technocrats, bureaucrats, and politicians planned to meet and make agreements behind closed doors at the Seattle Convention Center. The WTO's agenda aimed to liberalize international trade laws and incorporate over 140 sovereign nations into a codified global trade network. After Clinton signed into law the Bush-initiated North American Free Trade Agreement at the start of his first term in 1993, by the end of his second term, he was ready to conclude the coup de gras of the neoliberal, laissez-faire trade policies. The WTO would create a harmonious and wealthy global community. The agreement was endorsed by Republican Speaker of the House Newt Gingrich but opposed by old-school pro-labor Democratic congressmen who landed on Clinton's political left.

Many less powerful members of this "global community" saw a different agenda at play—namely, a corporate elite looking for cheap labor and less restrictive environmental control. Seattle was hosting a monumental deal that would impact the entire global community, all without bothering to confer with the population they lorded over. The companies were getting bigger and more powerful, and the proletariat was being pushed out of the picture—that is, until forty-five thousand people converged around the convention center in the commercial district on the first day of the conference, November 30, or N30.

A coalition of labor unions, human rights activists, indigenous peoples, environmentalists, nationalists, church groups, NGOs, even one group called Turtles and Teamsters—an almost comically diverse amalgamation of groups—initiated direct action demonstrations to keep the limousines and gas-guzzling bulletproof SUVs from getting into the conference without a struggle. The anti-WTO protesters peacefully shut down traffic by blocking intersections. Hundreds chained themselves together using concrete and steel pipes attached by carabiners that only the traffic blockers themselves could untether. They weren't blocking freeways or major commuter throughways, but they did successfully blockade the intersections surrounding the convention where the conference was underway.

By the afternoon, entry to the conference had become such a clusterfuck that police took action. They used pepper spray and tear gas to more rapidly disperse the crowd. The demonstrators were forced out of the area surrounding the WTO meeting, and by nightfall, they were forced a mile away to Seattle's Capitol Hill.

There was also a more destructive minority that capitalized on the chaos. Black-bloc-masked malcontents smashed the windows of banks and a Nike store, looted a Starbucks, overturned newspaper stands, and spray-painted cameras of local news teams who were foolish enough to get too close—causing millions in damage. But the cops were preoccupied with one objective—ensure the predominant trade organizers, the ones allied with the president rather than the costumed turtles, could make it to the talks. So the window smashers were left to go about their destruction, and the traffic blockers were dealt whatever force was required to keep the conference afloat.

The next day, D1, President Clinton was due to give a speech. Air Force One arrived at Boeing Airbase in the dead of the night. City officials issued a curfew. Two hundred unarmed National Guardsmen and three hundred state troopers were brought in to support Seattle police.

Clinton delivered a speech from the safety of his luxury hotel at the Four Seasons in Seattle, in which he reflected upon his vision for this prosperous global community. "Today I want to talk a little bit about the work that we're all here to do, launching a new WTO round for a new century—a new type of round that I hope will be about jobs, development, and broadly shared prosperity; and about improving the quality of life, as well as the quality of work around the world; an expanded system of rule-based trade that keeps pace with the changing global economy and the changing global society."

The "rule-based trade" was actually code for "cheap trade" via manufacturing in countries that lacked labor and environmental protections fought for and won by organized labor in the United States. Yet the smaller African, Asian, and Latin American countries, perhaps emboldened by the teamsters and turtles outside, stalled the conference. It ended without a conclusion. The protesters cheered at the news, thinking they had won a victory over the globalist multinational cabal. Not so fast.

The media ran continuous coverage of one dumpster lit on fire and of the black-bloc bullies smashing windows, all lumped in with the peaceful protesters whose sole aim was a nonviolent boycott of the protest downtown. And isn't it funny that, back then, the Ol' Gray Lady—the *New York Times*—slandered the protesters by mixing them in erroneously with rioters. The *NYT* report claimed that demonstrators "hurled Molotov cocktails, rocks, and excrement at delegates and police officers."

Whoopsie! The *Times* issued a correction two days later: "The authorities said that any objects thrown were aimed at property, not people. No protesters were accused of throwing objects, including rocks and Molotov cocktails." Three-time Pulitzer Prize–winning NYT egghead Thomas Friedman wrote an op-ed citing why the protesters were wrong to oppose unmitigated free trade. That was easy for him to say. Friedman made millions selling books and writing articles about the merits of globalization.

After what came to be known as "the Battle of Seattle," the police chief—a.k.a. the fall guy—Norm Stamper, resigned in disgrace. The whole world had seen Stamper's police force exercise their crackdown with impunity on behalf of the international visitors and at the expense of the protesting American citizens they gassed and sprayed in the streets. There, in the commercial district near the Columbia River, a beachhead was constructed in defense of the corporation, and the coalition of protesters were pushed away like silt in a surge.

On January 29th, 2000, Bill Clinton was introduced by World Economic Forum leader Klaus Schwab in a thick Swiss-German accent. "Mr. President, we want to truly use this meeting as a catalyst to consider new ways to spread the benefits of globalization." The problem here was that Clinton was the president of the United States, not of the whole world. History proved that the protesters in Seattle had won the Battle of Seattle but not the war waged on behalf of the American middle class.

The downstream effects of these trade agreements were dandy for the corporations who sold cheap shit to the American consumer, because they were manufactured under duress in sweatshops overseas or down south of the border. Although viewed on a longer timeline, the same process slowly eroded any chance the American middle class had to ensure their family was on stable financial ground.

Seventeen years later, during his 2016 campaign, Bernie Sanders railed against the wholesale of American jobs in favor of cheap retail. "Trade with China cost 3.2 million American jobs." But as Wikileaks emails revealed, Hillary Clinton's campaign sandbagged Bernie, and there was no chance she would undo globalized trade initiatives favored by the uniparty and strengthened under her husband's two terms. Trump also campaigned against Clinton's selling out of the American worker in the name of liberalized, globalized trade.

The city of marble monuments and continuously expanding budgets remained ignorant of the Americans suffering to pay bills in the slowly rusting and rotting industrial power houses during the previous twenty, thirty, even forty years. The Democrat politicians who went to DC to represent these flyover districts slowly followed the money, transitioning from the party of the working class to the party of the global technocratic elite. Yet the entire apparatus began clutching its pearls when Trump's victory defied every Beltway poll. During the campaign, he surely exhibited the moral compass of a dirty rock at the bottom of a swamp, but the fact that he won in spite of his obvious faults was lost on the establishment because they couldn't possibly be culpable; they were the smart ones, and only dummies and deplorables voted for that bastard Donald J. Trump. Nowhere was this more apparent than in the commercial tech hubs of the west coast.

Whether it was Amazon, Microsoft, the banks, the boutique cafés, or the goliath clothing brands—in 1999, any company that benefited from cheap foreign labor learned a lesson: if you don't want the activists on your doorstep, then you must join them. In August of 2020, even

Boeing made a pledge of $10 million to BLM-related causes when CEO and President David Calhoun triumphantly declared, "At Boeing, we acknowledge the toll that systemic racism and social injustice have had on people of color, particularly black communities here in the United States." Note how he said, "Here in the United States," given that Boeing had a storied history manufacturing bombers that killed both black and brown people indiscriminately in faraway lands.

All the biggest international banks pledged multimillion-dollar donation plans to Black Lives Matter and related causes. Jared Diamond of JPMorgan Chase took a knee with other employees in public solidarity with BLM. Starbucks rolled out a special edition BLM protest shirt that was mass produced in Haiti. Suburban white ladies could buy said shirt for the cost of three grande lattes, then show off their virtue for the cause at the local Whole Foods in their 90-plus percent white towns. The only problem being that the shirt was made in a country where 95 percent of the citizens are black, and the average salary is $150 per month. The shirt's mere existence exhibited the economic slavery of cheap labor exploited by Starbucks, which ensured that Haiti remained mired in poverty despite winning the only successful slave rebellion in history. For the absolute farce of a wealthy and harmonious global community that Clinton invoked at the WTO, one needs to look no further than Haiti: the 151st poorest country in the world per capita, with thirty-two of the remaining forty poorest countries in Africa.

It was as if the gruesome death of George Floyd suddenly woke the rich white executives out of a multi-millennium slumber, and they decided—all at once—to start donating to black causes out of the pure goodness of their hearts. That's not to say that the donations were a bad thing, at least as long as they went to legitimate nonprofits, which some did. Although Black Lives Matter's own financial filings proved it to be an organization that was boldly and undeniably corrupt.

Even though it was 2020 and the internet videos should have been free and open, like the early internet days, it turned out that the conversation about the divisive election issues were more programmed than any time before. Of the corporations that ran American media, the largest one that represented the political right, Fox News, as well as the oldest newspaper in the United States—acquired by Fox News/News Corp boss Rupert Murdoch—*New York Post*, zoomed in on our coverage of this new iteration of lawlessness in Seattle. But only because it satisfied their agenda, which kept America divided and tuned in. The nuanced difference between rioters and protesters was less convenient than the oppositional narratives that fit ever so nicely into a red or blue ballot box.

While we walked back to the CHAZ, it was already clear Shelby had recorded the most viral clip of the evening. The call and reply's implication that the ruling class would be "chopped," or beheaded by guillotine as they were during the French Revolution, surely contributed to the clip's virality. With over 650,000 views on Twitter, Fox News' Sean Hannity's producer sent Shelby a message and booked her for an appearance the following night on Hannity's prime-time show.

Viewed from a business perspective, our audience had significant overlap with Fox's viewership. Though we would soon learn that an appearance on a program like Hannity would effectively blackball us from the other major network news outlets, namely, any that did not rhyme with "Shocks News." The earned media from Shelby's news hit added an essential commercial success to our Seattle sojourn, though it would also become part of a trend where the larger media companies distilled portions of our content to the public only when the clips served to prove a partisan point.

The coalition of Teamsters and Turtles was a forgotten memory. As long as Donny and the cops remained the focus of the 2020 culture war, the multinationals could avoid finding themselves in the crosshairs of a class-based uprising as they had two decades prior.

June 14, 2020, 11:09 PM PST: Heart of the CHAZ, Seattle, Washington

> Which is better—to have laws and
> agree, or to hunt and kill?
> —Piggy, *Lord of the Flies*

I recorded a portly black man who carried an AR-15 rifle. His girth was clothed in a gray sweatshirt with the hood cinched down to his eyes and a bandana pulled up over his face. Affixed to the weapon was a drum magazine capable of holding at least forty rounds. The circular mag rested atop his rotund tummy while he stood casually outside the police station.

As I published the scene on Twitter, I heard some commotion near the police station. After I hustled up the hill to the northeast corner of the police precinct, I found Shelby. She was recording a fight. She employed her signature move, where she held the phone vertically along the straps of her backpack while recording in order to appear less obvious.

The fight started after someone slipped inside the perimeter fence surrounding the station and added graffiti to the already copiously spray-painted walls. Another individual intervened by publicly scorning the vandal. As the face-off escalated to physical contact, a few observers entered damage control, searching for anyone with a recording device. I was nervous for Shelby, but as the censorship brigade turned their attention to an individual with a larger, more eye-catching camera, she slyly holstered her phone.

Amid the ensuing brouhaha, distant but more frenzied screams reverberated off the boarded-up businesses northeast of our position. Jorge was the first one to hear the turbid echoes and take off. Shelby and I were quick to follow.

The source of the embroilment was actually a few blocks outside the border of CHAZ. As we ran up, a pack of two dozen people howled while they smashed a chain-link fence that surrounded an auto shop. As I neared the fence, I could see a smaller group inside with cameras and lights aimed in the direction of two men, one of whom was armed with a rifle. They stood next to a massive F-250 Super Duty pickup truck with the doors flung open and hazard lights flashing orange on their pale skin. I recognized Jorge's crooked helmet bobbing among the handful of people filming inside the fence.

I wasn't exactly sure what whipped everyone into such a frenzy, but as the crowd on the outside of the chain-link grew more rambunctious, I searched for a way to Jorge's position. I ran ten yards down the sidewalk where the fence was shaking less violently, and I quickly scaled over. Jumping barriers had been a valued skill ever since I successfully evaded police by vaulting a picket fence at age seventeen (though my other buddy got caught, and I had to turn myself in the next day).

I jogged up next to Jorge. The older and taller of the two shop defenders had an AR-15 rifle slung over the front of his body, this one with a less rotund magazine than the one I saw earlier, perhaps containing twenty rounds. But his tactical strap supported the weapon in front of a vest that held extra mags, as well as his own cell phone camera aimed back at the surrounding streamers. His left hand clutched the stock of the rifle while his right hand rested on its shroud. He yelled at me as I approached his periphery for an angle that showed both the mob and the men standing their ground. "Get back! Don't try to get behind me. I don't want anyone behind me." Given that he was heavily armed and this appeared to be his property, I politely accommodated his demand.

The younger and smaller man carried no visible weapon. He addressed the cameras more amicably with his version. "I am not against your protest. What I am against is that Jay Inslee [the governor] has let it get to this point. So, that is all I have."

The man with the gun quickly added, "Have a good night." Then he took his hand from the shroud and waved the gaggle of recorders away. The cries from the other side of the fence calmed down, and I wondered how these men mollified the mob.

As we walked back to the hotel, the three of us pieced together the full picture before Jorge and Shelby posted their reports. Allegedly, someone broke into their shop and attempted to light a fire. After the two men caught the intruder, they held him at gunpoint until the police arrived. That is, until the mob showed up at their gate long before the cops, demanding the alleged arsonist's release. The men decided to give in to the crowd rather than wait God knows how long for the officers of the law.

Based on Jorge's information, the cops were not keen on showing up at all. The perpetrator was released once the two men defending their business realized that they were greatly outnumbered and had no other choice.

Mob justice prevailed, though it was difficult to imagine what would have happened if the man with the rifle had not kept everyone at bay. For thousands of years, mankind crawled its way out of caves and mud huts to create this thing we called civilization — supported at its foundation atop a collective bargain by which society established laws, and the members of that society either followed those laws or faced consequences. The leaders of the most powerful civilization in the history of earth—in order to score a political win and or appear virtuous—had torn up that social contract and dashed it into the streets, only to be used as kindling for the angriest and most desperate of their constituents to build great pyres at the heart of cities around the country. Now the only thing that was missing was a match, or a magnifying glass, or even a pair of specs.

June 15, 2020, 5:00 PM PST: CHAZ, Seattle, Washington

> Maybe there is a beast. Maybe it's only us.
> —Piggy, *Lord of the Flies*

The area bustled with activity despite it being a Monday. Jorge learned from Katie Daviscourt that she was planning a return to CHAZ with more flags. Through research on Twitter and Instagram (where Jorge lived), he informed us that the black guy who sported the log pole was named Maximus, an Air Force veteran and mixed martial arts instructor.

Upon reentry to CHAZ, one of the first people I encountered was the big boy with the AR and drum mag from the night before. This time, he sported an AK-style rifle, which had an even larger drum magazine that almost made his tummy look small. If that wasn't enough, he had two more normal-sized mags stuffed into the pockets of his jeans. Combined with his gear, he probably weighed 280 pounds and carried at least a hundred rounds. I approached unobtrusively and asked if I could interview him. He wore the same hoodie as the previous night, cinched around his face, along with a neck gaiter pulled above his nose. He nodded his head.

"So are you out here to defend yourself, or are you out here for a cause?"

I could barely make out his muffled reply from behind the mask. "I'm here to support the Second Amendment. Notice how they marched on the Capitol? I'm doing the same thing."

After the brief statement, he turned away from the camera. Though I suspected his comment, "They marched on the Capitol," referred to an instance of armed protesters who occupied the Michigan State Capitol in opposition to COVID lockdowns in April, I chose against pushing the issue. Instead, I followed my rule of not pressing people who were more heavily armed than I was.

As I walked away, another large man approached the fat boy with the AK, who turned around and greeted him like an old friend. Though not as portly, this guy was taller, about six two, and at least 250 pounds. He wore the sleeve of a white T-shirt as a face mask, a black shirt, black pants, and a thick bundle of dreadlocks tied in a ponytail. He scanned the crowd as the pair stood behind a spray-painted piece of plywood that read ANTIFA 4 BLM.

I pulled out my phone and recorded their interaction. Dreadlock Man removed a silver handgun from his pocket that looked like a subcompact .45 caliber, though its actual size was hard to tell because of his large hands. Whatever it was could definitely take down a mule—it looked cartoonishly small compared to the AK. He brandished the firearm to his friend. The barrel aimed toward the entire campground where dozens of people congregated, unaware that they were down range. The short video showed such a wanton disregard for general weapon safety that it received over a half million views on Twitter.

In anticipation of the flag gang, part two, Shelby, Jorge, and I reunited. From atop the hill next to the precinct, we could see red, white, and blue advancing toward the Zone.

Instead of a giant wooden flagpole, Maximus wore the American flag wrapped around his body like a cape. Rather than a rifle, Max carried a megaphone attached to a sling over his shoulder, though it was mostly obscured by the red, white, and blue enshrouding his upper body.

Brandishing the flag was already earning Max more attention than Dreadlock Man's chrome-handgun display or fat boy's behemoth of an AK. If that wasn't enough, Maximus topped it off with a bright red Trump 2020 hat.

This time, Katie carried no flag at all and looked more like a CHAZistani than a conservative activist. She was dressed in all black. Her windbreaker jacket had the collar zipped all the way up with a hood that covered her face. I barely recognized her save a few locks of blonde hair protruding from beneath the hood. She was not as eager for a repeat as Maximus was.

The pair was accompanied by additional counterprotesters. They included a short, skinny guy sporting a "FAKE NEWS" hat and a gay-pride shirt. Two black women with dreadlocks clad in black walked alongside the group, shouting toward the entrance as they approached, "All you need is Jesus! Jesus is king! Praise Jesus!" A gay conservative and two boisterous black Christians? This was a curveball I had not suspected.

The flagitators' security was bolstered as well. This time, five beef biscuits flanked the flags. Among them were four guys dressed in black garments with gold lettering that said "PROUD BOYS."

During the 2016 election, former Vice News founder and conservative bomb thrower Gavin McInnes started the Proud Boys, identifying them as an all-male Western chauvinist brawling club. Some of its members ironically call it a men's therapy group.

In April of 2018, I met Gavin briefly at a party sponsored by a think tank. I approached him with a six-month-old 'stache that barely made it onto the visible spectrum. I introduced myself and asked him how I could grow better facial hair (he had an absurdly prominent mustache that was gelled up into a curlicue like in the olden times).

He replied without hesitation, as if he had the answer prepared ahead of time, "You gotta eat more pussy."

I stood with my mouth agape. He took my hesitation for weakness and subsequently launched into a diatribe about how young kids like me don't know the importance of eating pussy anymore. I went home after the interaction and, perplexed by what a ridiculous character he was, looked into some of his recent public appearances. Common theme were claims "Violence solves everything" and "We need more violence from the Trump people."

After I watched the litany of bullying statements that he vomited into the discourse, I surmised that the pussy comment probably arose from a deep-seated anger, perhaps rooted in sexual frustration that had nothing to do with my sorry excuse for a mustache.

By 2020, the Proud Boys were not quite at a level of national noto-riety, but they were infamous among politicos after four years of well-documented street brawls with the antifa cells in the hard-left hotbeds on the West Coast, as well as a notable skirmish where two Proud Boys were sentenced to years in prison for assaulting black-clad protesters outside a Gavin McInnes speech at the Metropolitan Republican Club in New York City in 2018.

The approaching PBs made no effort to hide their affiliation. The distinctive black-and-gold Proud Boys logos on their clothing indicated that they were here to confront and antagonize the citizens of the CHAZ.

The first PB was about six feet tall, but a wide frame still visible in a baggy, black Proud Boys hoodie and a black hat with a black gaiter hiked up above his nose and ears. Given these boys were supposed to be proud, I was surprised that some of them chose to mask their faces.

The next was a six-foot guy in a tight-fitting polo shirt that was not flattering. It was more than a beer belly—it was a keg belly (the PBs were also well known for consuming copious amounts of brew). He wore a black gaiter pulled up under the rims of his sunglasses and the low brim of his hat. He wore black everything except the gold on the collar and the smallest Proud Boys logo.

Alongside him marched another man about six, one, wearing a black denim jacket with a huge gold Proud Boys Seattle insignia, plus plastic-reinforced gloves, designed to inflict as much damage as possible in the event of a brawl. Unlike his associates, he was maskless, showing the scruff of a man who just didn't care. I would later identify him as a PB faithful nicknamed "Noodle Arms" from a video where he smacked a BLM sign out of a woman's hands in a shopping mall parking lot.

The fourth, shorter Proud Boy also wore a tight black-and-gold PB polo. He would have been the least intimidating, except I noticed the outline of a handgun in his front pocket beneath something shy of a full beer gut—it was a beer paunch. He was wearing the same American flag bandana around his head as the guy with the Yankees jersey who defended the flag gang the first time around, but he had a mask on during the first incursion, so it was hard to tell. He had a bushy mustache and stomped along in his khaki shorts like a little guy with a gun that made him feel big.

The only man who didn't don Proud Boys gear wore a bright red San Francisco 49ers hoodie. Also maskless, he was a hulk of a man standing six feet, five inches tall and weighing at least 260 pounds. I recognized him as the Samoan immigrant ironically nicknamed "Tiny," the de facto Proud Boys leader in the Pacific Northwest. I was familiar with his unmistakable likeness from videos circulated online during the Trump years in which he tossed aside black-bloc dissidents like a bully in a schoolyard. Tiny had a rap sheet of violent crimes as long as the sleeves of his oversized hoodie.

Not surprisingly, the crowd inside the CHAZ did not take kindly to the entourage. Two dozen CHAZ/BLM supporters rushed to the border to protest the counterprotesters and their Proud Boys affiliates. Some verbally accosted the unexpected intruders more than others. Also on location was a transgender organizer/demonstrator/rioter named Nikki, who was popular on Rose Twitter (Rose Twitter is a community of users whose profiles featured a rose emoji to signify their alignment with democratic socialism). Her rap sheet was not quite as long as Tiny's, though she certainly committed plenty of crimes associated with rioting and counterprotests in Portland and Seattle.

But Nikki was preoccupied with someone other than the Proud Boys. She pointed across the crowd, claiming that a heavily disguised man on the periphery was the infamous Andy Ngo.

The man in question didn't have an inch of skin exposed, wearing ski goggles, a heavy neck gaiter, black winter jacket with the collar and hood zipped up, black gloves, black gym pants and black shoes.

I walked for a closer look when Jorge tapped me on the shoulder and whispered that it was, indeed, Andy Ngo. I was familiar with Andy as a notorious citizen journalist who reported adversarially on left-wing radicals who were arrested on the West Coast. Antifascist activists hated Andy because he gained a large following on Twitter with regular posts of agitators' mugshots and descriptions of their alleged crimes. Nikki didn't like Andy because he posted their mugshots multiple times.

Six months prior, I set up the camera for an interview with Andy in our DC studio. With a black eye and scabbed face, Andy looked like he had just lost a lopsided boxing match. Videos of the injury showed a black-bloc mob savagely assault Andy on a public street in Portland in the name of the fight against fascism.

During the interview, which focused on political violence, Andy spoke slowly due to a traumatic brain injury from the assault. He was a first-generation Vietnamese American and homosexual. In the left's identity-obsessed culture, these qualities would normally purchase Andy praise were he not so tenacious in exposing left-wing violence, but that didn't keep Rose Twitter from ubiquitously calling him a fascist, a Nazi, or a white supremacist, or some combination of these.

⁝⁝⁝

With the powder keg of contentious characters filled to the brim, Jorge, Shelby, and I fanned out, discreetly acknowledging things could get a lil hairy. I attempted a livestream, but the signal was too weak, probably due to the high density of people also streaming and uploading. I live-tweeted the event instead. As long as the videos remained under thirty seconds, they would upload.

My first post to Twitter was a video of Maximus walking in: "Just Now: MAGA Hat and American Flags about to enter CHAZ."

The next video showed the convergence of the two opposing groups. The guy with the guitar case who'd brandished his handgun earlier put his hand on Max's shoulder. "Get a close-up. He's a karate guy, and he's not comfortable in his own skin right now." He poked Max's face, and Maximus winced for a moment like he was about to swing, but he kept his hands low under the flag.

As more people surrounded the uproar and began asking questions, Nikki Jameson refocused their attention on Maximus, pointing at him and muttering to another man in all black.

Maximus was using the megaphone to ask, "Who pays you, Nikki Jameson? Who is Nikki Jameson?"

Insults started flowing in from unidentified bystanders. "Why are you here?"

With one hand still clutching the strap of the guitar case on his back, he used the other to wave for attention. The man pleaded for peace among the ocean of screamers, activists, and streamers while simultaneously yelling louder than anyone else. I spread my fingers on the screen and zoomed in on the handle of the pistol. I posted the video with the caption, "People are armed and tensions are escalating."

The following clip showed the shortest Proud Boy, his handgun printed in the pocket below his beer paunch. While I zoomed in on the weapon, the guy with the guitar case yelled at Maximus and his red hat, "[Even] if Trump has an agenda for black America, I won't vote for him!"

I posted the video with the caption, "Individual wearing Proud Boys shirt also strapped."

As the situation became more unstable, I recorded continuously for the next twenty-eight minutes. I would later pull clips from the most notable moments and post them on Twitter. A video summary would be published on YouTube and Facebook.

Maximus clutched a microphone near his chest with the spiraled cord attached to the megaphone under his flag cape. A streamer with a gray goatee and a beret atop his bald head shouted from behind his camera rig, "If you march with guys with Nazi tattoos, that is not justice! You are marching with douchebags. That's what the Proud Boys are."

Maximus drew the mic to his mouth, "Relax! Relax! Black lives matter! Black lives matter!" The group continued up the hill toward the precinct. Without large flagpoles, they were able to walk more freely.

The black-clad Proud Boys followed. Though they remained as silent shadows with hands clasped, their heads pivoted back and forth as they scanned the swarm. Tiny faced away from the camera in the background of my shot. He was engaged in an argument with someone far smaller than he, though whoever it was became invisible behind Tiny's fridge-sized red hoodie. The two black women were under Tiny's watch, screaming about Jesus to whoever was behind the massive hoodie.

Maximus, who seemed to have no political home beyond the flag draped around his back, squeezed the button and activated the megaphone's receiver. A lightning bolt tattooed on his hand spidered around the sinewed fist of an avid boxer. "If you don't know already, reforming the education system is more important than defunding the police right now."

I elevated the camera for a better view, revealing at least a hundred spectators with various levels of interest. Dozens of other cameras and cell phones poked above the swelling mass, like submarine periscopes rising to the surface in the middle of a storm.

Someone behind me shouted, "Fascists. You are the modern-day Brown Shirts." I turned the camera around to show who compared the group to modern-day Nazi stormtroopers but could not locate the source.

I directed my cell phone camera toward Maximus and asked for his version. "Hey, Max, can you explain to the viewers why you are out here today?"

He replied unexcitedly, "Because I have to. I have to be out here. Because no one else is doing it." In the background of the footage was the artwork by the painter I interviewed on the first night. The artist's idealism during that interview seemed distant from the present scene, though it occurred in the same place only three days earlier. I noticed the art had not been painted over or graffitied, despite his predictions that the work would not last through the night.

Unexpectedly, the black guy with the guitar case and the poorly concealed handgun switched loyalties. He no longer carried his guitar case, and he now held what looked like a Bible or a large textbook. For the sake of clarity, which is nearly impossible, I called him Brandish Man.

Now, Brandish Man stood alongside the much shorter pro-America demonstrator with the FAKE NEWS hat and gay-pride shirt. They both faced a group of ten protesters, most of whom were white.

Brandish Man accosted the entire group. "None of these are black people! Notice that!"

The white guy with the pride shirt, emboldened by the fact that he had just acquired an unexpected ally, turned his camera for a selfie. "We are here at a Black Lives Matter protest. Everyone here is white!"

He turned the camera back toward the crowd. A person of dark complexion from the opposing group slapped the FAKE NEWS hat off his head. "I ain't white, motherfucker!"

I shuffled my way alongside the Fake News Guy for a closer shot as he bent over and retrieved his hat off the ground.

I must have gotten too close, because a short, skinny young man squared his shoulders to me. I noticed him on my periphery but ignored him until he aggressively bumped the arm that held my phone.

He wore a shiny black Patagonia windbreaker. The hood of his high-end hiking jacket covered a second, tight-fitting black hood, which made him resemble a postmodern ninja who needed rain protection. As I looked down at him dubiously, the bill of his black hat was pulled low over his forehead, which left visible only the pale skin around his eyes behind a pair of specs. I named him Black Bloc Boi.

Now inches below my face, Black Bloc Boi barked, "Are you a Proud Boy?"

I understood the severity of his accusation. It was now common to be assaulted for the crime of association with the wrong political tribe. As I peered down through his spectacles, I replied in a stern but quiet tone, "I'm a fucking reporter. Get the fuck away from me. I'm doing my job."

To my surprise, Brandish Man came to my side. He towered above us both as he readjusted his repurposed T-shirt mask and bellowed, "Listen, we are all here for Black Lives Matter."

The bespectacled Black Bloc Boi turned from me to my unexpected defender. "I know we are—"

Brandish Man interrupted him, "Listen, you're making us all look bad bringing that bullshit."

Black Bloc Boi attempted a response but was again cut short. "No, listen. You're arguing. You're doing all that. We don't need that. The guys that looked like you [white black-bloc bois] are tagging all the buildings and all that."

I panned the camera down as Brandish Man held the book in his left hand and poked his finger repeatedly into the waterproof zipper of the young man's expensive jacket. "If you aren't ready for it, we love you."

Brandish Man put his hand on the young man's shoulder, almost endearingly. "But step away. I'm built for this shit. I done already turned three of them away." He lowered his hand from the shoulder back to the boi's sternum, this time jabbing his thumb and finger into Black Bloc Boi's chest even harder than before. "And if they want to pull them things out, we can pull them things."

Someone from behind the camera pleaded, "Let's not pull them things."

I assumed that the "things" that Brandish referred to "pulling out" were the guns in their pockets. Either that, or he was literally preparing the crowd for a dick-measuring contest.

After this final rebuke, Black Bloc Boi sunk backward into the crowd. Simultaneously, I heard Tiny yell something inaudible but tonally urgent twenty feet away. He held his arms outstretched, utilizing his huge wingspan and frame to separate the two female Christian activists from a group who yelled back in their direction.

One of the Christian women uttered an angry retort to a guy with peroxide hair and a septum nose ring. "I'm not pushing you, but you're not gonna push me!"

Tiny began shepherding the Christian women toward the east, past the precinct, where the crowd was less dense.

Tiny's retreat emboldened the crowd, who pushed against his brawny body. The other Proud Boys corralled the rest of their gang. That's when the pushing really began.

I had my camera locked on the shorter Proud Boy with the beer gut and the pistol. With one hand, he pushed bodies and secured the other hand firmly on the handle of the firearm, which now poked out of his shorts pocket. I aimed the camera at the exposed firearm when Brandish Man noticed the same thing.

In a bizarre 2020 version of an old Western standoff between cowboys, Brandish Man stepped in and secured his nonbook hand on his own sidearm. The chrome handle glimmered threateningly as if he was casting for a new role as a BLM Billy the Kid. He stared down his nose at the much shorter Proud Boy, who stopped in his tracks.

"We good, kid! We good, kid! Hey! Hey! We good, kid! I know he bad!" He took his hand off the gun to point at Maximus and then back on his firearm, "But I don't know about you!"

Surrounding the showdown, an angry sea of protesters and counterprotesters swayed from one push to another. The nearby "security" checkpoint that marked the border was abandoned, presumably because all able-bodied CHAZistani security guards were currently involved in the struggle against what they deemed a fascist, right-wing insurrection.

The flag crowd linked arms with the Proud Boys and supported each other against the shoves. This only made the opponents push more violently. Someone yelled, "Break them up! Break them up!"

Maximus stood outside the human chain. He no longer had his hand on the megaphone receiver and instead hid both hands menacingly under the cover of his flag. Maximus maintained a Zen-like disposition as he flowed like water between the thrusts, washing from side to side but continuing slowly toward the exit. The plastic and metal barriers, which marked the border of the CHAZ, were only a half block away.

With the exit in sight, the Proud Boys began plowing through anyone in their path, unsuspecting bystanders included.

While the mass moved slowly forward, numerous heckles likened the flag/Proud Boy/Christian coalition to Nazis and fascists. Brandish Man, who apparently couldn't make up his mind, unexpectedly abandoned the standoff and turned his tirade back toward the CHAZistanis. "You are upsetting the peace! You are a safety hazard!"

I spotted Nikki, the prominent transgender antifa agitator, barking orders to no one in particular while gesturing toward the exit. I ran ahead and jumped onto a concrete road divider for a wider angle. There were a hundred people in tow chanting, "Black lives matter," and the flagitators began speed walking for the exit while the shorter PB was shouting, "Don't run! Don't run!"

Metal barriers clattered off the crossroads as the Proud Boys blasted through the border between the CHAZ and the Free World. Nikki stepped aside as Tiny barreled past. The sound of an ambulance siren blared on a megaphone.

Brandish Man backpedaled and brought his head down to stare down Maximus, who responded in an elevated tone of voice for the first time. "Be careful! Be careful! There's a reason why I'm quiet."

"I know who you are! Cuz you fight! You fight!"

While Brandish Man goaded Maximus to swing on him, I leveled my camera for all hell to break loose. Maximus chose a different path. He turned his back on the mob and walked back to the wide-open American road. I wondered what Brandish Man might have been doing if the pandemic never happened. Where did his guitar go? Would he be carrying that guitar case to gigs? That is—rather than packing a weapon that could kill more effectively than the microscopic virus, then bringing it to a protest and starting shit with everyone there? If George Floyd died in 2019 instead of in 2020, would any of these people be out here?

Four months into the pandemic, this invisible virus had not just invaded bodies and destroyed the lungs of our most frail and vulnerable, it wiped away entire industries and metastasized fear and fury inside the brains of every American. It spread not only through droplets of spit and snot but also over the airwaves and fiber optic lines of our media until every American was infected—and the most anguished knew of no other option than to take to the streets and scream.

Once the group was safely on the street corner outside the CHAZ, the shoving stopped. But the "Black Lives Matter" chants continued. The Proud Boys fanned out while they backpedaled in case anyone pursued too closely. The foot orchestra slightly resembled small team infantry tactics, but mostly, the PB movement looked sloppy and ill-conceived.

The pro-flag protesters rounded a corner and entered a parking lot. Maximus, Katie, and the two Christian activists loaded into a white Ford Escape.

The lingering opposition yelled at the occupants of the Ford SUV while it exited the parking lot. No one attempted physical contact with the vehicle because the group of Proud Boys still surrounded the moving car. They marched alongside like Secret Service security following the president's limo, a.k.a. the Beast. The Ford Escape exited the parking lot as an activist issued a final heckle. "They're all fascists!"

As the car disappeared from view, the dissatisfied dissenters lost interest and drifted back toward the CHAZ to get back to work on utopia. Shelby, Jorge, and I discussed who should follow the five Proud Boys. Jorge suggested that he head back into the Zone, where he planned to regroup with Julio, a Town Hall reporter, and gather reaction interviews. Shelby and I would follow the Proud Boys.

June 15, 2020, 7:16 PM PST: Harvard Avenue Two Blocks from CHAZ, Seattle, Washington

> "Fancy thinking the Beast was something
> you could hunt and kill!"
> "You knew didn't you? I'm part of you!"
> —*Lord of the Flies*

We walked a safe distance behind the Proud Boys as we posted videos of the most recent developments. I tweeted a short video of Maximus and company exiting the area along with the caption, "The flag bearers and flags are safely leaving the CHAZ."

Only one other person also followed the Proud Boys. He wore common street clothes, which made his political affiliation unclear. But given his calm demeanor and casual attire, Shelby and I did not expect any further confrontations.

With our heads buried in our phones, a car alarm rang out along with hot-tempered hollers fifty yards up the road. We both entered a dead sprint. Though this was certainly not our last foot race, I would call this one a draw because I had a few steps on Shelby at the start and only barely beat her to the scene, turning my cell phone camera on record as I arrived. Three Proud Boys—Noodle Arms, Tiny, and the shorter Proud Boy with a handgun in his pocket beneath his paunch—surrounded the plainclothes man, who was backed up against a white minivan in the middle of the road. His cell phone landed on the pavement next to the vehicle. Noodle Arms dealt a right hook to the man's face. His head smashed into the side of the van before he spun away from the vehicle in search of his phone.

The two other Proud Boys patiently watched the melee, one of them lifting his hoodie and revealing a handgun, while the taller one with a keg gut and black-and-gold polo reached down and picked up the cell phone. The man pleaded for his device as it was tossed over his head into the center of the road. The phone landed just in front of where I stood.

As he ran toward me and the phone, Noodle Arms connected a right cross with the man's cheek. I took two steps back as the fatter, shorter Proud Boy with the polo shirt and the pistol arrived at the phone first and picked it up. Still determined to retrieve his stolen property, the guy bear-hugged the pistol-packing Proud Boy, who turned away and used his body as a barrier to protect the phone. In doing so, he also exposed his firearm. Both men fell to the ground. The guy went from grabbing at his phone, which fell back on the pavement in the scuffle, to grabbing in the direction of the exposed gun.

Someone shouted, "He's reaching for the gun!"

Tiny jumped onto the dogpile and pulled the guy out of his bear hug like a rag doll while Noodle Arms rained down haymakers, connecting with multiple strikes. The guy collapsed on the pavement. Simultaneously, the taller, keg-gutted Proud Boy picked up the phone one last time and spiked it into the asphalt with all his might, shattering it to pieces.

Now that the deed was done, all of the Proud Boys retreated to the minivan. The battered guy struggled to stand back up. Noodle Arms ducked into the driver's side of the vehicle and retrieved a telescopic metal baton. He glared in our direction as we stood there filming.

Shelby and I both threw our hands up as a signal that we had no intention to intervene.

Apparently satisfied that we were not a threat, Noodle Arms spun the telescoping baton into his armpit, turned around, and hopped behind the wheel of the van. As the guy finally made it back to his feet, Tiny stood menacingly over him, keeping him at bay with his size alone as the rest of his crew entered the van. Tiny was the last to get in before the van sped off. It had no license plate.

The battered guy turned toward us with his face bleeding profusely. As he staggered in our direction, he clearly showed signs of someone who was seriously concussed, something I was familiar with after a lifetime of ice hockey and reckless antics.

I asked the guy if he was OK, and he responded slowly, "Yeah."

I asked him what happened but gave up after he was too shell-shocked for a coherent response. Three other individuals who also heard the beatdown showed up moments later and called the police.

As we waited for Seattle PD, I asked Shelby if she thought we should turn our footage over to the authorities. "Of course, we would do the same thing if it was antifa who beat this guy up."

Though I agreed with her premise, I replied with something that bugged me. "But isn't it also possible that guy saw us tailing the Proud Boys, realized we were reporters, then antagonized a fight that he knew we would film?"

Shelby acknowledged that it was definitely possible, but that we could never know for sure. This was also true. I had to at least voice my final concerns before we went forward.

"If he just so happened to end up in the wrong place at the wrong time, then why did he go for that PB's gun?"

Shelby certainly was not the type to dwell on these sorts of hypotheticals. She knew that, given we were fifty yards back when the fight broke out, ultimately, there was no way we could know what started the brawl. She also knew that, even if the guy who was savagely beaten had wanted a fight, he would never tell us as much.

After we posted the footage and turned it over to law enforcement, Shelby and I reconvened with Jorge. A quick internet search showed internet news articles and police reports stating that half of the guys we just filmed committing assault were currently on probation.

Shelby played it off with a shrug, implying we had done our job, and that was that. All Jorge could get out was, "Damn, bro." I experienced the sunken isolation that I knew from when I picked a fight with someone far bigger and more skilled than me on the ice, then played the rest of the game with a chip on my shoulder, knowing that I was a marked man. Only in this case, it wasn't a big guy with a hockey stick—it was a bunch of justice warriors with guns. One thing we all agreed on was that we should leave the CHAZ for good.

Over the course of our stay in Seattle, we managed to piss off both the CHAZistani security guards and now the Proud Boys. I enjoyed the Claws, but this no-law thing got real, quick.

After the assault, despite only a handful of hours of sleep during our week in the Pacific Northwest, I was kept awake replaying one terrifying question over and over in my brain: *What would have happened if that guy got hold of the PB's gun?*

June 16, 2020, 11:25 AM PST: Seattle International Airport, Seattle, Washington

Piggy was dead and the conch was smashed to powder.
                                            —*Lord of the Flies*

We arrived at the airport for our flight home the next morning. While Shelby never got her interview with the Lord of the CHAZ, Raz, everything we experienced proved that it was practically a leaderless movement.

In *Lord of the Flies*, Piggy was killed while he held the conch, which represented compromise and order on the island. Despite the boys' initial optimism with no grownups around, the absence of law inevitably split the boys into two warring tribes. By the time they were rescued, three boys had been killed—the boy with the birthmark burned in the fire that was started to signal the outside world, Simon was stabbed to death after he warned the boys about the fact that the beast was inside all of them, and Piggy was crushed by a rock as he demanded that the boys start acting like adults.

Despite the good "vibes" in the CHAZ, ultimately, fear and barbarism overcame Benny's "facilitation" and peace. Shelby had put it plainly on her Sean Hannity appearance the night before, "There's definitely a lot of peace, particularly during the day. We've seen a lot of productive conversations. There's a Conversation Café. But that's definitely not the whole story. We see, as the evening gets on in particular, there's a lot of tension. Just last night, things changed in the blink of an eye." She finished the interview with a final prediction: "It doesn't look like this is going to let up anytime soon."

As Shelby predicted, the lawless conditions persisted after we left. Within two weeks of our departure, there were multiple shootings and the homicides of two young men at the CHAZ.

On June 20, a nineteen-year-old man named Horace Lorenzo Anderson was shot four times by another nineteen-year-old man who worked as a volunteer for the "security" team tasked with defending the citizen-run autonomous zone. When police showed up to investigate the shooting, they were confronted by a violent protest. As if the first homicide and a series of shootings were not enough, it took one more death before the government decided the CHAZistani experiment needed to be shut down.

On June 29, a sixteen-year-old boy was shot and killed at one of the checkpoints, the same checkpoint where we saw multiple armed men who claimed they were defenders of the postmodern paradise. The car the deceased young man drove was riddled with bullets. According to witnesses, all of whom were sympathetic to the protest, the boy attempted a drive-by shooting before he was gunned down. We will never know what actually happened because the incident was not captured on video and no impartial witnesses were present. No one was prosecuted for the homicide. Despite the fact that the autonomous zone was established in the name of Black Lives Matter, both of the young men killed were black.

The entire experiment, along with the Conversation Café, was dismantled when police came in and tossed the checkpoint barricades aside on July 1, 2020. Cops moved back into the precinct. As Seattle Police Chief Carmen Best stated in a letter to the Seattle City Council members published in her book *Black in Blue*, "Before this devolves into a new way of doing business by mob rule here in Seattle, and across the nation, elected officials like you must call for the end of these tactics."

She had sent the letter too late. Under her orders, Best's police department abandoned the precinct in the spirit of de-escalation. After that, the deadly consequences were a foregone conclusion. Before the summer was over, Police Commissioner Best penned her resignation. "All of us must ensure that this righteous cause is not lost in the confusion of so many protesters now engaging in violence and intimidation, which many are not speaking against." Best, like Police Chief Doug Stamper, was the fall gal, a victim of the same corporately endorsed BLM movement with whom her department sought de-escalation.

Absent any law enforcement, these protesters, who called for the abolishment of police, established their own form of armed security. Late into each night, the "partylike atmosphere" would give way to a more hostile one, and, as Best predicted, mob justice became the law of the land. As in any power vacuum, those who had weapons overpowered even the most passionate calls for de-escalation. This Machiavellian model of nature showed its face in the heart of Seattle's progressive protest.

Yet legacy media scantily mentioned the growing disorder inside the CHAZ and many other protests across the country for fear of a politically incorrect opposition to BLM's cause.

When the partylike atmosphere turned into a deadly shooting range, there were no apologies to the families of the black kids who were killed.

As long as the press aimed the limelight exclusively at police-on-black violence, the stock-optioned white rich folks could signal their care for black people, even though they lived in safe houses in the suburbs where the cops would immediately respond to their calls.

The massive corporate entities headquartered in Seattle, notably Amazon, Boeing, Microsoft, and Starbucks, flocked to support the BLM movement—then said nothing about the death of these black Americans who were killed at a protest in the name of black lives. At the time of the writing of this book, there is no evidence that these companies donated to the families of the deceased.

The city simply disbanded the experiment and moved on as if nothing had happened. Progressive city leaders pointed their fingers to the other side of the political aisle while homelessness skyrocketed, and small businesses were destroyed by heavy-handed lockdowns in their own backyards. In *Lord of the Flies*, the boys were only rescued because a passing warship saw the fire that burned out of control and scorched the whole island.

On the ride home, we were once again afforded a near-empty fuselage. We spread our tired bodies out. I should have comfortably drifted to sleep. I could not. We only had so much room to stretch because everyone else was commanded to stay at home. The people on the ground remained lawfully at home, where they ordered necessities from Amazon and watched glass screens, all focused on the spectacle of the crazy violent shit we were witnessing, which we were powerless to change. I couldn't get the dread I felt filming that brawl out of my head. The more we continued recording, the more we were feeding the beast.

RIOT DIET

Entering CHAZ on the first night.

"BLACK LIVES MATTER" mural with cans of paint.

"DEFUND NOT DECAF."

The "NO COP CO-OP."

The "Conversation Cafe" —midconversation.

"SEATTLE ~~POLICE~~ PEOPLE DEPARTMENT EAST PRECINCT."

Epic!

CHAZ—bumping on the first night.

CHAZistani border crossing.

BLM Snack Van in the foreground; old Suburban with red beard man on the roof, and guy with Desert Eagle pistol standing guard on the right.

Desert Eagle pistol holstered via needlepoint belt.

BLM Snack Van.

A border checkpoint from the backside—with a Suburban roadblock in the background and "barriers" galore.

My drone shot of the CHAZistani dominion from above.

The Flagversaries entering CHAZ, flanked by guy with the Yankees jersey as security on the left.

The moment the flag was snatched from Katie, with Cossack Ushanka holding Starbucks cup on the right.

Shelby blocked the flagpole/log as if swatting a lob shot on the tennis court. *Screenshot from footage by Shelby Talcott.*

Middle finger for the cops inside the Seattle West Precinct.

A mob outside the auto shop, with an alleged arsonist sitting down on the right.

Rifleman defending the auto shop.

"IF THEY START SHOOTING, STAND BEHIND ME" —while holding a baby. *Photo by Shelby Talcott.*

"ANTIFA 4 BLM."

Brandish Man earning his name with his drum-sized drum magazine buddy.

Maximus entering CHAZ for the second time—this time sporting a flag cape instead of a flag log.

Brandish Man vs. Black Bloc Boi.

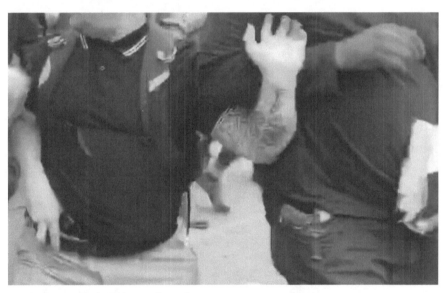

PB and Brandish Man packing heat.

Proud Boys beatdown as one PB protected his sidearm.

Beatdown, continued.

5. AMERICA'S ARCH OF CONSTANTINE

Occupied Protest at New York City Hall Park

June 28, 2020, 1:45 PM EST: Union Station, Washington, DC

Over the great bridge, with the sunlight through the girders making a constant flicker upon the moving cars, with the city rising up across the river in white heaps and sugar lumps all built with a wish out of non-olfactory money.

—*The Great Gatsby*

Midway through the twentieth century, Washington DC's Union Station saw over 15 million passengers walk through its doors every year.

In 2019, there were 5.2 million. The year 2020 would see that number cut in half to 2.6 million.

The station was almost deserted. As I approached the iconic entrance of the station just a few blocks from the United States Capitol, a homeless man writhed on the pavement, eyes rolled into the back of his head, with snot and spit sputtering from his nose and mouth. I looked around to see if anyone else noticed the imperiled man struggling to breath beneath one of the hulking four-story arches on the front facade of the station. One person walked by with a rollie bag and gave him a passing glance but did not stop.

As the homeless man's head rolled side to side, his breathing sounded constricted. I bent down and propped his head up on the dirty rucksack next to him. I flipped him sideways into the "help position" that I learned in first aid training to become a surf instructor. His breathing returned to a relatively normal cadence. I put my fingers on his throat, avoiding the mucus that rolled down his chin. His pulse seemed strong. Maybe it was uppers.

Another passenger stopped and asked if I needed help. I instructed them to call 9-1-1. The Good Samaritan agreed to wait for first responders because my train was departing soon. I rushed into the station but started to slow down as I walked through the newly renovated interior. The vaulted ceiling rose nearly a hundred feet above the shimmeringly clean marble floors. A white granite roof, freshly coated in gold-leaf paint, brightly reflected the early-afternoon sun that poured through the multistory iron and glass portico on the west side of the station.

The station's beaux arts architecture was typical of the late period of the French monarchy, with significant Roman and Greek influences. The spotless and empty Union Station echoed the same late-empire decadence while a homeless man suffered from a near overdose right outside its doors. I hoped this summer would not end as the French Revolution did, bloody beheadings and all.

I boarded the Amtrak train for New York City and headed straight for the bar. I ordered a Dogfish Head 90-Minute IPA, the highest alcohol content of all the beers available, in order to drown out my troubled thoughts about America's collapse. I would meet Shelby, who was already up north visiting family. Jorge was out of town. Our destination was the one-block New York City Hall Occupied Protest, a smaller version of the five-block CHAZ. The protesters gathered ahead of the New York City government's passing of the 2021 fiscal year budget deadline at 12:00 a.m. on July 1, 2020. Their demand was simple: reduce the NYPD's $5.7B budget by at least $1B—or else.

I sat at one of the tables in the café car, watching videos and news reports that showed a fenced-off area in front of New York's City Hall. Dozens of tents and picketers staked out a cop-free settlement on the southern tip of Manhattan. Though police avoided entering the zone, thus making it technically "autonomous," a noticeable difference from the more expansive and unattended area in Seattle was a large contingent of officers stationed in front of New York's municipal buildings, only a brick's throw away.

City Hall's proximity to the protest added symbolic and aesthetic power to the demonstration. As with the CHAZ, when news of the NYC protest reached the level of national curiosity, our team was keen to show our audience what was really going on inside.

As the four-hour train ride from DC to New York's Penn Station concluded, I nursed the last of a third bottle in the café car. I took my last sip of bitter, lukewarm beer as the hot summer sun drooped in the western sky. To the east, a thick haze cloaked Manhattan Island. A recent rain from a passing storm evaporated off the Big Apple's pavement in the dwindling glow. The steam that emanated from the hot concrete formed a thick condensation. It collided with the cooler air over the East and Hudson Rivers and shrouded the colossal iron skyscrapers with foreboding mist.

Before the train descended into the tunnel from New Jersey to New York, I peered at the Manhattan skyline one more time. The red, white, and blue lights of the Freedom Tower's spire shone through the fog, a tricolored lighthouse at the southern tip of Manhattan, shining brightly while the barren streets below suggested a far darker future.

September 16, 1861: Construction Site Next to City Hall, New York, New York

The Tweed Courthouse broke ground on the eve of the Gilded Age, a period when many of the country's richest and most powerful industrialists launched their corporate empires from the twenty-two-square-mile isle. But while Wall Street was on its way to eclipsing London as the wealthiest city in the world by 1920, the city was also home to some of the poorest neighborhoods in America. Tweed cheated his way to become the third largest landowner in New York City, though his corrupt construction deals lifted thousands of immigrants out of poverty. These new immigrants were paid a semilivable wage to construct the buildings that Tweed owned.

William Meager "Boss Tweed" was one of the most crooked politicians in American history. He rose to power through Tammany Hall, a political machine that controlled the votes of New York City's swelling immigrant population. Tammany provided for the city's most downtrodden populations, namely the Irish, who flooded the most broken-down neighborhoods in New York after fleeing the Potato Famine of the 1840s. Tweed greeted the Irish with jobs and welfare services in exchange for votes. By the time he became the head of Tammany's general committee in January of 1863, Tweed had his greedy fingers in nearly every major building project in the rapidly expanding metropolis. The Tweed Courthouse, also known as the old New York County Courthouse, was no exception.

During the protracted decade-long construction of the courthouse, Boss Tweed swindled millions of dollars from shady deals and inflated costs. The city's initial construction budget of $250,000 ballooned to a final tally of over $13 million. The price of brooms and cleaning alone exceeded the original cost estimate for the entire building. The courthouse became a lasting symbol of the political corruption that accompanied and abetted the vast accumulation of wealth around New York–based companies after the Civil War.

Despite Tweed's immense power in New York, he was eventually convicted for these fraudulent construction contracts. The same unethical transactions produced the courtroom in which he was sentenced to twelve years. One night in December 1875, the warden allowed Tweed a courtesy visit to his family's home in

Manhattan, which the disgraced politician exploited to slip away and flee to Spain. But when he arrived on Spanish shores, Tweed was recaptured and brought back to the United States, reportedly after Spanish officials recognized him from cartoons drawn by Thomas Nast, an illustrator for *Harper's Weekly*.

Boss Tweed famously said of Nast's work, "I don't care a straw for your newspaper articles, my constituents don't know how to read, but they can't help seeing them damned pictures."

Advances in printing technology made it possible for cartoons to be quickly drawn up on current events and printed for mass consumption. Through caricatures like one called "Wholesale and Retail" from 1871, Nast brought public attention to Tweed's illegal deals. The first image in the cartoon was captioned "Wholesale." It portrayed Boss Tweed walking out of the New York City Treasury with fat-bellied pockets while billy club–wielding police stood at attention. The second image, titled "Retail," depicted a man leaving a bakery with a bulging loaf of bread under his jacket while two officers prepared their cudgels for an arrest. Standing at six feet and over three hundred pounds, Tweed was easily caricatured by Nast, the barely five-foot-tall cartoonist.

Nast also popularized the use of the donkey as a symbol for the Democrat party and invented the elephant when the Republican party was initiated in 1854. A century and a half later, the most fundamental and universal "pictures" were not hand-drawn cartoons but digital memes—internet videos and images that instantly captured the zeitgeist in a way that no printed words or online story could.

Printed newspapers and magazines no longer controlled mass media because platforms like Twitter and Facebook drew many more eyeballs and commanded far more power than any single publication ever could. New Yorkers who protested the two-tiered criminal justice system in July of 2020 camped their protest in the Tweed Courthouse's front yard. History wasn't repeating itself, but the present seemed to reflect the past through a fun-house mirror.

June 28, 2020, 9:01 PM EST: New York City Hall Occupied Protest, New York, New York

The city seen from the Queensboro Bridge is always the city seen for the first time, in its first wild promise of all the mystery and the beauty in the world.

—*The Great Gatsby*

After we dropped off our gear at my mom's place in the West Village, we rode along in the vacant subway car. The city that they called "The City That Never Sleeps" looked to be soundly asleep. Shelby and I had linked up at my mom's apartment. She was out of town, and I'd asked her if we could use her apartment to avoid the cost of a hotel in New York City. I framed it as a charitable contribution to our little video team. Eliminating the exorbitant expense of habitation in Manhattan helped make our venture cost-effective and an easier sell to my bosses. We were headed straight for the mini version of the CHAZ adjacent to The Tweed Courthouse and New York City Hall.

When we arrived at City Hall Station, the stairway that led directly to the heart of the occupied zone was blocked off. I snapped a photo of the stairs barricaded by umbrellas, assorted trash, and metal barriers stacked to the tile ceiling.

Although the normal exit for the city hall of one of the richest and most powerful cities in the world was impassable, the elevator still functioned. Black graffiti was scrawled on the gray concrete floor of the lift. It read "FUCK NYPD." On the glass window, a message in yellow spray paint bore the now-familiar acronym "ACAB" (All Cops Are Bastards). As we ascended to ground level, I experienced a combination of emotions similar to when I walked into the CHAZ. I felt the anticipation of an adventure, a new cultural experience, and the fear of going undercover to document something that was tenuous and new.

I subtly began recording with my phone camera at 9:06 p.m. As the elevator doors opened to the street level of the Brooklyn Bridge-City Hall exit, we were greeted by a large American flag hanging upside down across the elevator's support columns. "BLACK LIVES MATTER" was spray-painted over the red-and-white stripes. The bottom third of the flag, including the stars that represented all fifty of the United States, lay on the soiled New York City sidewalk.

Propped in front of the sullied American flag was a cardboard political campaign sign, which read "JUSTICE FOR SENIORS" in red with "Killer Cuomo" spray-painted in black letters underneath. The "KILLER CUOMO" sign referenced the thousands of seniors who, under Governor Cuomo's watch, died in New York nursing homes at the start of the pandemic. The shoddy sign served as a gravestone for the old folks whose COVID deaths were covered up to preserve the reputation of yet another crooked New York politician.

Two bright yellow banners bearing the names George Floyd and Breonna Taylor (a woman killed by police during a raid in Louisville on March 13, 2020) adorned the elevator's overhang. The banners waved in the mild summer breeze like languid pandemic prayer flags. The slacked wind filled my nostrils with the smell of rotting garbage tinged by the skunk of pot smoke.

As we emerged from behind the nylon banners, we entered what looked like a cross between a festival and a late-night flea market, condensed around a grassy half-block area that served as a campground on the north side of the protest. As in Seattle, the overwhelming majority of the population wore some form of cloth mask over their faces.

Our initial worries that we would see CHAZ-style security checkpoints were quickly put to rest.

In place of sentries with guns and walkie-talkies were New Yorkers reclining in lounge chairs. Shelby and I looked at each other with a shrug, quietly communicating that this was an entirely new experience into which we were about to dive headlong. It might even be fun. Unlike the street-wide roadblocks we saw in Seattle, here, a few beach umbrellas and large cardboard signs were propped up along the park's low chain barrier.

Without any armed guards on duty, I felt comfortable enough for a Facebook Live broadcast with the title "Take a Tour of the New York City Hall Occupied Protest!" I first focused on a four-foot-tall black foam-core sign. Painted in neat white letters, it read:

DEMANDS

1. DEFUND THE POLICE!!!
2. DEMILITARIZE COMMUNITIES

3. REMOVE COPS FROM SCHOOLS!
4. FREE PEOPLE FROM PRISONS & JAILS!
5. REPEAL LAWS CRIMINALIZING SURVIVAL!
6. INVEST IN COMMUNITY SELF GOVERNANCE
7. PROVIDE SAFE, ACCESSIBLE AFFORDABLE HOUSING

The eighth demand was obscured by a pile of garbage bags and plastic bottles.

Next to the list of demands at the edge of the grass, mobile devices were connected to a tangled mass of cords that were almost as diverse as the city's population. The outlets at the end of the charging cables received electricity from a municipal power source.

We walked slowly, carefully avoiding stepping on protesters catching some winks in the various and confusing sleeping arrangements. Barely a single blade of grass showed beneath a quilt of picnic blankets, camping tents, and lawn furniture. A few large plastic tarps hung between the five trees and two light posts scattered through the park.

Someone led a chant, "Who protects us?" while a few of the campers responded, "We protect us!"

When we emerged from the other side, the southern half of the block was made up of a concrete plaza. Only in Manhattan could this be considered sparsely populated, but compared to the cramped campground, it resembled an urban countryside scattered with villages separated by a few feet. Some of these small groups painted the sidewalk while they sat on the ground or on folding chairs, while others stood around chatting and puffing smoke.

The eastern edge of the occupation was marked by the intersection of Chambers Street and Centre Street, which split flows of traffic from the Brooklyn Bridge into uptown and crosstown directions. The entire sidewalk was lined with moveable barricades. With official-looking stenciled blue letters that read NYPD along the metal rails, it appeared that the police had erected the fencing to keep the protesters contained within their fiefdom and away from cars that streamed from the nearby bridge.

In between locked bicycles, the barricades were festooned with paper signs bearing a variety of messages like "Fuck The Police They're America's Rapists," and the more generic "BLM." The only empty spaces along the barricade were occupied by a series of tables that offered up everything from baked goods to pasta dinners to criminal justice advice.

While the NO COP CO-OP in Seattle was overseen by the mild-mannered individual who explained how the store-bought Chewy bars and canned food were donated to the inventory, the New York City version was identified by a sign that read "THE PEOPLE'S BODEGA." Two women behind one of the tables proudly called out their offerings as if they ran a hotdog stand in Central Park, "Mac and cheese! Chicken! Cole slaw! Macaroni salad!" The other shouted, "Doughnuts! Doughnuts! We got doughnuts!"

To the west of the home-baked treats was a collection of artworks that rested in an unpolished state. The most prominently featured piece was a portrait of George Floyd that stood on an easel, painted in what looked like an updated rendition of a Renaissance portrayal, some solemn martyr who probably got burned alive in one of the Old World inquisitions. Four large glass candles you would expect to see in a boutique home-goods store rather than a filthy patch of concrete illuminated the graffiti on the firmament below, "Rest In Power."

Directly south of Tweed Courthouse was a smaller municipal building, the New York City Hall. The oldest continuously inhabited city hall in the United States, at the time of its completion in 1812, it was the tallest building in New York. Its baroque architecture was less grandiose than later historic buildings with huge Romanesque arches, but the more intricate style gave the building a certain elegance and air of history. It looked out of place among the shiny skyscrapers that dominated the financial district.

A temporary ten-foot fence enclosed the city hall. A small army of about a hundred police stood guard behind the steel mesh. They seemed entertained by the whole spectacle in the park. The ragged little tents were recently assembled but appeared as ancient as a bedouin camp alongside the old courthouse and city hall. The cops seemed to be guarding an archaic stronghold encircled by the modern iron structures threatening a final incursion.

I concluded the live video, and we moseyed back to check out the art. In addition to creative signs like a cardboard cutout of a sun that said "ABOLISH THE PRISON INDUSTRIAL COMPLEX" in fancy cursive letters, there were numerous canvases at various stages of completion.

There were no signs indicating that the works were for sale, leading me to believe that they had been painted for the sole purpose of beautifying a space that was anything but.

I walked over to a man who was putting the finishing touches on a particularly tormented piece. The most notable features were a naked female angel with a black ski mask who wielded a huge sword, a blue-shirted pig with a word bubble that said, "oink I'm a racist," and a hand-painted caption below that read "Abolition Is Creation."

I asked him if he painted the whole thing, and he told me that it was "open-sourced," meaning many different people had contributed to the work. He asked if I wanted to make an addition, and being a recreational painter of oceanscapes, I took him up on the offer. Just below the oinking pig, I painted a bright blue wave, more like one you would see in a tropical locale than anywhere near New York City.

He asked, "Do you surf?"

We bonded over the love-hate relationship between us and the fickle brown-water waves we rode in New York. Meanwhile, I labored over a picture of a far cleaner and more beautiful curl. As I put the finishing touches on the foamy whitewater of the breaking wave, the artist nodded approvingly.

He commented that the wave looked more like something from a dream. I agreed. The rest of the painting seemed painfully candid. I explained that I felt obligated to inject some beauty amid all of the real-world suffering. The artist's appreciation for my work, despite its lack of political connotation, imbued in me a certain kinship with the protesters at the New York City Occupied Protest.

The Zone itself did feel notably more chill and relaxed than the vibe inside the CHAZ, where the revolutionary activist types outnumbered the artists/bakers/creatives. Here in Manhattan, the Rat Race mentality filled the streets with people on their way to the next hustle, too busy for worries about what anyone else in the crowded streets was up to.

Shelby and I witnessed an entirely peaceful protest that night. But as I reviewed our Facebook Live broadcast, the video performed poorly compared to our content that showed more violence and anger. The most upvoted comment on the livestream, with a paltry eighty-two likes, stated, "This looks like a legit cesspool!!! Yikes, this is our youth? Where did we go wrong? I'm voting red all the way down the ballot and I hope you do as well."

Though the commenter was certainly right about the lack of cleanliness, her words also illustrated the division that dominated our discourse. Her profile picture showed an elderly woman about my mother's age. Did she believe any positive progress emerged from the countrywide protests that took place in the late sixties and early seventies when she was young? Maybe. But not this protest. Why not?

Trump was seventy-four, and his opponent, Joe Biden seventy-seven; they were of the same generation as the Boomer who commented on my video. Both advertised campaign slogans that framed themselves as resurrectors of America. Whether it was "Make America Great Again" or "Build Back Better," both of these slogans addressed the same problem— in 2020, the American Dream badly needed resuscitation.

On our way home, we crossed through Christopher Park in Greenwich Village, where a massive street party was underway. Amazed by a large gathering that had the hallmarks of a celebration rather than a protest, I pulled out my phone and recorded the scene.

Hundreds of people danced around a bus with scantily clad individuals on a stage built atop the roof. A man who wore nothing but a G-string and a cloth mask danced barefoot seductively on the very edge of the stage as the crowd sang along to Kevin Lyttle's "Turn Me On." Shelby and I danced as we walked through the almost entirely male crowd, enjoying the closest thing to an actual party that we had experienced since the start of the pandemic.

June 29, 2020, 12:15 PM EST: New York City Detectives' Endowment Association Headquarters, New York, New York

> "Can't repeat the past?" he cried
> incredulously. "Why of course you can!"
> —Gatsby, *The Great Gatsby*

We walked into the headquarters of one of the NYPD's three major police unions, the Detectives' Endowment Association, after Shelby suggested that we get law enforcement's perspective on the occupied protest. Since we interviewed demonstrators, we should also get the perspective of officers who would be impacted by the protest's demands. Shelby scored an interview through a connection where she grew up in Nassau County, Long Island, the western portion of which had been home to New York City's police force and first responders for generations.

The night before, hundreds of NYPD officers guarded New York City Hall, Tweed Courthouse, and the surrounding buildings in the complex. In total, the officers outnumbered the protesters. Though the tightly packed campsite violated the city's COVID-19 ordinance that banned large gatherings, the NYPD officers stood by as the protesters inside the zone drank, smoked marijuana, and spray-painted public property.

This relaxed attitude toward the BLM protests came from the mayor of New York City, self-described socialist Bill de Blasio. Ten days prior, he announced plans for bright yellow BLM murals—the same style as the mural Mayor Bowser painted in BLM Plaza in DC—spanning entire city blocks in each of the city's five boroughs. Since the start of the summer, de Blasio repeatedly signaled his support for BLM demonstrators' right to assemble in large gatherings, despite the global pandemic. On June 15, he banned the city-hired COVID contact tracers from asking individuals if they had attended any Black Lives Matter protests. When asked at a press conference why religious services were not exempt from the COVID ban on large gatherings, the mayor replied, "When you see… an entire nation simultaneously grappling with an extraordinary crisis seated in four hundred years of racism, I'm sorry—that is not the same as the understandably aggrieved store owner or the devout religious person who wants to go back to services."

Apparently, the police gave the occupied protest concessions not afforded to other segments of the population; much like the cops who never interfered with Gatsby's ostentatious and alcohol-fueled parties during the height of prohibition because politicians enjoyed the parties themselves.

Shelby opened the interview with Paul DiGiacomo, the commissioner of the police union, with a question about the protest's demand for a reduction of the NYPD's budget by one billion dollars. The commissioner responded with a prediction: "With less cops, there are going to be less people to have as backup out on the street. It's going to be dangerous not only for the police patrolling, for the detectives, the policing in general, but most importantly, it's gonna be more dangerous for the law-abiding people of this city."

Since countrywide calls to "defund the police" at Black Lives Matter demonstrations were catalyzed by George Floyd's death, Shelby next asked the commissioner what he thought about Floyd's killing.

He responded, "What happened to Mr. Floyd is despicable, and it was terrible behavior by any member of society, let alone a police officer. And I think that police officer's actions set back law enforcement fifty years."

After the interview concluded, I checked the math on the commissioner's statement. The time frame of fifty years harkened back to the civil rights movement of the late 1960s. Notably, hundreds of "homosexual youths" set off the Stonewall Riots on June 28, 1969, fifty-one years minus one day prior to our interview. I realized that the night before, Shelby and I serendipitously walked through a celebration of this monumental moment in the advancement of civil rights for gay people in America and around the globe.

⋮⋮

Fifty-one years prior, the Stonewall riots ignited a worldwide movement on behalf of gay rights. On June 28, 1969, it was just another weekend of revelry at the Greenwich Village gay bar known as the Stonewall Inn, that is, until the NYPD stormed into the bar and began arresting patrons and staff members alike. At the time, it was a grungy neighborhood of artists and counterculture activity in southwest Manhattan. Officers regularly arrested gays in Greenwich Village's Christopher Park for the crime of "masquerading," a statute that had not been updated since 1845.

The inn was run by the Genovese crime family, one of the notorious Five Families that ran New York's mafia underworld for decades. The bar had no running water, and the glasses were rinsed in a dirty bin of water behind the bar and then used to serve the next patron. That gay men were forced to socialize in dirty places run by this criminal network symbolized the city's discrimination against gay culture. Resentment toward this treatment as second-class citizens finally boiled over into violence on the night of the Stonewall Riots.

Plainclothes officers who carried out the sting entered the inn at 1:28 a.m. and attempted to detain a few drag queens who were especially resistant to the police presence. Other patrons heard the commotion and rallied in support of the queens. When news traveled outside the bar, hundreds formed an unruly mob outside the doors. They tried to break into the night club but were blocked by the thick wooden door. With only one way in and out of the night club, the police barricaded themselves inside along with the remaining patrons. Bricks smashed the windows, and incendiary devices like Molotov cocktails and flaming garbage were thrown inside. Police drew their revolvers and prepared for the worst.

The Tactical Police Force of the NYPD showed up as reinforcements just in time. A street brawl ensued. The violence descended into a riot, and sporadic clashes with a phalanx of riot cops behind shields went on for hours. By the time the streets were finally cleared at 4:00 a.m. on Sunday, June 29, thirteen people were arrested, and four cops sustained non-life-threatening injuries.

The event was largely ignored by the established media. *The New York Times* only made a brief mention of the riots on page thirty-three of their Sunday edition. The minuscule article took a tone that was discernibly dismissive of the now-historic event. "Hundreds of young men went on a rampage in Greenwich Village shortly after 3 a.m. yesterday after a force of plain clothes men raided a bar that police said was known for its homosexual clientele." An examination of New York's alternative media painted a much different picture.

The tabloid *New York Daily News* featured a photo of the riot on its front page that Sunday morning.

On July 3, the *Village Voice*, an alternative weekly paper, featured multiple descriptive exposés on its front page. In an article titled "Full Moon Over Stonewall," a reporter named Howard Smith became trapped inside the inn with the heavily outnumbered officers. He wrote, "During the 'gay power' riots at the Stonewall last Friday night I found myself on what seemed to me the wrong side of the blue line. Very Scary, very enlightening."

He went on to describe the moment that the commanding officer, Deputy Inspector Pine, was faced with a grave choice. "I can see the arm at the window. It squirts liquid into the room, and a flaring match follows. Pine is not more than ten feet away. He aims his gun at the figures. He doesn't fire. The sound of sirens coincides with the whoosh of flames where the lighter fluid was thrown.

"Later, Pine tells me he didn't shoot because he had heard the sirens in time and felt no need to kill someone if help was on the way. It was that close."

Not only did this illuminate the destructive nature of the riot, but it also showed a human side to the officers who gay New Yorkers viewed as the embodiment of their oppression.

The Stonewall flare-up reached national attention thanks to alternative media. Within a year, actual reporting of the event galvanized a series of gay-rights demonstrations from DC to Chicago to L.A. and San Francisco. Within two years, there was an increased number of gay-rights advocacy groups in every major American city. But in Christopher Park on June 28, 1969, prevailing American culture, as well as the institutions of the media, were less sympathetic to the cause than the police who were trapped inside. After all, the cops were simply executing a warrant at an establishment that indisputably had no liquor license, and the laws against "masquerading" that they enforced against gays were written over a hundred years before they patrolled the streets.

The commissioner that Shelby interviewed showed a similarly human response to the death of George Floyd, suggesting a parallel between our time and that of the counterculture movement that took place in the late 1960s. Both of my parents attended Woodstock '69 and protests against the Vietnam War. The older Americans were conservative and viewed the protests with disdain, favoring the post-WWII-era notion that every young American should marry young, buy a house with a white picket fence, and start a nuclear family. By 2020, New York City was known as one of the most gay-friendly cities in the world, and that same area of the West Village had become some of its most desirable real estate.

In both 1969 and 2020, the protesters on the street battled with police because they viewed them as the custodians of the institutions that they sought to change. But the key difference between the unrest that

I witnessed and what my parents experienced was that Mayor Bill de Blasio and the establishment media viewed the 2020 version favorably, while the 1969 protests ran counter to the generational gap in America at the time.

The hippies became yuppies and out of this transition was born the idea that the family unit was antique. Uniqueness was no longer counterculture—it was mainstream. De Blasio and anyone else who had a bone to pick with Trump became a BLM champion, though as of yet, yielding no prescription beyond press conference support and murals that said Black Lives Matter. As I edited the interview, cutting between Shelby and the commissioner's cameras, it was evident that even the cops could see the festering wound of police brutality in America. They were the hand of enforcement, yet they were just as powerless to change the system as those black Americans whose lives had been ended or destroyed by the boot of the law.

It was hard to tell whether the 2020 NYC Occupied protest would bring actionable change, as did the original Summer of Love and the subsequent years of anti-war, pro–civil rights protests, especially because the New York City government and the greater media feigned support of their demonstration—while also benefiting from the power structures that grungy campground in front of City Hall claimed to oppose.

June 29, 2020, 5:15 PM EST: Washington Square Park, New York, New York

> I had that familiar conviction that life was beginning over again with the summer.
> —Nick, *The Great Gatsby*

Before traveling to the protest at City Hall that evening, Shelby and I walked to the International Youth Group's police protest in Washington Square Park in Greenwich Village, just a few blocks away from the site of the Stonewall Riots. We walked underneath the Washington Arch, constructed for the centennial anniversary of George Washington's first inauguration and modeled after the triumphal arches that were erected throughout the Roman Empire during the height of the Imperial period. Seventy-seven feet above us, the inscription on the attic story bore a quote by America's first president at the Constitutional Convention in 1787: "Let us raise a standard to which the wise and honest can repair. The event is in the hand of God."

The crowd was only 120 people, but what they lacked in numbers, they made up for in youthful enthusiasm. They danced blithely with the music when we started recording at the center of the park. In typical New York City fashion, the organizers of the protest came out with a huge band, complete with multiple trumpeters, saxophonists, percussionists, and a legit full-size double bass player. The band was in the middle of a jazz riff when dark clouds rolled over the park and let loose a torrential rain.

Suddenly, the sky darkened, and the cloud burst its moisture on the park. The musicians hurried their instruments to shelter underneath some of the protesters, who popped open umbrellas, though they probably brought them along for the purposes of shielding themselves from the police rather than Mother Nature. Shelby and I, on the other hand, were woefully unprepared. We resigned ourselves to soaking in the warm rain.

Rather than dampening the mood, the deluge only made the crowd more enthusiastic. They chanted loudly above the sound of the torrent, "What do we want? Justice! When do we want it? Now! If we don't get it? Shut it down!"

The man who led the chant with a megaphone finished with a declaration, "Power to the people!" At that very moment, the sun peeked out from behind the clouds, and the megaphone man cried out, "Even if it rains, the sun shines yet again!"

I panned the camera to the sun, which peeked through the gloom. I pondered the possibility of a silver lining in the tempest of 2020. Where was the line between protest that inspired forward progress and destructive antics that only served counter to the protests' demands? As we exited the park after the protest, the sculpture of George Washington on the north side of the arch had been defaced with red paint, though most of it was already washed away by the summer squall.

June 29, 2020, 11:00 PM EST: New York City
Hall Occupied Protest, New York, New York

Gatsby believed in the green light, the orgiastic
future that year by year recedes before us. It eluded
us then, but that's no matter—tomorrow we will
run faster, stretch out our arms further…

—*The Great Gatsby*

A few drinks with dinner armed us with a healthy company-sponsored
buzz when we arrived at a much larger and louder demonstration in front
of City Hall, nearly a thousand New Yorkers. The NYPD budget deadline
that protesters demanded be reduced by $1 billion was twenty-five hours
away. Shelby and I knew it would be a long night.

"Defund The Police" was projected in six-foot-tall blue letters onto the
facade of the thirty-nine-story New York City Municipal Building across
Chambers Street. The hulking yet elegant structure was constructed at
the turn of the century to accommodate the expansion of the city's public bureaucracy, which consolidated all five boroughs under the single
umbrella of the City Of New York in 1898.

As it neared completion in 1913, the *New York Tribune* referred to it
as the "greatest and most costly office building in the world." An article published in the *Christian Science Monitor* around the same time was
headlined, "New York's Municipal Building Symbolizes Ideal Of A Great
City." It triumphantly reported, "Nearly 600 feet above City Hall Park,
New York City, a statue of Civic Fame stands silhouetted against the sky.
The feminine figure, wearing a laurel wreath, holds aloft in one hand a
crown with five parapets, each one of them a symbol of one of the five
boroughs of New York."

Traffic between New York's two most populous boroughs was slowed
to a standstill as demonstrators remained in the crosswalk long after the
signal turned green. After a few cycles of obstructed green lights, NYPD
officers intervened and escorted the crosswalk blockers back to the sidewalk. But once they were removed, at least ten or more would replace
them in the middle of the road. This sequence repeated a few more times

before the cops finally gave up, forming their own human chain across the intersection. Traffic across the Brooklyn Bridge was halted indefinitely.

Near the center of the protest, we overheard an argument about whether the demonstrators should move the barricades marking the edges of the Zone into the empty streets. One side argued that an expansion of the borders into the roadway would force a violent confrontation with the cops, while the other pointed out that drastic action would be required if they wanted their demands met.

The energy was far more hostile this evening. Rather than filming openly, as I had the night before, I recorded secretly. A crowd circled around a spirited debate between a woman, who had a megaphone, and a man who apparently wanted to drag the barricades into the intersection, which was now totally empty save the line of police officers.

The man arguing for drastic action wore a green bandana for a mask with black jogging pants, a black T-shirt, and a dark baseball cap. He pleaded his case: "I think being responsible is not letting cops into our space."

As police dutifully dragged out their own barricades and secured the ramps onto and off the Brooklyn Bridge, Green Bandana and his allies saw the stopped traffic as an opportunity for a complete takeover.

The woman who wanted demonstrators to avoid conflict wore a similar outfit to Green Bandana, all black, though she had a spectacular Afro that plumed through the back hole of her black Nike cap. She pulled down her mask and blared through the megaphone, "How the cops in our space? Is there any cops over there? Our sleeping bags are over there. Are there any cops over there?"

She gestured toward the tent area at the center of the occupied zone and answered her own question, "No!" She glared at the man with the green bandana before she continued. "So don't go over there. Why you still over here looking at me like I'm stupid? Now if you want to stand in the streets, you can stand in the streets. The streets is fair, our streets. But all I am saying is don't go close to giving them a fucking reason. That's it."

Two bystanders approached Green Bandana, and though the camera did not pick up what they said, their body language suggested that they asked for him to stand down. Green Bandana remained quiet, allowing the woman to initiate the common chant, "Whose streets? Our streets! Whose streets? Our streets!" The volume increased with each refrain.

Twenty NYPD officers stood in front of the barriers at the mouth of the BK Bridge. Half of them had riot shields and helmets with the visors flipped up. The other half carried clubs. Some wore cloth masks while others wore notably more stern expressions than the night before, probably because this time the protesters outnumbered them by a concerning margin. They conversed quietly amongst themselves.

It seemed that Green Bandana's plan was implemented in spite of the previous opposition. A group of five protesters quickly dragged the barricades, originally placed by the cops to surround the encampment, into the street. "Come on! Go! Go! Go!" The officers instantly heard the loud sound of steel dragging along the pavement but allowed the further incursion, presumably to avoid a confrontation. Or maybe they were just too tired to care.

A contingent of demonstrators inched their way to within a few feet of the officers in between them and the Brooklyn Bridge. Some saw a chance to capitalize on their victory and conquer the bridge itself, which was now empty.

A guy with long dreads, a tight, dark-green long-sleeved shirt, and designer jeans observed the opportunity at hand, "We are not afraid of them! Nobody is afraid of them. We got a thousand people!" Then he turned to the cops. "Y'all got a hundred people! We not afraid!"

Closest to him was a smaller man who wore tight skinny jeans, a tight, white wifebeater, and safety goggles like you would use in chemistry class raised onto the top of his head. He addressed cops a few feet away. "Question! Question! When y'all beat our ass" — then he waved his hands at the tents in the protest zone — "y'all gonna beat their ass too? That's what happens, right?" He answered his own rhetorical question. "So then the whole point of this gets taken away because we got our ass beat. For what? Why are all y'all in these streets right now? What is the message?"

Someone from the right side of the frame in my video shouted toward the police across from him, "Leave, leave!"

I panned back to the police behind the barrier while someone else joined the angry jeers, "Get the fuck out!"

The cops mostly ignored what was in front of them once they realized the protesters' lack of cohesion and clarity. More than a few cops yawned as the hour approached midnight. Only a few feet away, two men sipped on 24-ounce alcoholic lemonades and beers while they lofted scattered taunts into the summer morning.

"This ain't justice!"

"How can you be protecting people when you got no mask?"

"No leadership!"

Despite lively debate, the protesters and the police remained in a stalemate. Each side had their territory for the evening, and as of yet, the police showed no signs of yielding the bridge.

Ninety minutes after midnight, Shelby and I heard a loud commotion near the camp. We sped over and came across two men tussling, encircled by a shrieking crowd. As I started my video, a woman shouted, "Guys! Stop!" The two men collapsed to the sidewalk, though it was not clear which one had initiated the takedown.

The man on the bottom was obscured by the man on top, whose white T-shirt was stretched and torn by the desperate efforts of the guy pinned below. The man on top forced his forearm downward and subdued his foe. Someone from the peanut gallery pleaded, "Get him out! Don't let him bite you! Don't let him bite you!"

From that, I guessed that the man was either drug addicted, mentally ill, or a combination of the two. As they broke up, the man on the bottom, who still lay on the sidewalk, appeared to be in his midforties. His clothes had the tatters and soil of a street person. A few people helped him up and escorted him out. After the scuffle was neutralized, the crowd initiated some PR damage control. They immediately eyed Shelby and me with our cell phones still recording. I attempted to hide mine, but it was too late.

A woman to our right debated with a muscled, imposing man, "What does he need to delete? What does he need to delete?" That was the last thing my phone picked up before I stopped recording.

As I turned to face the man, the female unexpectedly snatched my phone out of my hand. I asked her if she was going to give it back, and as she replied, "No."

I responded with a move I learned growing up sandwiched between two brothers who constantly repossessed my stuff without permission. I asked, "Are you sure?"

While she was preoccupied by a response, I snatched the phone back from her clutch. She loudly demanded that I needed to delete the video of the fight or else. But once she sensed my desire to retreat, the woman turned to Shelby, who stood her ground at the empty intersection of Chambers and Center streets. Fifteen people faced Shelby as she made her defense. "This is a public street in America. I'm not deleting anything."

My eyes darted back and forth for potential threats, and I spotted two young males, one of them shirtless with clenched fists, who circled behind us and out of my field of vision.

I'd witnessed multiple people sucker punched in similar situations, so I took drastic action. I bear-hugged Shelby and dragged her backward. She may have been a professional athlete, but I had the adrenal performance-enhancing drug coursing through my veins. Shelby said something about being fine and not needing my help, but I could not hear her words because I was screaming at the top of my lungs, specifically at the individuals who had circled behind. "Get the fuck back! Get the *fuck* away from behind me!"

Though she made fun of me for losing my cool, I'd suffered one too many head injuries and did not want another.

The red lights of an ambulance stationed about a half block away were our nearest safety. Either because nothing fazes a New Yorker or because I was being overdramatic, the EMTs and cops didn't even bother to give us a second look. Thankfully, their presence was enough to deter any further pursuit.

I will admit I did sort of lose my cool. But I also pointed out to Shelby that it would most likely have been me who got sucker punched in the head and not her. She laughed out loud, which was rare, probably because the thought of me getting punched in the head amused her.

We remained by the safety of the ambulance and told the internet what we'd just experienced. On the way home, we contemplated pulling the plug on the entire trip but decided that since the budget deadline was now only a day away, we could stick it out.

Back at the apartment, I gave Shelby the bed out of chivalry or because I felt bad about freaking out. By this point, she was showcasing more stoically male characteristics than I was. I attempted to sleep in the living room on the couch, tossing and turning as the street noise occasionally rose above the low din of the window-unit air conditioner. I felt embarrassed by my momentary freakout, but I was mostly preoccupied by fear. It was now clear that the New York City Occupied Protest was not as benevolent and carefree as I thought.

June 30, 2020, 4:40 PM EST: New York City Hall Occupied Protest, New York, New York

And I like large parties. They're so intimate.
At small parties there isn't any privacy.
—Jordan, *The Great Gatsby*

After I laid eyes on the thousands of demonstrators and so much media, my elaborate disguise felt silly. With the deadline for the New York City budget less than eight hours away, we showed up to a multitude of local and national news vans with cumbersome cameras on tripods across the street from the park.

Shelby and I had overhauled outfits in the hopes we could avoid being recognized from the night before. I bought a funny-looking Australian outback hat at a drugstore along with a new gray camo neck gaiter I had hiked up to my cheeks.

Some vandals got busy after our involuntary departure the previous night. New graffiti covered the road and the surrounding buildings. Scrawled on the white limestone wall in front of the vast arches of the municipal building, black spray paint said, "De Blasio = Cucko," "cuck" being a lewd term for a man who allowed other men to have sex with his wife. Next to that, there was a pig cartoon with Xs on its eyes signaling a dead pig, along with the acronym ACAB.

Across the street, a vehicle that looked like an ice cream truck sold goodies to the passersby, but instead of popsicles, it advertised photos of multicolored lollipops with multicolored letters: "Weed World Candies." Parked in front of that was a converted minibus with a rooftop dance floor, similar to the one we saw at the Stonewall gathering in Christopher Park two nights prior. Two people danced on the stage with large speakers that blared techno music. One of them wore nothing but a G-string. I nudged Shelby wondering if it was the same person we saw twerking on the top of the bus at the Stonewall celebration, though it was hard to tell because he'd worn a mask during our first encounter.

Up the street, a small expedition of protesters strayed from the main area and directed some colorful language at a lone counterprotester donning a construction hard hat, a sleeveless flannel, and a sign that read "I SUPPORT/TRUMP/POLICE OFFICERS/ALL LIVES MATTER." The larger the crowd around him became, the louder he shouted, "Trump 2020!"

A vehicle slowly approached the exchange. A man dressed as Spider-Man stood out of the sunroof holding a cardboard "BLACK LIVES MATTER" sign. When the counterprotester saw Spider-Man's sign, he called out, "All lives matter! All lives matter!"

Two white-shirt police officers and a patrol officer approached the hubbub from their police line in front of the Municipal Building.

The BLM superhero implored the Trump supporter for peace instead of antagonism. A woman behind the camera pleaded, "Yeah, listen to Spider-Man!"

One of the white-shirt cops whispered something to the isolated Trump supporter, at which point he turned around and followed the police across the street. I followed them as the Trump supporter finally conceded. "Look, I made my point. I'mma head home."

Shelby was posting the details of the heated exchange when she saw reports of a protest on the Brooklyn Bridge. From the ramp on the New York side, we peered down the empty bridge, save approximately thirty people who marched from Long Island to Manhattan. While thousands of commuters' days were ruined as a result of a few dozen demonstrators, I certainly enjoyed gazing upon the bridge's nostalgic beauty, free of any modern cars. Trump's Make America Great Again (again?) campaign slogan also harkened nostalgia for another time. Fundamentally, Trump was a builder by trade, yet history showed that the construction of America's great cities was rife with fraud and graft.

During renewed economic progress following the Civil War, America's most corrupt political figure doled out tens of thousands in bribes. Tweed greased the gears for the building of a roadway that linked Long Island to Manhattan. He hoped to skim millions from the project. But before his plan came to fruition, Tweed was indicted for corruption.

The day after the Brooklyn Bridge opened to pedestrians, horses, and electric trolleys, an article in the *Baltimore Sun* on May 25, 1883, summarized the celebration. "Having waited since January 3, 1870, for the completion of their new great bridge, the citizens of New York and Brooklyn were yesterday jubilant." Not everyone was "jubilant," as the paper reported. The Irish community composed half the workers who risked their lives to construct the bridge. The Irish were pissed because the grand opening was scheduled for the birthday of Queen Victoria, the Queen of England at the time. As someone with the last name of McGinniss, I can confirm that the Irish are not terribly fond of the British Crown.

On May 3, the *Boston Daily Globe* published both sides of the quarrel. "The Central Labor unions of New York and Brooklyn decided that their patriotic American consciences would be unutterably scandalized by the opening of the Brooklyn Bridge on May 24, because it is the Queen's birthday." Meanwhile, the Irish protest of the opening also spurred significant animosity. "Fifty Irish members, with characteristic bigotry and stupidity, voted against the premiere [of the bridge]."

At the time, the recently arrived Irish were confined to the bottom rungs of society. City officials made no effort to heed the demands of the anti-Royal protesters; the celebration proceeded as planned on the Queen's birthday.

Moments before traffic began its centuries-long flow, President Chester A. Arthur crossed the bridge and shook the Mayor of Brooklyn's hand. The future mayor of New York City, Abram Hewitt, delivered a speech that praised the achievement. "It stands before us today as the sum and epitome of human knowledge, as the very heir of ages, as the latest glory of centuries of patient observation, profound study, and accumulated skill, gained step by step in the never-ending struggle of man to submit the forces of nature to his control and use."

Thousands of Irish chose to stay in their tiny apartments rather than attend the celebration where a multihour pyrotechnic show was blasted into the night sky from the center of what was the longest suspension bridge in the world. Additional fireworks were launched from the two towers that anchored the suspension cables to the bedrock, then the tallest structures in the entire city.

Viewing these articles through the rearview mirror in 2020, it was apparent that the Irish faced persecution when they first arrived, but black Americans were born with darker skin and had a much harder time assimilating or finding shelter in the cities they migrated to after the Civil War. One hundred and forty years later, New York City had rocketed from the financial center of an emerging industrial power to the most diverse and richest metropolis in the world; the iron sky rises in the financial district dwarfed the Brooklyn Bridge's limestone and granite towers. But days before Independence Day in 2020, the fireworks that launched when the civil disobedients arrived through the arched gateway from Brooklyn to Manhattan were sparked by adversaries of the established order rather than its celebrators.

⋮⋮

As the BLM demonstrators marched across the span between Long Island and Manhattan, many carried signs that said things like "FUCK YOUR WHITE SUPREMACY" and "DEFUND NYPD FUCK 12." The term "FUCK 12" translated to "FUCK THE POLICE." A handful of bicyclists served as a buffer on the front and back sides. Beyond them, traffic was blocked by police squad cars and NYPD vans that inched along, sparing no resources for the protection of the antipolice protest.

From the safety of their extensive security detail, a marching-band-style drummer kept the beat for their chants. "The people united...will never be divided!" As the small detachment reached Manhattan, the BLM protest, which had grown so large it spilled out from the police barricades and flooded the entire roadway, erupted in a collective cheer.

When the march ended in front of the municipal building, I staked out the pillars that supported the vast arches because their base was elevated eight feet above street level, an excellent vantage point for our audience. Shelby climbed up the other side of the pillar in spry fashion. From our heightened position, I saw the scale of the entire gathering. Over two thousand people spanned a half block in the northern direction up Chambers Street and a half block to the west down Centre Street.

At the traffic light in front of us, a man hung one arm from the crosswalk signal while the other held a megaphone. He donned the same distinctive sports goggles and black bandana wrapped around his forehead that I recognized from the day before. The prospect of an altercation with his above-average size and strength, plainly visible under his tight-fitting "BLACK LIVES MATTER" shirt, had troubled me when he was among the crowd that forced Shelby and me out the night before. I did not want to tangle with this dude.

He leveled the megaphone and opened with a call and response. "If you!"

And the crowd responded, "If you!"

Megaphone man continued in this fashion. "Show a sign of fear."

"And are afraid."

"Then go the fuck home."

"We are here."

"To protect everyone."

"And keep these police out!"

He paused for a moment. I spun the camera 180 degrees, revealing the NYPD police officers who loitered in the shadows of the arches behind me. Beat-up white Ford vans idled their engines and blasted AC, filled with cops who were prepared to protect the halls of the city's bureaucracy.

The megaphone man resumed his call and response exercise, but the pause allowed for another chant to spark up from a block north up Chambers Street. "Whose streets? Our streets! Whose streets? Our streets!"

The man with the megaphone threw up his arms in protest of the unsanctioned protest chant. A male voice from up Chambers Street shouted into his own megaphone, introducing a dueling of the electronically amplified voices. "You're too fucking quiet!"

The megaphone man in front of me responded, "Yo, listen! You, up there! Yo!"

But the chant persisted, "Whose streets? Our streets!"

He lowered the megaphone in frustration and jumped off his perch. I zoomed the camera in on his swim through the densely packed demonstration. Amid the huge swath of attendees, I noticed Spider-Man standing on the roof of a car and six scantily clad individuals who danced on the stage atop the mini school bus.

When I zoomed back out a woman with long blonde dreadlocks, pink pajama pants, and a pink bra jumped up the streetlight. She had her own megaphone, into which she shouted, "All you over there need to *shut the fuck up!*"

The chant in the distance finally stopped. The crowd near us cheered for the reestablishment of order. The woman with the bright bra and pajama pants thanked the crowd as the original megaphone man returned from his mission. Growing up in the suburbs of the Big Apple, the chant-battle provided further evidence for my suspicion that every New Yorker's got somethin' to say.

He took over the perch with a renewed fervor. "Don't hold a fucking line and say you're gonna stand with the people, and when the police fucking push up, y'all run back! If you're gonna run from the fuckin' police, and you're not gonna stand for the fuckin' people, get the fuck outta here, and go home!"

The audience roared in approval. Riding the wave of support for his tough rhetoric, the man pointed to the police under the archways of the Municipal Building behind him. "I want to put my foot on his fucking neck like he [the cop] do us. I wanna put my foot on his back like he do us. I wanna hang him from a fucking tree like he do us." The audience cheered with chilling zeal.

Shelby and I hung out on the pillar for hours because we would lose our primo vantage point the moment we dismounted. Her clip of the man saying he wanted to hang a cop from a tree went viral as the midnight deadline for the Fiscal Year 2021 budget approached, and Twitter was abuzz. The demands of the entire occupied movement hung in the balance, a referendum on whether the city government would capitulate or stand against the police budget reduction and face the consequences of the thousands amassed in front of City Hall.

The crowd became increasingly more restless as day transitioned to night. One individual climbed up onto a post that housed city traffic surveillance cameras. Using a broom that was doused in orange paint she stained the two bulbous lenses. Thousands cheered on her act of vandalism. I was acutely aware that my role covering protests required that I refrain from becoming a protester myself, but as an avid opponent of Washington DC's traffic cameras, I couldn't keep myself from screaming with glee.

When the stubborn summer sun finally yielded to darkness, the crowd stormed into the archway underneath the city's largest office building, the very heart of the bloated budget that the protesters wanted to be reduced by over a billion bucks.

Hundreds of NYPD poured out of their vans before anyone made it to the actual doors of the building. The NYPD utilized clubs instead of the riot shields I saw more commonly used in DC. The personal nature of the club, compared to being shoved by an officer behind a plastic shield, appeared to allow the cops to shepherd protesters out of the no-go areas without sparking a fight. A stalemate beneath the arches ensued.

Shelby and I could see movement near the rear of the protest up Chambers Street. It appeared that the massive police presence in front of us meant fewer policemen up the road. We finally descended our perch for further investigation.

Opportunists were dragging police fences, construction barriers, and whatever else they could find into the street. I captured a video of a black-bloc crew stomping toward the construction project.

They all carried darkly painted wooden shields. I zoomed in on a slender tall man with a gas mask, an ACAB patch, a medical cross patch, and a small antifa flag on his black backpack. Despite the hot weather, his pale skin was barely visible beneath the layers of black clothes.

By 12:30 a.m., a border wall was taking form a full block north of the municipal building where NYPD stood its ground. Though the barrier was makeshift at best, it spanned the entire width of the street. Given that it blocked a throughway for cars coming in and out of Manhattan, Shelby and I knew that police would not let these roadblocks stand come rush hour the following morning. While New York politicians showed leniency toward the demonstration, they would definitely intervene once the protest stopped the flow of commerce and the filling of the city's coffers.

We still had no news of the long-awaited police budget, so we sat down on one of the hastily constructed roadblocks on the northern end of the expanded territory. After some discussion over a few cans of White

Claw with fellow riot buddy Julio Rosas from Town Hall, we decided that we needed a few hours of sleep before rush hour the next morning.

On the first night in town, I viewed the New York protest as more amicable and open-minded than what we saw in Seattle. By the third night, the baked goods and artworks were replaced by a series of bloodthirsty speeches, walls, and shields. What I thought was a demonstration aimed at creation was now focused entirely on confrontation.

The protests during the late 1960s and early 1970s represented a struggle between counterculture and the institutions that slow-walked civil rights reform and persisted in the Vietnam War. The 2020 redux was not so clear-cut. Was the Trump supporter, outnumbered five hundred to one at this particular protest, the true counterculture in 2020? Or was the antipolice rhetoric of the crowd that evening representative of more genuine opposition to the existing power structures that kept average Americans down? I could not identify exactly who in the discourse represented the American renewal that drove millions across seas and through jungles for a fresh start.

July 1, 2020, 4:30 AM EST: Municipal Building Plaza, New York, New York

About halfway between West Egg and New York the
motor road hastily joins the railroad and runs beside
it for a quarter of a mile so as to shrink away from a
certain desolate area of land. This is the valley of ashes.
— *The Great Gatsby*

We jumped out of the Uber car on Broadway because a newly built roadblock kept us from driving farther down Chambers Street. Even at this final hour, expansionist activists patched up their defenses with whatever large objects they got their hands on.

We spent the ride downtown searching Twitter for intel on what had transpired inside the protest zone while we were gone. Though neither of us could find anything that showed the situation on the ground, it appeared that the NYPD's funding had been reduced by hundreds of millions of dollars. We thought this would be a victory for the protest. But many of the activists who reacted to the news within the first few hours were livid that their demands for a reduction of a billion dollars was not met. On this much they were right, city funding for the NYPD was reduced by about $300 million, from a whopping $10.5 billion in fiscal year 2020, to a still whopping $10.2 billion in fiscal year 2021.

I followed a group as they stacked the metal barricades, repatriated plastic construction dividers and city trash cans, and overturned newspaper dispensers. Though car traffic in the city had been significantly reduced since the start of the pandemic, if these barriers remained during rush hour, tens of thousands of commuters and truckers would be stuck in gridlock traffic.

Only a few small groups of demonstrators were working on the outer wall, but hundreds remained inside the camp. At least fifty umbrellas were set up along the metal barriers, adding an initial layer of protection to the mass of people and tents that waited anxiously inside. As we waited for the arrival of the NYPD, downtown Manhattan was eerily quiet save the sound of metal clangs reverberating off the graffitied limestone walls of Tweed Courthouse.

For the next hour, we waited on the top of the steps of the circuit courthouse across from the protest, hoping to film the police approach and remain hidden in the shadowed alcove at the top of the stoop. The lull of the predawn light was suddenly interrupted by the sound of whistles and the common police refrain, "Move back! Move back!"

I put my phone in Record mode as the NYPD emerged from the arches of the Municipal building to our south and the corner of Broadway to our north. The first wave of officers only carried billy clubs.

From behind the umbrella wall, hundreds of waiting protesters repeated in unison, "Why are you in riot gear?" Someone blared a siren from a megaphone.

The cops marched over a ten-foot-high graffiti message at the intersection of Chambers and Centre streets that read "BLACK LIVES MATTER FOREVER" as they tossed aside plastic barriers and street cones and dragged metal barricades out of their path. The few individuals who still remained outside took one look at the approaching line of blue-clad billy clubbers and ran back to the huddled masses.

Two officers spotted our hiding spot on the stoop almost immediately. One cop about 6′2″ with burly forearms and an American flag cloth mask pointed his billy club at us and shouted, "Out! You! Now!"

This was followed by a second, even taller cop with no mask and a tattoo sleeve on the arm who waved his club at us. "Keep moving!"

I replied politely, "Yes, sir! Yes, sir!"

It was always a balancing act getting as close as you could to capture the action while also not pissing off the police too much. I found that the formal address helped immensely, practiced during the moments I would plead in my prepubescent voice when my older brother had me cornered. The only defense I had against his superior size and strength was to appear helplessly respectful and therefore undeserving of a beat-down. Shelby shrieked with her version, "OK! Press," though her style had the innocent intonation reflected in a more feminine little sister touch. I tiptoed around the cops as they turned their attention to one photographer who kneeled on the ground aiming a camera with a long lens and didn't look ready to "Move back!"

The giant tattooed cop gently shoved the kneeling photographer with his club. The kneeler flopped to the ground almost comically, resembling a European footballer selling a foul, and made all the funnier by the fact that he was simultaneously snapping photos of a cop inches away with a telephoto lens (designed for zooming in long distances). He lay lifeless on the ground for a few moments, then got back up, repositioned himself closer to the cops, kneeled down again, and resumed taking photos. When the same burly cop returned from removing a plastic road divider and realized that the kneeler was not only still there, but closer than before, he turned and threatened another shove. The kneeler didn't even flinch, so the cop turned the club horizontal to his body and shoved the photog back down. A higher-ranking officer intervened, pulling the club-happy cop back to the police who gathered at the edge of the park. I looked around for Shelby, but she had disappeared in search of a better angle of the cops descending on the camp.

As the police gathered twenty feet from the wall of umbrellas, bikes, and metal barriers, I realized that I needed a better vantage point. I spotted the converted school bus where the scantily clad individuals danced the day before. Lo and behold, Shelby was already on the stage. A group of

NYPDs assembled at the front of the bus, just far enough away for me to sneak up the ladder in the back. A few rungs from the top, I relaxed my grip thinking I was ascendant and free. Suddenly I felt a hard yank on my canvas backpack and lost my grip. I tried to rotate my body during the eight-foot fall, but failed miserably and instead smacked into the pavement with my side. I smashed my left elbow, which was already a mass of flappy skin and fluid after a drunken men's league elbow pad malfunction in 2015 (the malfunction went unnoticed due to a few too many Natural Lights before my Sunday game).

Rather than concern for the boo-boo on my elbow, the female officer demanded that I walk away.

At that point it was clear the cops weren't, to use the New York vernacular, fuckin' around. I stumbled back to the trusty Corinthian column at the Municipal Building on the other side of the street. My raised angle revealed the cops' blue uniforms were stacked around the park up to seven deep. At the front, a continuous line of police shields boxed in the two exposed sides of the protest in an L shape, which was backed up against the fence of the courthouses like the pagan forces of Maxentius who were defeated by Constantine. Constantine, a more experienced commander than the self-anointed heir to Caesar Maxentius, kettled Maxentius' army with their backs to the Tiber River. Maxentius demolished the stone bridge at Milvian to ensure a definitive victory, though it ultimately ensured that they had no effective path to retreat. Constantine went on to unify the Roman Empire for the first time in forty years, while the anti-Praetorian emperor Maxentius drowned trying to flee.

With hundreds of NYPD officers, the column of dark blue appeared to outnumber the mostly black mass of protesters and turtled umbrellas. I could see Shelby looking at her phone, probably tweeting an update on the top of the minibus. I eyed her primo camera position enviously, legs hung off the edge of the stage as if she was relaxing at a picnic on a lakeside dock. But I spotted no-man's-land in between the cops and the camp; perhaps it was my chance to recover from my devastating defeat versus the female cop.

I entered through the back of the protest near the City Hall, then snuck through a gap in the barricades. The police line was to my right, with matching clear plastic shields that said "POLICE" in light blue letters and matching dark blue uniforms. The protesters were to my left, whose uniforms were varied but shared one main characteristic—from science lab safety goggles to ski goggles to bike helmets and plastic face shields, to wooden shields and gas masks—everyone possessed at least one item that would better equip them for a confrontation. Wherever there was a gap in the metal fences and improvised shields, some bold souls lined up their own bikes, seemingly feeble barriers to dam the ocean of hundreds of blue uniforms and blue shields poised a few feet away.

As I came to the end of no-man's-land, which was incidentally at the front of Shelby's minibus, one activist curiously yelled in the direction of protesters rather than police. Since it was usually the other way around, I went up to the individual who looked like a black male, though they wore a dress and a red wig, and asked if they were willing to talk. With a nod of approval, I started recording. We stood between the city's old institutions, personified by police, and the young protesters, who wanted those institutions reduced or torn down.

"So what side are you on here? We're kinda just in the middle." I gestured the camera down to the desolate area of pavement.

The individual extended one arm in the direction of the lawmen and the other in the direction of the rabble-rousers. "I'm on nobody's side. I'm neutral. I'm here for what's right."

"So what do you think about this movement here?"

"I think that it's pathetic, that it's crazy." The activist pointed to the protesters on the left. "They is putting their life in danger for no reason." Then they gestured their hand to the cops on their right. "Black and white and different races. And they can't even see that. They gotta provide for their family too." Now gesturing back toward the protest group, they continued, "They wanna go get high, and steal money, and party all night long!"

I zoomed the camera out for a wider view. The uniformed wall of police stretched into the background where the New York City Municipal Building and its huge Romanesque arches towered over everyone, a skyward token of the sheer size and power of the government.

At approximately 6:30 a.m., the flow of traffic resumed unabated from the Brooklyn Bridge. Morning commuters ogled the medieval-looking standoff as they rolled by.

I ended my video with the frame centered on the enigma wearing the dress who, by all exterior appearances, should have supported the protest movement and yet, as a free-thinking American, stood out here and voiced their own view.

Whether on the side of the police like the outnumbered Trump supporter or the person who stood by my side in no-man's-land, these individuals still possessed the autonomy to voice their opinions, no matter how unpopular they might be. Spider-Man and the dancing individual in the G-string made it evident that the other side of American culture was also free to allow such a diverse mixing of ideas to take place in the streets.

A cloud of cigarette smoke wafted by and I realized, after all the pandemonium, how badly I craved the calming head rush of a tobacco cigarette. Unfortunately, I had smoked my last cig on the way home the night before. I turned around and asked the smoking protester if I could bum one. "Long morning," I said.

He reached into the front pocket of his navy blue Carhart one-piece suit, something like a house painter would wear, and pulled out a mashed-up cigarette. He handed it to me along with a lighter. Upon examination, I was relieved that the sorry-looking cig was still intact.

The first rays of the sun peeked over the buildings and washed the Tweed Courthouse in golden morning light. I lit up the cig and tossed the lighter back to my new friend, then whistled to Shelby on top of the minibus. When she looked in my direction I instructed, "Portrait mode." This was an indication that she should take a portrait-style photo of me with her iPhone. She snapped a photo of me with my chin up in my best tough-guy pose, cigarette smoke billowing above the police shields behind me. With my Australian outback hat and Tamba Surf shirt, I resembled the host of an avant-garde nature program examining the wilderness of the coronavirus-ravaged jungle. Just like the activists and the cops, I asked for the photo because I was telling my own story from no-man's-land.

With the wheels of commerce that rolled off the Brooklyn Bridge and the police officers behind me, I inhaled the smoke and let out a sigh of relief, realizing that the cops appeared content in their defensive position. For the time being, the NYPD would let the occupied protest continue within the confines of the park.

Given the government's concessions to the protest, perhaps this wouldn't be like the bloody French Revolution; the French aristocracy realized that revolution was afoot only when it was too late. Perhaps it would be more like the end of the Roman Empire, which deteriorated slowly due to corruption and infighting before it finally succumbed to hostile forces outside its borders. But unlike the collapsed empires of the past, my interview in no-man's-land proved that in America citizens still had enough freedom to take to the streets and voice their individual opinions. I basked in the rising light for a moment, buzzing from tobacco and incensed by the potential for our generation to push culture and politics. The early morning was filled with the sound of cars rolling and was occasionally overwhelmed by the sound of protesters shouting for a new way.

July 1, 2020, 10:10 PM EST: Municipal Building Plaza, New York, New York

So we beat on, boats against the current,
borne back ceaselessly into the past.
—*The Great Gatsby*

We arrived at the Municipal Building a bit early for Shelby's Fox News hit scheduled for 10:30 p.m. on Laura Ingraham's show. Characteristically jarheaded in tone and wisdom, our boss Geoff gave Shelby one simple piece of advice: "Just stick to what you saw, your objective observations. Slow is smooth, smooth is fast."

Shelby was dressed in a gray T-shirt, the same attire she wore while covering the protests. I appreciated that she chose authenticity rather than getting dolled up, like the cable news hosts presenting themselves in conventionally bright dresses and caked makeup.

A Fox camera op with a rig that was worth as much as all of our video department's equipment combined was set up with large LED lights in front of the high-arched plaza at the front of the building. The police had the area in front of the colossal arches blocked off, but protesters peered toward the lights from behind the barricades. Though they were out of earshot, I could see them waving their angry fists at whoever was about to make an appearance on the vile and disgusting Fox News, a massive media company who by all accounts supported the cops gathered in the municipal plaza. The protesters' appearance was remote and minuscule, far beyond the bright metallic hues illuminating the cable news position, and dwarfed by the imposing architecture above.

The Municipal Building was one of the last buildings constructed as part of the "City Beautiful Movement," which was characterized by the same beaux arts, late French Renaissance architecture of Union Station in DC. The goal of the movement was beautification of the rapidly growing urban environments in America's cities, contrasted by the rapidly expanding slums that housed the underclass of new arrivals.

At the front of the building was a towering arch modeled after the Roman Arch of Constantine, completed in AD 312. The arch was a replica of one of the last architectural achievements built by the decaying Roman Empire. Though Constantine quelled the civil war and reunified the Eastern and Western Roman Empires one last time, the city of Rome would be sacked less than a century after its completion. At one time I ventured that the arch appeared to new immigrants as a symbol of America's might and the place that made dreams. Now it looked aging and dirty, stained by a one-hundred-year stream of combustion engines rolling across the Brooklyn Bridge.

⋮⋮

The NYPD reinforcements stood outside the old Ford vans that housed their riot gear. They laughed at a video on one of the cops' phones, the sound bouncing through what felt like a massive marble mausoleum.

While the camera operator attached Shelby's mic, the cluster of cops waved me over. A redhaired officer with an Irish name who looked about my age held up his phone. "Hey, is that Shelby Talcott?" His phone showed her Twitter profile. Shelby's cover photo portrayed her geared up to smash a tennis ball over the net with a fierce look on her face. He scrolled down and showed me one of Shelby's tweets with a video captioned "Fights ensuing on the ground, I'm on top of a bus."

The video showed Shelby's lofty angle, and the cop's coworkers below. While they removed one of the fences near the edge of the protest zone, they were engaged by a handful of umbrella-wielding defenders of the City Hall Park. The cops bumped up against them with their shields and swung the occasional club for control of the metal barriers that encroached the street, yet another Summer of Love 2.0 rendition of tug of war. A disgruntled defender of the autonomous zone furiously swatted police with their umbrella, which within a few strikes folded on the blue boys' riot helmets like a pool noodle.

The cop chuckled and gestured back to the rest of the police, "We were absolutely laughing our asses off watching this in the riot van earlier. That's awesome you work with her." This was the dark humor that cops and doctors used to get through the grizzly encounters of their day to day. While the internet sleuths and commentators responded with outrage, the cops had no such luxury. They had to either find comedy in the absurdity or succumb to it. The Irish who became cops and construction workers during Tweed's time had opposed the opening of the BK Bridge on the Queen of the British Empire's birthday. Now half the country viewed this Irish cop as the embodiment of imperial injustice.

To me, the funniest part was the idea that Shelby was some kind of celebrity to them. My friend and coworker of a younger age somehow became an impactful figure, for these cops, anyway.

I entertained their grim humor further, describing how I attempted a climb onto the same van, but a strong female officer yanked me off and nearly fileted my haggard-looking elbow. All the other cops were listening by now. They thought it was even funnier that I almost got wrecked by a girl.

Shelby informed me from in front of the camera that Raymond Arroyo was filling in for longtime Fox News host Laura Ingraham, who was on summer vacation. I wished Shelby luck. Despite the unexpected substitute host, she didn't seem nervous. Then again, I never knew how she felt because she never conveyed emotion.

During the appearance, Shelby stated matter-of-factly, "They [the protestors] don't want you sharing video of them fighting because it hurts their cause."

For hundreds of years, New York City was a place where people came from all over the world for their own piece of American opportunity. While Manhattan's vast wealth and ever-taller buildings made it a hotbed for corruption and shady deals, NYC's diversity also made it ground zero for the advancement of the rights of immigrants, blacks, gays, and numerous other groups of Americans who jumped into the Rat Race to up their lot. Wall Street was the center of America's wealth, but the city was also the cutting edge of the country's arts and culture. By 2020, these differences of opinion and race had been corporately merchandised to create dueling realities that everyone could watch 24/7 from a pocket-sized phone.

The unsleeping New York City and its busy streets were a living, breathing testament to the resilience of America, and its continued reinvention. From Tweed paying off his contractors all the way down to the guy who sold the brooms, to the owners of Stonewall paying off the cops to serve the gays in a dirty joint with no license, now we were stuck with another New Yorker handing out bribes, but this time it was Donald Trump, the current president, yet another shady New Yorker who built his wealth with fixed real estate deals that molded Manhattan's skyline. Only this time, Trump was arranging the payoff of a porn star, and his braggadocious NYC attitude was news-ratings gold.

I peered beyond the camera lights and past the imposing replica of the Arch of Constantine. I could barely make out the pale stars, drowned out by the city's bright lights and the nearly full moon.

July 2, 2020, 10:27 AM EST: Penn Station, New York, New York

> But above the gray land and the spasms
> of bleak dust which drift endlessly over it,
> you perceive, after a moment, the eyes of
> Dr. T. J. Eckleburg...blue and gigantic.
> — *The Great Gatsby*

We boarded the Amtrak and slowly churned along the dark tunnel that ran under the Hudson River. With the NYPD's budget deadline reached, we headed back to DC along tracks that were laid by laborers from a few generations prior.

On July 10, *The New York Times* put a photo of the new BLM mural before Trump Tower on their front page. The headline of the accompanying article stated, "Using Broad Strokes, de Blasio Has Words for an Old Adversary." The mayor commented while he helped paint the mural himself, "Black lives matter in our city and black lives matter in the United States of America. Let's show Donald Trump what he does not understand. Let's do it right in front of his building for him."

In a tweet, Trump said the BLM mural was "denigrating this luxury avenue" and that it was a "symbol of hate."

Mayor de Blasio fired back during an appearance on CNN, "That is pure racism.... The president, rather than having a chance to acknowledge America's original sin, he literally made it worse by suggesting that honoring black people on 5th Avenue would somehow make it less valuable or luxurious."

The "original sin" of slavery was indeed alive and well. The same cold-hearted mercantile system of profits that existed under the cotton economy of antebellum America still ran the show. De Blasio pointed at Trump as the bad guy and offered peace offerings to BLM, meanwhile he relied on an armed four-man security team to protect him every time he went to the gym. The police were merely the blue-collared enforcers of moneyed, white-collared institutions that supported Black Lives Matter, as well as those that scurrilously opposed it. Everyone who bought LED TVs, moved to a safe neighborhood, and enjoyed massive restaurant chains were tacitly endorsing the global international economic slavery ring, leveraging debt like a billy club as it plundered the whole globe.

In a flourishing post–Civil War New York, Tweed kept most of the press friendly by paying them off. By the 2020s, heartless corporations like Facebook and Google kept the ad dollars flowing to publishers, so long as they didn't stray their coverage outside the algorithms that fed the two-party lines. If any of the businesses whose brick-and-mortar storefronts were shuttered by the pandemic wanted to succeed in the everything-online world, they'd need the approval of these same companies to surface their product in the same algorithmic machine.

As in Seattle and DC, national attention was diverted from the protest of the police budget to a feud between the local Democrat leader and the sitting president of the United States. On July 22, the New York City Occupied Protest would be cleared by the NYPD. *The New York Times* moved on. The front page of *The Times* on July 22 and July 23 featured photos of Trump's next face-off with the local government, this time in Portland's fiery unrest. The front-page headline on the day that New York's protest evaporated into thin air read, "Sent to Quell Unrest in Portland, Federal Agents Fan the Flames."

From what we witnessed on the streets so far, the youthful protesters clashed with cops because they wanted to tear up the tracks laid by their parents and grandparents and to chart their own course for America's future. This demand for agency was demonstrated by the thousands gathered in front of City Hall, where they listened to speeches filled with violent rhetoric aimed at their perceived adversaries, the cops. From this, I gleaned that our moment of unrest was still mapped by the old paradigm, by which we were all told the wrongs in America could be righted if they could destroy their political enemies, narratives that were oppositional by corporate design. Though I was yet to witness how high the flames would climb.

Below Penn Station, there was a heavy darkness, condensed into a thick mist by all the steel and the stone above us, ushered by the old politicians and built up by huge companies before most of us had been born. While the train crawled through the abyss, I was stuck in the void between the Trump Train that chugged ever harder to the right, while the Delaware to DC Amtrak regular "Amtrak Joe" Biden dragged the Democrat machine toward the pro-BLM left— both of them gaining steam and billowing ever-thicker smokescreens as the election heated up. It was hard to imagine how this movement could instill change of the broader system that supported it, or what mechanisms our generation could use to build something new upon the valley of ashes accumulating between the two divergent tracks.

Rising in a clear, blue sky, the sweltering sun hit my face as the train emerged from the bowels of New York City. The heat of its rays warmed my troubled mind like the steady gaze of my departed father, whose generation made both progress and mistakes in their pursuit of a better America than the one their parents had. Though I was unsure if our generation would rise to the challenge when we became the ones who conducted the discourse, the iron horse continued its slow roll forward on the tracks. Once it was free from the tunnel, the diesel locomotive accelerated toward the marble columns and domed arches of the capital of America's Empire.

Breonna Taylor and George Floyd banners on the left, then Cuomo nursing home COVID murder sign in front of an upside-down BLACK LIVES MATTER American flag with Stars and Stripes on the sidewalk.

"THE PEOPLE'S BODEGA."

Sign-painting symposium at the New York Occupied protest.

Primo NYC real estate—doobie circles, politics, sidewalk painting, etc.

Civil unrest sleepover.

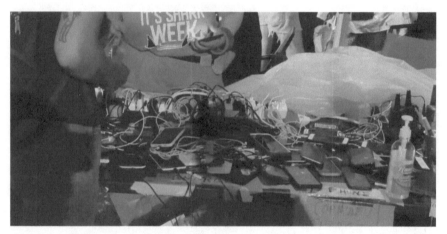

Charging station.

"PRESS" "office."

My contribution to the open-sourced street art (the wave at bottom left of top canvas).

Shelby interviewing NYPD Detective DiGiacomo.

When the megaphone man declared, "Even if it rains, the sun shines yet again!" — Washington Square Park.

A fight breaks out inside the zone atop "FUCK 12" graffiti.

My CVS disguise the night after we filmed the fight.

Occupied protest the day before the budget deadline, with NY City Hall in the background.

Spider-Man vs. Trump Man in front of the Boss Tweed Courthouse.

G-string on top of a bus.

The Brooklyn Bridge shut down as protesters marched from Long Island to Manhattan.

An anti police march arriving in Manhattan with protection from…
the NYPD!

Massive crowd with Megaphone Man leading the protest.

A crowd storming into the NYC Municipal Building.

Cops restored order under the Arch of Constantine.

Expansionist activities a block north of the Occupied protest.

Shelby and I threw up our hands. "Yes sir!"

Boys in blue remove barriers from the roadway; a telephoto photographer in foreground.

A megaphone in no-man's-land with the Municipal Building in the background.

Shelby about to go live beneath the vaulted arches of the Municipal Building.

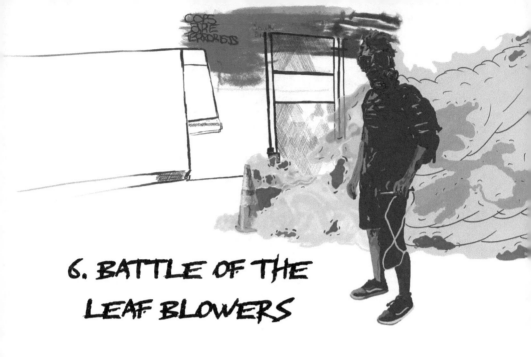

6. BATTLE OF THE LEAF BLOWERS

Tear Gas Paradise at the Federal Courthouse in Portland

July 23, 2020, 5:50 PM, CST: Terminal 1, Minneapolis-St. Paul Airport, Minneapolis, Minnesota

It is a dark time for the rebellion.
—Opening Titles of *Star Wars Episode V: The Empire Strikes Back*

During our layover from DC to Portland, we were thrilled to find a sign of civilization in the form of an open restaurant at Minneapolis-St. Paul airport. The start of the pandemic caused a shutdown of airport eateries; it was nice to be reunited with my old friend, the preflight beer. Shelby got a white wine, Jorge got a Jack and Coke, and I sampled a local IPA beer. Given that we saved hundreds by taking a flight with a three-hour layover, I figured we could live libatiously on the company tab.

238

We were due to arrive in Portland at 7:00 p.m. PST so we could capture the evening's demonstration. The spectacle of violence in front of the federal courthouse persisted since George Floyd's death, and showed no sign of stopping. In mid-June, the Portland City Council attempted to assuage protests by cutting the city's law enforcement budget by $15 million. But this was not enough for the demonstrators, who demanded a $50 million reduction in police funding. Unlike Seattle's leaders, who simply abandoned the police precinct that was under siege, the federal courthouse was not under local jurisdiction. The increasingly violent clashes between black-bloc-clad revolutionaries and law enforcement brought national attention to a small area of downtown Portland.

Though they demanded a huge reduction in the local law enforcement budget, the nightly demonstrations, which often descended into riots, were focused on the Mark O. Hatfield Federal Courthouse. The federal justice system has no input on local budgeting, for police or otherwise. The adjacent county courthouse and nearby police precincts remained mostly untouched, while the ground floor of the Hatfield Courthouse was covered in graffiti and scarred by fires. The city was dubbed "Little Beirut" when its residents came together in large demonstrations against the presidency of George H. W. Bush, the largest protests in Portland since the Vietnam War. What was happening in July of 2020 was far more warlike than the dissent that nicknamed the city after the bombed-out capital in the years after the sectarian Lebanese civil war.

Days earlier, President Trump called in officers from the Department of Homeland Security to defend the structure, which only incentivized more direct action. Portland's demonstrators perceived the move as an invasion by Trump's federal troops. Each side of the media had incessantly covered this new development, which helped meme the struggle into a symbol for Trump's reelection bid.

The biggest story of the previous week on the anti-Trump airwaves was a viral video that showed camo-clad federal agents in Portland as they detained an individual then loaded him into an unmarked minivan. For outlets like CNN, MSNBC, and *The Washington Post*, this clip was proof of President Trump's fascistic crackdown. This side of the media propagated a narrative that Trump and the federal officers were the evil

Empire oppressing a "mostly peaceful" demonstration in the name of black lives.

Meanwhile, the more pro-Trump media circulated videos of the progressive mayor of Portland, Ted Wheeler, attending the Black Lives Matter protest in front of the courthouse. Images of him bawling his eyes out from residual tear gas while a mob shouted him out of the protest area became fodder for Fox News, readers of the *Daily Caller* website, and other conservative outlets. The video affirmed the prevailing pro-Trump narrative that rioters, not peaceful protesters, were the dominant force in downtown Portland. For this half of the media, antifa was inciting a group of anarchists intent on burning the courthouse, a symbol of law and order, to the ground.

While we downed our drinks at the Minneapolis airport bar, Shelby did the math on how many nights Portland had taken to the streets for "direct action" in the name of Black Lives Matter. It had been fifty-six days since the first protest, which took place on Thursday, May 28, three days after George Floyd's death. He died just over six miles from the airport bar where we sat right now.

Shelby and Jorge spent a few nights in Portland the previous week. After their return, Shelby insisted that we needed the gas masks if we wanted to go back. I scrambled during the days leading up to our flight searching for masks that could protect us from the CS tear gas, an extra-spicy variety that was chlorine-based. The smoke cannisters used in DC could be tolerated without protection. As Shelby made clear in a joking manner, "The gas out in Portland hits different," as if it was some kind of more potent strain of drug rather than a riot munition. The joke was especially funny because we often questioned whether or not Shelby was addicted to the adrenaline rush associated with chaotic situations.

I ordered a second round of drinks while we practiced putting on our new old gas masks with our eyes closed, per the instructions of our Marine boss, Geoff. Shelby and I pulled out the ragged M40 masks that I purchased at a local military surplus store just outside DC. I was lucky that I found even these shoddy Desert Storm–era models, because gas masks were a hot commodity during the summer of 2020. Jorge, on the other hand, obtained a much more modern E-50 gas mask from one of his Instagram followers who was in the Border Patrol and appreciated Jorge's work. The eye window on his mask went all the way across the face, whereas ours had separate pieces of tempered glass for each eye. Jorge's mask was far spiffier, but Shelby and I joked that even the best visibility in the world wouldn't fix Jorge's poor writing skills (Jorge's egregious typos were an ongoing joke between Shelby and me). He had been staying on my couch in DC since May, so I didn't even feel the least bit guilty about giving him the same rough treatment I would my little brother.

Before we boarded the plane, I snapped a photo of us. The final round of our preferred drinks was partially finished on the table in front of us. The expression on my face was apprehensive but smiling wryly, Jorge looked like a kid on Christmas, and Shelby resembled an expressionless poker player ready to place a big bet on the table.

May 30, 1948: Vanport, Portland, Oregon

The unforgiving flood from the Columbia River washed away fifteen lives, forty thousand cookie-cutter homes and their automobiles in an instant. The new settlement was completely destroyed in the flood brought on by Mother Nature's wrath, but the disaster was made all the more tragic by the government's incompetence.

The community had been hastily built for workers in the shipyards that supported America's unprecedented industrial mobilization during World War II. It was the nation's largest wartime housing project, built on a flood plain between Portland city limits and the Columbia River.

While Europe was ravaged by the war, the manufacturing of the ships that brought bombs and soldiers across the Atlantic created job opportunities on the American home front. During this time, Portland's black population increased nearly tenfold, from twenty-one hundred to twenty thousand. Black men, most of whom were not allowed to fight on the front lines because of the color of their skin, picked up their lives and moved to Portland so they could earn a steady wage. Most of these new black residents lived in Vanport.

As the *Oregon Statesman* reported two days before the disaster, "'You will have time to leave,' said the notice distributed by the Vanport housing authority to every household on Sunday morning. 'Don't get excited. You will be warned if necessary.'" In fact, residents received only a thirty-minute warning.

After the Vanport disaster, displaced white residents had little difficulty finding new options in Portland. Black families were forced into already densely packed neighborhoods like Albina, one of the few places where they could settle legally. During this time, the Portland Realty Board followed a code of ethics that banned the sale of real estate to black residents in certain areas of the city. Even in Albina, blacks were not allowed entry to many of the white-owned businesses. In 1950, the city council passed a nondiscrimination ordinance that would have allowed them access to these spaces, but Portland voters promptly repealed it.

.·. .·.

Portland did not take on its modern progressive identity until the revolutionary period between the late sixties and early seventies. From 1969 to 1973, the average age of Portland City Council members dropped by fifteen years. Mirroring this youthful transfer of power on the political level, young people hit the streets for "direct action" protests against civil rights abuses and the Vietnam War.

One of these demonstrations cascaded into a multi-day riot in the area of Albina beginning on June 14, 1969. There was widespread smashing of windows and looting. A handful of homes and businesses were torched by Molotov cocktails or set fires.

In a miscarriage of justice that would make the federal officers Trump dispatched to Portland look like angels by comparison, a black man named Kent Ford was beaten, jailed, and charged with inciting the riot. When he was released on bail, Ford held a press conference on the steps of the Portland Police Department. "If they keep coming with these fascist tactics, we're going to defend ourselves," he said. It turned out that Ford wasn't even present when the riot began, and he successfully sued the Portland PD. His incarceration prompted the founding of a Black Panther Party chapter in Portland. At the time, FBI Director J. Edgar Hoover described the national organization as, "the greatest threat to the internal security of the country."

A few blocks from where Ford gave his speech years earlier, at the Mark O. Hatfield Federal Courthouse the 2020 Black Lives Matter protesters took "direct action" of a different form—over one hundred consecutive nights of street battles with local, state, and federal law enforcement officers. The namesake of the building, Senator Mark O. Hatfield, was a leading pioneer on multiple anti-discrimination laws. Although Portland became known as a politically progressive city, its history reflected a more primordial and less forgiving past.

The metropolis-to-be was carved out of the wilderness where the original European explorers once repaired a broken mast of the sailboat they used to explore the greatest of all rivers in the Pacific Northwest: the Columbia River.

Jesse A. Applegate described the location when he visited it in 1843: "There was nothing to show that the place had ever been visited except a small log hut near the river, and a broken mast of a ship leaning against the high bank. There were chips hewn from timber, showing that probably a new mast had been made there. ... We were then actually encamped on the site of the city of Portland, but there was no prophet with us to tell of the beautiful city that was to take the place of the gloomy forest."

July 23, 2020, 9:15 PM PST: Mark O. Hatfield Federal Courthouse, Portland, Oregon

A thousand worlds have felt the oppressive hand of the Emperor as he attempts to crush the growing rebellion."
—Script for *Star Wars Episode V: The Empire Strikes Back*

We stashed our additional gear in the nearby hotel then we headed to a corner store for water, craft beers, and cigarettes. I figured a Portland protester would probably prefer the trendier micro brews over the more traditional White Claw spiked seltzers. I also bought some smokeless tobacco that I could stash in my lip when the gas mask would prevent me from a nicotine injection via cigarette. After almost two months of covering civil unrest, I had developed a healthy nicotine addiction to calm my anxiety and stay awake.

As we walked up to the park in front of the courthouse, we could tell that the crowd was huge. The sounds of the chants echoed across the office buildings downtown, most of which were boarded up, covered in graffiti, or both. We rounded the corner of Main Street and almost the entire park, which spanned two city blocks, was filled with thousands of demonstrators. The small amount of light that remained from the long summer day showed that the crowd was far larger than anything we had seen before. Even the biggest marches in DC, New York, and Seattle were less than half of the approximately four thousand demonstrators that congregated before us.

A small group who looked like organizers stood on the elevated edifice at the entrance to the county courthouse, which was next to the federal one that had been under siege over the last fifty-four nights. The demonstrations had been gathering in the park to support Black Lives Matter and protest police brutality towards people of color. The federal courthouse had an eight-foot protective fence around its plaza, but the county courthouse had nothing but boards on the doors and windows. We waded through the thick mass of onlookers toward the leaders.

As we neared the front, a line of a few dozen middle-aged women with bright yellow shirts occupied the first few rows. They wore assorted gas masks, respirators, and bike helmets. We would later find out that this group called themselves "Frontline Moms." The rest of the attendees were a mixed bag, but the overwhelming majority dressed in normal street clothes and did not look as ready for battle.

We found some space behind a huge Doric column just across from the entryway. Everyone in the group of speakers was black, though the overwhelming majority of the audience below appeared white.

The activist closest to us stood on the edifice with an upside-down American flag draped over his body, a dark blue construction hard hat on his head, and a megaphone slung over his shoulder like the SJW (social justice warrior) version of a battle sword in its sheath. The guy next to him waved his own upside-down American flag. He was dressed in all black save an olive drab military surplus overcoat that hung down to his knees. The third man, standing closest to the audience, wore an oversized camo T-shirt and had ski goggles perched over the beanie on his head. He looked like a foot soldier out of the trenches in *The Empire Strikes Back*, the Star Wars film in which the rebels defend their stronghold against Imperial forces on the ice planet Hoth. As he raised the megaphone to his face, a large sign up against the ledge near his feet read "TRUMP IS A CANNIBAL."

Similar to the New York City–style of protest, this speaker employed the call and response technique, though his included far fewer profanities than the East Coast equivalent. He shouted into the bullhorn, "When I get frustrated, I go ahhhhh! Are you all frustrated?"

The audience replied, "Yeah!"

He gestured to the back and asked, "Are y'all frustrated back there?"

The crowd answered, "Yeah!" this time even louder.

He looked down to the yellow-shirted moms in front of him and asked, "Moms, are y'all frustrated?"

They screamed, "Yeah!" in a notably higher pitch.

Then he screamed, "Ahhhhh!" and turned the mic toward the crowd so they could also scream, "Ahhhhh!" I clipped the video and uploaded it to Twitter, which initiated my video coverage of the civil unrest in Portland.

I posted a second video from later in the speech when the activist declared, "They [police] violated our constitutional rights, so we got the right now to disturb the peace! And we will! Until they give us justice, we will disturb the peace!" Then he started chanting, "Black lives matter!" The crowd replied with the same chant, with thousands of voices thundering through the city square.

After the speaker with the ski goggles finished, a woman wearing blue jeans and a colorful shirt stepped up and took the megaphone. I would later see this same woman in a video online in which she was arrested for jumping onto a police motorcycle.

She instructed the audience to take out their phones and turn on their flashlights. Her melodic, feminine voice was a welcoming change from the raspy voice of the previous speaker. As if she was a mother singing her baby a lullaby before bed, the woman crooned the same phrase over and over, "Hands up. Please don't shoo-oot. Hands up. Please don't shoo-oot."

Everyone else eventually joined in. Thousands of white LED lights waved along with the harmony of the song. They reflected off the singer's large, light brown afro that vacillated in the light summer breeze, like a buoy bouncing up and down in a calmly undulating bioluminescent sea. The swaying LED lights combined with the harmony of the thousands of voices was almost hypnotizing. The moment felt more like a religious gathering than a protest.

With the thousands of peaceful demonstrators and no police yet in sight, I wondered aloud to Shelby and Jorge, "Where are the federal cops I heard so much about?" Having already witnessed the inevitable late-night siege of the courthouse, Shelby and Jorge assured me that I would see them soon.

After the speeches concluded and the sun's glow disappeared, the crowd flowed from the entrance of the county courthouse to the non-scalable fence that surrounded the adjacent federal one. We followed the Frontline Moms as they linked arms and formed a continuous human chain along the fence. Behind them, a group of gas-mask-wearing individuals dressed in black bloc assembled in the shadows of Lownsdale Square, a park just across the street from the courthouse.

Most of the casual spectators for the speech had dispersed; the demonstration shrunk to less than a thousand people. By this point, those without gas masks, helmets, or eye protection were in the minority. Those who remained were dressed like they were ready for a fight. The scene was still mellow, but I heard some screaming farther down the fence.

I came across a tall black man named Phillip, a conservative activist who I recognized from disputes with left-wing protesters in various internet videos from Portland and Seattle. He had his arms stretched out with his back against the fence as if he was protecting a child from gunfire. Phillip wore street clothes, and unlike almost everyone else, did not wear any form of mask. I subtly hit Record as the group of protesters heckled him to put on a mask.

Phillip replied indignantly, "Well if you don't want to get sick, then don't get close, I guess."

Another protester from behind me chimed in, "Why are you on the wrong side of history?"

"We can find a solution together! We do not have to listen to a few people who yell, 'Burn this down!' There are problems. There's injustice around the world, but causing more injustice, that don't do shit."

Someone off camera shouted, "He's a Trump supporter right there! This Nazi has been banned on Twitter!" Phillip's eyes darted back and forth. Though he stood his ground, I could tell he was unnerved by the simmering anger.

Another voiced an unexpected proposition. "I want to give them [the federal government] a chance! It's one time." The individual was apparently suggesting that Phillip may have a point, and they should pursue peace rather than antagonizing the police just this "one time."

Someone called out in disagreement, "They're the federal government! We can't trust them!" Dozens of people in the crowd started booing Phillip. Even some of the Moms joined in with the jeers. The female speaker who led the bioluminescent lullaby earlier stepped into my camera frame and stood in front of the fence next to Phillip. She pulled her mask below her chin then addressed the boos, "It doesn't matter what he believes or not, you have to let them protest the way they want."

Another black guy with bleach-blond hair backed up the afroed activist. "Everybody protests in a different way, and we have to be, like considerate of that. Like I don't personally care if people throw shit, but he does! He's not going to do that but we just have to be considerate of everybody."

A woman yelled from behind me, "He's gonna get pepper balls up the ass! He's gonna get tear-gassed!"

The bleached-blond black guy agreed. "Tear gas is inevitable. It's the feds. We are all going to get tear-gassed no matter what."

Such a multitude of voices took me by surprise, given how the Portland unrest was covered in the mainstream press, characterizing the crowd as either a monolith of anarchy and violence or peaceful proponents of positive social progress.

The dialogue in front of the fence revealed a more complicated truth. A sizable minority, including one of the organizers, lobbied for peace instead of violence. But as far as the corporate press was concerned, the reality was far simpler—the protesters were either benevolent opponents to the fascist Trump, or they were violent domestic terrorists keen on burning the courthouse to the ground.

But I did not see any large expensive cameras typical of the well-funded media conglomerates like *The Washington Post, Wall Street Journal, The New York Times*, Fox News, or CNN capture this more nuanced debate. Though these news outlets represented ideological stances from across the political spectrum, their binary approaches all resulted in the same outcome: The further polarization of America's understanding of Portland's protests.

By midnight, the Moms were replaced by the hardcore gang who banged their shields into the fence with increasing violence. Phillip gave up on his crusade for peace and departed in short order.

Amid the loud clangs of plastic and wood smashing into steel, someone near the front lines shouted, "The only good cop is a dead cop!" The officers of the law he was referring to were still hauntingly hidden somewhere inside the doors of the courthouse.

Another individual down the line tossed a flaming cardboard box over the fence. More debris was tossed onto the pile. When the flames of the garbage fire grew, the crowd cheered triumphantly.

Capitalizing on the energy, someone cried, "A-C-A-B," and the entire crowd chanted in reply, "All cops are bastards!"

The mob synchronized the collisions of the shields with the beat of a melodic chant. A tsunami of sound echoed off the graffitied concrete walls and into the trees in the park behind us. The entire length of the fence waved back and forth like waves stirred up by an approaching storm.

The imminent intervention from police meant it was time for the gas mask routine that I had practiced with Jorge and Shelby. I tossed it on as camo-clad men who looked more like combat troops than cops stormed out of the front doors. The sound of the shields hitting the fence was instantly drowned out by the thunderous boom of flash bang grenades. In addition to flash bangs (nonlethal grenades that produce a bright flash and a loud boom to disorient and deter anyone nearby), officers tossed and fired tear gas grenades over the fence as they filled the courthouse plaza. Exploding munitions flared brightly through the thick smoke emanating from both the garbage fire and the chemical gas. The spectacle resembled temporal lightning slashing through dark clouds.

Within minutes it was difficult to see more than twenty feet ahead. And that would be without staring through the two semi-opaque portholes of my old gas mask. The steady barrage of flash bang and tear gas grenades only emerged from the smoke moments before they flew over the fence, which made it hard to determine where they would land ahead of time. Once they hit the street or landed in the adjacent park, protesters, though I think at this juncture it is appropriate to deem those who remained as rioters, utilized heat-treated welding gloves that quickly scooped up the piping hot tear gas grenades then tossed them back over the fence. A half dozen gasoline-powered leaf blowers started their engines and blew the gas back toward the courthouse.

Police arrived at the fence aiming what looked like paintball guns through the gaps in between the mesh panels. These guns shot little plastic balls colloquially known as "pepper balls" and had a much higher rate of fire than the tear gas launchers. Pepper balls, also known as "riot balls," are plastic balls designed to shatter on impact. The needle-like shards they produced when they broke on impact would irritate the skin and eyes, sometimes for days afterwards.

A barrage of these riot balls collided into shields, umbrellas, and unprotected bodies like massive hailstones exiting a smog of chemical chaos. Those who did not have shields sported umbrellas, and those without either were at the mercy of a maelstrom of hundreds of pepper balls whizzing through the air.

As most of the few hundred left in front of the fence retreated for coverage, I panned my cell phone camera and revealed a man who walked by himself out of the smoke carrying a large American flag. In the background shone the graffiti-covered BLM Snack Van under the spotlights pointing from the courthouse to the street. Unlike the others I saw that night, his flag was not hung upside down. In his other hand he carried a gas leaf blower. The blue plastic that housed the engine matched the flag almost majestically. Hockey shin guards covered his legs, and a black duffle bag was slung in front of his pelvis as some kind of makeshift protection for his nether regions. On his head he wore a baseball batting helmet. His eyes were covered by lab safety goggles with a heavy black mask hiked up over his nose. In the background, a small contingent of umbrellas and shields huddled for safety on the side of the road.

The flag-wielding feller of federally funded toxic tear gas used the blower to push the smoke back at the police as a garbage fire on the plaza side of the fence basked him in a warm light. Strobe lights and lasers flashed from the park behind him. I couldn't help but marvel at the sight, a rebel clearing the streets of the dark smoke brought forth by the brute force of the federal government. A firework exploded behind him, and for a moment, it looked like the Fourth of July. But after he cleared the tear gas in front of him, the flag bearer turned his leaf blower toward the garbage fire and used its wind to stoke the flames.

My mesmerization by the patriotic performance was ended when someone inside the huddle of umbrellas screamed, "Fuck you!" Once the mob was beaten back from the fence, the cops disappeared back into the building as quickly as they had exited.

In no time at all, the rioters resumed their siege of the barrier, though they were now scarcely more than a hundred strong. It took an hour of fence banging and sporadic small fires before the federal officers reemerged for a new offensive.

The high pitch of a whistle screeched above the low roar of leaf blowers. I saw cameras and cell phones aimed down the street, and I sprinted in the same direction. When I got around the corner of the fence, I saw two dozen cops who marched in a straight line across the street, venturing beyond the plaza into the city for the first time that evening. The red and blue lights of a police SUV that followed slowly behind them sliced through the tear gas smoke like searchlights peering through the fog to an uncharted coastline.

The moment I started the video, one of the rioters tossed a glass bottle that shattered in front of the police line. One of the camo-clad troops fired a tear gas canister off the pavement in front of him. As it ricocheted off the ground and flew down the street, the metal canister whooshed within a few feet of my camera lens.

I panned the camera so the audience could see who was on the receiving end of the volleys. The fence that was being shaken violently until only moments ago was deserted except for one man who stood defiantly alone. He wore a bike helmet and ski goggles on his head. The only other protection he had was a pair of shorts, a T-shirt, and a bike that he held in front of him like the world's worst shield.

In the background behind him, someone scooped up an active tear gas can and tossed it back. I spun the camera following the canister as its smoke billowed through the air then landed at the feet of police, who returned fire with tear gas launchers and pepper ball guns. The pepper ball, fired by CO^2 gas, produced a discernibly more staccato cackle than the tear gas launchers, which were propelled by explosive shells and had to be breech-loaded with a new round after each discharge.

I panned the camera back to the poorly protected man, but when he came back into the frame he was heaped on the road groaning in pain. He returned to his feet slowly, rising only as quickly as needed to avoid being swallowed up by the approaching wave of police.

Once the cops reached the front of the courthouse, they fanned out and combined forces with another two dozen officers who emerged from the other side of the building. Over fifty strong, they formed a line at the same spot where the Frontline Moms had linked arms earlier. Every officer was kitted up with a gas mask, tactical helmet, body armor, gloves, and big heavy boots, though not a single one had a riot shield.

The siege squad repositioned themselves as close as possible, tucked behind umbrellas and wooden shields to my left. The cops reloaded their tear gas launchers and pepper ball blasters to my right. One of the cops closest to me, about 20 feet away, reignited the clashes when he unexpectedly tossed a flash bang directly into the middle of the umbrellas. Another officer threw a tear gas grenade in front of them, the resultant smoke hissing and writhing like a man-made serpent slithering through the concrete sprawl.

Someone inside the dark park with a boombox played Star Wars' famous "Imperial March," which occurred every time Darth Vader arrived on screen in *Episode V: The Empire Strikes Back*. The officers of the law walked slowly through the park until they had forced the rioters a full block away from the fence.

With the agitators scattered, there was little risk of being identified if I ran a live broadcast. I typed in the headline, "Federal Officers break up protests in Portland, Oregon," and commenced the stream to our audience of over five million Facebook followers. Within a few minutes, thousands were tuned in.

The Facebook Live commenced with over a hundred cops on the two blocks in front of the county and federal courthouses bifurcated by

SW Main Street. The federal officers wore camo and stood in front of the federal building while the county sheriffs wore navy blue and stood on the side of the county circuit court. None of them we could see wore name tags.

To their north, the greenery of Lownsdale and Chapman Squares was filled with less than a hundred resilient rioters who inched closer and closer to the line of cops.

A large white balloon filled with paint had popped at the intersection of SW Main Street and 3rd Avenue, which was directly between the front of the two courthouses. From a police speaker mounted on a nearby squad car a cop declared sternly, "You, in the street! Get back!"

Another paint bomb flew from outside the frame of my shot and splattered just behind a tear gas grenade expending its last remaining smoke. "The Imperial March" from *Star Wars* resumed after the line of cops fired a fresh volley of munitions and marched into the park.

The umbrella gang backed up at the same rate as the advancing police line, with about fifty feet between the two groups. I stood between the groups and panned my camera between them. Comments about the absurdity of the situation rolled in on the live stream as a strange game of riotous soccer unfolded in front of me. As quickly as a canister was fired into the shields someone would kick or throw the munitions back at the launchers.

Given that I had a gas mask and was wearing all black with no PRESS markings, I did not expect to be differentiated from the dissenters. I was about to suffer the consequences dearly. One of the cops reloaded and swung his 40 mm tear gas launcher in my direction. Still streaming to Facebook Live, I shook my gas mask side to side in a silent plea: "No! Please don't shoot me!"

The officer aimed the weapon and fired directly at me, rather than the normal protocol of bouncing the shell off the pavement to diminish its velocity. The aluminum canister smashed into my arm, tearing and burning my flesh. My arm gushed blood. I let out a scream, "Ah, fuck!"

The blast knocked the watch right off my wrist, and it fell on the sidewalk along with the searing hot canister. When I bent over to grab the watch, I am pretty sure that the same cop quickly reloaded and fired again, though I was still looking down when another shell collided with my thigh. It was like getting hit with a rubber bullet except instead of Styrofoam it was piping hot metal.

I cried out, "Ah! Fuck!" Though I would agree that swearing on camera was a lapse in professionalism, I also must note extensive studies that support the pain-killing property of swearing, including one published in the National Library of Medicine in 2011: "For many people, swearing (cursing) provides readily available and effective relief from pain."

As I lay in a heap, the camera rested on the sidewalk. A flash bang grenade lit up the black screen. Our viewers did not even notice that their cameraman just got wrecked by two tear gas shells.

The cops continued forward so I stumbled with urgency back to the umbrella gang at the corner of SW Main Street and 4th Avenue. I rested for a moment up against the side of the circuit court building.

When the police arrived on the curb, I struggled back onto my feet and put my hands up. One of the cops turned in my direction then waved me away with the electric torch on the front of his launcher.

"Yes, sir!" I dutifully replied as loudly as possible through the gas mask, still not sure if my radius bone had been fractured. I fled one block farther north to the corner of SW Main Street and 5th Avenue for refuge, but came across another skirmish in the middle of the road. I tried to locate Shelby and Jorge but they were off on their own missions, capturing different angles of the mayhem in the solitary effort to share some semblance of these silly street battles. It seemed a bit less silly now that my arm and leg were throbbing and oozing blood.

The live video finished with an incredible clash between a shield wall of twenty protesters wielding wooden, plastic, and nylon umbrella shields, which spanned the entire width of SW Main Street. They endured the final face-off against a police force nearly double the size.

The Feds extended themselves two blocks from the federal property they were tasked with defending. They ended the standoff with the shield gang when an officer near the curb tossed smoke and tear gas grenades directly in front of his feet rather than toward the opposing force. The right side of the police line unexpectedly turned and sprinted back toward the courthouse, followed by ten more. The last cop to head down the street would tap the next guy in line, then another tear gas grenade as ten more officers departed in the second wave. The last contingency of cops peeled away as one brave rioter ran out in front of the shields and kicked the smoking gas grenade in the direction of the retreat.

The shield umbrella gang emerged from their defensive positions and cautiously pursued the police. Realizing that the tide had turned, one of them hoisted an upside-down American flag and waved it vigorously. "The Imperial March" restarted from a boombox that had apparently gone mobile, interrupted occasionally by the clangs of exploding munitions as the cops turned and fired to cover their withdrawal. Every time the cops turned around, the advancing black-bloc-clad column would momentarily stop, place their shields on the ground for maximum protection, then spring back up when the cops resumed the departure.

This peculiar late-night dance concluded when a smoke canister landed at my feet. I turned the camera down for a close-up of the can as it sputtered chemicals into the night air. Behind the wall of smoke, the police withdrew back into the garage on the rear of the courthouse.

When I reconvened with Shelby and Jorge, neither of them was surprised to see me dripping blood from my leg and arm. I had a track record of showing up to the newsroom with harebrained injuries and there was still work to be done. We realized that a resourceful rioter had cut a large gap in one of the fence's steel mesh panels at some point during federal officers' campaign outside of their domain. We puzzled over the cleanly cut hole. Did someone actually bring a metal saw out to a demonstration?

Despite the defensive vulnerability, only a few dozen faithful returned from the diaspora to continue their siege. Two of them snuck through the gap in the fence pulling a plastic trash can in which they collected combustibles for a sizable garbage fire. The extensive graffiti on the facade of the courthouse became illuminated as they added debris to the blaze. PIGS was scrawled hastily next to BLM in black letters on the white stone facade of the building. The gold lettering that read Mark O. Hatfield Federal Courthouse glimmered, untouched, three stories above.

∴

When it was completed in 1997, the courthouse was named after former Senator Mark O. Hatfield, who had served a long career as a champion of civil rights for black Americans.

When Hatfield was at a university in nearby Salem, Oregon, during the 1940s, he witnessed Portland's racist legacy against black Americans firsthand. After a frat party one night, a young Hatfield had to drive his friend, the accomplished black concert artist, actor, professional football player, and activist Paul Robeson, out of Salem for a place that he could spend the night. Robeson could not find a hotel in town because blacks were still banned from any accommodation within the city's limits.

Once he started his political career, Hatfield spearheaded and passed legislation that would eliminate discrimination based upon skin color at public accommodations within the city of Portland.

After he became a US Senator, Hatfield also voted for the Civil Rights Act of 1968 and the Civil Rights Restoration Act of 1987.

⁝⁝⁝

I hit Record as I stepped tentatively inside the fence. The cornerstone of the courthouse, dated 1997, had been graffitied after the death of George Floyd. It read "THE PEOPLE'S COURT," written in black-and-white paint above the words engraved in stone, "UNITED STATES OF AMERICA."

A Caucasian rioter who wore only a black T-shirt, black pants, and a black flat brimmed hat, waved a large piece of cardboard as one would stoke a kumbaya campfire while he chanted, "Say his name!"

The few people nearby responded obediently, "George Floyd!"

I wondered for a moment what he would be doing normally if not antagonizing DHS officers, but it appeared he was in his elements among the trash ash, man-made wind, and fire. He displayed an eerie satisfaction when someone off camera tossed a traffic cone, a full trash bag, and a large plastic electric fan onto the fire. I was surprised by how the fan lit up like kindling, which added a whole new 2020 definition to the term "fanning the flames."

Inside my head my mind was racing. I had so many questions. The main one that kept coming up—What the fuck is this guy doing to help the cause? The back of my brain wanted to join him because I had no answer, and I was always better at lighting fires than putting them out.

The white arsonist burning trash in the name of black lives marveled at his work and approached one of the metal cylinders for a seat around the fire. The cylinders were originally placed in the plaza for fortification against vehicle-born attacks, but before this year they were only utilized by courthouse employees for the enjoyment of a leisurely lunch break outside. He feasted his eyes on the fire then looked over his shoulder and commented to no one in particular, "That's a hot fire!"

As if the police inside waited for the moment the garbage arsonist felt comfortable, they poured out of the building and rained pepper balls on his anarchic parade. The fire starter fled over the fence as riot balls pelted his body and steel mesh around him. Either he was drunk or tougher than I am, because he barely flinched when the balls shattered on his flesh. I flinched violently when a few of the same balls collided with my arm that was still bleeding from earlier.

I shouted, "Ah fuck," which, as we have established, helped numb the pain. I narrowly avoided arrest as I snuck through the hole in the fence. Four cops provided covering fire as another extinguished the flames. The plumes of smoke attracted more dissenters to the fence.

A woman with PRESS written on her helmet shouted from behind a gas mask, "Shame! Shame!"

By 3:45 a.m., the air was still thick with a foul smog. A block and a half long police line stood in formation despite the dwindling numbers of antipolice demonstrators. The few dozen who stayed milled about inside the park, sipping on suds and smoking cigarettes.

I commenced one more live broadcast so the audience could see the results of a night of "direct action" in downtown Portland. The streets were covered in debris and a layer of white chemical powder that almost looked like fresh snow.

Only two people remained actively engaged with law enforcement. One of them was a white man who claimed he was a veteran. He wore gray-scale urban camo pants and a black T-shirt and knelt on both knees in front of the feds, his hands clasped in prayer. The other individual was a black guy who wore a flat brim hat and a light gray fleece, strangely normal street clothes given that almost everyone else at this hour had some form of respirator, gas mask, or eye protection.

The veteran remained silent, blue lights of a nearby police cruiser illuminating the solemn expression on his face. The black guy paced the police line behind him as he exclaimed between puffs of a cigarette,

"Blessings! We appreciate what you do! But use your finesse! You guys have finesse! Blessings!"

Compared to the violent agitators earlier, at this late hour I was bemused by the guy who offered blessings rather than belligerent anti-police rage.

As I scanned across the trash-strewn intersection, a small group rushed to the corner of the fence at the other end of the courthouse. I ran down and came across a white woman wearing a respirator and ski goggles who waved hydrangea flowers a few inches in front of a group of federal officers' gas masks. She pranced in front of them, dancing to no beat in particular while she plucked the purple petals and threw them at their uniforms. The cops turned their backs acrimoniously and walked backward toward the fence. She skipped after them, one of the officers watching her movements closely as he backpedaled. When the woman thrust the bouquet of flowers to within a few inches of the only officer still paying her attention, he tackled her to the ground.

The silent veteran got up from his kneeling position and arrived as the flower woman hit the ground. He entered the tussle and attempted a rescue. In a moment, a dozen officers swarmed the pair. The veteran and the flower woman were forcibly dragged back into the courthouse through the hole in the fence.

At 3:53 a.m., I bent over and picked up the abandoned bouquet from the ground. Given my proximity to the courthouse, some feds behind the fence shone a spotlight on me and the beat-up botanicals. I held up the brightened petals in front of the camera. Though they were wilted, their vibrant purple color radiated in the filthy, smoky surroundings. Just before I ended the livestream, the only parting commentary I could come up with as I showed the audience the flowers was a perplexed, "Welp?"

Shelby, Jorge, and I sipped on some of our warm leftover beers on our way back to the hotel. My arm and leg had finally stopped bleeding. After my dad needled dozens of stitches on the kitchen table growing up, I hated hospitals and figured these flesh wounds would heal up, though today I still wear the scars. I guess you could call them lil riot gang tattoos. The alcohol turned out to numb the pain far more effectively than the swear words. I lit up a cigarette and posed for a picture outside the hotel, bleeding and with a scraggly riot mop for hair that was covered in chemical powder. Jorge and Shelby laughed at my haggard appearance, a living testament to the adage, "Play stupid games—win stupid prizes!"

The blood rushing to my head from the nicotine made it feel as if I was hanging upside down, reeling from the roller coaster of experiences on our first night.

The twenty-three-minute video would garner over a quarter million views and 3,500 comments. The top reply was from a middle-aged woman who wrote, "I can't believe this is my America. These people don't even know what they are protesting about. They are destroying our country."

Though this was one of the tamer comments, it was a good encapsulation of how our audience felt about the unrest in Portland. But for the other half of the country, these social justice demonstrators were more than justified in their violent confrontations with law enforcement because of the racist and murderous legacy of America's criminal justice system.

What was lost between both narratives was Portland's own legacy of racism against black Americans. It seemed that the conflict's rise to national prominence had given the protesters a tangible enemy in Trump's federal officers, but this projection of federal force had removed the city's own history from the equation.

After all the black speakers left for the evening, a mostly white crowd would engage in battles with police night after night. The city's black population had been scarce ever since the Vanport disaster and the racist property policies in Portland in the 1950s. Quaint suburbs around Lake Oswego were nicknamed "Lake No Negro" because only 1 percent of its residents were black even by 2020. Oswegans would hear none of the echoes of munitions and screams from under the steep roofs of their homes among the evergreens on the edge of the pristine lake; their sheltered chalets were protected by the Oswego PD. They had their cake and they were eating it too. Regardless of who the real bad guy was, what was even less clear was how these mostly white demonstrations, in a city with less than 6 percent black population, would achieve better conditions for black lives.

July 24, 2020, 11:19 AM PST: Burlington Northern Railroad Bridge, Portland, Oregon

This may smell bad, kid, but it'll keep
you warm until I get the shelter up.
—Han Solo, *Star Wars Episode V: The Empire Strikes Back*

On the short run from the hotel to the waterfront, a steady breeze cooled my chemically burned skin. The refreshing 68-degree weather was thanks to the WNW wind that came from the northern Pacific, through the mouth of the Columbia River and across downtown where it cleared the tear gas far more effectively than any leaf blower could.

I woke up at 7:00 a.m. PST for my daily meeting with the video team working remotely around the country. Our content from the previous evening had been demonetized on the two platforms where we made most of our money, Facebook and YouTube. Both platforms had policies that would remove monetization and/or issue a strike (three strikes and your business is toast) on videos that showed things like excessive violence or bullying. Our previous coverage had not reached that threshold, but the scenes in Portland, even with the least offensive headlines we could come up with, like "Police Break Up Crowd Outside the Portland Justice Center with Tear Gas and Flash Grenades," were deemed too extreme for monetization.

My co-director Sean and I conferred with the CEO Neil and EIC Geoff and determined that we could replace the lost revenue with exclusive tours of the protest zone for the most ardent subscribers. We'd launched a "Patriots Only" subscription model a few months prior and realized that selling subscriptions through an uncensored look into the warlike scenes would be a viable model to keep our coverage afloat.

After my morning meetings, I was bleary-eyed but could not go back to sleep—still too wired from the previous night's pandemonium. Perhaps the sight of the Columbia River would revive my riot-addled brain.

I got my first look at the river as I jogged up to a lush green park that led up to the Burlington Northern Railroad Bridge, the first bridge of any kind to cross the lower Columbia River.

The Burlington Bridge was built in 1908, a new century testament that American settlers had finally conquered the wilderness of the Northwest. Prior to America's total domination of this region the battle was against whatever elements the wilderness could dole out, including the Native Americans that lived there. When the Nez Perce tribe was ordered out of the Portland area by General Howard of the US Army, the Nez Perce Chief, Joseph, fought back. On June 17, 1877, his band of warriors killed thirty-four soldiers in one skirmish. It was one of the Natives' last significant military victories against American troops on their campaign to tame the West.

By the turn of the century, the westward trip could be made from the comfort of a train car. The native populations had been vanquished by disease and brute force. Most of the pioneers came from the Old World where the sheer magnitude of the new American continent was beyond comprehension. The size of the Columbia River Basin alone is larger than the entire country of France. Yet America's grandest mountains and rivers were conquered by these men and women who, along with immigrants from China, constructed a transcontinental network of thousands of miles of bridges and tunnels during the course of one lifetime. A generation prior, the trip to Oregon had required a perilous multi-month journey by horse-drawn wagon.

Even after America's technological might destroyed the Native Americans' civilization, Chief Joseph formed a bond with one of General Howard's successors, Lieutenant Wood, who relocated to Portland in the 1880s. By the twenty-first century, the friendship between the descendants of Lieutenant Wood and Chief Joseph endured, linking the lineage of the former enemies long after their ancestors' deaths.

The jog along with the flow of the river revealed more of the city's historic bridges, constructed during the twentieth century to accommodate automobile traffic into the city that boomed from the industries harvesting huge forests, and mining beneath the majestic mountains.

I turned inland en route back to the hotel and gazed up to a brick-laid Romanesque Revival clock tower, the most notable feature of Portland Union Station. When the beautiful old brick train terminal was completed in 1896, the city became the railroad hub of the Northwest.

I ran across a pedestrian bridge below the looming tower as my reverence for the picturesque bridges and railroad station was interrupted by a foul smell. Descending the stairs from the bridge to street level, I was inundated by a stench.

Around the corner back toward the downtown area I came across the source—a large parking lot that was converted into a homeless encampment with government-issued tents packed together in a semiorganized fashion. Though there were also porta -potties in the lot, the entire city block reeked of excrement. The smell of superheated shit rushed me back to a visit to a Palestinian refugee camp in Amman, Jordan. The main difference was that the Palestinian camps were dustier, but more orderly. The Portland version had trash strewn in every pathway between the makeshift homes; this was the first proof that I saw of what I heard was a huge homelessness problem in Portland.

As I continued my jog through Chinatown, I encountered many more tents of various sizes and levels of cleanliness, though these were camped directly on the sidewalk, rather than off the street in a designated area.

Chinatown had housed Portland's original underclass, the Chinese immigrants. A fire in 1873 burned the entire area I ran through, over 250 dwellings and 100 retail stores. A secret society that opposed the employment of the Chinese was suspected of arson, though no individual or organization was ever formally charged.

The same streets were now littered with a new underclass, the homeless. Men and women of all races loitered outside their tents where they begged passersby for help. Their appearances were generally ragged, and pedestrians zigzagged through their encampments or simply ventured into the street to avoid the saddening scene.

Much like my experience with the man who overdosed inside of DC's Union Station, the dichotomy between the poverty-stricken drug addicts living in tents outside the grandiose imperial architecture of these landmarks indicated a grim reality…our greatest cities were rotting from the inside. While Portland had been a city once divided by race, this new underclass spanned across all ethnicities and lived in shelters as rudimentary as the wigwams of the natives that were decimated by the American settlers. The "Union" that the name of these train stations invoked had become a union in name only. By 2020 the country was disunified, mired by economic and spiritual regression, perhaps permanently.

I wondered how many of the desperate rioters I saw the previous evening lived somewhere on the streets of Portland. While the city's founders endured unimaginable adversity in the creation of the modern city, it was clear that many of its current residents were faced with a new set of challenges—joblessness, homelessness, mental health crises, spiritual poverty, and drug dependence. I shuddered at the thought that the overwhelming majority of them would never overcome these issues. This was an epidemic that had no cure.

The chemicals from the night before burned as I rinsed off with cold water. After a spicy night of coverage, I would always put off showering because the irritants in tear gas and pepper balls were designed to get even spicier when mixed with moisture. This would specifically irritate a person's most sensitive areas, the mucus membranes (eyes, mouth, nose). Any kind of shower or water would spread the burning liquid across every inch of skin. Jorge and Shelby were blowing up my phone, rushing my painful cleanse along so we could check out the area in daylight for the first time.

On our way to investigate the status of the afflicted fence, we walked through the park in front of the courthouse, Chapman Square. We passed at least fifteen camping tents in the shade of the trees. A dozen individuals lounged among sleeping bags on park benches. I noticed two brightly painted plywood shields next to the bench where two ragged women begged park goers for whatever they could spare.

A huge terraced tent set up in the middle of the camp resembled what you might see at a football tailgate constructed by drunken college kids. We recognized the spot as Riot Ribs, which went viral online after they began feeding demonstrators on the Fourth of July 2020. They had been serving free food to protesters, homeless people, and pedestrians at all hours of the day for nearly three weeks. Over that period of time, the establishment raised over $300,0000 through an online GoFundMe campaign.

There were six grills smoking with various meats and vegetarian options. One of their covers said in hand-painted white letters "GO HOME FEDS." Propped up next to one of the other grills was another large wooden shield. I wanted to do a food review of the famous, or infamous, Riot Ribs, but after I took one look at the dirty, grease-stained kitchen, I decided I would wait for a time when I had more sleep and the courage derived from what, in my younger, more testosterone-infused days, I called "Beer Balls."

In front of Riot Ribs at the heart of the square, three men openly sipped on tall cans of beer. One of them, who wore black shorts, black shoes, black socks, and a black hat, held a cigarette in one hand and a twenty-four-ounce Budweiser in the other. The man sat beneath a thirty-foot-tall sculpture that memorialized the Portland Regiment who fought during the Spanish-American War. It was spray-painted on all sides with various forms of graffiti that said things like "LITTLE MEN/ BIG GUNS," "1492," and "GET OUT OF OUR CITY." The small cannons that surrounded the statue had been splashed with black paint, which dripped down the marble foundation before it dried, resembling a wound that never received attention.

The Spanish-American War erupted in 1898 after 266 American servicemen were killed in an explosion on the USS *Maine* in Havana Harbor. At the time, Cuba was part of the dying Spanish Empire and America was a rising power. Although an investigation revealed that an internal fire exploded the munitions on the American destroyer, the newspaper headlines rushed to their own conclusions.

The two most notable papers in New York, born from the same streets as that little cartoonist Thomas Nast took down Tweed's fat ass, published jingoistic headlines that drummed up war with Spain. With no factual basis, the *New York World* wrote, "Maine Explosion Caused by Bomb or Torpedo?" The *New York Journal* decried, "Destruction of the Warship Maine Is the Work of an Enemy." The public outcry pushed the country into a war that was short and successful. All of a sudden, American Imperialism and sensational journalism seemed like the winning strategy.

William Randolph Hearst and Joseph Pulitzer owned the *New York Journal* and the *New York World*, respectively. The two men birthed the term "yellow journalism" when the advent of color-printed newspapers stoked a bidding war between Hearst and Pulitzer for the acquisition of a wildly successful cartoonist named Richard Outcault. While Thomas

Nast carved black-and-white cartoons into wood for a weekly paper, by the late 1800s technological advances meant they could be rapidly drawn and printed in color in the daily paper. Outcault's most popular comic was called *The Yellow Kid*, portraying, in full color, the life of a kid in the slums of New York. The competition between the two papers, as well as their profits-over-truth mentality, established a pattern of corporately sensationalized reporting the likes of which the country had never seen. And 122 years later, high-speed internet presented a new way for publishers to make money. There weren't two competing papers—there were tens of thousands. As technology changed the way Americans consumed their news, yellow journalism became clickbait.

Clickbait was a seemingly benign term, but its origins were as old as news. Stories that tapped into instinctual lizard brain fears and desires were far more likely to cause a reader to buy papers, or a user to click. If we wanted to get clicks on our videos, if we wanted our business to succeed, the key was the thumbnail, or the first image a social media user encountered while scrolling rapidly through their feed. The most successful thumbnails instantly pissed off the passerby, or for our mostly older, mostly male viewers, displayed a young, hot chick. When you had both of those elements combined, we called those thumbnails "Boomer crack." I wasn't a journalist or a video director. I was like a low-level drug dealer. Mark Zuckerberg was Pablo Escobar selling his users bias-confirming hyperbole and tits.

***

My meander around the statue was cut short when the guy with the tall boy Budweiser pointed his cigarette at my camera and said, "Fuck Ted Wheeler! Ted Wheeler is a bitch! I challenge him to a UFC fight!"

I thought about asking the man why he had such choice words for the mayor of Portland, Ted Wheeler. But his belligerency had already attracted the attention of people who peered at my recording phone, so I continued across the street to check out the fence.

We filmed construction crews who were patching the hole from the early hours of the morning. They told us that the metal had been cut with a saw. We all laughed at the ridiculous commitment of whoever brought the metal saw to a political protest.

We headed to a nearby bar where we could post our construction update while we grabbed a bite and a coupla cold ones. After a few months in this peculiar line of work, we became accustomed to the "riot diet," characterized by fried food as the standard fare. Most of the small businesses near protest zones were boarded up, so typically we only had time for one or two hot meals at odd hours. That left us with limited options, either bars or fast food. Besides, the fatty fried stuff was the only way to satisfy anyone who is sleep deprived and adrenalized from the constant threat of arrest or injury.

We entered the bar and were greeted by the owner who spoke in a thick Levantine accent. Upon inquiry, I learned that he grew up in Amman, Jordan, where I studied for a semester in college. I spoke in Arabic and he laughed at a white guy mimicking the strange and guttural sounds of his native tongue.

I asked how business was since the pandemic, and he relayed that the bar had enjoyed a steady customer base from the federal officers who stayed in a hotel nearby. After they defended the courthouse every night, they would come in on their days off and unwind over bar food and a few beers. He noted that, as an immigrant owner of a small business in a city with rising crime, he loved the police and was happy he could provide them with a hot meal. According to our desert-born friend, the federal cops were afraid of visiting other bars around town because they assumed that they may be ID'd and harassed. This helped explain perhaps why none of the officers we saw wore name patches on their uniforms.

The woman tending the bar overheard me speaking the strange sounds of the Jordanian Arabic dialect with her boss, and I got the idea she might let me take her on a date. It had been nearly half a year since the start of the pandemic, and I was a lonely, single dude. On the receipt, I scribbled my number along with a note in Arabic that asked her out to dinner, which I knew my new Jordanian friend would have to translate for her later.

July 24, 2020, 10:06 PM PST: County Courthouse Portland, Oregon

> How am I supposed to know the
> good side from the bad?
> —Luke Skywalker, *Star Wars Episode V: The Empire*
> *Strikes Back*

Approximately five thousand people packed tightly into the park for the Friday night demonstration. After a slow trudge through the city square, we made our way to the same elevated position as the night before, directly across from the speakers. This time they had a spotlight that shined on their improvised urban stage.

Hundreds of Frontline Moms were clad in their yellow shirts with plenty of gas masks and helmets to go around. They linked arms for photo ops from dozens of cameras. The blue-hued limelights cast an ominous tone. A mom in the middle of the arm-linking matriarchs wore a sign around her neck that read "DON'T/SHOOT/MOMS/BLM."

The photos above the headlines in all the well-established news outlets featured these almost entirely white, middle-aged women in the weeks that we were in Portland. Of course they did. The moms wore bright yellow and stood at the "frontline" of every speech almost every night—they couldn't be missed.

Where were the black moms? Probably working or taking care of their kids, I thought.

But the big cameras with the bright lights and the moms with their colorful shirts would disappear from sight as soon as the tear gas grew thick later in the evening.

The speaker with the raspy voice and ski goggles from Thursday stepped up with a megaphone. He got the crowd riled up by performing a rap that was his own version of DMX's "Rough Ryder's Anthem," shouting the updated chorus, "Stop cops! Shut 'em down! Open up shop!"

Once they caught on to the revised lyrics, the demonstrators chanted the updated rap line for nearly a minute, becoming even more musical once participants clapped along with the beat. Again, I got the vibe of a religious revival rather than a political protest, which made it harder to believe that it would turn into a smoky hellscape in a few hours. After they were warmed up, the crowd chanted, "Vote Trump out of office!"

While the speakers continued, a significant portion of the audience already spilled over to the area of the Federal Courthouse. We noticed way more shield-wielding black-bloc bois and gurlz out this evening, so we climbed down from our roost and repositioned next to the fence for the start of the siege.

Though it was a minority of the huge, more peaceful crowd that we saw below the makeshift stage, more than one thousand people surrounded the courthouse. As the speeches winded down, hundreds began smashing the fence.

Drums thumped in the background amidst chants of "Black lives matter!" providing the front line with a driving beat. They synchronized the collision of their shields in two-second intervals. The top of the fence waved back and forth 45 degrees in each direction with every coordinated crash. The violently undulating steel looked as flimsy as a wood and wire dune fence enduring a hurricane that just made landfall.

Someone shouted, *"Fuck your wall!"* right next to my camera's microphone. The mob was certainly trying to their best to "fuck" that wall as hard as they could.

A half-dozen road flares had been tossed into the courthouse plaza. They bathed the unadorned square columns that supported the building in a dark red light. A rioter tossed a red smoke grenade that landed next to one of the flares, then a firework exploded overhead and rained down fiery orange sparks. Green lasers and blue strobe lights blasted their beams at the dark doorways that housed the feds in waiting. The pyrotechnics lit up the interior of the courthouse just enough to see a few camo uniforms preparing for their offensive. It looked like Darth Vader just unsheathed his red lightsaber before he emerged from a smoky red glow.

I was prepared with my gas mask and camera rolling when the feds streamed out through the door. Pepper balls whizzed into the fence then exploded into powder. Anyone without gas masks, or at the very least eye protection, retreated from the irritants with haste.

Those who stuck around continued their assault on the fence, which was now partially broken at its base and flopping wildly from side to side. One guy, clad in all black, tried a flying drop kick. Perhaps he imagined that he was in an action movie, but he timed it completely wrong because when his kick contacted the fence it was swinging back in his direction. He catapulted away from the courthouse and landed hard on his back in the road, but sprung up instantly. He revised his tactics after this and went with an alternative form of "direct action"—throwing traffic cones at the federal troops on the other side of the barrier.

The leaf blowers came back on, their low din periodically overpowered by a PA system that calmly stated, "This is the Federal Protective Services. Do not attempt to damage or remove, enter, or climb the fence around the federal courthouse. Failure to do so may result in arrest or the use of crowd-control munitions."

I guffawed behind my gas mask…too late for that!

As the feds creeped closer and continued with a high rate of fire, they finally separated the determined rioters from the fence. An unbroken line of scores of shields and umbrellas supported by a phalanx of leaf blowers lined up on the other side of the street. They assumed defensive positions as the feds aimed their guns through the gaps in the wall and continued the pepper ball onslaught at close range.

I filmed from behind the umbrella line. The upper portion of my body was exposed but I accepted that I would get pelted for a firsthand perspective. I played enough paintball as a kid, so I did not mind the welts, but the peppery powder that differentiated the riot balls from normal paintballs began irritating my exposed skin. When my dad purchased the guns for Christmas in 2003, he ensured his was equipped with an electric trigger that achieved a much faster rate of fire while "Santa" brought much cheaper and slower mechanical triggers for my two brothers and me. But when one of us finally plugged Pops with a few paintballs, we would be laughing about his painful groans for weeks. I was outgunned even then, but at least I had something to return fire. This time all I had was a cell phone. On the bright side, the footage I recorded from the front lines would sell "Patriots Only" subscriptions to pay for the trip.

The shield wall inched closer as MC Hammer's "Can't Touch This," blared somewhere inside the park behind us. A man who sported a bulletproof vest with "PRESS" emblazoned on the front ventured out only feet away from the cops. He did not look like your typical riot journalist.

His helmet had a giant fake orange mohawk, a punk rock version of a Spartan helmet from Ancient Greece.

He plastered a large, transparent plastic shield up against the mesh fence. Through the plexiglass, he gave the officer on the other side a middle finger and danced provocatively to the music.

Plenty of right-wing personalities had complained about so-called "antifa press," who antagonized police rather than simply documenting what took place, but this was the first time I had seen it in real life.

The scene answered the question of why the cops tagged me the night before.

A law enforcement officer came up to the other side of the fence and blasted a thick stream of orange pepper spray at the mohawked antagonist, but he was virtually unaffected because of his gas mask and long sleeves. A few other individuals who were nearby were not as well equipped, covering their faces to no avail. They scurried back behind the umbrella wall where a few "medics" came to their aid (although the only visual indication that they were medics were a few pieces of red duct tape that formed a cross on their helmets and backpacks).

As if the crazy meter wasn't already cranked up to max, I heard the squeal of a saw striking metal pierce through the music and the mayhem. When I got closer, I saw sparks flying around a man with a gas mask and a small circular saw. While the DHS officers were distracted on the other side of the plaza, he huddled under the protection of four colorful umbrellas and three shields pressed up against the fence. His electric circular saw sliced easily through the bottom where the fence met the horizontal supports on the ground. It appeared on the verge of falling over. At least twenty more cops poured out of the front doors. They marched up to the sound of the screeches. The saw man sheathed his tool and fled, but the deed was already done. After a few dozen synchronized shoves, the metal separated from its base and the fence sagged in the direction of the courthouse. Some of the officers now held clubs, presumably in the event that the fence came down and they had to resort to dark age truncheons instead of guns.

As the police forced the mob and their saw squad to the other side of the street, I recorded a flash bang grenade fly over the fence, panning my camera to the street as it landed on someone's head and exploded at the ground next to a cluster of turtled shields and umbrellas. I did not realize it at the time, but that flash bang hit Shelby directly on her plastic helmet, which we just bought at a Portland military surplus store. She had a hard time hearing for the rest of the evening but still thought the footage was hilarious.

One hour and eleven minutes after midnight, a tall and chunky county police officer lumbered through the trash-laden plaza of the federal courthouse holding two leaf blowers. As he slowly plodded through the courthouse plaza, plastic bottles and broken glass crunched under his heavy steps. He resembled a tired employee shuffling between cubicles for the first cup of coffee on Monday morning rather than a man in the middle of a fight against what many in right-leaning media referred to as "domestic terrorists."

A rioter with his own much larger and more powerful backpack-mounted leaf blower entered the left side of my video and bashed into the fence. The Monday Morning Riot Cop turned around slowly and aimed both his blowers at the angry rioter on the other side of the fence. The law-breaking leaf blower operator gave the middle finger to his federally funded competitor. I stuck my phone through a seam inside the fence for a clear shot of the response.

Unentertained by the hostile gesture, the leaf-blowing law enforcement officer turned his back and rested one of the blowers on a metal cylinder, like a union worker putting down a lunch pail. But he only had a moment for rest because a rebounded tear gas canister flew over the fence directly at his head. The cop dodged the canister nonchalantly as if avoiding an errant paper ball thrown at the office trash can, then lurched over to the smoking grenade and aimed his leaf blowers so they blew the gas back at the fence. The cop disappeared and the camera showed nothing but an impenetrable cloud of CS gas. I ended the video as the sound of shields smashing metal clanked in the microphone.

Two hours and fourteen minutes after midnight, law enforcement unexpectedly withdrew back inside the courthouse, which provided the umbrella gang with an opportunity for refortification. A line of twenty-four shields and ten umbrellas formed a horseshoe shape around the intersection at the corner of the fence, which sagged inward with plastic bags, street cones, and other trash collected around its base. The shields, two of which were the same decoratively painted ones I saw near the homeless tents that morning, were planted firmly on the ground. Umbrellas were stacked on top, forming a near-perfect turtle formation that would be the envy of any Roman centurion.

Directly behind this formation roared a bonfire fueled by garbage and some large wooden pallets. As I aimed the camera at the fire, someone dropped a fresh pallet on top. Another individual wearing black jeans, a black hoodie, and a black mask hiked up high over their nose doused some kind of lighter fluid on the bonfire. As the flames climbed higher toward the night sky, the crowd cheered with jubilation.

About fifteen members of the media were illuminated as they aimed cameras at the blaze. Including me, the media appeared to account for about one-third of the people that were still in front of the courthouse, broadcasting surreal images of a small group of rioters for all the world to see. By framing the shot solely around this one fire in a city of 635,000, even a quiet night by Portland standards could be made to look like the apocalypse in Little Beirut.

It took fifteen minutes before the cops were back out in the streets. I sprinted down the block with a handful of other streamers and reporters, including Shelby and Jorge, as we recorded the dramatic approach. Twenty-five cops marched uniformly, two-deep the entire width of the street. Someone played "The Imperial March" in the background, which I learned also functioned as an alarm that signaled the stormtroopers were on the way.

The turtle gang showed no sign of yielding their defensive position in front of the fire. In all of the previous confrontations I saw in Portland, aside from the flower lady and the hapless veteran who was tackled the night before, the violence occurred at a distance and from behind gas masks. Compared to the NYPD in short sleeves and nothing but truncheons and helmets, the bizarre charade of blocking projectiles and sending them back was far less personal. The distance of the violence and the gas masks allowed each opposing side to view the other as an avatar of a bad guy rather than a human being. Similarly, the audience was likely to lob horrendous insults in the comment sections of our videos, though as compared to the internet, it's far more difficult to say such things to someone's face.

When the cops briskly marched within twenty feet, one by one, the shields lifted up and backpedaled around the fire. The line of feds halted and leveled their weapons fifteen feet in front of the flames. Lights from the sirens of a cruiser lit their backs up blue, but the blaze in the middle of the road glowed the front of their uniforms bright orange. The cops and the rioters seemed to be on the very edge of America, the line between order and anarchy. The military fought against the Native Americans deemed subhuman savages as they conquered the west. The DHS officers outmatched their opponents using gas and gunpowder to bend perceived forces of chaos to their will. But the frontier in 2020 was not such a clear-cut battle between America's ceaseless expansion and its adversaries. It was a struggle against fellow countrymen, an internal crisis of meaning whose only solution was to prove the other side as corrupt.

Meanwhile, the rioters crouched behind their shields and the flaming trash heap. Outmatched with their makeshift defenses, these antipolice demonstrators believed they were standing up to our corrupt postcolonial capitalist system, the same system that decimated the Nez Perce and marginalized Portland's black residents for over a century. Their fight: either find meaning in skirmishes they were bound to lose or remain greasy cogs in the soul-crushing system of the modern mundane.

After a minute-long pause, one of the officers in back tapped the shoulders of the front line, then the volleys resumed. The camouflaged cops advanced more slowly around the garbage fire. As they shot their breech-loaded 40 mm grenade launchers and riot guns through the smoke, the sound of riot balls colliding into wood was followed by screams of pain. A man remained on the ground as the shields continued backward. Though he clutched his leg in anguish, the cops did not stop their march. He had no time to lick his wounds lest he risk arrest, so he sucked it up and sprint-limped out of sight. Federal fire extinguishers turned the garbage fire to a pile of molten, smoldering plastic in no time at all.

The rioters were clearly no match for the riot munitions. More and more began deserting the clash. By the time the skirmish arrived at the corner of the next block, the rest of the shields and umbrellas scattered out into the empty streets.

When push came to shove, all they could do was yell profanities, throw bottles, and retreat once the cops came out in front of the fence. This realization gave the surreal experience an air of theater, like when I found out that R2-D2 in *Star Wars* wasn't an intergalactic droid but actually just an old midget in costume.

What was happening in Portland was more akin to the actors who played the role in a movie, with the politicians and the corporate decision-makers as the producers of the show. The same people came out night after night and put on a spectacle of violence for the general public, locked up at home and eagerly fixated on the next clip that would confirm the us-or-them biases that each side was electronically fed.

Based on the shields that were stacked up next to the haggard-looking homeless women at the park earlier that day, many of these people came out for a riot because they had no home, or anything else to lose. As the world watched the madness, the justice warriors were given the archetypal feeling of significance that every modern person craves, but few can attain; they got exactly what they wanted when the media recorded the cops cracking down with impunity.

Ultimately, the police always succeeded in extinguishing the fires and sending the dissidents battered into the night. But once videos of their brutal superiority reached the internet, the cops who followed orders from on high provided the narrative that Trump and his storm troopers needed their tyrannical rule overthrown.

The woman with the flowers and the veteran from the night before were the only ones I saw actually confront the officers, but even in that case the Democrat-funded bail reformers would have them out of jail by the next day. The stage for these nightly confrontations had been set by the politicians, and the ratings-eager media were keen on broadcasting their viewers' favorite version of the play.

What became the most viral video of the trip was titled "The Battle of the Leaf Blowers Is On in Portland," with the caption, "Protesters play volleyball with cops using tear gas canisters." The headline was the brainchild of Grae Stafford, a British fellow holding down the fort at *Daily Caller* HQ in DC. He was up late editing and uploading our footage to various social media platforms, supervising and cooking up pithy titles like a riot Mary Poppins. The video received over 1.4 million views on one Facebook page. Given the less tragic and more comedic nature of the bizarre scene, it stayed monetized. Usually this would fetch a few hundred to a few thousand bucks, depending on the watch time. This one crazy video produced the cash to keep our news company's Facebook-funded riot pornography operation rolling along.

Of the 6,300 people who commented on the post, the top comment was made by a middle-aged man whose profile picture portrayed him smiling with white hair and a button-down shirt: "They need a Water cannon. Or more officers to be able to surround and arrest. Throw [a] thing at an officer of the law is assault. Arrest them immediately. And transport them a thousand miles away to a waiting jail in a county where the judge is not in Soros' pocket."

The fact that this comment acquired the most likes was a good indication of how our audience felt about the protests/riots that took place night after night in front of the courthouse.

In the eyes of our mostly Boomer and conservative audience, if anyone represented the evil Emperor on the ideological left, the wrinkly skinned tyrant who rules over Darth Vader in *The Empire Strikes Back*, it would be the influential billionaire referred to in this comment, George Soros. His wealth funded millions of dollars to nonprofits that reportedly posted bail for the rioters after they were arrested in Portland, Minneapolis, and other cities that saw destructive unrest. Across the country, Soros also funneled millions to political campaigns of local and federal prosecutors that favored a soft-on-crime approach.

While Joe Biden was campaigning for president, in the eyes of our audience, George Soros was the real bad guy who pulled the strings behind the scenes; much like the hooded Emperor who commanded Darth Vader via holographic message as he prepared the invasion of the rebel stronghold in *The Empire Strikes Back*.

From the more liberal and anti-Trump perspective, perhaps Steve Bannon, the architect of Trump's shocking 2016 campaign victory and host of the hit online show *War Room*, would best fit the role of the evil Emperor. His pale, haggard appearance and dour demeanor certainly made him a good fit for the character.

The silliness of the federal government employing leaf blowers for their crackdown on political violence created the curiosity gap that caused so many people to click the video. The sight of tear gas tossed back and forth like a fourth-grade game of hot potato was hilarious, but it got so many clicks because it was also infuriating.

Perhaps instead of playing "The Imperial March" when the feds marched out of the building, it would be more appropriate to cue the theme from *Spaceballs*, the 1987 film produced by comedian Mel Brooks that satirized the *Star Wars* franchise.

The film portrayed Darth Vader like a self-conscious little dweeb who wields a dainty lightsaber from his crotch, making his sword fights in the movie appear childish, and about as masculine as a six-year-old boy trying to aim over the rim of the toilet to take a pee.

While the situation in Portland may have looked like a satire, it was actually real violence that was incensed by national politicians and cable pundits who hyperbolized their enemies as terroristic threats. The anger on the streets was turned into political fodder that stoked the fury of our cultural factions. The fact that the media had become so fixated on the riots motivated Portland's rioters; they finally found the attention they believed their cause deserved.

I realized my contribution to this fear-mongering media machine, but I bore on. Since we felt that the rest of the media was either editorializing or selectively showing only half the story, we saw no other option other than to keep the camera rolling and let the tear-inducing clouds of gas blow in whichever direction the wind took them.

By 3:00 a.m., the staging ground for the nightly spectacle was entirely empty save a few sorry-looking folks who milled around in the park. I utilized the abatement for a video of all the trash and discarded munitions inside the courthouse plaza. I stuck my phone through the slits in the fence for a clear view. As I zoomed my camera in on a charred pile of trash, I heard something sputter next to my feet. I found out what it was before I had time to investigate when I saw a bright red, white, and blue flash fly up around me then heard a firework explode. When I looked down, my legs were covered in a thick orange soot. I stamped my feet to make sure I was OK, and only felt a minor sting from a few of the sparks.

All I could hear after it went off was a loud ring. After review of the video, I exclaimed after the explosion, "Who the *fuck* threw that?" Though I did not hear myself say it at the time.

About twenty feet away, a woman screamed bloody murder, as if her legs had actually been blown off by the firework. As it turned out, she was fine, and so was I. Though I'm convinced that my hearing is no longer as good as it was before I went to Portland.

Shelby and Jorge ran over when they realized what happened. My hearing returned after a few minutes, and we decided that we should call it a night. We resumed our new tradition of sipping on warm alcoholic suds on the walk to the hotel. As I cracked a beer and examined my legs, I realized that I was wearing the nylon pants that I found in my dad's closet after he died. The nylon fabric was burned from the explosion, but definitely still functional enough for riot attire. On that summer morning, I christened them my *lucky* riot pants.

My *lucky* riot pants swished loudly as Shelby, Jorge, and I laughed about all the crazy things we saw that evening. Shelby and I laughed especially loudly, probably because we couldn't hear so well from the flash grenade and fireworks.

July 25, 2020, 8:13 PM PST: Tope Bar, Hoxton Hotel Rooftop, Portland, Oregon

Why you stuck-up, half-witted,
scruffy looking nerf herder!
—Princess Leia, *Star Wars Episode V: The Empire Strikes
Back*

The bartender reached out after deciphering the Semitic coding of my note, so I arranged for a date with her on Saturday night. She recommended a trendy bar on the rooftop of a luxury hotel downtown. I could tell it was trendy because of the monosyllabic and ambiguous name, Tope.

It was a serene evening and when my date went to the bathroom, I recorded a video of the breathtaking panorama. A block to my south, the second tallest building in Portland, Bancorp Tower (nicknamed Big Pink), reflected the waning light off its rosy glass. In the east rose the faint summit of Mount Hood. The snow-capped peak shone orange from the sunset and appeared as a cosmic lighthouse far beyond the metropolitan anarchy surrounding the protests. On the shadowed streets below was

Old Chinatown, where I had jogged around vagrants begging outside their sullied shelters.

Shelby was skeptical about pursuing romantic interests on a work trip, admittedly a legitimate point. But I told her it would just be for a few drinks, and I could catch up with her and Jorge by nightfall. Jorge could have cared less. In fact, he was quite enthusiastic that one of us single guys was headed for a real-life date in the midst of the loneliest months in modern times.

I was starting to enjoy the crisp northwest breeze that was predominant in Portland's summer, far more refreshing than the prevailing south winds that did nothing to cool the muggy summers in DC. I savored the deep breaths I took through my nostrils, an indulgence I avoided when mouth breathing to avoid the putrid sulfur and chlorine gas from the man-made munitions. I felt exceptionally emboldened because I was about four cocktails deep.

It almost felt like I was back in the normal, pre-2020 world, where we could party merrily without fear of infection or societal calamity. Spellbound by my recess from the riots, I headed back inside for another round of specialty cocktails. Under the foolish notion that I still had the same tolerance for booze that I had during my bartending days, I also took some shots with the bartenders before I brought the drinks outside. The hard liquor was made more potent because I only drank softer beer or wine since the lockdowns.

My memory is hazy on how I returned to the hotel, but I came back to reality when I woke up just after 2:30 a.m. to missed calls and angry texts from Shelby. She was wondering where the hell I was. My date and I were on the top of the covers on the bed, fully clothed; she was sleeping soundly. What happened? I called Shelby to find out her location, but she didn't pick up.

I logged into Twitter looking for her latest update. My heart plummeted when I saw the mayhem in Shelby's video. It read in all capital letters, "BREAKING: THE FENCE IS DOWN IN PORTLAND." The video showed the street in front of the courthouse with almost the entire block of fencing folded over into the street. A flash from a tear gas canister inside the courthouse plaza dispersed a wall of smoke and obscured Shelby's camera from the few dozen rioters behind shields and umbrellas across the street.

Her next Tweet stated, "This is an absolute battle right now in Portland." The video showed twenty members of the shield gang inched all the way up to the felled fence, while law enforcement showered them with pepper balls.

Her Twitter thread continued with a video posted fifteen minutes later: "Federal officers sweep the park and push rioters away from the courthouse. One sprays me in the face with something. I have my mask on, but the skin that isn't covered is burning."

The video showed a postapocalyptic scene with chemical ash and powder covering the grass in the park like snow. Shelby closely followed officers as they marched through the Riot Ribs kitchen. The officer yelled through his gas mask at Shelby to "Get back!"

Through the haze under the tent of Riot Ribs HQ, the stainless-steel refrigerator in the background showed a glib reflection of orange from the electric string of lights.

Shelby's subsequent Twitter thread showed everything from officers violently detaining a rioter, to a few cops covered in multicolored paint from exploded balloons. One video showed a federal officer with humiliated body language; his shoulders sloped forward as he lazily held his shield, which was made opaque by various shades of house paint. He looked like a guy who had a terrible day at work, a sullen human rather than an aggressive hand of the callous institutions designed to keep us down.

By the time I contacted Shelby and Jorge, they were ready to come back to the hotel. I apologized and explained that I innocently passed out, but she was mad as hell, and rightly so.

I struggled with the prospect of failing my coworkers. Part of the role I thought I served was to ensure Shelby and Jorge's safety. Yet I abandoned them when things were most chaotic, and therefore most dangerous. I put a frivolous thrill ahead of my professional pledge. As a video creator rather than a reporter, I always erred on the side of immersing myself into the chaos rather than separating myself from it. While Shelby stood in the midst of the madness then made sense of it in her reports, I relished it so my camera could show what it felt like inside the belly of the beast. The embrace of entropy caused me to fail in the cooperative mission that we established before covering the riots.

When I laid eyes on them, Shelby stared solemnly from behind a thick coat of orange pepper spray and Jorge was too tired to even lift his eyes beneath a pepper powdered and crooked helmet. I would like to say this yielded an inflection point for me, where I turned my back on the destructiveness of substance abuse—my family's legacy of escaping the emptiness of tragedy and death with drugs. But in reality, my shame for having failed Shelby and Jorge, as well as my hopes for her forgiveness, did not result in a course correction of my behavior, at least not yet. For the moment, I remained in Portland, and my flirtation with the Marshall of Madness was about to enter full swing.

July 26, 2020, 1:45 PM PST: Mark O. Hatfield Federal Courthouse Portland, Oregon

> You were very lucky to get out of there.
> —Luke Skywalker, *Star Wars Episode V: The Empire Strikes Back*

The metal melted back together under the intense heat of a welding torch as the workers added new plates to the joints at the foundation. Shelby and Jorge relayed that it wasn't saws that took the fence down the night before, but good old-fashioned manpower. With a few ropes affixed to the top, the rioters were able to yank the whole thing down in a tug of war fashion, similar to what was attempted in front of the Jackson statue in Washington, DC, back in June.

After I finished a "Patriots Only" tour of the reinforcements in front of the courthouse, I met with Andrew Duncomb, a black conservative activist known as "the Black Rebel," for an interview that we would publish for our general audience on Facebook and YouTube. Less than twenty-four hours before publication, he was knifed right in front of the federal court of law.

Despite the fact that Duncomb was black, his political views were enough to get him stabbed. He displayed the real-world impact of Portland's culture war when he winced in pain as he shook my hand. He showed me the fresh wound on the middle of his back where he claimed a seven-inch blade narrowly missed his kidney.

Andrew was determined to conduct the interview at the location where the assault took place, only a hundred feet from the courthouse. We met a few blocks away. As I prepared the DSLR camera and Andrew's microphone, I tried to talk him out of it. Given the small crowd of demonstrators around the area, I was worried that if Andrew was identified, things could escalate to violence (again). As if the situation wasn't tenuous enough, Duncomb also insisted that he hold a large American flag over his shoulder.

I implored that the flag would only draw more attention. He agreed but countered by saying that if we were on a public street in America, he should be able to fly the flag wherever he pleased. He made a decent point.

As we walked to the courthouse, Andrew was joined by two brawny white dudes who had been waiting in the car. One of them carried what looked like a paintball gun, but when I asked, he told me it was a "riot gun," meaning that it fired the pepper balls we saw police use. In addition to the large American flag over Duncomb's shoulder, the conspicuousness of the man's riot gun elevated my concern.

My heart raced as we drew stares the moment we arrived. I hit Record and began with questions as soon as possible. The hospital wristband was visible on the hand that supported the pole. The flag hung at a 45-degree angle halfway out of the frame.

We opened with Andrew's version of what led to the stabbing the night before: "We were being stalked by an antifa group after I had been doxed [revealing a person's identity online]; they put my information out there to look for me filming. They don't like conservative journalists coming out there and reporting. And so after them following us around for a while, we were going back to the car and they were still following us. I didn't feel comfortable with them following us back to the car, and so I came right over here where we are at" —he gestured to the sidewalk next to us— "and put my hand over his shoulder and said, 'Hey what's up, buddy? Why you guys keep following us around,' and he pulled out a knife and stabbed me right in the kidney. Or not in the kidney, but he aimed for my kidney."

At this point in the video after editing, I cut to my footage of the open wound. I realized the imagery would probably get the video demonetized on YouTube and Facebook but included it so the viewers could see the real-world impacts of political division. The six-minute interview concluded as Duncomb implored people to stand up for their rights, even against threats of violence. "We have to put our foot down and not allow this stuff to happen. If conservatives are under attack on the streets just for filming, then we have a huge problem when it comes to this Marxist socialist type agenda that they're trying to force upon us through threats of violence and attacks."

By this point, a crowd of about fifteen people formed around us and shouted insults like "Nazi." We exited the area the moment I stopped recording, and I was relieved no one followed us back to the car, maybe because of the riot gun. I headed back to the hotel and edited/uploaded the video. I puzzled over the day. I guess black lives matter, but only if they support Black Lives Matter?

July 26, 2020, 10:19 PM PST: County Courthouse Downtown, Portland, Oregon

Luminous Beings Are We. Not This Crude Matter.
—Yoda, Star Wars Episode V: The Empire Strikes Back

It was a blistering 99 degrees that day, which probably accounted for the smaller numbers; the crowd was half the size of Friday and Saturday. Wearing a gas mask and a helmet in the heat was like wrapping yourself in Saran wrap for a day at the beach. Or perhaps it was Sunday, and they were all at church, but probably not. Who needed church when you had a much larger and more culturally acceptable congregation right in front of the courthouse every single night? Maybe those who stayed at home or in their tents were just tired from the weekend shitshow. I know I was.

My neck was sore from supporting the heavy mask and my shoulders were cramped from holding my phone steady. I begrudgingly began filming the same guy with the raspy voice as he stepped up to the megaphone atop the stairs. He wore a Black Lives Matter T-shirt and used his low, grumbling voice to rile the smaller crowd with a dependable "Fuck Donald Trump!"

The people replied, "Fuck Donald Trump!"

He continued. "We ain't negotiating with Donald Trump or the feds! Get the fuck out of Oregonnnnn!"

The crowd cheered. There were only about thirty Frontline Moms this evening, but they were fully geared up and jazzed with enthusiasm.

After the speeches around 11:00 p.m., a few hundred diehards formed around the fence. This time we perched on the edifice at the corner of the county courthouse. The pulled-back perspective would provide viewers with a better look at exactly how many people assaulted the fence, and what tactics they used. We felt removed up there, like spectators at a football game.

For the moment, the crowd remained mostly well behaved, and barely anyone even touched the fence. A trumpet and a drum made from a plastic bucket played some tunes as the crowd continued with their chants.

I jumped off the ledge to snap a photo of an unconventional riot outfit: nothing but boots, a helmet, a gas mask, and a speedo bathing suit, or as I called it, a "banana hammock." I was sweating my balls off and wished I could wear my favorite board shorts instead of heavy black cotton.

By midnight, some banged shields into the fence while others shot fireworks and bottle rockets into the courthouse plaza. Each time a firework exploded in the plaza with a colorful crack, the crowd would erupt like their team put the pigskin through a field goal.

Perhaps the police were especially sensitive after the fence came down the previous night, because they emerged from inside the courthouse after a handful of fireworks exploded in the plaza.

There would be much less leash for the pyros tonight.

We were impressed by how quickly the crowd threw the tear gas canisters back at the platoons of officers grouped inside the plaza. The trumpet from earlier belted a cavalry call that rallied the lesser but more dedicated rioters to hold the line. The police bunched up behind clear plexiglass shields for protection.

A firework flew in from outside the frame and landed beneath a cop cluster. One of them looked down and went for a kick just as it exploded in a bright flash of red, white, blue, and green. Though they were equipped in full gear, I could tell a few of the closest ones were rattled because they dropped to their knees. The others tightly encircled them in the defensive position that a tactical unit would resort to when under ambush with nowhere to hide. Their ears were probably ringing like mine had after the intimate encounter with fireworks the other night.

Due to the small number of diehards, the threat of the fence coming down this evening was virtually nonexistent. Yet the agitators were still able to elicit a violent response from police by simply increasing the volume of fireworks they shot at them. Now that the police were in the plaza, the pyrotechnics exploded almost as regularly as the tear gas and flash bangs.

I captured video of a fire that spontaneously combusted at the far end of the plaza. A small flame was visible flying over the fence before it exploded into an instantaneous ball of fire covering an area about the area of a small car. A pack of ten officers stood within twenty feet. They all turned in surprise then signaled for a fire extinguisher.

The cops must have recognized their vulnerability after this incendiary development. The platoons retreated back into the building briefly before they emerged from the garage in the rear. The new offensive spread the width of the street. Rounding the corner to the front of the courthouse, they handily dispersed the protesters/rioters/actual domestic terrorists who tossed the homemade firebomb.

We sipped on our beverages. The experience felt like we were in a luxury sports suite watching a game from afar, only with much warmer drinks and explosive devices instead of a ball. While the fireworks could cause hearing damage, some minor burns, or even perhaps blow off a digit, this was the first time I had seen a Molotov cocktail. At that point we realized it was becoming closer to a gladiatorial game.

That same evening Fareed Zakaria discussed the situation on his Sunday CNN program, "GPS." "Today on the show, Portland, Oregon. Federal agents in violent nightly clashes with protesters. Now President Trump says he could send seventy-five thousand agents around the country. Is this an abuse of power, or does the president have the right to restore order?"

Unwilling to give any concessions to violence instigated by rioters in front of the courthouse, Zakaria's characterization of Trump's troops initiating the "violent nightly clashes with protesters" was no mistake. His monologue was read from a teleprompter script.

Zakaria brought on Obama's former Secretary of Homeland Security, Jeh Johnson, to discuss. Johnson repeated this narrative: "Fareed, you're right that, in Portland, there have been enduring, consistent demonstrations in the aftermath of George Floyd unlike most other cities. And it has continued, for the most part, peaceful. And whether or not that warrants deploying large-scale federal law enforcement, I think, is a very, very difficult question."

Johnson made no mention of the dozens of riots declared by the Portland PD before Trump called on the Department of Homeland Security to defend the courthouse. The injection of federal officers undoubtedly increased the tensions. But prior to their arrival was nothing near "for the most part, peaceful." That would be like calling a football game, "for the most part, no contact," simply because many of the players stood on the sidelines while the rest of their teams smashed into each other each and every play. Almost none of what happened in Portland were merely "demonstrations," but rather demonstrations-turned-riots with the consistency of an atomic clock.

While Johnson sat there whitewashing one side's complicity in the violent clashes night after night, he was also a sitting member on the board of directors for weapons manufacturing (specifically, lethal missiles) juggernaut, Lockheed Martin. Clearly, Johnson had no problem investing millions of dollars in a company that built bombs to kill people overseas, but when federal agents used nonlethal munitions to prevent literally hundreds and sometimes thousands from lighting fires in the plaza of a federal courthouse, well that was where he drew the line.

On this Sunday in July, football was not the spectator sport that drew eyeballs from American viewers. Instead, the leaders of our media industry had devolved into lionizing blatantly corrupt political figures. Their media cheerleaders hurled insults as toxic as CS gas back and forth between the opposing echo chambers. In this game, only one team could win, and the path to victory was written in the corporate playbooks that ran increasingly incendiary rhetoric about the civil unrest.

July 27, 2020, 12:29 AM PST: Corner of SW Main Street and SW 4th Avenue, Portland, Oregon

I am your father.
—Darth Vader to Luke Skywalker, *Star Wars Episode V: The Empire Strikes Back*

The man with the trumpet, who we cleverly referred to as Trumpet Man, stood in front of a boarded-up business while he spoke to Jorge for a "Patriots Only" interview, "Inside the Mind of a Portland Rioter." He was shirtless, a pair of safety goggles and a bandana hung around his neck. According to him, police shot him in the face with a pepper ball.

With shards of plastic still stuck in a gnarly, partially healed gash on his unshaven cheek, Trumpet Man explained what happened. "They started to do their stormtrooper march…and I see this fed raise up the barrel of his pepper ball gun and shoot me right in the face. I went down and dropped my horn and had my leaf blower in my hand too."

Jorge then asked why Trumpet Man believed he had been shot. "My dad was a cop growing up. I actually tend to sympathize with them. These guys are psychopathic. They want to hurt people."

The disparate statement that he "sympathize[d]" with police but also believed that they were "psychopathic" revealed Trumpet Man's own internal struggle. America's political agitation divided families as well as communities. Upon further research, Trumpet Man was the trumpeter I had seen sounding the horn of victory at the livestream of the genesis of the CHAZ in Seattle. Not only did he come out every night in Portland, he also traveled to different cities for his fight against his father's own profession.

Months later, I would see Trumpet Man in a video on Twitter, which showed a homeless encampment in Portland, with government-issued tents similar to the ones I saw near the train station. The camera zoomed in on the activist's distinctive long blond hair while he shouted, "Trumpet Man!" Apparently with no home or discernible job, in the Black Lives Matter movement, Trumpet Man found a purpose beyond his own difficult life. Much like Luke Skywalker, he had forsaken his father because he believed that his dad had turned to the Dark Side. The righteousness of his cause was reinforced in TV studios that broadcast coverage of his escapades and profited from his cause.

Those who were physically injured by this violent discourse were not the media juggernauts who sat in their TV studios, or the stable incumbent congressmen whose offices were protected by armed guards and insured by government healthcare. It was the individuals who took to the streets, so desperate and disillusioned by the system that they willingly faced tear gas and pepper balls until 4:00 a.m. Or it was the blue-collar cops who, night after night, collected their paychecks battling against mobs shouting the popular 2020 chant, "All cops are bastards!"

At least Darth Vader risked his own skin when he enforced his rule through violence against the rebel enemies. Neither Donald Trump nor Joe Biden would ever bear personal witness to the real-world ramifications of their political attacks. Neither of these presidential candidates appeared. They would never actually stand in them. Those who manned the foxholes were those with broken families and economic hardship, who found a renewed purpose within the political fervor of "this is an existential threat."

When the bombastic rhetoric manifested into bloodshed, questions about why the tragedy happened would, for both sides, be answered by pointing the finger at the other political tribe.

July 27, 2020, 12:31 PM PST: Marriott Hotel Near Downtown, Portland, Oregon

Wars not make one great.
—Yoda, *Star Wars Episode V: The Empire Strikes Back*

I set up a camera, placing gas masks and helmets in the background for an aesthetic touch. We had nowhere near the budget for a studio rental so Shelby's luxurious one-person room would have to suffice. The interview would be headlined "Portland Resident Wants to Move to Alaska to Get Away from Protests." Our subject was a thirty-something who worked in the federal building that was under siege night after night. A bright red rose tattoo on her forearm and jet-black dyed hair made her look more like one of the hipster demonstrators we might see outside the courthouse at 1:00 a.m. rather than a government bureaucrat who worked inside of it during normal business hours. She was accompanied by her fiancé, a downtown garbage truck driver who had his own experience with Portland's unrest.

After a few questions about her background, Shelby asked about harassment from the most radical aspects of the demonstration. "You mentioned antifa coming up to you and saying stuff. Some people in the media have sort of downplayed these riots, that the violence and antifa is just a 'myth.' What do you think about that?"

She chuckled at the idea. "I was actually just having a conversation about what Jerry Nadler [a US congressman] just said, how it was a 'myth,' and it reminds me a lot of…when in the French Revolution where King Louis and Marie Antoinette, they couldn't see past the palace of Versailles. You know they couldn't see past their gardens and their feasts and their parties. Meanwhile, the people in the streets are starving to death and fighting. It makes me really sad that these people say that they represent their district, they are so far removed from reality that it's a joke."

Her reference to a clip recorded by independent media journalist Fleccas, showed House Judiciary Committee Chairman and New York Congressman Jerry Nadler characterize antifa as a "myth." The clip went viral, because it showcased Nadler's detachment from the very real violence that politically charged groups like antifa were committing in America's streets. These groups were decentralized and shadowy by design. Since very few of these masked individuals would ever admit on camera that they were actually "antifa," it was easy for the ruling class to claim ignorance while the perpetrators committed arson and assault from behind a black mask and all-black attire. Nadler's supposition was based on the Democrats' narrative, which painted the BLM protests as virtuous, while blatantly ignoring the fact that antifa had hijacked the BLM narrative, at least on the ground where they could practice violence based on the ethos of destruction before all else. Meanwhile, the right wing had the boogie man of antifa as a major threat to the Union.

Our interview subject's use of the French Revolution as an example was especially poignant, because we heard the same reference to the death of the French monarchy invoked by BLM speakers across the country. While they disagreed on the best way forward, opposite sides of the spectrum shared the perception that America's elites were like the French monarchy, out of touch in their comfy ivory towers. The French proletariat were in the streets outside the Bastille, and 240 years later, Americans were storming courthouses and landmarks in DC.

July 28, 2020, 12:12 AM PST: Front Doors of Mark O. Hatfield Federal Courthouse, Portland, Oregon

Hmph! Adventure. Heh! Excitement. Heh! A Jedi craves none of these things. You are reckless!
—Yoda, *Star Wars Episode V: The Empire Strikes Back*

Officers retreated back into the building after they extinguished the fires and fought the mob back from the fence. There were a few minutes of silence until the crowd moved slowly back to their perch atop the concrete barriers, which construction crews placed in front of the non-scalable fence that morning in hopes that it would prevent the entire thing from coming down. This had the unfortunate effect of giving the rioters a platform upon which they scaled the fence and dropped debris into the plaza to start fires and blasted fireworks directly at the front doors. I stood next to a few shield-wielders atop the concrete and began handing out beers so they might accept me into their gang. Though they knew I was some form of press, they immediately warmed up to me because of the bountiful beers.

I was fiddling with the straps on my gas mask when the front doors of the courthouse exploded in a massive fireball. Luckily, no police were present because the Molotov cocktail engulfed the front doors in a fireball that spanned fifteen feet. Though I did not capture video of the incident, a clip posted on Twitter by a user named @Brittany3l showed the incendiary device's detonation. Immediately afterwards, the onlookers' riotous cheers sounded as if they had just witnessed young Skywalker destroy the Emperor's Death Star.

When police came back out, my new anarchist buddies and I cracked a few more warm Portland IPAs, reveling in the toxic tear gas that burned our naked eyes and mouths. Through tears and snot we joked about our violation of the Center for Disease Control's recommendation to wear masks even when outside. The pain of COVID isolation felt real, while the scene of burning garbage and pyrotechnics seemed more like a bad dream.

I cracked another beer and headed beneath the trees with two shield gangers who were craving a smoke. After we sat down on a patch of dirt next to a garbage fire, they agreed to record their thoughts on the fray. It must have been the most toxic interview of the pandemic because with each breath of garbage we probably shaved minutes off our lives. The fire was about the size of what we would call a "bonfire" to keep us warm on a cold night at the beach, except it was burning mostly plastic instead of wood. The light wind on that evening did little to clear the smoke, so we simply breathed it in as we spoke.

They were both shirtless. One had "gas this" written in faded black marker across his pale white chest, which was mostly just skin and bones. His buddy was much fatter and appeared to be Hispanic. They were both significantly younger than I was, but one thing we shared was a mutual conviction that the politicians that were still running our country had done so for too long. I aimed the camera lens at all three of us, though I did not record with the reverse angle in selfie mode because being able to view the shot was less important than filming blind with the superior forward-facing lens in low light.

"What do you think is the biggest—"

But the chunkier of the two rolled a lighter through his fingers as he interrupted me. "Yo, I'm gonna go on a cigarette hunt."

I was out of cigs, so I continued with the skinny fellow. "What do you think is the biggest bullshit thing that the media says?"

He replied without so much as a pause. "I went to CHAZ, Capitol Hill Autonomous Zone, and they were like, 'That place is just a violent mob. That's all it really is.' But it was kinda more organized than that, but honestly, people did get shot, but it is what it is."

Noting his obvious contradictions, I pressed further. "How did they lie about it?"

"Well, they compared that place [CHAZ] to like squalor and poverty. It kinda was, kinda, but not really. It was a protest. Duh! People are gonna be shitting on houses and eating cold food, you know."

The portly guy returned with a cigarette clutched in his fingers and promptly interrupted for his two cents' worth, "No, listen, listen, listen, tell the people of America that we are here fighting for our rights, our constitutional...our civil rights, and we're trying to reach...we're trying to pay for all the bad shit that we did."

He pointed at the camera and popped the cigarette in his mouth after he finished his point, but suddenly pulled the bogey back out to round it out. "Cops are fuckheads, man. They just want to lock you in a cage."

"So, what's the biggest lie they're telling about here?"

The skinny guy chimed back in. "The news media says that we're losing but I just watched the people of Portland push the police back into the police station, so I thought, *how ridiculous.*" He was referring to a police retreat earlier, though it was probably better characterized as a peculiar late-night dance.

I cut to the real question I wanted to ask. "So did you guys see that explosion, though, out there?"

The skinny guy replied, "I saw a lot of cool explosions."

"Did you see that one right up against the wall though, that big one?"

He paused for a moment. "I think I know what you're talking about, yeah."

"What do you think about that? You think that would hurt the cops if it fuckin' blew up on them?"

The skinny guy cast a ponderous gaze toward the courthouse as he replied, "Probably, yeah. Oh my god. yeah. I wouldn't want to stand there. That's all I have to say. I didn't throw it, so I had nothing to do with it, but—"

I utilized the pause to rephrase my question. "What would you think if that did blow up around the cops. Like, what if one of the cops died?"

The skinny pale guy chuckled. Two people with garbage lids for shields walked by in the background as the portlier guy pointed his still-unlit cigarette at the lens of my cell phone. "Fuck it, if one of them cops got killed, good! They're fuckheads anyway. They shouldn't be here."

The skinny guy laughed even harder, then weighed in. "I don't want to say it out loud, but yeah, that's why we're challenging Trump." He puffed on a nicotine vaporizer that was all the rage with the Gen Zs.

His portlier buddy gave his final point. "Listen! Listen! Donald Trump sent them [law enforcement] from Washington, DC, to stop us, man. They ain't gonna stop shit."

At this, he put the cigarette back in his mouth and sparked the lighter but failed to light the cig.

I took the next question to the federal level as he fiddled with the flame, "Do you think it's Trump's fault that this is all happening?"

The fatter guy pointed his yet-to-be-lit cigarette at the camera. "It's an intermix of a buncha bullshit." Then he finally sparked the cigarette.

His skinny friend added, "Yeah, I think everyone was kinda at this boiling point and then something just fuckin; pushed them over the edge. It was bound to happen. Yeah, like coronavirus, George Floyd, of course, that was horrible."

His friend expounded after he exhaled his first drag. "I'll tell you what it is. It's just people generally is just tired of all the bullshit. Tired of the government stripping them of their dignity. Just to make a couple dollaz." He took another huff of the cig and sat back in his lawn chair, seemingly satisfied by his final point.

I sensed their interest in talking to me had run its course. "Well, boys, I hope you guys stay safe."

The skinny guy replied, "you too," then gave me a fist pound and puffed his electronic cigarette, its light blue color reflecting off his colorless and dusty pale skin.

The fat guy bid farewell as he gestured his noncigarette hand with a peace sign. "Hey! Much love! Peace to the world! The whole world is watching! I hope you get a billion views, homie!"

I did not realize that a portion of our interview would be rebroadcast in prime time by Sean Hannity on Fox News the following night. Though it would not get "billions of views," it would certainly get millions—almost all of whom would view the young men as the face of the fifty-something nights of rioting, even though they arrived the day prior.

I ventured to the heart of the dark park where beneath a grove of trees were the smoking grills of the Riot Ribs kitchen. I popped the top of another warm one, anticipating that whatever food I was about to review would require some liquid courage to help wash it down.

By this time, I was two sheets to the wind. In this case, the chemical wind wafted me toward a culinary experience like no other, sampling Riot Ribs in the midst of—you guessed it!—a riot! Since the establishment raised over $300,000 on crowdfunding websites as well as donations through money transfer services like CashApp and Venmo, I figured they would have plenty to offer. I had been meaning to do a taste test, and now that it was my last night in Portland there was no excuse.

Through my gas mask, I exclaimed, "Extra-spicy baby! Check this out!" As I panned the camera from me to the grill to set the scene, a stun grenade exploded above the Spanish-American War Memorial only feet behind us, but the small crowd around the kitchen didn't even acknowledge the munition that was designed to discombobulate them.

In my inebriated state, I figured the gnarlier the scene, the more entertaining the content. I flipped my gas mask up on my head and shouted over the rap music playing inside the kitchen. "Hey, you got any of them Riot Ribs?"

The grill operator, not visible on screen, was surprised that someone actually wanted to eat one of these things. "Not yet, bro, not yet. We got some dogs, though." Another flashbang exploded nearby.

He shrugged and flipped open the grill nonchalantly, which revealed about a dozen sorry-looking hot dogs and sausages roasting over glowing orange coals. They were charred to the point that it was difficult to recognize what color or variety the dog had been when it was first placed on the grill, probably hours ago, before any of the tear gas went off.

There were no buns in sight, so I reached out my free hand in front of the camera lens. The grill operator looked at my hand suspiciously because it was covered in white pepper ball residue.

I replied in my best tough-guy voice, "My hands are a little bit spicy but that's all right." He dropped it from the tongs into my fingers.

"Thanks, buddy." The grease bled from the charred dog onto my fingers, oozing fat that swallowed up the dust from the shattered riot balls. It glistened in the light like some kind of dirty French delicacy born out of violent revolution.

I wandered over to a few people gathered around a garbage fire and figured it would be a suitable ambiance to sample my delectable treat. I turned the camera back in my direction and prepared my audience for what was about to go down. "Yo, I'm about to sample this Riot Dog right now. It's been sitting on that grill for probably about four hours."

When I sank my teeth into the dog, the first thing I tasted was the poisonous chemical flavor of tear gas. I narrowly avoided a gag as one of the men around the fire sensed my misfortune. "Oh shit! How is it?"

I couldn't even muster a word to describe how disgusting it was, so I simply shook my head. The gas mask perched atop my mop for hair swayed from side to side as if emphasizing my discomfort. In the background of my shot, a man with two plastic shields perched against his hip tightened his gas mask in the smoldering light.

I forced out a commentary, my mouth still full of a mashed-up blend of crummy hot dog and synthetic munitions. "I cannot even describe to you. I mean I have to swallow it, but it is so bad. It tastes like it was roasted over that garbage right there. That's what it tastes like!"

He laughed at my discomfort. I feared that I might vomit right on the flaming plastic in front of us, so I hurried away from the group as I searched for a suitable place to spit out the partially chewed doggy.

Yelling over the half-eaten hot dog in the midst of all the mayhem, I gave him some context. "Dude, I've been looking for a proper burial for this Riot Dog for the last like five minutes and I finally found it! It is the worst hot dog I have ever eaten in my entire life. It tastes like tear gas."

The man replied curtly, "Um, it's feeding the homeless people."

With my joke deflated and realizing I had indeed read that Riot Ribs gave excess food to homeless people in Portland, I conceded his point. "Oh, that's very true."

I pointed the dog at the fire in search of a more agreeable topic. "That's kind of nice, though."

He replied, "Yeah, isn't it great?"

Now that the fire had been successfully consolidated by the pyro posse, it burned brightly. I threw the half-eaten Riot Dog onto the flames, and it sputtered grease as it burned. I bid farewell from behind the camera, "RIP Riot Dog. Goodbye."

Someone in the background shouted, "Hey, if anyone got any lighter fluid, bring it down!"

My journey into the heart of Portland's chaos ended with half of a tear gas-soaked hot dog burning to ash in front of the federal courthouse.

The interview I recorded that night would be used by Fox News to put a face on Portland's nightly battles against the federal enforcers of the law. But the more time I spent awash in the chaos, the more I would learn that under dire enough conditions, the dark side could consume anyone.

July 29, 2020, 8:37 PM EST: Glover Park, Washington, DC

Beware of the dark side. Anger, fear, aggression;
the dark side of the Force are they. Easily
they flow, quick to join you in a fight.
—Yoda, *Star Wars Episode V: The Empire Strikes Back*

Back home, I recorded a video gliding along the empty streets with my hands off the handlebars of my single-speed beach cruiser. After a common afternoon rainstorm, it was the dead of the humid summer in DC and most of those who had not already fled the pandemic-paralyzed city were locked up at home. I was en route to my old roommate and Jackson statue wheelman Rosie's house. He invited me over for a viewing after I told him that Fox News had requested to show my interview with the skinny and fat guys in Portland.

I was nervous about what was technically my first on-camera prime-time news interview, albeit recorded around a garbage fire. The A-block segment included a clip of Attorney General Bill Barr at a hearing on Capitol Hill where he cited recent news reports, "injured police including just this past weekend, perhaps permanently blinding three federal officers with lasers."

The screen cut back from the sound bite (footage that plays with audio on a newscast) to Hannity in his New York City studio. "Blinding law enforcement officers. Think about that. Look at this disturbing new video from *Daily Caller* tonight, showing demonstrators laughing about anticop violence. Ask yourself, do you find this funny?"

In the two-box frame next to him, Shelby's footage of a cardboard fire inside the fence played as B-roll.

Then Hannity cued a ten-second sound bite that began with my question, "What would you think if that did blow up around the cops, like one of those cops died?"

The skinny guy in the frame laughed at my question, the lower portion of the side of my face visible in the top of the frame. The news headline on the graphic below read "PORTLAND RIOTER LAUGHS AT THE PROSPECT OF INJURED, DEAD POLICE OFFICERS." In the top left, a credit read "Richie McGinniss/THE DAILY CALLER."

His fatter buddy who was sitting just behind in the frame pointed his cigarette at the lens and weighed in. "Fuck it (though this portion was bleeped), if one of them cops got killed, good."

The screen returned to Hannity, who repeated the young man's line sarcastically as he threw his hands up. "'If one of them cops got killed, good!' Is that the country we want?" The headline text displayed next to Hannity read "47 ARRESTED, 59 OFFICERS INJURED IN SEATTLE PROTESTS THAT TURNED VIOLENT / KIRO 7 NEWS STAFF."

I felt uneasy about the brevity of the excerpt. With the time-sensitive cable news format, it was not surprising the show pulled such a short clip. But the way the clip was presented begged the question: Was I providing content that furthered the aims of the Evil Empire?

My interview with these young men made them the face of the militant terrorists in Portland. But they didn't throw the Molotov cocktail. While throwing an incendiary device at police is an inherently evil act, I also knew that those kids, who could barely light a cigarette, certainly were not the real bad guys that the American public should fear.

I recalled plenty of stupid things done out of anger during my younger years. Growing up at the birth of the twenty-four-hour news cycle, which vilified the "other" to keep viewers affixed to their television screens, fear of radical terrorism was as American as apple pie. On the morning of 9/11, the principal took my middle school into the gymnasium and told us that two planes crashed into the Twin Towers. A handful of the kids in the room, whose parents worked in the buildings, began crying as their adolescent wails echoed off the hardwood floors. Administrators ferried them into back offices for consolation and phone calls. The rest of us put our heads down, some of us sobbing at the sound of our classmates' innocence disappearing into the back hallways of the school. I entered adolescence as America invaded Iraq and Afghanistan. CNN, MSNBC, and Fox News all saw eye to eye on one thing: Radical Islamic terrorists were public enemy number one.

When our leaders tried to sell a war for "democracy" in Iraq, they masked their real ambitions with phony intelligence reports and patriotic rhetoric. Our media did not ask the tough questions of our government then, because anything other than "supporting the troops" was politically incorrect. Thousands of American soldiers were killed or maimed for life. Hundreds of thousands of Iraqis also perished, millions were displaced, and today their country remains in shambles.

During the same period, the corporate interests of multinational big oil and the military-industrial complex profited immensely; the news media's complicity helped sell this phony war. I wanted to kill these bad guys myself, so I moved to DC and studied Arabic and Middle Eastern History at Georgetown University. But in studying the language and the history, I learned that America inherited a broken postcolonial order from the French and British Empires. After I spent five months studying in Amman, Jordan, and traveled throughout the Middle East, I realized that this problem could not be fixed from within our own government, which would continue with the system that benefited the institutionally privileged, but killed the poor men and women tasked with enforcing their perpetuation abroad. Instead, I took an internship at Al Jazeera Arabic and chose to work in news media in the hopes that the next time our country confronted a crisis, the Fourth Estate would use the uniquely American foundation of free speech to stand up for the American people. Now it seemed that my work was helping to tear them apart.

September 16, 2010: Haifa, Israel

You must feel the Force around you. Here.
Between you, me, the tree, the rock, everywhere,
yes. Even between the land and the ship.
—Yoda, *Star Wars Episode V: The Empire Strikes Back*

I saw a far more deep-seated and intergenerational conflict during my five months in the Middle East my junior year of college. The home in the sandy outskirts of Haifa in northern Israel belonged to family friends whom I visited multiple times during my study abroad. Incidentally this was also near the best surfing in Israel, though given the small waves in the Mediterranean Sea, it was comparable to the best ice hockey in Dubai. When I strapped my surfboard into the seat of the cab from my apartment in Amman to the Israeli border, the Palestinian driver looked at my board with the same puzzlement as Captain Cooke and his men had when the Europeans first observed the naked Hawaiians surfing in 1779.

I arrived at my temporary family's house and they welcomed me with open arms, despite my uncharacteristic luggage. Like me, they had a family of three boys. I immediately settled into the inter-brother dynamic and felt at home around the table with the whole family.

At dinner on the first night, I told them that I was planning a trip to Beirut and southern Lebanon in a few weeks. The middle brother, Ofer, exclaimed, "I love Lebanon. It is so beautiful!"

I was confused, given that Israeli passports were not allowed entry into Lebanon. "Ofer, what do you mean? You're Israeli. You can't go to Lebanon."

As he realized I had fallen right into his Israeli-humored punch line, Ofer replied with a wry smile, "Of course I visited there! During the invasion in 2006!"

The younger brother, who had never seen war and served as an immigration agent, didn't laugh quite as hard as the older two who served as combat troops.

Ofer was in the special forces and carried out multiple combat missions during the July 2006 Israel-Hezbollah War. Their dark sense of humor was evidence of the small area of land this family lived on, and had to fight over for generations to ensure our peaceful night in their home. I enjoyed the feeling of a family home, which I had not experienced in months abroad in the desert. Before the mom, Viv, tucked me into the spare bed, she even showed me why the water-starved Israelis are the best dishwasher loaders in the entire world.

On my second day with the family, I toured the Golan Heights with the dad, Dani. He fought against the Syrians in the 1973 so-called Yom Kippur War. The Arabs, however, referred to it as what translated to "the War of Attrition."

We drove in his small car along a dusty route in northern Israel and parked on the side of the dirt road. Dani panted as we walked up the steep side of one of the few hills in the area and gazed out at the almost lunar landscape. He gathered his breath and pointed up the hill. "And right here two of my friends were killed by the Syrians. One got shot in the head right in front of me. I got blown up with shrapnel in my arm. The Syrians are tough bastards."

Dani showed me a grisly-looking scar on his upper arm before he continued. "And down there, I was in a field hospital for my wounds and a helicopter crash next to me and explode. A few more of my friends died in the crash." Dani hung his head sadly, his already broken English further impeded by his choking up. I bowed my head silently out of respect for his lost friends.

After our tour of the Golan Heights in the hot sun, we got back into Dani's tiny car. His big pale body seemed out of place cramped into the driver's seat while we bounced through the dark red dirt.

He took me to the final location of the tour, which appeared as a small group of sad looking fig trees in the middle of a dry and lifeless landscape. But as we walked closer to the small grove of trees, I realized that there was an oasis hidden in their shade.

Dani stripped down, old man gut bulging around the elastic straps of his tighty-whities underwear. He slowly lowered his aged, war-torn body down and placed his feet into the small watering hole. I was confused by his actions until I saw a school of fish congregate around the dry skin of his feet. I joined in the strange ritual. We sat under the shelter of the trees. The water sprung from the depths of the earth and cooled our bodies while we talked about happier tales, family, friends, and our favorite places to visit in New York. The fish slowly snacked on the calluses of our tired feet.

We fluttered our legs back and forth as the minnows tickled our feet, changing the conversation to our favorite destinations in New York, which we both agreed was the best city in the world. I loved Middle Eastern food, and Dani was a big fan of Italian cuisine. Dani knew my mom, and we laughed about her hard-nosed but hilarious working-class Guido Buffalo sense of humor. Dani's sadness seemed to melt away in the shade from the hot sun, his furrowed brow relaxed as the beads of perspiration rolled from his bald forehead into the desert oasis. I couldn't wrap my head around the tragic circumstances that he experienced, but I knew that sharing it with me had given him a certain solace, as if passing the pain along gave him some respite, like an old farmer finally passing the burden of heavy toils onto his son.

Once the fish finished their feast, we dunked our heads in the pool. I felt cleansed, having shed some of the dead skin and sweat from our journey through the desert battlefield. We put our shoes on and took the dusty road back home.

October 7, 2010: Tyre, Southern Lebanon

"Through the Force, things you will see. Other places.
The future, the past. Old friends long gone."
—Yoda, *Star Wars Episode V: The Empire Strikes Back*

We marveled at the Temple of Jupiter, the largest temple in the history of the Roman Empire despite being thousands of miles from the capital of Rome. Three weeks after my stay in Israel, I traveled to Lebanon to see the other side. We stood in front of the most prominent building among the ancient ruins known as Baalbek, a few hours outside of Beirut, Lebanon. I was accompanied by my buddies Keith, Levi, and Andrew, who were training in the Arabic language for various branches of the armed forces. It was my junior year of college and for four semesters I studied Arabic five days per week for an hour a day (not including homework, on which I was perpetually behind).

In addition to visiting the temple, I insisted we take the trip so I could lay eyes on the 800-ton blocks used in the construction of the outer walls and foundation that supported the structure. These megaliths were some of the biggest stones used for the construction of any building since the dawn of mankind. It was a mystery when they were placed there, though it was suspected to be long before the Roman Empire conquered the known world.

Atop the temple's four sixty-foot pillars that remained intact were ornately carved, hundred-ton blocks that formed the roof of the temple. The question of how the Romans hoisted these stones aloft was almost as big a mystery as the megalithic stones, which were transported over a mile from the quarry where the largest limestones originated. Purple granite pillars, which appeared machine-fashioned at first glance, lay in broken pieces throughout the complex. Archaeologists suspected that this rare type of granite was carved from an Egyptian quarry hundreds of miles away.

The security at the site was virtually nonexistent so we climbed around the huge, mysterious stones like archaeology junkie monkeys. As I sat atop one of the megaliths on the outer wall, I wondered what the pristine and colossal columns in DC would look like in a few thousand years. Would America only leave ruins like those of the Roman Empire? And who had hauled the even more giant stones before them? Little did I know that only one decade after my time in the Middle East I would witness citizens storm some of my own nation's most sacred pillared halls.

After our exploration of the archaeological site, we got back into the van and the hired driver asked where we wanted to go next. I had my plan in mind, now I just had to get Muhammad on board with my mission—discover the other side of the fight that I came to the Middle East to understand.

Though many of my friends were pursuing military careers, my Arabic was the best, thanks to two full years of intensive classes at one of the top programs in the United States. I asked if Muhammad could help us with our mission, which was simple, head into Hezbollah territory and see what it was like in person. Hezbollah was a Lebanese Shiite political party and paramilitary group that emerged from the power vacuum of the Lebanese civil war. It was a proxy militia funded largely by Shiite Iran and was infamous for carrying out brutal terrorist attacks on military and civilian targets around the globe.

Having already traveled through Israel, I was interested in what the other side of the multigenerational war looked like. I felt comfortable enough with the strapping young soldiers-to-be in my company.

We arrived in the coastal town of Tyre, one of the oldest continually inhabited cities in the world.

Going on my gut alone based on our ninety-minute conversation in Arabic, I decided I trusted our driver, Muhammad, as the guide for our investigation into the terrorists we were told about on the news.

Just a few blocks from the Mediterranean Sea, the van pulled up to a square in the middle of an apartment complex. In the center of the square, there was a small market with a few tents and folding tables. Bright yellow Hezbollah flags that hung from the tops of the tents waved in the trade winds.

Given that I'd purchased an Israeli Defense Forces T-shirt a few weeks prior, I thought it fitting to purchase a Hezbollah shirt as a souvenir from the other side of the battle. In the last days before what you said on Twitter could get you canceled, I did not weigh in the fact that the purchase of my three-dollar T-shirt could be interpreted as a tacit endorsement of the suicide bombing committed by Hezbollah that killed 241 United States Marines in Lebanon in 1983, the same brutal suicide tactics that killed my friends' loved ones on 9/11. Much like the young dudes who stupidly laughed at the Molotovs in front of the Portland courthouse, I was at that time an energetic and reckless kid who rebelled against the narratives that were pumped out of multimillion-dollar studios by multinational corporations.

After my purchase, the salesman and I discovered a shared appreciation for *Al Tufah Kabeer* ("the Big Apple"), so he invited me in for tea. The rest of my travel group was scattered around the market. I saw my opportunity, and since I was young and dumb, I perhaps did not properly weigh the risk versus reward. I looked the man in the eyes and decided he would not kidnap and behead me like I had seen in so many grisly internet videos. Because of the trust gained through my proficient Arabic, he asked me to come alone while the rest of the guys tried their best to haggle in broken slang over the various bright yellow Hezbollah swag on display.

The two of us sat down in his small living room, which was sparsely adorned but impeccably clean, especially given the dustiness of the streets just outside the front door. As he heated water for the tea, I looked around at the intricate geometric patterns on the Islamic pottery he had on display.

My host delivered a tray with small, clear glasses and a silver teapot. After he carefully poured the steaming mint tea, my new acquaintance asked if I wanted a Cleopatra cigarette, though they pronounced the *p* with a *b* because there was no letter for *p* in Arabic. It was common for

Arabs to offer these cheap cigarettes in cabs and casual conversations. I only smoked my first cigarette a month prior on my twenty-first birthday because I grew tired of repeatedly refusing the offers.

After just a few puffs, my head was spinning. The host told me a story about how he shot at Israeli commandos from his window years prior. He showed me holes in his living room wall where he claimed they returned fire. They looked more like deep craters than holes from a bullet. He explained that a *bundukia kabeera* ("big gun") made the giant cavities just above where we pleasantly drank tea.

He briefly disappeared into a back room. My heart rate jumped wondering what he was doing back there, accelerated by the nicotine now coursing through my veins. He reemerged with an ancient looking AK-47. My initial fear subsided when I noticed the antique rifle lacked the distinguishable banana-shaped magazine to feed it with ammunition, which in turn might be used to shoot me. All the more astounding, this guy claimed he not only fired the weapon, but did so against one of the most advanced militaries in the entire world. While he fired what looked like a gun manufactured in 1947 from his living room, the Israelis invaded with fast boats, grenade launchers, armored vehicles, body armor, night vision, air support, and the list goes on.

The man spoke with the same furrowed brow that Dani did, simultaneously excited to share his old war stories and pained by the traumatic memories they brought forth. He had fought from the window of his own home. The Israelis had invaded from the sea. His ancestors had lived in this ancient town for as long as he could see into the past. The passion with which he spoke and the thousand-yard stare he gave when he described the details of the 2006 war gave me a sense of why he was so radically at odds with the Israeli war machine. This much older man had fired his much older gun at young commandos who were far better trained and armed—with the youth and technology that he could never match. I sensed he was exaggerating the whole thing to compensate for the fact that he had actually experienced a tremendous loss. Though I obviously didn't agree with the savage suicide bombing tactics that I knew Hezbollah carried out in the past, this encounter also put a human face on what I, as an American, understood as the evil side of the struggle.

The man had sad eyes when he finally finished frantically miming and describing the ordeal in rapid, guttural Arabic. The language itself seemed to mimic the sounds of the battle he described. He sat back down and clasped the glass of tea but did not drink. He looked at me as if he wanted acknowledgement that he fought hard and that I understood. I was afraid by the prospect of his humanity. I was more comfortable with the caricature of a screaming angry terrorist. This was a man in his home who, like Dani, wanted to share his story to offload some trammel. Or at least he wanted me to help him carry a small portion of it with him by understanding why he fought and that his cause was just.

My cigarette was burned down to nothing so I extinguished the butt in a crystal ashtray and bid the self-proclaimed Hezbollah hero farewell. As I exited back into the dry heat, I struggled to regain my feet under my spinning head. In the time it took me to smoke a cheap cigarette down to a nub, my understanding of the Middle East was turned upside down.

July 29, 2020, 10:31 PM EST: Glover Park Georgetown, Washington, DC

Fear is the path to the dark side. Fear leads to anger.
Anger leads to hate. Hate leads to suffering.
—Yoda, *Star Wars Episode V: The Empire Strikes Back*

After I watched Sean Hannity's show on Fox News, I pedaled my beach cruiser back home from what was technically my first prime-time interview. My name and face had just been seen by millions, but the short portion of the video I recorded of the two young men in front of the Portland federal courthouse was used to cast them as the very face of evil in our country's struggle between left and right. I felt more remorse than satisfaction. I was no different than the cog that pulled the chain and moved my bike tire forward along the road, except rather than forward, our country was moving sideways—in two different directions.

Exactly one month after this interview in front of the courthouse, in downtown Portland, a man named Michael Reinoehl, a supporter of the far-left group antifa, would shoot a man named Aaron Daniels, a member of the far-right group, Patriot Prayer. Reinoehl would die in a shootout with federal officers a few days after that. According to a *New York Times* interview with Reinoehl's sister, the protests in front of the courthouse, "made him feel like his existence meant something again."

Somewhere out beyond the quiet streets of Georgetown in DC, past the Rocky Mountains, and up the Columbia River into the Pacific Northwest, "The Imperial March" was bound to play again in front of the courthouse. Rioters like Trumpet Man, who declared war on his own father's profession, or the angry young men that Hannity showed on his program, were compelled to action by the good-versus-evil narratives that played each night on the prime-time news. With their underdog status and their almost cartoonish technological disadvantages, were the Hezbollah guy and the Portland dudes the righteous rebels (like Luke and his ragtag band of embattled warriors in *The Empire Strikes Back*)? Or were Luke's values of honor and duty embodied by my Israeli middle brother Ofer, his father Dani, and the dutiful yet unenthusiastic Monday Morning Riot Cop?

Like young Skywalker, Americans were presented with a chance to rise above the sins of our forefathers. Our American factions were derived from more recent conflict, born from the paths our parents and grandparents chose. At one time arguably the most anti-black city in America's West, at the very least Portland's mostly white Black Lives Matter demonstrators and rioters proved that the city and the country could rebel against the scars from the past. But did that mean that extremism was the only proper response? For my friends in the Middle East, the conflict was carved deep into their DNA after thousands of years of warfare and fallen empires. I could not grasp their struggle, and the American version seemed to be trivial and insane at the same time.

In Amman, Jordan, in 2010, I befriended the man who sold pirated DVDs on the street corner near where I lived, just a few hours' drive from the Israeli-Lebanese border. One night he offered me the original *Star Wars* trilogy. As we negotiated over the price, he told me, "We Palestinians, we are the rebels. America and Israel are Evil Empire."

I was a believer in my homeland's freedom and opportunity. But I also understood why the American empire's military support of Israel would lead my Palestinian DVD friend to that conclusion, because he was born into the other side of a millennia-old battle between the Arabs and the West.

I asked him a question in my simplistic Arabic when I paid for the movie. "You move to the United States if you could?"

"Yes," he replied. "New York. Fresh start."

Although he viewed America as the bad guys, he still wanted a taste of the American Dream—a "fresh start" where he could live alongside Jews and Christians and atheists, and every other religion under the sun, all hustling along the busy streets in search of something better.

In America, if we could rise above the tragedies, we could gain a "fresh start" from the conflicts of our past, no matter how Vader-like our fathers' actions may have been. My Middle Eastern friends were not so lucky.

As I cruised home to my quiet, safe bed that night, I was blissfully unaware of the fact that I was about to come face to face with the death and destruction that takes place when the rule of law evaporates, and the void is filled with age-old anger and fear.

But I wouldn't witness it on the Israeli-Lebanese border, or even in front of the courthouse in Portland. Instead, it would be in a sleepy little city on the shores of Lake Michigan.

The first night in Portland, with megaphones leading a protest from the steps of the county courthouse.

A second angle of the crowd stretching to the federal courthouse (top right).

A bioluminescent sea of cell phone lights.

An "undulating" fence in front of the federal courthouse.

Using a leaf blower to stoke the flames while holding an American flag.

Feds emerging to clear the front of the courthouse.

A bike (on left) failed to block riot munitions, while a tear gas shell skipped off the ground (on right).

Old gas mask holding up pepper-ball-powdered hair—well, not so much.

With a plastic fan burning, a traffic cone entered the flames just before the rioter exclaimed, "That's a hot fire!"

Veteran and Mr. Blessings at the police line in the early hours of the morning.

Flowers in front of the cops—a moment before the arrest.

Veteran tried to rescue the flowers and the woman, moments before both were dragged back into the courthouse.

"Welp"—flowers on the pavement at the end of the final broadcast for the first night.

FAFO = Fuck Around and Find Out.

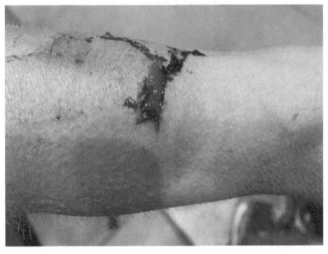

Me arm has seen better days.

Portland Union Station.

Tents in Chinatown.

Riot Ribs (on right), Spanish-American War Monument (center), and scattered tents (background left).

"Fuck Ted Wheeler!" with a Budweiser beneath the Spanish-American War monument.

"FRONTLINE MOMS" soaking up the limelight.

A flash bang exploding inside the umbrella gang.

The umbrella gang defending against a torrent of pepper balls and tear gas.

"Antifa press."

A metal saw sent sparks cutting through the non-scalable fence.

Monday Morning Riot Cop.

"The Battle of the Leaf Blowers."

Plenty of cameras capturing the bonfire.

The turtle gang preparing to defend the bonfire behind them.

The turtle gang, continued.

Feds preparing to extinguish the bonfire in front of the federal courthouse.

Feds forcing the turtle gang away from the bonfire.

The turtle gang making a last stand.

Feds vanquishing the turtle gang.

Hanging with the same "epic" knight from the CHAZ.

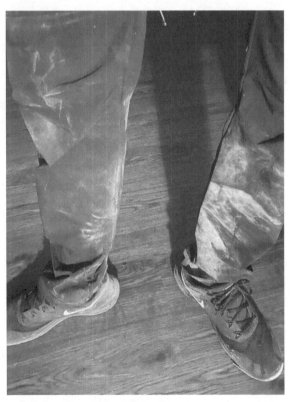

Lucky riot pants after a fireworks explosion.

RIOT DIET

Duncomb walking away from the federal Courthouse wearing his hospital bracelet—accompanied by riot-gun security.

Banana hammock, boots and gas mask.

Fireworks exploding among officers inside the plaza of the federal courthouse.

Rioters lighting garbage fires and launching fireworks from atop a concrete divider.

The last night in Portland—a garbage fire, which became the site of the Riot Dog's final resting place.

Farewell, Riot Dog.

That's a wrap in Portland—Riot SqUAd OUT!

Technically my first prime-time cable news interview—me on the far right, with the wispy mustache. *Screenshot from Fox News Hannity.*

7. BE WATER, SPREAD FIRE

The "Fiery but Mostly Peaceful" Riots in Kenosha

August 19, 2000, Afternoon: Eastern Long Island, New York, New York

It was a blue bird day in the heat of summer on Long Island when my dad showed me a lesson that would direct my decision-making in Kenosha twenty years and one week later. The beach was crowded with a seasonal swarm of city folks, international tourists and occasional locals monitoring the crowd and grumbling about the yuppies and Euros who would invade their town for eight weeks per year. Though the waves were small, there was a new sandbar at our favorite beach. I tugged on my dad's swim shorts and badgered him to take me out for a surf. He told me to be polite and wait until he finished his conversation, then resumed speaking with one of our family friends who was a local artist.

Unexpectedly, my dad stopped midsentence and sprinted toward the shoreline, which was about a hundred feet away. I remember, at first, being infuriated that he hypocritically interrupted his own conversation. Our artist friend stood as confused as I was. I saw my dad run into the water and address someone face down in the deep eddy between the shoreline and the new sandbar.

I sprinted over the soft, hot sand as fast as my ten-year-old legs would allow. By the time I arrived, my dad was barking orders at the crowd that was forming, a few of whom waded next to him in waist deep water. He examined the lifeless body, which was face down on the surface seemingly paralyzed or dead.

"I think he broke his neck diving into the sandbar. I am going to roll him over very slowly and then we are going to bring him onto the beach. Make sure to keep his neck as straight as possible."

By now, what appeared to be the family of the injured young man were at the waterside screaming in a staccato foreign language that was unidentifiable to my young ears. My dad, consistently calm and collected, urged them to settle down while four other people assisted him in slowly guiding the patient up the beach. Dad stood holding the young man's head, helming the rescue effort like the trained medical professional that he was. They laid him down carefully on the hard sand above the receding tide. Thankfully, there were multiple Manhattanites on the scene, all trying their best to get a call out on their expensive cell phones. A pot-bellied, middle-aged Wall Street–looking guy with sleek shades finally got through.

The ambulance arrived, and my dad oversaw the EMTs while they put the patient into a specially designed spine board stretcher with a padded area to immobilize his neck. The EMTs carried his paralyzed body up to the ambulance, which was waiting in the sandy parking lot. Before lifting him up, my dad asked the stretchered young boy, who didn't appear to be older than his early twenties, "Can you wiggle your toes for me?"

The boy blinked his eyes, but his toes did not move.

As they loaded the patient onto the stretcher, a first responder attempted to take my dad's name. I was surprised to see him wave her off and politely say, "Nope, I'm good." As he walked away, I remember being confused as to why he was unwilling to tell the amazing story of what he just did.

According to the local newspaper, the *Southampton Press*, the boy was a European visitor who did not speak English. Elizabeth Grodsky from the fire department's EMT squad stated, "He was lucky to have been pulled out of the water by an orthopedic surgeon who happened to be at the beach; I don't know the surgeon's name." Elizabeth continued with her version of events, "[he] was conscious, but did not feel his limbs." The ambulance reportedly arrived in no time at all, but after the exit was impeded by weekend summer traffic. "Medical technicians gave up trying to drive [him] to Southampton Hospital and instead had him airlifted to Stony Brook." Written the day after the event, the article stated that the young man was listed in "satisfactory condition."

As we walked away from the beach and the ambulance my dad said, "Let's go, boys." Frustrated by the abrupt ending to the potential for shreddable waves, on our drive home I asked why he refused the interview in the parking lot. I wanted to brag about how my Pops was a hero, but how was I going to do that if his name didn't get printed in the paper? At a stop sign he turned around to the back seat and told my brothers and I, "I never got sued in my whole career and I'm not about to start now."

By 2020, the anger I felt that day had changed to admiration. I recognized that he passed up the limelight in order to ensure his family's financial future. A few weeks later, we received a call from the family of the young man. Though we never found out how they tracked him down, the family stated in broken English that they were very thankful because their son was walking again. In the heat of the August summer, my dad saved that boy's life among the crashing waves, because he responded quickly but also calmly and rationally. Or, as my Jarhead boss Geoff put it, "Slow is smooth, smooth is fast." After the gunshots went off near the beaches of Lake Michigan 20 years and six days later, I would do a pretty poor job of following that advice.

May 30, 1900: Kenosha, Wisconsin

The first Rambler rolled off the assembly line at the Jeffrey plant in downtown Kenosha at the dawn of the automobile age.

Americans were no longer tied to the railroad and were free to traverse the vast continent according to their maps. As one of the first assembly-line vehicles ever produced, the Rambler accounted for over one-sixth of the cars manufactured in the United States in its first year, 1902. By 1905 the sales had doubled, thanks to a new innovation for the time, a steering wheel rather than levers for maneuvering the vehicle. Its maker, Jeffrey Automotive, was the second-largest auto manufacturer, eclipsed in size only by Oldsmobile. Ford would not overtake Jeffrey Automotive until it produced the Model-T in 1908. Thomas B, Jeffrey, the founder of Jeffrey Automotive, was an immigrant from England.

During this time, over 60 percent of the Kenosha population were either immigrants or the children of immigrants. The manufacturing jobs provided by the automotive industry as well as a commercial tannery turned this small town on the Michigan River into a place of promise, but only for those who could tolerate both the freezing winters and the extra journey from the ports of the east coast to the heartland.

A multitude of churches and synagogues, many of which stand today, were built as the influx of migrants sought a place to worship and maintain the traditions of the old country. Their construction reflected the craftsmanship of another time, with large stones, stained glass, and pointed steeples that rose to the sky, like miniature American versions of the grand temples and cathedrals built over thousands of years in the old world.

The courthouse in Kenosha was rebuilt on the coattails of this new wealth in the early 1920s. The neoclassical architecture and two-story marble hallways were ordained with hand-painted frescoes and carved stone pillars. It stood at the center of town like a shiny new symbol of the American legal system—a beacon of adherence to law and order.

The lasting limestone churches and government buildings exemplified growing opportunity. The auto industry generated by the Jeffrey Automobile Company, later renamed Nash Automotive Company, and finally absorbed by Chrysler, were at one time the source of well-paying jobs that put food on the table for countless immigrant American families. But inevitably, these companies could not compete with the much larger multinational car giants like Ford, Toyota, Mercedes, and the like. Inspired by architectural achievements of the empires of the past, the landmarks in Kenosha remained standing long after the plants shut down and the immigrant population moved to areas with more to offer. Kenosha could no longer compete with the vast complexity of the commercial world developing on America's coasts and beyond its shores. The people who remained there suffered the aftermath.

August 24, 2020, 8:08 PM CST: Kenosha County Courthouse, Kenosha, Wisconsin

Out of the night that covers me,
Black as the pit from pole to pole,
—William Ernest Henley, *Invictus*

As the sun gave way to a waxing moon, the 20-foot marble pillars of the Kenosha courthouse were illuminated behind forty law enforcement officers dressed in black. They used plexiglass visors and shields that the Sheriff had ordered to block incoming debris like frozen-water bottles and scraps of metal. It was eight minutes past the countywide curfew, effective for all nonessential personnel. Shelby, Jorge, and I had just arrived from Chicago airport after seeing reports of Kenosha on fire the previous night.

The first night of serious unrest, Sunday, August 23, brought riots in front of the courthouse followed by widespread arson in the surrounding commercial neighborhoods. A viral video sparked the destruction—an incident on Sunday morning where a man named Jacob Blake was paralyzed and in critical condition after police shot him seven times. Cops wrestled with Blake as he tried to enter a vehicle, which belonged to the mother of his children with the kids inside. The police were on the scene with a warrant for charges of felony sexual assault, trespassing, and disorderly conduct for domestic abuse. Blake had allegedly forced himself into the home of his baby momma and abused her multiple times. The video showed two different attempts to taze Blake. His shirt was torn in the tussle before he was shot seven times. Just like everything else in this moment of selective outrage, the internet turned Blake into a saint who was senselessly shot by the pigs, even though anyone who watched the video could see that Blake was literally brawling with officers as he attempted to enter a vehicle with minors inside.

The Associated Press reported on the cell phone video that showed the shooting from afar. "Seven shots can be heard, though it isn't clear how many struck Blake or how many officers fired." The protesters claimed that it was a senseless shooting. According to police, he was shot for resisting arrest and attempting to enter his car while he was armed with a knife. A medical report stated that he was shot four times in the side and three times in the back. The demonstrators chanted that Blake was shot seven times in the back as they aimed their ire at the Kenosha County Courthouse, just a block away from the police station. Then rioters then set fire to surrounding mom and pop businesses and cars.

On Monday morning, the Democratic governor of Wisconsin, Tony Evers, delivered a statement, which concluded, "I have said all along that we must offer our empathy; equally important is our action. In the coming days, I will demand just that of our elected officials in our state who have failed to recognize the racism in our state and in our country for far too long."

Democratic presidential nominee Joe Biden also weighed in, stating that the cops involved "need to be held accountable."

When Shelby, Jorge, and I reviewed the footage and read the headlines, we made the decision and booked a last-minute flight. We scrambled to catch our plane and landed at Chicago O'Hare airport in the late afternoon. We made quick work of the hour-long drive to Kenosha. I rented a black Chevy Malibu, which I liked because when I rolled up behind someone in the fast lane, they would get out of the way; it was the same car that was used by many cops. We quickly dropped our bags at the Stella Hotel just a few blocks from the protests in front of the courthouse. The Stella had operated out of the sturdy old building for over 100 years.

Governor Evers had reportedly called in 125 National Guard to aid law enforcement, though upon arrival I was yet to see any sign of them on the ground. A few hundred demonstrators were scattered on the street and in the town's civic square. A man wearing a hoodie and a mask squirted water on the line of cops who ducked behind their shields. Another man wearing a hoodie and shorts pulled down his mask and jeered, "You scared of a little water, buddy? Chill out with the fuckin' pepper balls, dude!" He must have been referring to the prior night, because there was no sign of pepper balls so far this evening.

As compared to Portland, the demonstrators were much more spread out. The park was at least twice as large as the one that faced the Mark O. Hatfield Courthouse, and they were also dressed more casually. Only a few of the Kenosha demonstrators had gas masks and their outfits were generally more colorful than the all-black shield/umbrella gang we saw late at night on the West Coast. With a high school directly to the south of the park, a dinosaur museum, old churches, and a stately library to its west, the environment surrounding the protest zone was less imposing than the tall buildings of the business district in Portland or New York.

At the same time we stood in front of the courthouse, Donald Trump Jr. took the stage at the Republican National Convention in Washington, DC, where he decried that the presidential election was a decision between, "church, work, and school," versus, "rioting, looting, and arson."

When darkness fell on Kenosha, agitators launched fireworks from a grove of trees in the middle of the park. Rioters threw rocks and bottles. I briefly removed my hockey helmet to affix the gas mask to my face as at least thirty more officers poured out of the courthouse. In an act of open defiance, one of the disgruntled masked men spray-painted BLM in white letters on the sidewalk directly in front of the police shields. They were preoccupied by the airborne ambush. Just above that graffiti read ACAB in freshly painted black letters. Though there were only a few hundred people protesting, the volume of fireworks and projectiles became as intense as we saw from the thousands of more well-equipped agitators outside the federal courthouse in Portland.

The police line increased to about eighty officers who stood in a line on the edge of the sidewalk. Additional officers poured out of the back of the armored vehicles that rolled onto the road in front of the courthouse. They began firing pepper balls and tear gas. Although these cops were county police, they looked more like the federal law enforcement officers in Portland, clad in green uniforms with gas masks and wielding pepper ball guns and tear gas launchers instead of billy clubs or shields.

Within twenty minutes, more armored personnel carriers rumbled onto the wide street and across the trolley tracks that used to bring workers to their stable jobs at the auto factory, though that plant had been shut down for over sixty years. Now, the vintage trolley ran only during daytime hours and remained mostly empty save the occasional school field trip.

⁙

This area had been named City Park during the Civil War when the surrounding houses were part of the Underground Railroad. The runaway slaves would finally find their freedom boarding boats in the nearby Kenosha harbor. The public space was renamed Library Park after an avid supporter of the Union cause, Zalmon G. Simmons, donated money for the construction of a new library and a monument for veterans of the war. Thousands of citizens of Kenosha came out on Memorial Day 1900 to see the new library, and the unveiling of the monument that honored heroes who helped rid the United States from the entrenched institution of slavery. An article published in the local newspaper on the day of the opening declared, "The day was the greatest day in the history of the city."

And 120 years later, the dinosaur museum as well as the library were damaged during the riots in the lead up to what would become the worst day in the history of the city.

⁙

As the crowd retreated into Civic Park, directly adjacent to Library Park, I commenced a video for *Daily Caller*'s "Patriots Only" subscribers. Given that *Daily Caller* was labeled by establishment sources like CNN and *The Times* as "right wing," the Silicon Valley folks at YouTube and Facebook allowed us to exist on the platforms almost as a necessary evil. We would routinely see our channel throttled after publishing scenes from the hardcore protests from Portland to DC, and almost all of our riot content would get demonetized anyways, so we put it behind a paywall to make money instead.

I zoomed the camera in on a graveyard of hundreds of glasses and plastic bottles lying on the sidewalk and street in front of the police shields. I yelled over the driving bass of a rap song that blared from a speaker, interrupted by the government's much louder munitions. "As you can see there are literally hundreds of plastic bottles on the ground in front of law enforcement, and now we have them using a variety of munitions including tear gas, some flash bangs, and also we saw some pepper balls."

A group of thirteen reassembled in the middle of the park where they opened umbrellas and used road signs to create a temporary wall. Pepper balls pelted the surfaces and one by one they slowly backpedaled to the rear of the park, where the rest of their less-daring comrades had already found refuge.

A man casually walked toward the police line dressed in what appeared to be some kind of long leather kilt, football pads, reinforced gloves, and welding goggles. He was carrying a broom. The broom was on fire. *What in the name of Americana?* I thought. He began sweeping the debris that protesters had thrown out on the street. I had to look up from my camera screen to make sure what I was seeing was real. The man gingerly swept the bottles and broken glass toward the side of the street while the straw of the broom burned more with each swing. As I panned the camera over to the police line, their expressions were unclear, but the volleys halted temporarily. One of the other protesters behind me shouted, "That's metal as fuck!" After the wicker was burned to nothing, the man concluded his fiery but mostly custodial exhibition and carried the charred broomstick back to the umbrellas clustered around the trees.

Just when it appeared that the small contingency of antipolice rioters/demonstrators were vanquished, I heard cheers from the side of the courthouse. A few hundred BLM protesters returned from a march through downtown. They carried signs, plastic shields, and umbrellas.

Reinvigorated by the new influx of agitators, the crowd was in the hundreds and police were outnumbered at least three to one. The coppers formed a tightly packed horseshoe formation around the front steps of the courthouse, flanked on both sides by armored trucks with an officer manning a spotlight and a tear gas launcher peering for targets from the top hatch. The distinctive rhythmic tumbling of the armored vehicles' V8 turbo diesel engines were occasionally pierced by hollers from behind umbrellas.

A fresh volley of water bottles, fireworks, and fractured stones flew toward the police line, prompting a voice from a loudspeaker, much more polite than the cops in Portland, New York, or DC: "Please step back across the street, thank you." But instead, an intrepid pack of fifteen umbrellas and a few road signs inched closer and shot a few roman candles toward the cops, who responded with more pepper balls and tear gas.

After the police initiated their counterattack, their munitions forced the road sign/umbrella/shield barrier into the middle of the park. Despite reinforcements, when the cackle of the riot guns and the booms of the launchers initiated, the mob again put up a paltry defense and retreated to the back of the park. But the cops' preoccupation with the umbrella/shield gang also created a vacuum that arsonists used to burn entire city blocks surrounding the protest-turned-riot.

Municipal garbage trucks had been parked on every intersection around the park to prevent vehicle entry into the protest area. They were quickly engulfed in flames. I filmed a truck breathing a five-foot plume of fire from the gas tank like a trash dragon. The red graffiti on the limestone walls of the court of law in the background declared, "Fuck the police bitch ass."

When the crowd retreated southward past the high school, the scattered mob began setting fire to automobiles, notably the Car Source 1 lot which contained dozens of vehicles. I ran back to the nearby hotel and grabbed a drone because the bird's-eye view would show the full extent of the arson. I sped through the peaceful art deco lobby, running away from its sanctuary because the city outside was rife with misplaced rage that was engulfing city blocks in the blink of an eye.

I reconvened with Shelby after we were scattered by the cops, but she already wanted to leave me behind and go interview small-business owners trying to save their storefronts before they were burned to ash. Halfway up the block, five shady-looking characters were gathering debris to light a dumpster on fire.

I prepared to fly my drone over one of the blazing lot at Car Source 1 when my own frustration set in. I realized the battery wasn't properly attached. I had improperly recharged it after we hastily put down our bags and headed to the protest. I was stuck with a 40 percent charged battery to fly the aerial camera over an entire city block of burning vehicles. It didn't matter. I purchased the drone two years prior after selling fifteen empty-keg shells when we moved out of our news outlet's old office. If it burned up, I could tell the boss that I had purchased it with recycled funds courtesy of our company's penchant for a cold one after a long day's work.

Shelby was growing impatient. With my voice raised over the sound of the drone hovering above us, I asked her to wait for me. I was preparing for one more flyover. She continued to walk away. The hum of the drone disappeared as it took off and was replaced by the hissing of burning tires in the adjacent lot; the definitive American symbols of gas-guzzling freedom would finally explode when their little remaining fuel caught fire.

I shouted this time, "Come on, Shelby, it's not safe!"

Shelby replied before I could finish the "f" in *safe* in her typical sassy but deadpan manner. "Stop babying me. I'm going."

I shouted again, louder this time, "Shelby, that's fucking stupid!"

She spun around and screamed back, "You're not even my boss! You can't tell me what to do!"

Technically, Shelby was correct. Geoff was her manager, but I recalled his line from the beginning of the summer, "If Shelby gets a black eye and you're not in the ICU, I'm going to fucking kill you myself."

I relayed that exchange to Shelby in an angry tone. As I repeated Geoff's quote, "I'm going to kill you myself," the dumpster fire folks paused their efforts and looked in our direction, as if we were the crazy ones. I couldn't quite make out their expressions behind cloth masks.

Although I realized my recounting of Geoff's words in that instance probably had something to do with what the young bucks were now calling "toxic masculinity," I had little time for regret. Shelby turned her back, and I would have to catch up.

The flight lasted only a few minutes due to the depleted battery and the shoddy craftsmanship of the Chinese-manufactured drone. I ran back to the hotel room to stash the cheap little gadget because carrying excess baggage in this kind of lawless situation would basically be an advertisement saying, "Mug me!"

When I came back out, to my surprise, an additional twenty cars were aflame in that same lot behind the hotel. I mounted a metal utility box for an angle of the expanded destruction and almost immediately a group of rioters congregated below me. Examining the three lenses of the fancy new Apple iPhone 10 that I'd purchased at the beginning of the summer, they told me that I had a nice phone. The next guy said something about how maybe they wanted it.

I replied, "What this one?"

Flashing the blue screen of the iPhone in their faces for distraction, I looked behind to scope an escape route. I dashed off the four-foot electrical box and sprinted away. As if I was auditioning for some fucked-up riot redux of *Forrest Gump*, I ran at a decent pace for two football fields before I slowed down. My phone had all my footage from that evening on it, and to me, that was worth more than capitulating to the would-be thieves.

By the time I regrouped with Shelby, she had already recorded our most viral clip of the night. It showed a small contingent of masked arsonists who broke into a furniture store where they used a dash of lighter fluid and a singular match that sparked a small fire on one of the chairs. The blaze spread to tables and other chairs, wooden cabinets, and office desks. After only a few minutes it spread across the whole store. The end of Shelby's video showed fire spitting out of every window until the business was no more.

Forty-nine minutes after midnight, a group of men wearing street clothes struggled to extinguish the burning vehicles in a different parking lot owned by the same used car business a few blocks from the Kenosha County Courthouse. Shelby and I approached the scene to figure out why these folks were risking their own skin to extinguish the combusting cars and save the auto shop structure a few paces away.

One man operated a power washer as a firehose while three other guys sprinted buckets and trash cans full of water back and forth. Each time they tossed water on the inferno, it would sizzle and sputter, but continue unhindered. They seemed to be fighting a losing battle as most of the cars on the lot were either actively burning or already burnt to a crisp. Shelby yelled over the noisy gas motor and the sound of pressurized water colliding with metal. "What are you guys doing?"

Covered in soot and soaking wet, the power washer guy stopped the water but kept it aimed at the car. "You see any fire department?"

At that, he turned back to the burning car. Shelby looked down at her phone, which I knew meant she was tweeting one of her signature riot vignettes. In this case, she was telling America the story of these sorry suckers who came out at 12 a.m. during a riot to save their boss' business. When we came back in the early hours of the morning, all the cars were toast, though the building did seem intact.

I returned to the courthouse where National Guard Humvees finally showed up. I recorded a final video before I found Shelby and Jorge to head back to the Stella Hotel. "Patriots, this will be the final broadcast of the night. We're back here in front of the courthouse, we've seen multiple fires set around the city and obviously things have died down here."

There were ten Humvees and a few dozen troops guarding the municipal building from a handful of laggards who remained. The courthouse was intact but garbage trucks smoldered along the block in front of them and the surrounding commercial districts were torched as much as the arsonists pleased.

August 25, 2020, 11:50 AM CST: Kenosha County Courthouse, Kenosha, Wisconsin

> I thank whatever gods may be
> For my unconquerable soul.
> —William Ernest Henley, *Invictus*

Passing thunderstorms arrived during the few hours that we slept, but not enough rain fell to calm the widespread conflagration. We arose and I guzzled a few cups of coffee, Jorge cracked a Red Bull, and unflappable Shelby (who didn't drink caffeine) had some water. We discussed a plan to interview the owners of the wrecked small businesses as well as community members volunteering to clean up the smoldering rubble. On our way to see the burned-out shops, we stopped to record construction crews erecting a fence in front of the Kenosha courthouse.

A forklift ferried pieces of metal mesh to and fro as I began a video tour of the new reinforcements for our "Patriots Only" subscribers. "As you can see new development here, they're building a fence around the courthouse. Actually, one of the construction workers over here just told me that, 'Guess what? This is the exact same company that erected the fence in Portland.'" I panned across the partially completed fence; through the metal grates was some scattered graffiti including "BE WATER, SPREAD FIRE" in large black letters next to the entrance. When the pan finished at the end of the block, the carcasses of four burned-out garbage trucks were slumped with their tires melted into a black tar on the light gray pavement of the boulevard.

We walked a few blocks past a group of volunteers scrubbing anti-police messages spray-painted on the side of the old schoolhouse. One of these volunteers would return later that evening to defend the three Car Source businesses with an AR-15. I didn't even notice him because we were on our way to the cinders of the furniture store.

Jorge found a gray-haired man sorting through the rubble of the furniture store, who turned out to be the owner. He agreed to do an interview, and Jorge attached a small wireless microphone to his T-shirt. All that remained intact were the steel I-beams and some of the concrete walls behind him as he described watching the destruction unfold in real time.

"I was listening to the police scanner on my app and I was watching a live stream happening on Facebook. We saw the protesters turn and come this way and…we could see there was some damage and windows were broken. It wasn't until after that that we realized the building was on fire and it wasn't just a few minutes after that the place was just a complete blaze." With sadness in his voice he concluded, "What I see I was not prepared for. I knew it was gonna be a disaster, but I didn't know what a disaster looked like until I saw it."

I prepared a drone flight over the charred skeleton of the store. From above, the dozens of burned-out buildings scattered between the boarded-up brownstones that were spared resembled pieces of charcoal and mesquite wood at the bottom of a Weber grill.

While Jorge's interview provided a human face to the destruction, from the viewfinder of my aerial camera controller it seemed nothing more than the beginning of a smoky and delicious meal. When I landed, I noticed the sign of the store in front of me, which read "B&L Office Furniture" in black letters. The ampersand was crossed out and the O was covered by an M scrawled with black spray paint. Underneath that, what had read "Chair Clearance Sale" was crossed out with red spray paint and replaced with a nonsensical swear. Now the sign read "BLM/ FUCK." The "FUCK" was so sloppily painted it was hard to read.

August 25, 2020, 8:49 PM CST: Kenosha County Courthouse, Kenosha, Wisconsin

> In the fell clutch of circumstance
> I have not winced nor cried aloud.
> —William Ernest Henley, *Invictus*

After the near mugging the previous night, I decided to wear my *lucky* riot pants. I hoped they would bring me good fortune in the fell clutch of chaos. The reporter for *The New York Times* decided she would return home because she knew Kenosha was about to explode. I couldn't blame her. Based on the escalation over the first two nights, it was a smart choice.

As Shelby, Jorge, and I spent the afternoon editing footage and posting stories, there was a thick atmosphere of dread that deadened our normally lively conversation. I drank more coffee, which probably made things worse, then I popped a Zyn nicotine pouch, which definitely made things better. Our normally cavalier attitudes were solemnly subdued. I opted for the plastic helmet I purchased at an Army surplus store in Portland rather than the hockey helmet because we weren't playing games anymore. Made from shoddy plastic, the surplus helmet looked like a playtime version of a helmet one would wear in a war. I donned a T-shirt with a huge BLM logo that I got in CHAZ, because tonight of all nights it would be paramount to blend in. On the back it had photos of black Americans who were killed by cops.

When we arrived at the courthouse, forty cops stood behind the non-scalable fence as a firework whizzed over their helmets and exploded in red and orange sparks. A man wearing a green cloth around his head and face smashed into the metal mesh with a shield fashioned from a blue plastic oil barrel that was cut in half. The flimsy shield did nothing to move the fence as he screamed, "Fuck you, you fucking pussies!" The makeshift turban that hid his identity might have resembled his idea of a Palestinian militant, but his Teenage Mutant Ninja Turtle T-shirt and the lab goggles atop his head discerned a man with less serious intentions than wiping Israel off the face of the earth.

With only a handful of malcontents molesting the fence, it looked like a 4:30 a.m. walk in the park for cops in PDX. But the Kenosha cops were a bit more trigger happy. They initiated tear gas launchers as if they were facing the invasion of the Mongol Horde. Without leaf blowers to blow the smoke back at the fence, the tear gas grew so thick that it became difficult for me to see more than twenty feet. The few hundred onlookers were armed with nothing more than various forms of goggles and hoodies instead of gas masks.

Among those few hundred, less than half were ballsy enough to brave the unending storm of nonlethals. Their shields featured far more variety and notably shoddier construction, from pieces of thick cardboard cut in creative designs, to trash can lids, multicolored umbrellas, and repurposed road signs.

The Portland shield gang with their turtled shield formation resembled a riot version of a Roman legion. The Kenosha equivalent looked more like disorganized Germanic barbarian tribesmen.

A steady police defense from inside the fence ensured that no large groups could take it down. There were cops on the top of the courthouse who fired tear gas and pepper balls downward, which made popping anyone who attempted tampering with the fence as easy as blasting fish in a barrel. Even still, the volume of fireworks and projectiles that this small crowd was able to deliver was impressive. The cannonade kept the cops busy as they repeatedly ducked behind their larger and sturdier shields. Through the smoky atmosphere on street level, I noticed the flashing red and green lights of a drone that took off from the roof and hovered high above, though it was impossible to hear because there was a strange and irritating siren emanating from a location I could not determine.

I filmed one man who placed the stick supporting a small American flag inside the mesh. Every time he flicked the lighter to burn the Stars and Stripes, a shower of pepper balls would collide with his black hoodie. The flag remained intact, because after a few tries, he was forced to run away in pain.

Completed in 1925, the Kenosha County Courthouse was as large and elegantly designed as the hulking Romanesque structures in Washington, DC. An article published on August 27 of that year by the *Kenosha Telegraph-Courier* was headlined "Finest Courthouse in West Is Verdict Here/Visiting Judges Hail Kenosha County Courthouse as Masterpiece of Architecture." The article opened, "The finest in the West! That was the proud pronouncement of the thousands of Kenoshans who took advantage of the invitation from Kenosha's County Board to be their guests on an inspection through Kenosha county's new $1,250,000 courthouse building dedicated today. … The courthouse looms up like a giant among pygmies, yet its proportions soften the effect upon the eye and give the building a tone of grace and simplicity that offer additional evidence of the foresightedness of the County Board and its engineers in selecting the designs of the building. Its twenty pillars majestically stand out in front of the building and the entire building is in perfect harmony with the plans for the Kenosha Civic Center, of which this is the first building to be completed."

As part of the same "city beautiful" movement that inspired the towering Municipal Building built in New York City around that period, the courthouse reflected a time when American municipal buildings were inspired by elements of the great French and Roman Empires of the past. They were built to last for generations to come. But as happened in France and Rome, American expansionism and excess came at a cost. The Black Lives Matter protesters seethed with anger because they believed that the cops and the courthouse epitomized the system that kept its knee on the neck of blacks and minorities since America began.

The "perfect harmony" that the building once embodied for the thousands of eager Kenoshans in 1925 was now representative of an imperfect division. Kenoshans and those who traveled to the city to protest fled when the situation became violent after the sun disappeared. The bad actors who remained vandalized the pillars and tried to bring the fence that protected the courthouse down. When they failed in these efforts, rioters and arsonists, battered by the police, ran out into the city and destroyed whatever they could. After 2020, Kenosha would be remembered for those who sought destruction and stoked flames. The demonstrators who sought peaceful change would be forgotten, just like the time when the courthouse was a symbol for equality under the law.

It became obvious that the cops were preparing something, quieting their munitions for a brief moment of peace as darkness fell. I looked briefly for Shelby and Jorge then gave up; they were on their own missions embedded somewhere inside the mob.

The Kenosha, state, and local PDs apparently decided they'd seen enough, marching from around the back of the courthouse and in front of the wall. Whereas in Portland the police were supported by normal police SUVs you might see driving in any American city, the Kenosha police were accompanied by armored vehicles known as Bearcats. I recognized them only from movies where the rectangular armored trucks would be utilized by a hostage rescue squad or a SWAT team storming a building to kill the bad guys.

They rolled to the front of the park accompanied by at least twice as many cops as protesters. I had never seen a contiguous line of cops this long, numbering well over 150 and spanning the entire width of the grand courthouse behind them. Blue-and-red sirens of eight armored trucks were diffused heavily by a cloud of chemical gas. The pristine building behind the military-style vehicles seemed out of place.

Each time the endless lines of shields inched forward, a second line of officers would toss flash bang grenades and blast riot balls while the front line of shields chanted, "Move back!" I sidestepped at the same pace. An armored Bearcat advanced slowly across the trolley tracks with the police shields in tow, but its progress was impeded by two daring demonstrators blocking its path. They held their umbrellas above their heads like an American version of Tiananmen Square.

While police decided on what to do next, the lull in pepper balls allowed the press to congregate around the Bearcat. Twenty-four cameras circled around the front grill of the armored vehicle. I panned my video from the press to the two protesters for a look behind the scenes of the antipolice play. Fifty feet in the background the wall of trash can lids, road sign barriers, and plastic oil barrels that were cut in half to form shields protected another eighty people, crouched defensively for the cops' next move. The curtain would come down on the stage of Civic Park when police initiated their final push. After clearing the umbrella obstructors with a few flash bangs, cops continued marching in lockstep with the Bearcats grumbling along. They only stopped after reaching the end of the park, where they broke into groups and hid behind armored personnel vehicles, shooting their nonlethal projectiles without stopping until they pushed the entire mob a few blocks more.

I wanted to post my coverage of the multihour skirmish onto Twitter before the hardcore rioters had time to regroup, but I couldn't get a cell signal. I ran back to the Stella Hotel to get Wi-Fi, figuring that I could also use it as an opportunity to locate Shelby and Jorge. We lost contact once the cops initiated their offensive through the park.

As soon as I logged on, I saw footage recorded by Elijah Schaffer that showed armed individuals standing guard in front of the used car business where we held the power washer interview the night before. The presence of citizen armed guards signaled an escalation of the story that Shelby and I covered the night before. It was the amateur fire brigade hustling to keep the business from burning to the ground. Tonight, it was something entirely different, and massively dangerous. Crowds of already angry rioters were confronting the riflemen with hostility that looked ready to boil over into something far worse. I rushed out of the nostalgic hotel lobby. Posting could wait until after I got to the bottom of the story unfolding nearby.

On my way to interview the armed guardians at the Car Source 2 parking lot, I followed the same path the rioters had after their recent retreat out of Civic Park. In their wake was a trail of burning cars, garbage trucks, and shattered glass. The street was quiet save the sound of exploding gas tanks and the hiss of air expelling from melting tires. I was on my way to ground zero for the Summer of Love.

A light southeasterly breeze blew cool air from nearby Lake Michigan, ushering away most of the tear gas and putrid smoke that emanated from incinerated livelihoods. I smelled remnants of burnt plastic accented with the familiar spice of recently deployed CS gas. I removed my gas mask despite the lingering chlorine clouds because I would need my face exposed to gain the trust of any riflemen who might be willing to do an interview.

I pulled my phone out of the *lucky* riot pants once I laid eyes on the Car Source 2. There were three armed individuals on the ground standing in front of the building, and three more on the roof, though it was hard to be sure how many, because it was so dark. My primary goal was to inquire why these average Wisconsin citizens decided to come out during a riot and defend this business with guns.

"'Sup, dudes. I am a video guy. I was wondering if anyone wants to do an interview?"

A baby-faced guy sporting an AR-15 attached to a tactical shoulder strap piped up. "Sure." He looked sun-starved and chubby from months of COVID lockdowns and fast-food delivery. To complete the image, he wore periwinkle medical gloves, and a fanny pack med kit, which struck me as a strange outfit at a riot with a bunch of pissed off young thugs and malcontents.

He looked at first glance like someone who played too much *Call of Duty* and decided to dress up like his idea of a postpandemalyptic provider of law and order.

"What's your name?"

"I'd rather not say"

"How old are you?"

"Old enough."

"Mind if I film?"

"Not at all."

I pressed the red button on my iPhone. I had no idea that the video I was recording would be viewed by tens of millions of people trying to figure out what went wrong in Kenosha.

I aimed my phone camera at the young man. "So, what are you doing out here? Obviously, you're armed." I paused to pan down to his gun. "And you're in front of this business we saw burning last night, so, what's up?"

Blue and red lights from nearby police vehicles bounced off his pale face and the boards on the windows of the building behind him, muted reflections of the city's futile efforts to maintain order.

"So, people are getting injured, and our job is to protect this business, and part of my job is also to help people. When there's somebody hurt, I'm running into harm's way. That's why I have my rifle." He grabbed the rifle with his bright-colored medical gloves and briefly lifted it from the tension of the shoulder sling. "Because I have to protect myself, obviously, but I also have my med kit." He spun the orange med kit in front of his body and nodded his head, pursing his lips affirmatively.

I continued with a growing nervousness in my voice. "And, uh, what about these other folks? Obviously, there are other people who are armed as well?"

"Their job is to protect me." I aimed the camera up the street and zoomed in on a man wearing olive drab standing in front of a burned-out SUV with a rifle perched in front of the extra magazines of ammunition on his vest. The mags were of the size that most civilians would refer to as "high-capacity" magazines.

"Gotcha. And then, uh, what about these guys on the roof?" I directed the camera above, my hands shaking slightly. The shadowy armed figures on the roof were barely visible through my phone screen, so I turned the camera back down to the interviewee. He replied before I could even get the frame of view back on his smiling face. "Their job is to provide overwatch and to protect me also."

"Gotcha."

"They're protecting everybody on the ground. We're protecting each other." He rubbed his medical gloves together, almost timidly as he searched for words. I interjected to continue the conversation, but I was preoccupied by my surroundings and didn't have a question ready.

"Understood and…and…"

He jumped in before I could finish. "We're running medical, and we're going in and we're getting people."

"And what about you? Are you…are you from the area?"

He replied abruptly again. "I am from the area."

This claim would become one of the most hotly contested facts of the impending homicide trial of the naive boy-man in front of me.

During the moment of silence, the young man crossed his arms and twiddled his latex fingers uneasily. He glanced around furtively as I tried to think of the next question.

"What brought you out here tonight… You just wanted to provide medical attention?"

"Provide medical attention to people that need it. If somebody's injured. Like if you get hurt, I'm grabbin' you." He said this last bit with a smirk and an uneasy chuckle.

"I got hit with plenty, uh… I'm gettin' hit with plenty of pepper balls. But…it's just bruises."

"Your eyes good?"

"Yeah. I got my mask. I'm good."

I tapped the bag on my leg containing White Claws, Zyn nicotine pouches and my gas mask.

The young man's eyes darted around nervously and started to mutter, "And that's about—"

I interrupted him for the question I really wanted to ask. "And have you encountered any issues thus far, with law enforcement or anything like that?"

"We had a group earlier that tried to set fire to the church." He pointed to his left in the direction where the protesters had been earlier. "So, we went to the church and we de-escalated the situation telling them they need to leave or they will be detained and then later arrested."

"This church, right over here?" I panned the camera to the silhouette of a church a block up the street with the gray shell of a toasted car and an ashen dumpster in the foreground.

"That church, right there. And we stopped a fire out all the way down at the school."

One of the buildings completed as part of the Kenosha Civic Center renovation was the city's high school.

When the new school building was completed on a cold, rainy day in November of 1927, the *Kenosha Telegraph-Courier* described the event with an article headlined, "Drizzle of Rain Fails to Dampen Interest as School Board Dedicates New High School." The article's tone was enthusiastic about Kenosha's future. "What it [the high school] shall be depends not only on the Board of Education, the Superintendent of Schools, the high school principal, the teachers, and the pupils, but upon all the citizens of Kenosha. If in the making of this fourth reel, we combine the fire and stamina of the Pioneer Age with the wisdom of the Cultural Age and the ingenuity of the Industrial Age, a picture of great beauty, utility, and inspiration will undoubtedly be produced."

⁞⁞⁞

As the future would have it, this same building was vandalized on the previous two nights of rioting. The young man who stood before me was part of the effort to clean up Kenosha High School earlier that day, and now he stood in front of a business that was charred by fire because in his mind the cops could not serve their stated role to protect the citizens and businesses of Kenosha. The church that he referenced was St. James Church, built in 1883 in order to accommodate the growing Catholic population that relocated to Kenosha in the hopes that America could provide their families with a better and more prosperous future. In less than thirteen minutes, one of the rioters these riflemen stopped from burning the church would set into motion a tragedy that would change Kenosha forever.

I tried to think of the next question, but all I could utter was, "Wow," because my attention was focused on a different gunman who walked into the background of my shot. He wore blue jeans and a black shirt, totally normal looking street clothes minus the rifle, and something that looked like a giant knife, the shiny chrome shimmering blue and red in his waist belt.

"And…do you think it would have been different if the police had tried to stop them from…from setting the fire?"

"I feel like there would have been a lot of casualties and a lot more people injured." His tone seemed unsure, with an intonation in his voice that sounded like a teenage valley girl talking about her feelings. He continued as he tightened his right hand around the strap of his med pack and rubbed his thumb up against his pointer and middle finger with his left. "So I think the police are fine where they're at. And then, let us run the medical because EMS is not coming in. This is considered a red zone to EMS and fire. They are not coming in."

I remembered the fire that those sorry suckers were trying to fight with garbage cans full of water last night and nodded in acknowledgement. "Yeah."

Once he got through my rapid-fire questions, the young man seemed more confident in his statements, though he was still glancing around. "So us citizens, we need to help each other."

Then he gestured off camera to the jacked dude who resembled a Blackwater security operator in some far-off failed country. The hulk approached with huge biceps that barely fit into a tight black shirt behind a tactical vest with extra magazines. A rifle was slung in front of a barrel chest, his appearance all the more seasoned next to the young man who continued his shpiel. "Me and him are out here running, and seeing if people need medical attention."

The Bicep Guy interrupted as he turned up the street, "Speaking of which, we need to check to see if anybody got hurt again."

The young man complied, "All right," and I prepared to conclude the interview. "Understood."

The young man walked away and looked back. "You wanna follow us? You're fine."

"Yes, sir, absolutely," I replied.

I felt weird calling someone so much younger than me "sir," but I was also uneasy about their weapons and the prospect of an armed venture into this incendiary wilderness.

They started to walk out of the lot, and I didn't want to give the impression that I was getting in the way, so I took a moment to stop recording and get my bearings. I pressed the red button on my iPhone and put it in my pocket. I took one last glance at the gun guys on the roof as I trotted after the patrol. The gunmen watched me closely.

We headed south to find the protesters that fled from the hundreds of police that cleared the town square. A Bearcat idled on the corner ahead. I felt more comfortable around the cops than around the armed civilians on the roof, so I grabbed my phone and pressed the red button again. I tried to resume the interview with an injection of some humor as I caught up to the two freelance riflemen.

"So, you guys are like medics who are packing, huh?"

I laughed at my own joke like I always do when I get nervous, and they both looked over their shoulders. Baby Face had a goofy grin, and it looked like he would have been smiling even if I hadn't made a shitty joke. Bicep Guy chuckled without any visible emotion and replied, "Yeah, kinda like that. Well, he's an EMT. I'm just kinda protecting his ass."

In fact, this man would end up abandoning the young medic at some point in the next ten minutes.

"So, you're a certified EMT?" Baby Face looked too young and fleece-able for someone who had witnessed blood and guts firsthand.

"Yap," he replied, seemingly unsure of himself, so I pressed further.

"So you're EMT certified? And do you work as an EMT normally?"

"No, sir, I don't. I'm a lifeguard normally. I got my ALS [aquatic lifeguard safety] a little bit ago."

"Gotcha."

Then the Bicep Guy weighed in on his own background. "And I'm former army infantry and I got a whole bunch of trauma training."

I replied as respectfully as I could. "Gotcha. Well, I appreciate your serv—"

A piece of a brick came out of the darkened area of the street and bounced off the armored personnel vehicle like popcorn thrown at the screen during a crappy movie premiere. It made a high-pitched clang that clarified that this was real life, and not a bad movie.

I recognized these gray brick fragments from the night before. My thirty-nine-dollar plastic army surplus helmet that I got with Shelby in Portland did not seem very protective now.

Shoulda worn the hockey helmet, I thought while I glanced around nervously trying to locate the next airborne hunk of stone.

Bicep Guy chuckled and said, "Oh, shit."

The PA speaker from the Bearcat commanded in a loud, tinny voice, "Put down the rocks! Watch out! Right behind that white vehicle they're throwing rocks at us! Be careful!"

Bicep Guy yelled out to the hidden rock hurlers, "Friendlies, friendlies!"

Baby Face followed. "Medic coming through! Medic coming through! Does anybody need medical? Does anybody need medical?"

Across the intersection, protesters and rioters in various states of affliction looked toward the yelling rifleman. Some of them had just been winged by pepper balls or rubber bullets. Others just coughed and wheezed, pouring water on their faces for relief, even though anyone who has done it before knows that moisture just makes it worse. Many in the crowd were now staring at the patrolmen with angry expressions. I could hear some of them muttering among themselves as we walked closer. The protesters/rioters/looters were clearly confused by the fact that my interviewees were carrying guns but also offering medical assistance.

Two hipster looking guys clad in spike-studded all-black denim vests, ripped up black jeans, and long scraggly hair walked over after hearing offers for medical attention. One had an eighties-style skateboard in one hand and two fire extinguishers hoisted above his head in the other. The punk rock firefighter held a cigarette in his mouth. It bobbed on his lips; the big cylinder of ash suspended at the tip of the cigarette was almost as logic-defying as his rock star appearance with his fire extinguisher and skateboard. He started talking shop. "We got guys putting out fires and shit. They're here to put out fires."

Baby Face replied, "They know." It wasn't clear to me who "they" were, but it was obvious that the punk rock hipsters and the militia medics had a common cause.

"He just got shot up," the punk rocker gestured horizontally with his skateboard toward his friend and then took a long drag of the cig. He exhaled the smoke out of the side of his mouth without removing it. When the injured punk rocker approached, Baby Face saw an opportunity to lend a hand. "You good?"

The second punk rocker replied nonchalantly, "I'm not shot."

A female hipster with a black leather vest and a black leather backpack strolled over to join the meeting of the minds. Her pierced belly button was showing, which struck me as a strange thing to see at a riot. She also carried a skateboard in one hand and a fire extinguisher in the other, like some kind of heroine in a *Mad Max* sequel.

"I thought you got rubber bulleted?" she said with a discernible alcohol- or drug-induced slur that turned the last three letters of her question into a single consonant.

"Oh no, I just got rubber bullet-*ted*," the second hipster said with greater precision and articulation of the final consonants. He pointed with the fire extinguisher at his opposite bicep. A welt was visible beneath the spiked cuff of his vest.

Baby Face lifted the punk rock patient's sleeve with his periwinkle medical gloves.

"It didn't even leave a welt; it just stung. It just fuckin' stung, I'm fine."

Based on the white-powder residue visible on his black clothes and the minimal size of the welt, I assumed that it had been a pepper ball and not a rubber bullet that had hit him. 40 mm rubber bullets pack a punch and the hipster's arm would have been twice the size if he had been pelted by one. A riot ball, on the other hand, is much smaller and less devastating, other than the irritating powder that it releases when it explodes. I called these "pepper bois" because your eyes tear up when they break on or around you, much like after eating a spicy pepper.

"A little pepper boi never hurt nobody!" I joked from behind the camera to enter the conversation. "Just a little spicy that's all."

The girl with the slurred speech who looked like a riot heroine recognized my attempt at humor, "A little salsa!"

"Yeah, a lil salsa," I acknowledged. I wanted to ask the punk rockers what they were trying to do with the fire extinguishers, but Baby Face continued up the street.

"Anybody need medical? Medical?"

I jogged to catch up and came across a strong smell of marijuana. I could see the cloud emanating from the south where more of the felled protesters were congregated. I watched the light wind carry a ganja cloud past me and inhaled deeply. "Someone's got some medical weed. I'll tell ya that."

The young man turned around. He grinned while he clutched the rifle with his left hand so it didn't swing with his body, "Fuckin' right." He continued to shout and wave his hand. "Does anyone need medical? Medical?"

I kept the camera on him. Two guys and a girl to our left were eyeing the AR-15 with scowling eyes above their cloth masks. I brought the phone closer into my chest to make it less obvious that I was filming. We approached the large congregation of protesters sprawling across the entire street and into the adjacent parking lot of another church. Baby Face was seemingly unaware of the stares. "Medical!"

My eyes scanned the closest protesters, half of whom peered in our direction. Most donned masks of some sort, but their body language alone indicated they were not happy. After being volleyed a quarter mile from the courthouse by riot control munitions, I can't say I was surprised that they appeared pissed about a young guy screaming "medical" while wielding what they probably perceived to be a weapon of war. A group in the parking lot to the right shouted threateningly in our direction.

"You were the one that just told us to get off the car."

A young homie wearing a white sleeveless shirt, yellow sweatpants, a sideways yellow hat, black mask, and reflective white shoes took a step in front of the three other guys in his crew. I noticed the guy to his right clutched what looked like a rock sling, a stone-aged weapon that employed a leather strap to swing heavy rocks and throw them much farther than possible with just hands.

The guy to Yellow Pants' left held two broken pieces of bricks in a clenched fist like he was ready to swing. The last dude squatted near the ground looking at his phone. He wore black pants and a bright blue T-shirt around his face. He had something in his waistband, which appeared to be a pistol, but it was hard to tell with the streetlights behind him. I didn't examine the group more closely for fear of appearing too inquisitive. Yellow Pants took another two steps forward, now positioning his empty hands as if he too was toting a rifle, mimicking Baby Face, who clung to his med pack and rifle defensively.

"I remember you, bro, you said get off the car."

Yellow Pants repositioned his mask as he muttered, "Fuck you talking about 'medical'?"

Finally aware of the hostility aimed in his direction, Baby Face took a 90-degree turn to his left and continued down the sidewalk. His walking away only incensed Yellow Pants further.

"Yeahhhhh," Yellow Pants said tauntingly, walking closer in his bright white shoes toward the young rifle toter, who was walking away and shouting, "Anyone need medical?"

"This motherfuckah thinks he in a movie. Yeahhhh, he thought it was sweet," he continued.

I wanted to hear more about the earlier confrontation that had Yellow Pants so angry.

As Baby Face walked away and resumed shouting, "Medical!" I wanted Yellow Pants' side of the story. I kept the phone aimed away from the group to keep from springing an interview on them.

"What, yesterday or today?" I asked.

Yellow Pants replied quickly, "Today!" I cautiously panned the cell phone over to face him.

"Dude had the gun was sayin' get off the car, get off the car. Now he talkin' about medical."

He was talkative enough to conduct an interview, so I aimed the camera directly at him and asked, "What car, over in the dealership?"

When I aimed the camera directly at the homies, the one with the bricks scratched his head with his nonbrick hand and eyed me distrustfully. The guy with the rock sling didn't look too happy either.

"Sorry, I…" I struggled for words but all I could do was mumble. I put my phone down and got into an athletic stance in case I needed to bolt (as I had done with the would-be muggers the night before). But I still wanted to hear what these homies had to say.

"If you want to interview, that's cool. If not, I'll put my phone away." None of them looked keen on the interview so I put my phone down and attempted to further diffuse the situation. With my hands hanging as stealthily as possible at my waist, I pressed the red button to stop recording.

With one last chance to salvage my attempt to extract information from the crew, I went with the break glass in case of an emergency approach. I asked, "Does anyone want a White Claw?" Brick Hands still looked ready to bash my head in, but his larger buddy stood up from his squat and appeared interested.

"Whatchu got?" The rest of the crew started to laugh at how my discernible fear combined with my efforts to provide them with booze. Yellow Pants tapped Brick Hands on the shoulder. "Yo, you tough, huh?"

Brick Guy backed down, and I couldn't tell because of the mask, but I hoped the oversized recipient of my peace offering was smiling as I cracked the Claw and handed it over.

Feeling safer now, I contemplated opening my last Claw to have a drink with the homies and get more info on the confrontation. When I went to grab the alcoholic seltzer, I saw Baby Face hustling south. He carried a fire extinguisher in one hand and his AR-15 in the other. I glanced back at the homies who were now looking in the same direction. They looked pissed, but not keen on pursuing their rival.

I waved at them and said, "I gotta go." I wasn't sure exactly where he was heading, but, given the fire extinguisher, I guessed somebody was lighting more cars on fire. I doubted he would be running that quickly to put out a dumpster fire. Trotting down the street, I tried to imagine all the possible outcomes of what was unfolding. I decided to call Shelby. I couldn't tell if she was still mad at me from our fight the night before because she scarcely showed any feelings, but I didn't care. Seeing the young man running all by himself, I had a bad feeling something was about to go down.

Clearly, Shelby was adept at looking after herself, but tonight was different. Tonight, there was a kid with a med kit claiming to be an EMT while running through the street with an AR-15 in one hand and a fire extinguisher in the other. I recalled Geoff's command about Shelby and the ICU as I pursued Baby Face. Reaching for my phone midstride, I heard something hit the pavement. I looked down behind me and saw my gas mask on the ground. I forgot to close my leg pack when I served the homies a White Claw.

After picking the mask up and resecuring my pack, I could no longer see Baby Face.

The phone rang for what seemed like minutes. Shelby finally picked up. "Hello." She answered in her stoic tone.

"Shelby, you OK?" I asked, slightly out of breath.

"Yeah."

"Where you at?" I asked. Shelby was self-admittedly horrible with directions. She would just shrug her shoulders whenever I asked about north or south or other such navigational terms that she claimed she wasn't wired for. I looked up at the street sign and tried anyway. "I'm on Sheraton, I think."

Shelby replied, "I think I'm actually just up the street from you." I felt a moment of relief, realizing she was close by.

"Something's about to go down, we should—"

I came upon a group of people in a poorly lit stretch of the road. I could barely make out Baby Face's tactical shoulder strap and rifle in the dark. I couldn't tell if he still had the fire extinguisher. Several people were yelling from the middle of the street. Someone screamed the N-word loudly. The relief I felt after hearing Shelby's stable voice was replaced by the terror one experiences when the fight-or-flight instinct is triggered in the brainstem.

From the middle of the road, there was a car lot to my right where rioters were smashing windows and torching cars. I noticed one man with a shirt wrapped around his head emerge from behind one of the busted-up cars. He advanced in the direction of Baby Face, who now looked like a deer caught in the headlights.

I told Shelby, "Oh fuck, I gotta go."

I hung up the phone and switched to the camera app on my iPhone. I thought I hit the red button and started recording.

Baby Face evasively juked in the opposite direction toward the car lot behind him. I ran after both of them, not realizing how quickly things were about to unravel.

August 25, 2020, 11:47 PM CST: Street in Front of Car Source 3, Kenosha, Wisconsin

> Under the bludgeonings of chance
> My head is bloody, but unbowed
> Beyond this place of wrath and tears
> Looms but the Horror of the shade,
> —William Ernest Henley, *Invictus*

As Baby Face turned away and ran, the shirtless man sprinted after him. I held my phone in front of me trying my best to steadily film, but my eyes were now fixated on Baby Face and his pursuer. I had been running all summer to stay in shape, practicing short sprints, even jumping hurdles or the common DC pothole to simulate a mad dash away from danger in an urban environment. But this time, I foolishly sprinted toward peril. As FBI surveillance drone footage revealed over a year later in court, in those last moments as the three of us dashed through the parking lot, I gained significant ground. I had limber, weak legs from months of the Riot Diet and general fatigue, but my hockey lungs, some fear, a dash of stupidity, and maybe even a bit of destiny, powered me forward, faster.

As I caught up, we entered a well-lit area of the Car Source 3 parking lot, Baby Face, his AR-15 slung at the ready, approached a cluster of parked cars. The shirtless guy threw a bag that landed with a crash that sounded like a glass bottle shattering on concrete. Baby Face spun around to see if he was still being chased and, seeing the man still running, he continued toward the lot's storefront, right next to three parked cars. A loud crack rang out from somewhere to my left. I thought it was a firework or a flash bang, but it was a man shooting a handgun into the air. Baby Face turned around just in front of the three parked vehicles. His gun was aimed 45 degrees at the pavement. I ceased my sprint forward when I suddenly realized that the shirtless man was not going to stop running toward the rifleman, who stood frozen by fear.

The shirtless man was in a crouched running position just before he dove forward toward Baby Face. He shouted, "Fuck you!"

Baby Face stood frozen for a moment. I saw his eyes wide with panic, his already-pale face even more white as he comprehended the advancing man's trajectory. The shirtless man was nearly in a flying Superman body position, hands outstretched as far as he could reach in front of him.

My eyes darted from the petrified Baby Face to his rifle. He swung his gun to the left to dodge the shirtless man's outstretched hands. Because I was behind both of them, it was hard to tell, but from my perspective it appeared that the shirtless man barely missed grabbing the barrel of the rifle. After his hands missed, he grabbed at nothing but air. The young man swung his rifle back and fired what I heard as three or four shots in rapid succession. It all happened in an instant.

I felt a sensation of something zip past my legs and heard a cacophony—the boom of the gunshot and the round colliding with something hard, like the sound of thunder overhead combined with the crash of an open ocean wave in the cosmic amphitheater of stormy Hanalei Bay. I looked down at my *lucky* nylon pants. Although my pants still had the burn marks from the firework that blew up at my feet in Portland, everything else looked OK. I stamped my feet on the pavement a few times to confirm that I had no pain, then looked back up to the body that was now lying face down and lifeless on the ground.

After the adrenaline kicked in, the thinking part of my brain shut off. My lungs felt like they were filling with panic instead of the hot August air as gunshots from a different weapon rang out nearby. I ran over to the man lying face down on the pavement in front of me, switching my phone from my two-handed position for optimal filming to holding it in one hand. In that moment, I liked to remember that I ditched my role as a newsman who was recording an event, and that I consciously chose to help the guy I just saw get blasted at close range. In reality, no thought process or decision-making took place. My mind proceeded on the circuitry that was wired during my young life leading up to that point, mimicking what I saw my dad do during moments of panic when I was ten years old on the beach.

With the continued gunfire, the area where the man collapsed had the added benefit of providing me with some cover. I ducked behind the cars and began looking for damage on his body. The gunfire ceased. There was an eerie quiet save the sound of my own breathing, and something that sounded like the gurgling of a gutted pig. Then I heard footsteps behind me. I screamed loudly, "Call 9-1-1!" But I remained looking down and only saw the pair of legs that belonged to the individual out of my peripheral vision. After issuing the command, I saw a hand enter a pocket and assumed that the phone was retrieved to call an ambulance, at which point I returned my focus to the dire situation at hand.

I screamed in a panicked voice barely recognizable as my own, "Are you OK? Just don't move man, don't move. All right, I'm gonna flip you over real quick."

He did not respond. A small hole in his neck showed barely any blood at all. Having seen plenty of action movies and hearing many of my dad's ER stories, the first semi-rational thought that went through my head was to search for massive exit wounds somewhere on the other side of his body, especially given that the young man fired his rifle at such close range. I figured that I would need some cloth to plug up what I encountered.

I stood up to remove my shirt, tossing my helmet off my head to allow free passage of my makeshift tourniquet. I muttered, "Fuck," just before my plastic helmet bounced off the momentarily silent street. I squatted back down. My voice cracked. "I'm gonna flip you over real quick, bro. I'm gonna flip you over real quick. Just gotta get pressure on this, dude."

As I rolled him over, I tried to calm the panic that wanted me to roll him over "real quick." I wished I had my dad's calm, slowly rotating the young man near the breaking waves. I struggled to steady my shaking hands and flipped him over. Someone else arrived as I started to look for the giant holes on his naked torso.

I asked, "Where's it at?" but the young man who just arrived next to me did not see anything on the man's pale body either.

He egged me on, "Where is it? Where is it?"

More people arrived screaming. I began barking orders, "Get a light on it!" But no one responded, so I shouted louder and more forcefully. My panic pushed the air from the top of my lungs to my raspy voice box that somehow found a higher pitch than normal. "Get a fucking light!"

A woman flipped on her cell phone light and pleaded, "Put pressure on it!"

This time I replied more softly, realizing that she was trying to help rather than escalate the chaos. "Where, dude? Where, where's the hole? Get the fuckin mask off!" I was referring to the T-shirt wrapped around his head.

The girl exclaimed, "There, in his head! Come on!" Other people in the swelling crowd gasped as we saw red blood on his forehead, behind the hole in the red shirt.

"Put pressure!" the cell-phone-light holder shrieked.

Someone else just behind my shoulder forcefully yelled over the pack of ten people all shouting various expletives and pleas, "You shot him?"

When I turned my head, I discovered, with horror, he was glaring at me. My reply had the slobbery sound of someone on the verge of crying, "Me? Fuck no!"

Then I heard one individual on the periphery exclaim, "Yo! There's a hospital right here!"

The frenzied field hospital was about to turn into mob justice, and I knew we were inadequate caregivers compared to the stable profession-alism of someone like my dad or my ER-trained brother, so I pivoted to the best way to an actual emergency room, which was directly across the street. I demanded, "Who's got a car? Who has a car?"

With my left hand I reached my shirt to the side of his head to staunch the wound. I also briefly lifted the phone in my right hand from his stom-ach. The camera showed the man's face with blood dripping from his nose. While my camera lens showed the whole face, my own God-given eyes only watched his slumped pupil. His eyes drifted upward following my left hand as it placed the Black Lives Matter shirt on his forehead to staunch his bleeding.

A black arm reached around the back of his head. "I got him! I got him!" I turned my own wide eyes from the wounded man's half-closed one to the face that owned the arm. He looked at me and nodded downward. "Put that down. Fuck that!" He pointed at my phone. I realized that I still had it clenched in a death grip in my right hand.

As I intertwined my paler Irish-Italian arm with his, I acknowledged, "I gotchu, dude," then put the phone into the side pocket of my supposedly *lucky* pants. The Good Samaritan was a black man who appeared to be about my age. When we struggled to lift him, the small-statured casualty was heavier than I anticipated. He slipped from my grip. When I examined why the body was so slippery, I realized my hands were covered with blood. The small hole in his neck was bleeding profusely. I tried to use his own shirt to put pressure on his neck while simultaneously holding the black shirt on the top of his head.

My riot rescue comrade confirmed he was ready for extraction: "I got him! I got him!"

We got him up and staggered forward.

Independent video journalist Ford Fischer, whom I had seen at protests from DC to the CHAZ, arrived at the frantic scene. My fellow Samaritan had his shoulder under one arm of the imperiled man while I had the other slung across my back. We used our inside hands to support one leg each as we shuffled across the parking lot, executing a sloppy version of a fireman's carry followed by a crowd of about two dozen people.

Someone shouted, "Medic!" then various expletives into the dark sky. The lights shone above the Car Source parking lot like a stadium in the middle of a quiet, sleepy town that only woke up for the "Friday Night Lights" of a high school football game. I was the senior lineman who saw nothing but the scrum of America's political circus gone wrong.

The man's skin was wet with blood, and he slipped in our arms. We stumbled as we arrived at the edge of the parking lot. As we slowed down to regain our grip, someone bumped me hard with their chest and I almost fell to the ground. Thankfully, the black Samaritan under the other arm had a solid footing and prevented me from falling on my face. A third man sensed our misfortune and helped us lift the imperiled man's legs.

With my ear pressed against the wounded man's right armpit, the low death rattle of his labored breathing and the high-pitched screams of the mob both hit my ears at the same time.

We shuffled across the dark area beyond the light of the hospital or the car lot in the middle of the road. I put my head down and surveyed the pavement in front of me, watching my steps closely to avoid another slip. The path for my shoes became brighter with each step as we neared the lights of the hospital sign. So much noise, from everywhere, choppers from above, sirens, but the sounds that live most in my mind are the shrill screams of one onlooker, "Help! Help!" and the sunken gurgle of the imperiled man's lungs filling with blood instead of chemically spiced air.

On the other side of the street, an individual donning a green tactical vest atypical of the protester's normal street clothes flagged me down. He stated that he worked for the hospital, insisting it would be faster if we loaded him into the truck. He gestured to a black Dodge Durango, then ran to the back of the SUV, and opened it up. Then he ran for the driver's seat, passing Ford Fischer's camera microphone, loudly commanding the mob that quickly surrounded the vehicle on every side, "Get back! Get back! Back! Back!"

Shelby was visible in the foreground of Ford's video; my sand-colored canvas desert rucksack that she borrowed was strapped to her placid demeanor within the turbulence of the frantic horde. I jumped in the back with the wounded man. I wedged my hand onto the frame of the raised tailgate to push us deeper into the trunk. The black good Samaritan lost his grip and couldn't get himself close enough to get in.

The hospital employee jumped into the front seat and started the deeper growl of the engine that ran the American-made SUV, then punctuated by honks because the front of the vehicle was still blocked by the messy mob.

Fischer attempted to walk his camera around to the back of the vehicle near my dangling feet. His camera was knocked to the side by a man wearing a black mask, black shirt and a black flat brim stomping toward the swarm behind the bumper. I felt something hit the side of my face. Then a second blow came just below my eye, even harder. The force of the punch caused me to collapse into the back seats of the car, the injured man's head still cradled in my left arm. As I turned to the origin, the man with the black flat brim and clenched fists sprung deeper into the vehicle to continue his assault. I gave him one of the signature little brother crab kicks that used to be my go-to defense against my far-larger older brother when I was lying on my back and unable to flee. As my foot collided with his chest, he fell backward. His final diving punch came up short of my face. I still have no idea why he was trying to punch me.

Fighting to keep from falling out of the back of the Durango after the last-ditch kick, I got my left arm simultaneously around the headrest and the man's head, then stretched my right arm and wedged my hand inside the corner of the back window. I wrapped my hands around the metal that moored me to the back of the seats like the leash of my surfboard when stuck beneath the stormy waves in Hawaii. As long as I could hold onto the board, when the maelstrom subsided, I would have my lifeline to the surface. I held his head tightly, my back pinned up against the back of the black seats as with the black volcanic rock of Kauai's reefs, hoping that if I held on long enough then perhaps he could be saved, perhaps the destructive chaos of the synthetic storm that hit Kenosha could be weathered unharmed.

The truck honked and lurched forward but stopped multiple times, with yells from the driver, "Go!" and "Move!" By the time Ford releveled his camera, the angry guy with the black flat brim could be seen swinging a disgruntled fist as the truck sped off.

Heading down the ramp to the hospital, I pulled back the fabric from the front of the man's face to reveal his eyes, which were rolled into the back of his head. The engine roared while the truck drove down the ramp. We stopped for a minute as the driver typed in the passcode and waited for the metal gate to raise. The man's eyes leveled and met mine. I hadn't tried this hard not to cry since I read *Invictus* to my dad the last night we were together on earth.

I did not know the man, but his demeanor told me that he was look-ing into the shade and was very much afraid. "It's gonna be OK, bro. We are gonna have a beer and laugh about it after this." I just wanted the man lying in the back of the SUV next to me to know that despite this place of wrath and tears, he was not alone. We had comforted my dad as his one eye followed the path toward the light, though when I saw this man's eyes disappearing behind his black pupils, where he was about to go I did not know.

Rolling through to the emergency room exit, a gurney attended by three wide-eyed medical personnel came through the automatic doors. I jumped out of the SUV. The hospital staff helped me load the body onto the wheeled stretcher. I watched the gurney roll down the hall into some unknown future, or a certain past, for the man with a bullet wound to his neck and head. I was haunted by the look of fear in his eyes. I will never forget the look, gasping for air while he disappeared behind the doors in the hands of the doctors and nurses in the operating room. I stood in the waiting room in shock. All I could think of was the imperiled man's terror as he confronted the horror of the shade.

I was left alone in the ER, accompanied only by the low buzz of the harsh fluorescent lights. I looked down at the red blood covering my hands, arms and body. "What the fuck!" I said to no one. Just as I reached into the pocket of my *lucky* riot pants to examine the footage on my phone, the automatic doors coming from the entrance on the other side of the ER slid open.

An officer entered, supporting a man who was clutching his arm. When the white lights landed on the escortee's arm, I could not believe what I saw. His bicep appeared to be gone. Though his humerus bone still connected his shoulder to his elbow, that was about all that was left of his upper arm, as if some kind of human butcher removed only that muscle and nothing else. They hobbled behind the same doors as the gurney had a few moments before.

I realized strangely at that moment that I was still technically at work. My first order of business was to call my CEO, who was a lawyer and would have the most immediate advice on how I should proceed. It took me a few minutes just to look up and dial the number because my hands were shaking so violently, and the blood smeared the screen of the phone. What was normally a simple task had become a feat of focus and might.

The phone barely rang twice before he picked up. "Neil, shit just went down tonight, and I recorded a shooting. What should I do? Do I need a lawyer?"

Despite it being after midnight on the East Coast, his voice came through clear and calm. "You didn't do anything criminally wrong. You were doing your job. I'm glad you're all right. Just cooperate with the police; tell the truth, and everything will be OK."

A green uniformed state trooper was staring at me as I stood there by myself speaking on my phone, shirtless and covered in blood.

I told my boss, "Thanks, Neil. I gotta go." I hung up the phone and before I even got it into my riot pants the cop was six inches from my face. He had a haircut that was long enough to let you know he was bald by choice, but short enough where it was clear he didn't like to fuss over things like hair on his head.

"What the fuck happened?" he asked.

I told him a brief version of what I saw ending with me stating that I recorded the whole thing.

"Show me," he said.

I went into the photos app, and with horror realized that the video only began after I arrived over the body and just before I took off my shirt. "Oh shit," I said as I frantically panned through my videos to see if there was anything else. It had to be a mistake. Just before the video that started after the shooting, there was a photo that showed a dim, trash-strewn sidewalk near where the chase began. With my mouth agape, the officer, who was looking over my shoulder, sensed something was wrong.

"I...I don't think I recorded it." I felt like I wanted to throw up as the officer impatiently stated, "Gimme that." He panned through my camera roll but came up with nothing.

After a brief back and forth where the officer informed me that he was taking my phone regardless, I gave up. I was at this point keen on taking the path of least resistance to avoid any more angry exchanges, most especially in the face of the cop's vehement demands. He took down my name and information then left with my phone through the same automatic doors. He encountered a few other police who gathered around. I took his departure as an opportunity to call my mom.

I asked the woman at the waiting room window if there was a phone I could use. She pointed to a landline in the corner of the room next to the bathrooms. Thankfully I had her number memorized from a time before digital phone books. When I went to dial, I realized that I still had blood all over not only my hands, but also my torso and arms. I stepped into the bathroom and looked in the mirror for the first time. The sunken, swollen eyes looking back at me resembled some naive but more aged version of myself. A terrified self-pitying young boy who could do nothing but cry as loudly as possible and wait for Mom and Dad after a bad nightmare. I soaped my arms, bare chest and neck. Blood and soap dripped on the bathroom floor as I dabbed myself dry with the rough paper towels. Although it was now silent in the restroom, my heart was still pumping, and I could barely hear anything over my own heavy breaths. I dried my hands and dabbed my eyes then looked back at my slightly cleaner self in the mirror. As I drew deep gulps of air, I looked from the mirror to my hands, which finally began to steady.

"Mom, don't worry. I'm OK."

She replied in her signature delirious tone that she had when I called her in the middle of the night, like the time I lost the pickup truck in the ocean during a massive winter storm. Though that time I had told her simply that I was OK, and I needed to speak with Dad.

"What's the matter, honey?"

"Mom, I witnessed a shooting. I need a lawyer."

My mom still sounded tired, "Well what about Dick?" Dick was our family friend who was a corporate estate lawyer.

"What the fuck, Mom! Would you ask a gynecologist to give you open-heart surgery?"

After a brief, tense discussion, we remembered that Brendan, the dad of an old friend from preschool, was a criminal lawyer. I called and left him a voicemail. By the time I hung up, I saw Shelby and our riot buddy, Julio Rosas, waiting at the hospital doors where the cops were congregated. I was surprised to see them, because the hospital was locked down according to the lady who directed me to the phone. In an uncharacteristic moment of softness for Shelby, she and Julio hugged me tightly. My bare skin felt vulnerable as I realized for the first time that it could have been me whose insides were torn to shreds by the young man's gun. But I was safe now and my heart rate finally started to slow down.

After our embrace, she literally offered me the shirt off her back, given that I would stick out like a sore thumb if I tried to go shirtless back onto the streets. The shirt belonged to her dad. So, I guess she technically offered her dad's shirt off her back. I cannot help but draw meaning from the fact that Shelby was wearing her dad's shirt, and I was wearing my dad's pants. Somehow, in this cosmically realigning moment in our own lives, our own ancestors were there looking after us in the form of the clothing we chose to wear venturing undercover during the uncertain danger of the fiery and not at all peaceful third night of riots.

The cops came up and said that they were going to bring me down to the station. Shelby kept her shirt because I would be safe with the cops. I bid my riot buds farewell. The air was clear of chemical agents and the light summer breeze felt cool and cathartic. I took in a deep breath of fresh air and, for a moment, I felt like I was in Hawaii surfing the empty waves after the storm cleared. But another set of dark clouds was brooding on the horizon. The sight of the waiting police cruiser sent a chilling reality into my mind. Because I did not capture the shooting on video, I could not show the cops what I saw, and I would instead have to narrate to them in great detail the horror that I saw.

I got into the back of the squad car and the frigid air conditioning goose-bumped my skin, here in the dark cold place they put you when you end up on the wrong side of the law. The interior light in the front of the car shed a warm light on a young officer's face as she looked through the metal grates and gave me a wry, comforting smile before she drove the cruiser across the town square to the Kenosha police station.

At 1:24 a.m., I sat in a windowless room with a desk and two chairs. They had taken my phone so I was left to stew in my own thoughts while I waited for the officer to enter and take my statement. I did not realize it, but the camera in the top corner of the room was already recording. The video I obtained through my lawyer months later shows me squirming nervously in the type of uncomfortable chair you'd expect in an interrogation room. The microphone picked up a great big sigh while I ran both hands through my disheveled hair, pulling on the riot-munition-dusted split ends. I thrust my fistfuls of hair upwards in the hopes that the tug on my mop would jerk me awake and everything would turn out to be a nightmare. But the burning sensation was only a slight distraction from the apprehension that this was real life. I took another deep breath and cradled my face in my hands. I finally relaxed my clenched jaw and neck, a much-needed rest after supporting my clunky old gas mask for nights on end. My neck would get sore when I was days into a surf trip, but no matter how sore I was when the swell showed up, I would have to shake it off and get ready for the biggest waves of all.

The smiling cop from the squad car came into the room. "I'm gonna grab you a water real quick. Do you want to use the restroom first?"

I'd barely drunk any liquids all night and didn't have to pee. "I'm good."

She politely added, "And just so you know, you're not under arrest. We tell people...when they are."

"Good to know. Thank you."

The officer was gone for a few minutes and I was taken by a desperate urge to slug the last White Claw in the gas mask bag still attached to my leg. She returned with a warm bottle of water and apologized. "This is the best we can do. It's not cold."

She handed me the bottle and I said, "Straight vodka, thank you very much."

She chuckled.

Yearning for human tenderness, I continued, "Thank you very much, Officer. What was your name?"

She replied, "Officer Wigher."

I introduced myself by raising my right hand as if testifying as a witness.

"Richie, nice to meet you."

"Nice to meet you."

"Nice to meet you too. Thank you."

I could have repeated, "Nice to meet you," a dozen more times to her because I was drunk on adrenaline and the comedown, and it *was* nice to meet her because she offered a portrait of order and discipline, a visual life jacket, as I emerged from one sea of chaos, certain to enter another.

I drank the lukewarm water and continually replayed the shooting in my head. My primal fears of life and death were replaced by a rational one. If I missed any important details, it could change the course of Baby Face's life. But he had just ended the life of a man I did not know and could not get out of my mind.

Instead of a warm alcoholic seltzer to placate the terrible images running through my head, I remembered that I also had a plastic can of Zyn nicotine pouches in my gas mask bag. I took a sip of the warm water and popped two six-milligram pouches into my top lip, a nicotine injection equivalent to ripping four ciggies at once. The police video shows me pacing and shifting around anxiously for a few minutes until I finally let my head fall back, when the hefty dose of nicotine salt pouches hit my veins all at once. I tried to sleep, but all I could think about was the pupils eroding the color of that man's irises. I kept my eyelids shut tightly. I would not cry in front of the cops. Seemed like bad form.

During the nearly two hours that I sat waiting for the detective, footage shows that I unsuccessfully tried to take a nap by lying on the coarse carpet, drank two bottles of water, put six Zyn nicotine pouches in and out of my mouth and moved my chair four separate times. I even did a few minutes of yoga in an effort to alleviate my neck pain. One hour and forty-five minutes in, I scooted the chair closer to the wall and found a comfortable position, my head leaning back and feet propped up on the table. As I finally drifted off to sleep, my last thought was that perhaps the man had not died. Maybe my life could go back to normal again.

I was stirred out of my nightmare when a detective with a shaved head, spectacles and a bulletproof vest over a white-collared shirt walked in at 3:13:26 a.m. CST. I blinked my eyes open and immediately jerked my feet off the table. Readjusting in my chair to sit up, all I could get out was a stifled, "Hey."

"Sorry," he said standing to the side of the table holding a stack of papers. He proceeded in a very gentle tone. "I'm Detective Cepress. Hey, I just got called in for this."

I replied, "Yes, sir," to signal that I was a (mostly) law-abiding citizen.

"We understand you recorded video of the incident. Are you OK with us downloading the phone?"

Confused by why the cop wanted to download my entire phone including everything I recorded that summer leading up to this incident, I replied, "No, I can just give you the videos. I'm not OK with you downloading my phone."

He switched to a less gentle tone. "OK. Then we are going to keep it and get a search warrant."

I wore an expression that combined puzzle and irritation, asking why.

He replied, "Because it has evidence of a homicide on it. Because if we downloa—"

I interrupted the detective. "Is he dead?" The video at that instance shows my stunned expression, eyebrows raised in shock, but sloping outwards reflecting the panicked worry I felt inside.

"Yeah," Cepress answered matter-of-factly.

I put my hands on my face. Though I expected the man I tried so hard to save would probably die, nothing prepared me for the moment when the news finally landed, officially, from a brusque cop who'd had similar talks with jittery, confused civilians like me hundreds of times.

Detective Cepress continued to speak about me giving them access to my phone. "So if we can download it, then we can get it right back to you, but I can't give it to you without pulling the video from it."

This started to seem like the soft-power tactics they use to coerce the guilty and the innocent into trashing their own constitutional rights, the stuff I only saw on crime shows like *Law & Order*. I wrapped my forearms around my ears and placed my elbows and forehead on the table. I only heard the blood pumping through my ears and felt a hyperventilated emptiness. What a terrible place that man was in before he died.

Cepress was standing over me sitting there, like a stern teacher interrupting a recalcitrant pupil's nap.

I tried offering a solution. "I mean, are you able to download it and delete the other files in front of me?"

"I can bring in our tech guy. I don't even know what that means."

"OK, can I talk to him?"

"Yeah."

Cepress left the room. I muttered to myself, "Oh fuck," as I replayed what I could have done better. If my dad or my brother had been there and made all the right decisions, could they have saved him? For my efforts I had an incomplete and inconclusive clip of a man's last moments of life.

Their so-called tech guy came in and we discussed various methods of transferring the files.

Despite me giving them my phone's password, he was unsuccessful in downloading the contents of the camera roll. I was relieved by their incompetence because it meant that they wouldn't be able to download the ten thousand-plus videos that I recorded over the previous months of unrest, the entire summation of my hectic summer toil. Some of it was backed up on the cloud, but most of it was not. The only videos that pertained to their investigation were the last few. After some lengthy explanation, they finally agreed to let me Airdrop the relevant files, which was a wireless transmission that took seconds to transfer to the tech guy's device. At 3:20 a.m., the detective sat down and turned on the computer to finally begin questioning me about what I saw. He started with my full name, DOB, phone number and address.

As I recited this basic information, my grief gave way to intention, and I began speaking methodically. To aid in my recollection I threw in two fresh nicotine pouches.

"OK, Richie, so obviously you're in town covering the protests and whatnot. Were you there all night long?"

I detailed how I came to meet the shooter during an interview less than fifteen minutes (though I told the officer I thought it was forty minutes) before the shooting.

"It was the building across from the big lot that was burned out."

"I think you're talking about the glass building with the garage door for cars?"

"Yeah, it was boarded up now."

"How old was he?"

"He looked like he was in his midtwenties, lower twenties maybe, baby face."

I described the scene, what looked like three gunmen on the roof, and a few more on the ground as I interviewed the young man. "I don't remember exactly what the line of questioning was, but it was something along the lines of, 'Why are you out here?' 'Why are you armed?' 'What do you think you are accomplishing by being armed?' And he cited that he was protecting that business."

"OK." Cepress began scribbling.

"He mentioned an instance earlier in the night at the church near the courthouse over there."

"Yeah."

"And then I asked him what would've happened if law enforcement had shown up, and he said that he didn't think they could have de-escalated it like he was able to."

"OK." More scribbles.

"I did the interview, and he said if you want to come follow, I'm also a trained medic and currently a lifeguard."

Cepress scribbled again.

"The other guy was a vet, and I believe he said military."

When we filmed a video series with competitive shooters in 2018, I remembered the strict discipline with which they instructed me to handle the rifle, as well as how easy the weapon was to shoot.

While AR-15s were hard to come by where I grew up in the North, after I moved south of the Mason-Dixon to DC, I would always relish the opportunity to travel to friends' farms and experience the terrifying ease of squeezing off rounds on an AR-15.

"I've handled plenty of AR-15s. I'm not, like, a gun nut, but I just noticed that he was kind of not handling the weapon very well." More scribbles.

"I'm not sure exactly at what point in time he picked up a fire extinguisher. So, he had a fire extinguisher in one hand and an AR in the other."

Cepress chuckled with puzzlement. "Hmm? OK."

I relayed that I didn't know where the big arms guy went but that I called Shelby after I saw Baby Face running down the street with a fire extinguisher then hung up abruptly when I saw his fire extinguisher was gone, "and as I put my phone down, I noticed that he [Baby Face] started to run... The individual who got shot was advancing toward him and he [Baby Face] actually dodged around, and then he ran backward." I noted the ensuing chase, and how the young rifleman turned around and stood to face his pursuer with his gun aimed 45 degrees at the ground.

When recounting the shooting itself, I stood up to demonstrate how the deceased lunged moments before he was shot, and how the young man went from aiming the rifle toward the ground before he dodged around the advance, leveled his weapon, and fired three, maybe four times in rapid succession.

I confidently told the officer about how I took two steps away from the path of the shooting as the shots went off. Then I recalled looking down at my feet while the pursuer collapsed to the ground, "and as he's raising his weapon, the first shot goes off and I think it might have hit the pavement because I felt something like, hit my leg, and my first thought was like, 'Did I just get fucking shot?' I don't know if I felt the wind of the bullet or, if it hit the ground and the cement hit me, something. But I definitely looked down at my legs like, 'What the fuck?'"

The interrogation concluded at 3:57 a.m. The detective slid his card across the table as he stood up from behind the computer. "So I'm gonna give you my information, and I'm gonna go check on your phone so we can get you outta here. I'm sure you're tired."

I grabbed the card and replied with a sigh, "Yes sir. Yeah, I'm going on like three hours of sleep a couple days in a row. After this shit, I'm gonna have a big fuckin' week. I'll tell you that."

I put his business card in one of the cargo pockets of my *lucky* riot pants. I got up and left the room. My mind racing, I was soothed only by the sound of the gentle swish of my *lucky* riot pants walking down the quiet hallway of the police station.

The kind officer, Wigher, drove me back to the hotel. We talked about what would come next. I grew nervous about the prospect of having to tell the world what I saw without breaking down. I felt alone in the back of the police car as the blue-and-red lights reflected off the solid stone of the municipal buildings surrounding the defiled town square. My dad was gone and I had never wanted him back more than I did at that exact moment. But at least I had his pants.

I was locked up in the back but the officer agreed to roll the window down. The wind passed by the burned-out cars and dumpsters, and it flickered their smoldering embers. The chemical clouds from the police munitions were replaced by the smoke emanating out of incinerated livelihoods and smoldering dreams.

The predawn light glowed fiery orange behind the parked police cars. Above the empty, filthy streets and the black fence, the silhouette of the courthouse loomed even darker in the dawn than when it was lit up at night. I bid the officer farewell at the hotel. Bare-chested beneath the brightening sky, I breathed in the cool, clean air that was blowing from the west down the Rocky Mountains then across the broad plains of the heartland of America, before it arrived in the burning city of Kenosha.

Sometime while I stirred restlessly in the hotel bed, the wind blew the dark smoke past the tiny waves on the beaches of the Great Lakes. I made a listless effort to sleep beneath the dark specter of a different kind that now hung over Kenosha, heavy with the burden from years of waning hope, now spiraling out of control around the eye of the biggest media hurricane of the year—rifle-born bloodshed and the young.

August 26, 2020, 12:38 PM CST: Culver's American Restaurant, Kenosha, Wisconsin

And yet the menace of the years
Finds and shall find me unafraid.

—William Ernest Henley, *Invictus*

Shelby agreed to join me at the popular Wisconsin fast-food burger joint on Sheridan Road, the same street a few miles from where the shooting took place. We passed by the scene on the way. I glanced for a moment and saw police tape around where the man collapsed, then turned my eyes back to the road and continued on.

I barely slept two hours because my phone was ringing off the hook with friends, family, and random people I barely remembered who saw videos of me in the frantic rush to the hospital. I had been copying and pasting, "I'm OK. Thanks for your concern," to respond as quickly as possible and avoid any real engagement. Everyone was asking me questions about what happened, but I just wanted to put it out of my mind. Some reporters, mostly from local outlets and conservative online news sites, also reached out. At the moment I didn't feel ready to do anything other than eat, slam a few brews then sleep. What does a sane, stable person do twelve or so hours after witnessing a homicide? I don't know. But I had yet to try the famous burgers at Culver's, so I convinced Shelby to head over there with me for some chow and suds.

As Shelby and I sat waiting for our meal outside, the beer tasted cold and crisp in the blaring sun above the royal blue Culver's umbrella. I was still trying to wrap my head around the difference between my memory of what I saw and what the experience made me feel personally. Since I only covered what I saw with the cops, I confided in Shelby who often served as something of a therapist at this point—even though it felt more like she was a sister when it came to lending an ear.

I explained that though I knew the dude who died had gray eyes, now when I replayed what I witnessed in my mind, I saw them as the same bright blue as my dad's had before he passed away. She nodded affirmatively, though I sensed some concern behind the unwavering gaze of her own blue-gray eyes.

I was happy to have some company, and I figured the sunshine, some cheese curds, and a double cheese burgie with all the fixings would set me right. I stopped at a liquor store on the way and picked up a Spotted Cow, the most popular local Wisconsin beer, because Culver's only sold soft drinks. I needed something with a bit more umph to wash down my meal and calm my tattered nerves. I hadn't ingested anything other than coffee, water and nicotine since the incident took place the night before.

The only person I shared my thoughts with was Shelby's boyfriend, David Hookstead, a fellow reporter and self-proclaimed "head of security" at *Daily Caller*. David was from Wisconsin and had been handling guns since he was a kid. I shot rifles with David, and his expertise with firearms spoke for itself. David woke up earlier than anyone else I knew, and immediately after I got home from the police station, we had the following exchange:

> David: "Are you guys safe?"
>
> Me: "Yes"
>
> David: "Did that guy live?"
>
> Me: "Nope. Cops told me I was a witness to a homicide. Dude was basically dead in my arms. He barely had a pulse."
>
> David: "Everyone on social media is saying he was a rioter trying to start something at a car dealership. Is that true, or was this a straight-up murder?"
>
> Me: "The guy he shot was 100 percent trying to grab his gun."

When our food arrived, I was scanning through news articles to catch up on how the media reported on the tragic events from the night before. Shelby was buried in her phone too. I took my first bite of the burger. The crisp lettuce and soft melted cheese combined with the juicy all-American beef tickled my taste buds, reminding me that there were still things in this world that could be simple and pleasant.

The article I was reading was from *Vice News* with the headline "A 17-Year-Old Aspiring Cop Has Been Charged with Murder in Kenosha." Four paragraphs in, I came across a shocking line, "In several graphic videos, he's seen opening fire on protesters; one was shot in the head, another in the chest." I took a bite of a crispy cheese curd and slugged my beer as I reread the paragraph. Was *Vice* really claiming that the young man "opened fire" on protesters?

I cracked another Spotted Cow with a frustrated twist of the bottle cap. I knew this to be "udderly" false based on the chase and attempt to grab the gun that I had witnessed firsthand. Shelby agreed that, despite her personal opinions on what took place, it was an egregious mischaracterization. I slugged more beer as I continued scrolling.

Video by Drew Hernandez went viral overnight, with over a million views on Twitter alone. From a distance of about fifty feet, it showed the chase between the shirtless man and the Baby Face into the parking lot. The shirtless man shouted, "Fuck you!" before what clearly sounded like four shots.

Drew's video was pixelated and somewhat hard to make out exactly how close the shooter and the deceased were to each other at the moment the shots went off. I felt a pit in my stomach that had more to do with dread than hunger, because the footage confirmed that it would be up to me to determine the finer details of what happened during the first shooting. One thing was clear, my efforts to step out of the way of the gunshots were far less successful than I confidently told the cops. The gunshots went off, and then I stepped to the right. I had told police that I stepped out of the way before the shots were fired—perhaps my own mind trying to take agency over a situation in which I had no control.

I took a long glug of Spotted Cow as I contended with my powerlessness in the moments the gun went off, then almost spit out my beer when I realized that the pair of legs that ran up behind me at the scene belonged to the young man and his still smoking gun. Recalling how I demanded, "Call 9-1-1!" so forcefully, I was tormented by the realization that in those moments, I was not the master of my fate, and my determination to get the story almost got me maimed for life. I turned off Drew's video. I could not bear to see or hear my frantic failure. Not now.

Independent streamer Ford Fischer, who ran around the block toward the sound of gunfire, filmed another angle of me and others rushing the victim to the hospital.

Elijah Schaffer, a reporter for Glenn Beck's online outlet *The Blaze* was in the Car Source 3 parking lot filming the breaking of windows and the torching of cars before the shooting took place. An hour before I did, he also interviewed the young rifleman who pulled the trigger.

Independent streamer and everywhere man Brendan Gutenschwager's footage captured the second and third shootings from close range. It showed the young rifleman sprinting down the middle of the road. A skinny man with long hair and no shirt dashed up from behind and hit him in the head. The young man continued to run but fell moments later. Another man wearing a gray hoodie ran into the right side of the frame and launched a jumping kick. A gunshot rang out just as his foot connected with the young man. The round apparently missed, because the Jump Kick Man promptly ran away. Moments later, another man with a dark hoodie swung a skateboard and hit the young man in the head. Another shot rang out; the man with the skateboard stumbled and collapsed. One more man with tan shorts and a black jacket ran up, reached for what looked like a handgun, then one more shot from the rifle rang out, and the man clutched his upper arm as he too ran away. The young man got up and continued running down the street. The video ended with him putting his hands up in front of armored police vehicles. With lights blaring, law enforcement drove past the young man.

Shelby did not record any video because she was worried I had been shot, running toward the gunfire to find me. Jorge and Julio had been conducting interviews right up the street.

All of us were present for the peaceful and violent protests around the country the entire summer, and we were also on the ground for the shooting that was now the top headline at every major news outlet in the western world. Despite the footage that clearly showed otherwise, this *Vice News* reporter sat in a desk chair on the salary paid for by a media property that sold for over $500 million, and told her readers that the young man was, "seen opening fire on protesters."

The only reason any of us were there in the first place was thanks to coverage by Wisconsin-native Kristan Harris, who covered the first day of rioting that sparked national attention. Nathan Debruin, born just twenty minutes north of Kenosha in Racine, took photographs of the man with the vaporized bicep as he pulled a Glock from a holster and aimed it at the young man before being shot.

The *Washington Post* was the only major outlet who had a reporter, Whitney Leaming, record consequential content during that night—a verbal altercation between the riflemen guarding the Car Source and rioters after one of the gunmen extinguished a dumpster that was on fire. Leaming dove behind some bushes when the shots went off, then filmed the aftermath of two men dragging the lifeless body of the second man killed through the street like a denim sack of potatoes that was too heavy to lift.

Collectively our footage would become the backbone of the entire trial to come. The content our group of independent and digital native news scrappers recorded had been used as fuel for the far-larger news corporations' narratives in the past. Though we all monetized the content differently, some erring more on the side of commentary than straight news, the capturing of dangerous moments was a critical aspect of the strange riot-roving business that kept us all afloat.

Thanks to my failed filming attempt, I was one of the only people who could speak as an actual witness to the first shooting. Terror about my safety that night boiled into resentful rage as I continued to scroll. We had all risked our butts, and yet the corporate media on both sides cared only for the details that satisfied their audiences to generate more clicks and views.

I finished my Culver's burger and Wisconsin-brewed beer. I was fed up. Shelby thought that the kid was an idiot but agreed that the situation was being portrayed through a partisan lens. I decided that I had to tell the public what I had witnessed. Initially, the only cable news requests I received were from Fox News. Not necessarily a bad thing.

My *Daily Caller* coworkers agreed that Tucker would be the best way to relay what I saw to the broadest audience. Tucker would be the obvious choice. Though he left *Daily Caller* by the time I started in 2017, as the original founder along with his long-time friend and CEO Neil Patel, Tucker attended our Christmas parties for the next few years, and occasionally stopped by the office to shoot the shit.

During a phone call with my family, my younger brother cautioned me on how my eyewitness account may be called into question because of Tucker's reputation among the broader mainstream press.

I told him defensively and slightly enraged, that none of those outlets wanted to hear from me anyways. While I may not have agreed with everything Tucker said during his five hours per week hosting Fox News' most-watched show, at least he said what he wanted, much unlike party-line-toeing guests I saw come in and out of the studio when I worked at NBC.

I shrugged off my brother's claims, perhaps naively not realizing that in 2020, where you worked and what shows you appeared on were more important than what actions you took when on the job, or what you said when you appeared on those shows.

I slugged another beer and had Shelby drive back to the hotel. I collapsed into my room, turned up the air conditioning, closed the blinds, and tried to rest. In the dark, cold room of the historic Stella Hotel, I tossed and turned, puzzling over why I saw those eyes as blue in my mind. Was it because my dad could have done more?

August 26, 2020, 6:14 PM CST: Chicago, Illinois

It matters not how strait the gate,
How charged with punishments the scroll,
—William Ernest Henley, *Invictus*

I was an hour outside Kenosha when I hit Chicagoland rush hour traffic. I took the opportunity to record a video of the Chicago skyline. The black-glass-and-aluminum facade of the Willis Tower rose 110 stories into the kind of gray-blue sky you see when the hot weather begins rapidly vaporizing the wet earth, but it is still a few days from rain. Growing up, I was puzzled by the building and its façade, which looked more like a quarter-mile-long obsidian knife from the Stone Age than it did a skyscraper. During that time, it was called the Sears Tower and was the tallest building in the world until 1998, having replaced the World Trade Center in 1973. By 2020, the Midwestern American brand Sears filed for bankruptcy. The tallest building in the world was now the Burj Khalifa in oil-rich Dubai, and the renamed Sears Tower was repossessed by an NYC-based private equity firm called Blackstone. The company's "equity" was more accurately described as a multibillion-dollar snowball driven by leveraged buyouts of things that became cheap after the American empire teetered on collapse in 2008.

My exhaustion was overwhelmed by awe driving into the Windy City for the first time. Fox News' *Tucker Carlson Tonight*'s team informed me that if I wanted to appear in their studio downtown (rather than by Skype on the shoddy internet at the hotel), then I would have to drive myself an hour and twenty minutes each way. Typically, Fox provided a black car service to and from the hit, but that was not an option because of the after-sundown curfew effective in Kenosha County, which the car would have to traverse in order to pick me up. Shelby had a hit on Martha MacCallum's Fox News show an hour earlier.

Because she couldn't make it into Chicago on time, Shelby was forced to gamble with the hotel internet. I would have to go it alone.

It was a lonely drive in the rented black Chevy Malibu, but at least I was wearing my dad's dark blue shirt. Of the two collared shirts I brought to Kenosha in my carry-on, I selected the navy blue polo that I found in my dad's closet along with the *lucky* riot pants.

It would be my first cable news hit interview aside from the one I did for *Russia Today* (RT) six years prior, when I was barely affording DC rent doing freelance video/drone work and bartending on the side. My buddy Ryan, who was a producer at RT News and also my former co-bartender, figured I would be a good guest booking for his story on the newly established commercial drone community. I flew my drone inside the studio in downtown DC for demonstration, then gave my opinion on how drones would be regulated moving into the future. Though during the RT interview I was terrified that my primitive drone with a Jerry-rigged GoPro camera and a sloppily soldered RC video antenna would malfunction or crash, the subject matter I was about to cover on Tucker was far more politically charged, not to mention that I would be speaking to an audience at least one thousand times the size (or more).

When I arrived at the studio, I went straight to the green room and chugged a few coffees with only fifteen minutes to spare. Due to COVID, the makeup artist who was in the green room informed me that she was only allowed to apply makeup to her previously scheduled guest. I did not particularly care for it anyways, but a gargantuan pimple formed on the top of my wispy mustache from lack of sleep, or from stress. I pleaded with the makeup artist for any kind of solution. She ripped off a piece of sponge and glommed on some flesh-colored substance. My craftsmanship in applying the makeup was no better than my sloppy soldering of the drone I flew in RT's studio. I could not get a read on what the makeup artist thought from behind her mask. She looked at me and said simply, "Good enough."

Feeling less than confident ahead of my appearance and with only a few minutes before taking a seat in front of the camera, I called Brendan, the criminal lawyer who was my oldest and best friend's dad. He advised me to use the words, "alleged shooter," despite the fact that I interviewed the young man the same night and was 100 percent positive that they were the same person. Brendan's advice to use the word "alleged" was spurred by the same paternal instinct when my dad refused to give his name after saving the young man at the beach. Brendan explained that even after the criminal trial was over, there could still be civil suits, and he didn't want me to get sued. He concluded that I should speak slowly and that it would be fine because since I was a little kid, he knew I was cut out for TV. More than anything else, I was stabilized by his steadfast voice in the absence of my dad's.

I sat down in the studio chair and used the reverse camera on my phone for a mirror. The collar of my dad's worn old shirt was wrinkled and sagging. I did my best to smoothly crease the collar then snapped a selfie at 6:55 p.m. CST just before going on air. I attempted a half-lipped smile but the expression of my eyebrows was sad, my eyes glazed over. When I was informed via my IFB earpiece that my hit was confirmed for the top of the show, I felt too numb to be nervous. If I had any butterflies in my stomach, they were either dead or even more sleep deprived than I was. The ratings that night would exceed 5.8 million viewers, up from his average viewership of 4.3 million that summer. Many of the additional viewers likely tuned in to see what went down in Kenosha.

Typically, Tucker would intro the show off the bat. But the first thing that played loudly in the IFB microphone in my ear were sounds from the chaos the night prior. Clips from independent journalists Julio Rosas and Drew Hernandez blared the sound of the personnel fence crashing back and forth, the crackle of a burning car, a dumpster fire put out by a fire extinguisher, and finally a firework bursting over an armored police truck. There was a monitor that displayed the show below the camera lens, but I was set to appear any minute. As I regularly explained to our reporters who did their first TV hits, a common mistake of novice guests is to look down at the monitor to see the host's face, because the viewer becomes distracted if the guest looks away from the lens. I stared at the dark iris of the digital camera lens and listened to the tormented sounds through the earpiece.

Tucker began his monologue. "Two people died, many of the details remain hazy. Big media corporations have done their best to downplay the violence in Kenosha and around the country. But there were a few reporters on the scene last night. One of them, Richie McGinniss of *Daily Caller*, was standing nearby when a man was shot in the head. McGinniss ripped off his T-shirt and used it to try and staunch the man's bleeding. Here's the scene."

The next clip showed Drew Hernandez's camera as he ran over to me addressing the body, which was blurred out but the audio was exactly what I avoided hearing again since the shooting took place: Terrified shrieking, gurgled death knells and all. Tethered to the chair in front of the camera, I was unable to remove or turn down the microphone in my ear. The sound of sadness and despair coursed through my ears and into my veins. My heart rate elevated, and instincts urged me to run. Then the sounds of the chaos stopped and Tucker continued his monologue. "Sorry for the painful video, but it's real. That man later died. At one point the 17-year-old who has now been charged tried to run from the mob; he tripped and fell in the street. A man ran up and smashed him in the head with a skateboard. The seventeen-year-old then fired his gun. Here's the scene." Footage of the second shooting revealed shouts of rage, gunshots, then shouts of fear—although I was relieved that at least it was no longer my own panicked voice playing in my ear.

"So, what does that amount to? We're unsure. A court will decide whether what you just saw qualifies as self-defense. As of tonight, we really don't have more details. We do know why it all happened though. Kenosha has devolved into chaos because the authorities in charge of the city have abandoned it. People in charge, from the Governor of Wisconsin on down refused to enforce the law. They stood back and they watched Kenosha burn. So, are we really surprised that looting and arson accelerated to murder? How shocked are we that seventeen-year-olds with rifles decided they had to maintain order when no one else would?"

Video showed a woman burning an American flag next to the fence around the Kenosha courthouse. She proclaimed, "Death to America!" Another said, "Kill the police!"

The broadcast cut back to Tucker. "That's not Iran, it's Wisconsin! It could have been a dozen other places in this country. The violence has been building unabated for three months now. Every day the mob becomes more radical. If federal prosecutors treated the organizers of BLM and antifa the way they treated Roger Stone, our cities wouldn't look like Kosovo tonight."

According to Tucker, Stone's treatment by the feds was a prime example of a two-tiered justice system.

Tucker continued. "But they didn't do that. Instead, they enforced standards selectively, in direct violation of our most sacred American principle, which is equal protection under the law. They ignored that. Across the country prosecutors responded to politically disfavored crimes with maximum aggression. And they ignored the rest."

Tucker gave some historical context: "A party that tolerates rioting has no future in a democracy. Human beings crave order; it's a prerequisite for life. They fear uncertainty above all. People will trade anything for relief from chaos. That's a fact of human nature. It's always true."

The video box next to him played Julio Rosa's video of a man attempting to dropkick the fence in front of the illuminated pillars facing the Kenosha courthouse. "And politicians who understand that, win. Rudy Guiliani got elected twice in an overwhelmingly Democratic city because he knew that underneath it all everyone hates lawlessness. Everyone. Richard Nixon knew that too. Nixon was not a charming man; no one ever longed to have a beer with him. Yet Nixon managed to win what is to this day the single biggest blowout in American history, the 1972 elections. How did he do that? It was simple. Richard Nixon was for order, his opponent was for chaos. It wasn't hard, it's not hard now. Yet that lesson seems lost on this generation of leaders. Our cities are burning because the people in charge have allowed them to burn."

The camera cut full screen to Tucker at the end of his monologue. "Most Americans are not bigots. Unlike CNN, they are not fixated on skin color. They don't really care—most of them. What you're watching is more sinister than that. What you're watching is the academic left, funded by big business, crush the last remaining resistance to their control of the country. And that resistance is an independent American middle class. That's who they really hate. This is not a race war, this is a class war. Remember that."

During the time after I heard the gruesome footage in my ear, I calmed my breathing. But with all the talk of race wars and class wars I struggled to pull my mind out of the horror of the Shade.

I realized that I was about to be introduced, as Tucker changed the subject back to the present day. "Richie McGinnis found himself in the midst of all of that last night in Kenosha. He runs the video operation over at *Daily Caller*. In the video we saw a moment ago we saw him trying to save that man's life with his T-shirt. Unsuccessfully, sadly. Richie McGinniss joins us tonight." I came up in the two box on the monitor underneath the camera. My facial expression appeared blank and distant, like I was looking through the lens of the camera toward something else.

"Richie, what did you see? First, we had the video we just played, which is just remarkable, what were the immediate circumstances around that?"

I spoke slowly as if I had something else on my mind, beginning with a few words of filler before I actually began to relay any actual information. "Well Tucker, we were out all night and I originally encountered the alleged shooter at a business that..." I started to stutter and panicked. For a moment I thought I would lose my train of thought, "Uh...at...uh... business that had been burned the night previously. And we actually saw some of those people who worked at the business—trying to put the fires out themselves. And the next night we...uh... I actually encountered the alleged shooter at that business and I actually asked him a few questions on camera. And later that evening I saw the same individual in the street drawing a lot of attention due to the fact he had what I thought was an AR-15 strung over his shoulder. And so, a lot of people were shouting at him, at which point I..."

As I got closer to recounting the shooting, I started to lose my grip. "At which point I, uh... Basically, you know...saw him start to run, heard the shots, and you saw the rest on video." I sped up describing the most critical part of the shooting because I just wanted to finish my statement without cracking my attempt at a steady and confident voice.

Tucker changed the topic of conversation, which provided me with instant relief that I would not have to go into more detail on the grisly scene I saw twenty hours before. "From the video, it's not clear that there are any police around. There's a big mob, people have guns, shots are going off, where were the cops?"

Despite the change of topic, I still found myself choking up. "Well... we actually... I'm in..." I took a deep gulp before I finally found my words, "Kenosha with Shelby Talcott and Jorge Ventura, two of my colleagues, and we've been asking people all around town, you know business owners who've had their places looted, where were the police? And they said it took two hours, it took an hour, it took the fire department three hours. So definitely they're there, but obviously not responding in any quick fashion. So the seventeen-year-old who I, uh, interviewed earlier in the night, he actually mentioned that he was there to maintain peace in the absence of police."

Tucker asked, "In one video that we played, he is being chased down the street, and he's hit in the head with a skateboard. Why was that group of people chasing him? Do you know?"

Realizing Tucker was referring to the second person killed, by which time I was already on my way to the hospital, my rattled brain attempted a coherent answer. "Well I believe that the video you are referring to took place after the initial shooting, so I think at that point they were basically looking for whoever who had a weapon on them and obviously the weapon that he had on him was very noticeable. But what I can say is prior to the first shooting that I witnessed, I did see a number of individuals pursuing the seventeen-year-old alleged shooter, and actually the individual who was shot, I did see advance on the shooter very closely."

I continued to stare blankly at the lens until the producers told me I was clear. I rushed to the rental car and called my mom, searching for consolation after what I thought was a stuttering mess. As any mother might, she told me I did great. Even with her support I felt weak and incapable of finding satisfaction or meaning from my prime-time premiere. The man was dead, and I could barely bring myself to figure out why. I missed a turn and drove thirty minutes in the wrong direction. The trip back to the hotel that should have taken one hour took me two and a half hours. It was almost midnight when I was stopped at a police checkpoint before exiting the highway into Kenosha County. I was held until he could confirm that my Congressional Press credential was legitimate. By the time I got back to the hotel, I longed only to return home to the safety of my own bed.

I had to get out of Wisconsin as soon as possible. The next day Shelby enjoyed one more Culver's burger before I drove her and Jorge to Chicago O'Hare airport for our flight back to DC. On one of the most crowded planes we had seen since the pandemic began, I could not find a comfortable position in my cramped airline seat. Far from being the captain of my soul, I was a passenger without control.

August 27, 2020, 10:19 PM EST: BLM Plaza, Washington, DC

A man wearing a light blue police uniform and a pig mask marched along the personnel fence surrounding Lafayette Square, a common rallying point for protesters because the fence blocking the park made it the closest view of Trump's White House, and the southern end of BLM Plaza. By this late stage of the summer, there were hundreds of signs hung from the mesh of the fence, many of them photographs of black Americans who were shot by police.

The fake cop paid no attention to the lively protest around him and instead swung his rubber pig nose back and forth as he scanned the Secret Service and Park Police officers lined up on the inside of the fence, as if they were the ones that needed monitoring. The eternally bucking horse of the Jackson Statue loomed beyond the cops, silhouetted by the floodlit White House a block behind.

When the exaggeratedly porcine cop started north toward St. John's Church, he scribbled with a pen onto a small notepad that rested on a protruding prosthetic stomach. A giant BLM flag waved in the air above us as I strolled up to him and asked, "What's the ticket for?"

With perfect comedic timing, he ripped off the page from the notepad, which I aimed at with my camera: Ticket/No good reason/$150.

As I passed the old church, I walked across huge, freshly painted white letters on the ground next to the giant yellow BLM mural that stretched two blocks to the north: "DEFUND THE POLICE #ABOLISH." A crew of three percussionists banged away on giant bass drums.

Farther north at the intersection of 16th and I streets, a few hundred people were gathered around a large set of speakers that blasted hip-hop music. Aside from the flags and the signs, the scene resembled a block party more than a political protest. Shelby and I met back up and agreed this felt like child's play compared to the shootings and the attempted muggings we experienced over the previous few days. The goal was to keep my mind occupied by continuing my work, but even while standing within the vibrant protest, I found myself preoccupied by the shooting in Kenosha.

Earlier that day, my best friend's dad and now my lawyer, Brendan, sent me the criminal complaint filed by the Kenosha DA against the shooter, Kyle Rittenhouse, who turned himself in to the Antioch Police Department the morning after the shooting. It named Antioch, Illinois, as Rittenhouse's residence, which was only twenty minutes away, but had the entire internet abuzz with the fact that the shooter had crossed state lines into Wisconsin in order to guard the battered Car Source businesses with an AR-15. As I sat in my backyard and discussed the filing with Brendan, I learned that the man he shot in front of me was named Joseph Rosenbaum, and for his death, Rittenhouse was charged with one count of first-degree intentional homicide, carrying a maximum of sixty years.

My uneasiness turned to outright dread when my lawyer read the next paragraph, which stated that I was also a named victim in the case. For the charge of recklessly endangering my safety, Rittenhouse was charged with a potential maximum sentence of an additional twelve years. A count of intentional homicide carrying a maximum life sentence was also added for the killing of a man named Anthony Huber, the one who had hit Rittenhouse in the head with a skateboard in Brendan Gutenschwager's video. The man who I saw missing a bicep in the emergency room was named Gaige Grosskreutz, and for his injuries, there was a charge of attempted first-degree intentional homicide. There were additional charges for recklessly endangering an unnamed victim, and possession of a dangerous weapon by a person under the age of eighteen. The total counts amounted to life in prison plus an additional 144 years.

I felt the pit of dread that one experiences when they lose control of a car or fall helplessly through the air. I was not only a key witness in a case where a teenager's life was held in the balance but also a named victim in a homicide that was rapidly gaining worldwide attention.

The complaint went on to describe select portions of my witness statement from the police station. "The defendant told McGinnis [the document misspelled my name] that he was a trained medic. McGinnis stated that he (McGinnis) has handled many AR-15s and the defendant was not handling the weapon very well." Given that I had made this reference when talking about Kyle's spinning around yelling, "Medic!" and running through the street with a gun in one hand and a fire extinguisher in the other, I also stated that I was "not a gun nut" and realized that the adversarial system of the courts was capable of producing narratives as polarizing as the pro- and anti-Trump press.

I asked my lawyer if we could issue some kind of correction because their characterization of my AR-15 expertise and exactly how Rittenhouse mishandled the weapon was inaccurate based on the statement I gave the cops. He said that while I could file a complaint to the DA's office, that may cast me as a biased witness, which would not be advised. Brendan made it plain that fulfilling my role as a witness would have to supersede a selfish desire to clear my name.

Logging into Twitter after our phone call was a bad idea; my inbox and replies were flooded with messages from people who had just looked into the complaint. One direct message said, "I saw that you claim to have handled AR platforms and that KR wasn't handling his very well. Serious question, where did you receive your training and how long ago was it?"

But anxiousness about my role in the criminal complaint was quickly supplanted by details on the first victim Joseph Rosenbaum, who was publicly identified in the criminal complaint. According to arrest records in Texas, Rosenbaum was previously convicted of sexual conduct with a minor. I thought at first this new information might alleviate my guilt about watching Rosenbaum leave the world, but I could not unpack the image of him bleeding in the back of the SUV that was scarred into my brain. I chose to dive headlong back into coverage of a protest of Trump's speech at the Republican National Convention in DC that night rather than dwelling on the impending trial or the pissed off people online.

My mind remained in a dark place as I sleepwalked alongside Shelby following the pack of a hundred or so protesters who split off from the main group and were marching around to the west side of the White House on 17th Street. They amassed around an exit where VIPs would leave the RNC event after Trump finished a speech officially accepting the 2020 presidential nomination for the GOP, during which he tangentially referenced the recent shooting. "The Republican Party condemns the rioting, looting, arson and violence we have seen in Democrat-run cities like Kenosha, Minneapolis, Portland, Chicago and New York and many others."

A woman stood feet in front of the gate that provided access through the fence to the White House grounds. She puffed a cigarette beneath a plastic pig nose attached to her head by an elastic band. Secret Service joined the Metro Police outside, chaperoning the suited men and summer-dressed women who began trickling out of the gates. Shelby and I gave our nonverbal "stay frosty" nods from behind our cell phones as the guests from the party began exiting the White House South Lawn. They were greeted by unimaginative jeers like, "Fuck you!" and "Fuck Trump!"

We saw Secret Service cops sprint north on 17th and we took off in pursuit. Though I complained that it was a floppy-footwear issue, Shelby beat me by a few steps to the scene. We arrived moments after the Secret Service handcuffed a man with black calf-high socks, black shorts, black flat brim baseball cap, and a black Portland shirt. He was screaming in his defense, "What do you mean? He punched me first! I did not touch that man!" Unconvinced by his version of events, the Secret Service escorted the man away. I complimented one of the Secret Service officers on how fast he ran despite wearing over fifteen pounds of gear on his waist and chest. Apparently, I was not as fast or agile as I thought I had been a few days before.

Shelby and I returned to the exit from the White House on 17th where the rest of the VIPs filtered into the night without any serious physical confrontations. Our riot buddy Brendan Gutenschwager, also fresh off the plane from Kenosha, recorded a viral clip up the street at a different exit, in which Senator Rand Paul of Kentucky and his wife were mobbed by thirty protesters as only a few police battled them back.

Just before midnight, fireworks in celebration of Trump's nomination blasted into the humid but cloudless sky above the Washington Monument. We ventured farther south on 17th for a better view, then climbed atop the huge brass lions perched on marble beds in front of the Corcoran School of the Arts. I tried to keep my hands from shaking as I filmed the pyrotechnic show for our audience, but the smell of sulfur and the boom of the fireworks rushed me back to the angry screams among the gunshots in Kenosha. The finale began in a spectacular series of red flares while a woman in the thinning crowd started a "Fuck Trump" chant with both middle fingers in the air.

August 29, 2020, 11:14 PM EST: BLM Plaza, Washington, DC

A 21-year-old *Daily Caller* intern named Phillip had just taken over a spare room in my house. He told me he wanted to see some protest action, so I agreed to take him along on what was likely to be a lively Saturday night. He sat in the front seat of my old BMW convertible and ogled the crowd as we rolled past the bustling Saturday night protest with the top down. After we parked up the road, I decided that on such a nice night, I would go as low profile as possible and leave my gas mask behind.

As Phillip and I walked up to the swarm of hundreds of impassioned people protesting Trump's nomination by the RNC, I felt dull and uncertain, as if proceeding into the spectacle through a foggy malaise. We walked to the corner of 16th and H streets at the southwestern corner of St. John's Church.

Within moments of locating Shelby by the desert pack on her back, we heard police chanting, "Move back!" I was alarmed and surprised to see the police line spanning all the way across H Street, where I had just driven minutes before. There was a commotion once the chanting cops neared the corner of 16th and H, the southern hub of BLM, where I saw the fake pig cop two nights before.

At least a hundred protesters ran away from the approaching police formation. A few of them stood their ground and engaged with the plastic-armored, truncheon-wielding Metro Police officers. One of these officers discharged a large can of mace that first hit one of the disorderly demonstrators, but then when he swung the can to hit the next one, the stream covered an impressive fifteen-foot distance directly into my face and camera. We all retreated north past St. John's Church, soaked in pepper spray and straining to see where we were running.

The refugees from the enforcement incursion fled to the preexisting group near a drum circle on top of the Defund the Police #ABOLISH mural a half block to the north. The crowd was enraged when they saw their comrades screaming in pain from the spicy liquid that burned eyes and skin. The cops had no mercy for the temporarily blinded belligerents, though, and continued their march north up 16th. They only stopped once they pushed the hundreds attending the protest two blocks to the north at the corner of 16th and K streets. Next to the giant yellow B of the BLM mural, this effectively marked the northern reaches of Mayor Bowser's BLM Plaza.

As I used my own snot to clear my eyes, I didn't even have time to locate our intern, Phillip, before an avenging group of about twenty gathered in front of the newly formed police border, which sealed everyone off from the two-block stretch of 16th Street that made up BLM Plaza. A few plastic bottles bounced off the plastic armor of the cops. Then a glass bottle came out of nowhere and shattered on the helmet of an officer directly to my right.

Almost immediately cops used launchers to discharge smoke canisters and lobbed flash bangs. The smoke flew over our heads while the flashy bangy bois detonated within feet of my feet. The mob only grew angrier instead of backing down.

Through the ringing in my ears, I could barely hear when the cops reissued their command, "Move back!"

They began marching lockstep through the first of six lanes on the normally bustling K Street. As I backpedaled garbling, "Yes sir" through spittle and drool, I regretted leaving my gas mask at home. It was not as bad as the synthetic chlorine tear gas in Kenosha or Portland, but combined with the mace, I was reduced to a slobbery, munition-handicapped version of Hellen Keller.

Behind the curtain of a smoke canister in the middle of the intersection, I spotted something I thought had to be some kind of riot-induced mirage—a foggy likeness of the distinctive graffitied sprinter van coined the BLM Snack Van that appeared in countless viral videos from the summer of riots in Portland. Through the writing of this book, I learned that I had crossed paths with that van in Seattle and Portland.

Only a week earlier, the most recent clip of the van showed it smashed by Proud Boys shields and telescopic metal batons during a Bronze Age–style skirmish against antifa in front of the Mark O. Hatfield Courthouse on August 22. Miraculously, during the seven days since the video was posted, the van repaired its shattered windows and traversed the entire North American continent to the spicy scene in DC.

The driver attempted a right turn from K Street onto 16th to avoid the phalanx of advancing cops.

Unfortunately for the Snack Van operator, a flock of fleeing protesters impeded his turn. The vehicle was stalled like a sitting civilly disobedient duck as cops marched across the double yellow line within a lane of the van. I squinted, unsure of what was about to happen, but too blind to aim. I opted to switch my camera to a wide angle for a broader perspective, the camera equivalent of buckshot to a hunter when the target moves too fast to aim.

One of the white-shirt officers ran through the police line. When he jogged up to the slowly rolling van, he swung his billy club backhanded, resembling an out of shape tennis player slamming a volley over the net. The truncheon pulverized the driver's side window of the Snack Van. Shattered glass rained down on the peroxide-dyed hair of the driver, and then the cop opened the door and yanked him to the pavement.

Given the Snack Van's infamy and the dramatic fashion in which its windows were once again smashed, we would sell this footage for thousands of dollars to the British website *Daily Mail*. Between that and the tens of thousands of dollars earned licensing our Kenosha footage, the violence and absurdity made it a profitable week for the team. But capturing this footage had taken its toll on those who recorded it. After the offensive was over, I located Shelby who still seemed fine, but I was a wreck.

And I still hadn't located my poor intern, Phillip. After they scattered the entire demonstration, police reformed a contiguous line of shields across the south side of the intersection of 16th and K. Traffic resumed on K Street while I tried calling Phillip to no avail. I took a moment to light a cigarette in the hopes that I could replace the acerbic taste of pepper spray with the bitter flavor of smoke.

I didn't even get a chance to smoke it down to a butt because a smaller group of three enraged BLM Plaza refugees approached the shields. The closest one to the cops wore a gas mask with pink respirators atop his head. I recognized it as a 3M brand because it was famously used by Walter White to synthesize crystal methamphetamine in the popular TV show *Breaking Bad*. The other two wore cheap plastic chemistry lab goggles with black masks that covered their head and face. I ditched the cig and began recording.

"Back the fuck up! We goin' off on your white ass!" shouted the first as he pulled the gas mask down over his face.

"Pussy! Pussy!" screamed the second.

"What? Boy what? Do something!" dared the third.

One of the black Metro PD officers raised a large can of pepper spray to his hip with his left arm while he held the shield with his right. He casually swung his arm side to side, dousing the trio as well as me and a few others. I recoiled. "Goddamnit!" I uttered in the complaining tone one might use when their office computer won't turn on. Three flash bangs went off in rapid succession nearby. I aimed the camera at the ground as I scurried back, then turned the lens to face me. I grimaced with one eye open and a Washington Capitals flat brim cap on my head.

The only commentary I could come up with was, "Fuckin' A," before more flash bangs detonated within ten feet while a woman screamed bloody murder in the background, "Fuck you!"

I decided that was enough and began blindly roaming K Street in search of young Phillip. I finally located him at a bus stop a block down the road. He and another young skinny independent journalist were bawling their eyes out while some "medics" dressed in all black with red duct tape crosses dumped bottled water on their faces.

"What the fuck are you doing? They don't need water!" I ordered the two young'uns to walk with me to the car where I had towels in the trunk.

"You just gotta wash your eyes with some snot, dry off, and tough it out, boys."

They were slobbery messes by the time they got to the car, where I applauded them for their bravery as they dabbed their eyes. Phillip's young riot reporter buddy showed me a tennis ball–sized welt from a rubber bullet that drilled his leg. The rubber bullets were plastic 40 mm pill-shaped plastic shells with Styrofoam tips, fired from the same breech-loading launchers that shot metal tear gas and smoke cans. I recalled how busted up I was when I got whacked by two metal canisters in Portland, so I agreed to drive him home. *They got rubber bullets in DC?* I wondered aloud. His welt spoke for itself.

After I dropped the young injured one off, my eyes were still foggy dodging the regular DC potholes, which were especially unkind to the suspension on my 17-year-old BMW. Suddenly, I saw the blue lights of a Metro Police car light up in the rearview.

I had been pulled over more than a dozen times during my twelve years in DC and never got one ticket. I worried maybe this time was different as I examined my extremely bloodshot eyes in the rearview mirror. I went through the standard protocol to keep cops happy, turn the car off, keys on the dashboard, flip the interior light on, and place both hands firmly on the steering wheel. But when the cop came up, his perplexed expression told me that the interior light only aided in revealing me and poor Phil's horrid conditions.

"What the fuck happened to you guys and why is he in the back?"

I looked to the empty passenger seat, then to Phil still crying in the back seat, and suddenly realized that this probably looked like the world's most emotional kidnapping.

"Sorry sir, I just dropped another guy off. This is my coworker at the news website where we work. Your coworkers just pepper-sprayed us big time while we were covering the protests at BLM."

"Is that why you were swerving?"

"No sir, I was avoiding the huge potholes along the bus route on K Street, because my car is very old and she doesn't handle them too well."

Amazingly, the officer laughed and, after he checked my plates (which came up clean because my copious speed camera and parking tickets don't count as moving violations) he told us to get home safe. *White privilege is real and I'm living it*, I thought.

Once we were free, I stopped at a red light, turned my camera to selfie mode and aimed it at my misty eyes. "Hey Phillip, how was your first peppy spray?" I pulled the camera above my head, revealing poor Phillip in the back.

He could barely open his eyes but persevered through snot and spit sputtering, "For the news, man! For the news!"

The video became an instant cult classic clip among the *Daily Caller* staff. After that they acknowledged that mild-mannered young Phillip was totally hardcore. I would ride with him again on our way to capture the Capitol Riot on January 6.

September 4, 2020, 1:30 PM EST: National Mall, Washington, DC

The Friday of Labor Day weekend I drove to the National Mall for a pretaped interview with CNN. Without the fear of breaking down on live television, my nerves were placid as a windless lake. I looked over at the Lincoln Memorial at a stoplight, then up at the Washington Monument as I drove my convertible toward the Capitol. I shifted from first to second then third gear enjoying the tinny roar of the inline six-cylinder engine under the hood of my BMW M3. With the aging combustion engine propelling me down Independence Ave, I was trying to wrap my head around the fact that I was only able to traverse the airwaves from one shore of the political spectrum to the other because of an egregious error of not actually recording the Kenosha events, not because I was the closest witness to the first shooting, or because I attempted to render aid. The facts I brought forth did not favor a particular narrative spun from on high. My appearance on the predictably anti-all-things Trump news network was scheduled only after my words on Tucker Carlson's show were grossly misrepresented in one of their news packages on the Kenosha shooting.

On Sunday, August 30, I received a text from a former *Daily Caller* reporter named Ford saying he saw me on CNN. When I looked up the report, feverish sweat droplets activated residual pepper spray from the

MPD-sponsored hose-down that Phillip and I endured the night before. My insides burned along with my skin.

"The witness to how the incidents began is Richie McGinniss, a journalist for the right-wing *Daily Caller*, who appeared on Fox News, and supported the conservative belief that the seventeen-year-old illegally carrying a semiautomatic rifle was actually there to keep the peace in a town the police left out of control." The piece went on to play Tucker's question, "Where were the cops?" to which I responded, "Definitely they were there, but they're obviously not responding in any quick fashion. So, the seventeen-year-old who I interviewed earlier in the night mentioned that he was there to maintain peace in the absence of police." The reporter continued, "Video footage from throughout the night shows the police were everywhere." This implied that my statement was somehow misleading. In fact, the police were "there" as I stated, but anyone who witnessed the events in Kenosha also knew that the cops utterly failed to respond to reports of property damage, arson, or any other crimes that didn't involve defending the courthouse. I related to Tucker why Rittenhouse decided to show up with a rifle, yet CNN framed this objective observation as support for the shooter.

For the first time in my life, I had to admit that my younger brother's advice was...correct. It was expected that CNN would use what they viewed as a pejorative qualifier, "right wing," (even though *Daily Caller* did not use "left wing" every time they referred to employees of CNN), but this rehashing of my words went much further than that. My appearance on Tucker was being framed as support for the accused shooter.

Fortunately, my Marine boss, Geoff, calmed me down during our Monday morning Zoom call the next day. I was soliciting his advice but spent more time ranting about how I wanted revenge than I did asking how to find a resolution. Rather than admonish me for the nakedly meager threat of going up against one of the largest media empires in the world, Geoff looked at me as directly as he could through the tiny iris of his computer camera. Even through the pixelated distortion of our call, his denim blue eyes pierced through my computer screen while he gruffly told me to hold my fire and go through the proper channel. Contact CNN's head of communications, Matt Dornic, instead. After walking me through the importance of emphasizing how and why CNN made misstatements about me, I cc'd Geoff on the following, perhaps at times emotionally charged email on September 1st:

Hi Matt,

Richie McGinniss here. I am the chief video director at the *Daily Caller*, but I also was witness to the horrific shooting in Kenosha last week.

Attached below is a clip from your airwaves this Sunday during an episode of *CNN Newsroom with Ana Cabrera*, which states, "Richie McGinniss, a journalist with the right-wing *Daily Caller*, who appeared on Fox News, and supported the conservative belief that the seventeen-year-old illegally carrying the semiautomatic rifle was actually there to keep the peace in a town that police left out of control."

But my statement in the sound bite you pulled is "The seventeen-year-old who I interviewed earlier in the night, he actually mentioned that he was there to maintain peace, in the absence of police." There are two issues here:

1) Any google of my name would show that I am not a journalist at the *Daily Caller*—I am the chief video director. They are discernibly different roles.

2) Every single appearance that I have had related to Kenosha, I have been extremely careful to only report what I saw during the shooting and what I heard from Rittenhouse during our interview earlier in the night. Given that I am now the key witness in a homicide, it is essential that I maintain impartiality and stick to exactly what I saw and heard.

In this report, you say that I "supported a conservative belief," as if I injected my opinion on the matter.

That is simply not true, and in fact, I was very clear to state that I was relaying what Rittenhouse told me. I stated, "He actually mentioned that he was there to maintain peace in the absence of police."

In order to rectify this, I would appreciate a correction or an opportunity to come onto your airwaves to speak for myself. I am surprised I have not been contacted by your network earlier, given that you have been running my Rittenhouse interview on all of your shows and I was the closest individual to Rittenhouse and Rosenbaum at the time the shooting started. You can also see in videos on the scene that I rendered aid to the first victim immediately after the shooting, while gunfire was still going off. I also was the one who carried that victim and transported him to the hospital.

Again, my role in this is to be an impartial witness. When your program suggested otherwise, I take that as an unfair and untruthful infringement on my role to simply state what I saw and heard on the night of the shooting.

Given the sensitive nature of this situation, I would appreciate your attention to this matter. If you have any further questions, feel free to let me know.

Best,

Richie

Within two hours, Matt from CNN responded, "They're chasing down. I'll keep on it. Thanks for flagging." I should have been satisfied with his speedy reply, but I was still seething with the same uncontainable anger I would feel when an opposing hockey player beat me to the puck and scored a goal, then skated triumphantly to celebrate before a cheering crowd.

I replied within five minutes, thanking Matt for his attention to the matter but also ending with the combative line, "If I were a reporter for another outlet, I bet you all the money in my wallet that I wouldn't have been treated in this way by CNN. You guys never even reached out to me for comment..."

The moment I hit Send a private email from Geoff hit my inbox: "One point of advice, don't lean on the word 'you' too much in emails to comms staff. Matt had nothing to do with this package. We want him to work with us."

Then Geoff sent another after reading my simultaneous message to him and Dornic: "Dude...now you're being combative. Patience."

I felt like a fool. Without outstanding talent on the ice, my amateur career as a hockey player was distinguished as an antagonizer by using poignant language to knock better players off their game. The downside was that sometimes this feisty tactic would lead me to lose sight of winning the actual game, and I would end up in the penalty box.

While I was blinded by rage, Geoff identified the plainly visible fact that Matt was just one employee of thousands and worked in an entirely different role than the journalist who anchored the report. To add to my professional media *faux pas*, I failed to follow Geoff's advice to avoid the use of "you" by sending a premature email.

That afternoon as I stewed in my poorly air-conditioned home office, the reporter who did the video package, Drew Griffin, reached out:

Richie,

I was forwarded your note.

Regarding the piece you refer to, it was not my intent to label you as advancing the view that Kyle Rittenhouse was acting in self-defense. It was to illustrate how your eyewitness account was being used by Tucker Carlson as evidence to support that theory.

As a fellow reporter, I understand your concerns. I would be happy to interview you, recorded on camera, to discuss your experience and to ask additional questions I have related to your coverage of the events in Kenosha.

Please contact me at your convenience so we can arrange.

Thank you again for letting us know about this.

Drew Griffin

I experienced a mix of embarrassment and satisfaction with Drew's timely and accommodating reply. Most of all I was grateful that Geoff convinced me to extend an outstretched hand rather than a backhanded slap. CNN and *Daily Caller* certainly had different perspectives as companies, yet Geoff's record of acting with integrity (although his Marine humor got a bit vulgar sometimes) earned him a good relationship with their head of comms. Geoff pointed me to a concrete avenue through which the seemingly oppositional companies could find common ground. From the smoldering rubble of the destructive discourse during the summer of 2020, I was given the opportunity for a new way forward.

The same day as my patch-up exchange with CNN, the president visited Kenosha where he participated in a round table that was open to the press. With the Stars and Stripes and a flag of the presidential seal over each shoulder, Trump touted his use of federal troops. "My administration coordinated with the state and local authorities to very, very swiftly deploy the National Guard surge federal law enforcement to Kenosha and stop the violence. And I strongly support the use of the National Guard in other cities."

The New York Times fact-checked Trump's speech with a claim that the Democrat Governor already called them in. "False. Mr. Trump is taking undue credit for the relative calm that has settled this week over Kenosha, a city roiled by protests and violence last week. The governor, not the president, sent the National Guard to Kenosha. And the presence of guardsmen was not the sole factor in tamping down the violence."

Both *The New York Times* and Trump missed the AR-15 in the room — the tragedy happened because neither Trump's late reinforcements, nor the Democratic governor's earlier National Guardsmen who defended the Kenosha Courthouse but let the commercial district burn, did anything to "stop the violence" when it mattered most.

During the same round table, Trump identified the business furniture store that was reduced to ash. "I just came from a visit to one of the businesses that was burned down, B&L Furniture. To stop the political violence, we must also confront the radical ideology that includes this violence. Reckless far-left politicians continue to push the destructive message that our nation and our law enforcement are oppressive or racist."

Shelby captured the match that eventually engulfed the entire business in flames, Jorge interviewed the owner the next day, and I videoed a remote perspective of the building's carcass from a hundred feet above. It burned so brightly and completely that the footage of the devastation went viral. Our business model required headlines that fanned the flames in an environment where oxygen was equivalent to videos of scurrilous behavior spurred by civil unrest. The most successful clips in this combustible atmosphere showed evidence of the other side of the political spectrum committing acts of violence and stupidity.

After hearing the president invoke the business that Shelby, Jorge, and I filmed, I discovered that the letters in the store's name, B&L, were the initials of the owner's mom and dad. This was just one totemic loss in a town that already saw its breadwinners outsourced by trade deals that benefited automotive shareholders, then was shut down by government mandate, finally burned, and put under the national media spotlight because of political gamesmanship between an opining governor and a hard-tweeting, former reality TV commander in chief.

The full picture showed that Trump's casting of both peaceful protesters and nothing-to-lose malcontents as "radicals" failed to acknowledge that all these people were taking to the streets for the same reasons that Trump voters, labeled as racist extremists by left-wing media and politicians, voted him in. An entire media establishment, built up over time, was based upon a business model of pointing the finger at the bad guy across the aisle, as long as it wasn't the corporate advertisers who paid the bills.

What President Trump framed as the incarnation of "radical ideology," arose from the grievances shared by his supporters, all part of the vast underclass spanning the entire political divide.

Trump's claim that the Democrats framed our nation as inherently racist was never fact-checked by *The New York Times* because during the summer of 2020, Democrat politicians and their media allies bombarded the public with coverage that suggested America was, indeed, inherently racist.. In an interview with Anderson Cooper on August 27, Democratic candidate Joe Biden suggested that Kyle Rittenhouse was part of a "militia group," and admonished Trump for not denouncing "white supremacy," framing Rittenhouse's shooting of three white men as a racially motivated crime. Biden visited Kenosha two days after his Republican rival on September 3.

Biden rambled for a few minutes about nothing to do with the city he was visiting before he again attributed the violence to race. "It also exposed what had not been paid enough attention to, the underlying racism that is institutionalized in the United States still exists, has existed for four hundred years. So, what's happened is that we end up in a circumstance like you had here in Kenosha."

Yet Biden's claim that racism "had not been paid enough attention to," negated the National Basketball Association, Major League Baseball, and Major League Soccer teams who canceled games the day after the shooting; the BLM murals painted in major cities across the country over the past few months; the hundreds of Fortune 500 companies who ran BLM-inspired ads; and the tens of millions of Americans who marched in the name of BLM, or at the very least posted a black square in support of racial justice from their social media accounts while sitting on the couch at home. The black square was an Instagram trend where users posted black squares onto their profiles in order to signify that they stood in solidarity with the BLM movement, as if taking a few seconds to post an all-black picture might suddenly rid the country of its racist past.

Biden appeared so oblivious during the round table that it was possible he did not even recall his key role authoring the 1994 Crime Bill, which created funding incentives for prisons that have since put tens of millions of black Americans in prison, more than Jefferson Davis would have kept in shackles if the Confederacy had won the war.

The solid granite column of the Civil War Memorial in the center of Kenosha stood as an imposing testament to the country's racist past. Yet the reality on the streets of 2020 was that skin color was just one component of the greatest class disparity since America's founding. The dominating ultrarich encouraged everyone to stay home, and the pervading plebeians served whatever role they could during the largest transfer of wealth in human history. The benefactors' gig economy revolution—those who were able to transition to working from home in their boxer shorts—were at the top of a system that decimated the middle class during the dot-com and 2008 financial collapses, two colossally greedy failed wars in the Middle East...all accelerated when the coronavirus brought government mandates that shut down millions of businesses around the nation. The technocracy remained satisfied as long as the masses viewed their problems through one zoomed-in angle, rather than a wider perspective that exposed the entire lopsided game. Across colors and creeds, the people I saw around the United States were disaffected youth confronting their harsh prospects through the only avenue presented as worthy of support by the elderly powers that be.

The same scenario played out in cities around the country, where Democrat politicians allowed these BLM-inspired no-cop zones in support of their political tribe, while Trump branded his own form of nativism by labeling all of the protests' attendees as violent radicals. Despite both sides claiming they took the necessary steps to halt the bloodshed, their zero-sum agenda did more to conjure a perfect storm of culminating fears. In all cases these environments eventually gave way to anarchy. The strongest or most heavily armed prevailed, countless businesses were destroyed, and some of the most destitute individuals ended up dead or scarred for life. Then, and only then, would the city shut down the experiment. After that, the programming moved on.

Lockstep with the dueling politics, the media fervor buzzed around the grisly homicides. National network crews flew in from the coasts, arriving in Kenosha like flies swarming scat made of decimated dreams. The stories were gritty and raw and the people at home craved something shockingly real to moor them from remote isolation to the real world.

I expected the politicians to reduce the most politically charged violence to a campaign stop. But in a time when every public figure with a big job was terrified of cancellation for saying the wrong thing, outside the box thinking was but a rare candle amid the downpour of bombastic rhetoric that inundated the two adversarial echo chambers. Now they were propagating the "politically informed" versions of how and why Kenosha was taken by fury. Piecing things together from pavement level, it became increasingly clear that the real cause of the Kenosha tragedy was broken homes and inescapable existential gloom on both sides.

It was the first time that I realized that for one side, Rittenhouse was becoming a BLM-anarchist-destroying folk hero, and for the other, a representation of everything that was wrong with the Trump-voting, AR-15-toting, redneck right. Rosenbaum became either a martyr or a pedo who deserved what he got. I was stuck in between with a simple truth that was detached from ideological ideation. Fulfilling the role of witness would be a far graver manifestation of growing up stuck in between two bros.

I found myself in the same circumstance when my older and younger brother would form an alliance against my stubborn adherence to a singular truth, attacking me from both sides. The older they got the more even the playing field became. By the time my younger brother was an adult, he was the smartest talker and my odds at winning became a long shot at best. Even on the rare occasion that I thought I had won one of those two-versus-one arguments on paper, my brothers would always walk away viewing me as the asshole who wouldn't budge.

Except now I was not fighting for what I wanted for dinner that night or arguing against my brothers about whether or not a cheeseburger was a technology (it is). This time, my embattled position defended a plain-as-day account of the young man I met who, in the middle of a lawless atmosphere, tried serving the role of cop, firefighter, and medic all at the same time. Then another man screamed profanities while chasing after him, reached for his weapon, and was shot dead directly in front of me. The simple approach of sticking to what I saw and heard is what gave me leverage to appear on CNN, who probably would never have given me the time of day were it not for their egregious manipulation of the observations I presented on Fox News.

Drew Griffin's version of my first appearance on CNN's biggest adversary, Tucker Carlson, had been wrong initially. But my assumption that CNN would inevitably give me the cold shoulder because, according to the 2020 standards of news media, they were on the other team, was also wrong. The same night of the shooting, a CNN correspondent stood in front of a burning building in Kenosha with the contradictory headline "FIERY BUT MOSTLY PEACEFUL PROTESTS AFTER POLICE SHOOTING." Griffin's interpretation was preordained when the media-establishment-dug partisan trenches along the BLM uprising months before the shooting took place.

Without Geoff dug in by my side advising me to aim high rather than complain, I would have slung mud to my paltry following by detailing how CNN did me dirty. When I was cornered against my brothers, my first instinct was to lash out. Now, my brothers were on my side, along with Geoff and my best friend's dad, all serving as my guides. Thanks to them I was walking across the wide-open, manicured lawn on the National Mall to greet two CNN employees behind a camera and a cluster of high-powered lights. I brought along our graphics guy, Sagnik, to film the entire interview from our end—as protection if CNN tried taking my words out of context again. I sat on the stool with a posture that reflected my renewed agency as I noticed the sound of rustling trees, which was far more settling than the droning AC unit of a cable news studio. Beyond the camera and lights rose the majestic United States Capitol. It provided a conspicuous reminder of the gravity of the American chaos in which I was submerged, though my eyes had to remain fixed on the black orb of glass that refracted my face to the digital camera sensor beyond.

When Griffin got on the line, he jumped right into a question after a brief introduction. "So how did you get into town and what was your assignment?" I could tell Sagnik didn't expect it either as he fumbled with my phone then began videoing from the side.

Turning to the CNN camera guy, I inquired, "Wait, are we rolling?"

The producer next to him confirmed that they were, indeed, rolling. Usually, I was the one behind the camera, but here I was in the news equivalent of an "away game," where I was on their field and they made the rules. One approach I would use in confrontations with larger, faster, opposing hockey players was known as the "face wash," where I would rub my smelly glove all over their nose and eyes behind the play. The move was never intended to hurt them, though the stench of another man's unwashed sweat was humiliating. I interjected while I still had the chance to take some command of the situation. "Real quick, Drew... I'm thankful that you brought me back on and I did feel that you made some misstatements about what I said previously, and you did imply that I injected some opinion in this, but my role here is to tell you what I saw and what I heard as a witness." This was my insurance policy. In case Griffin selectively edited the ensuing footage, Sagnik's cell phone video would ensure that I at least entered my viewpoint into the public record. I felt at ease once I got it off my chest and Sagnik steadied the camera phone, even though my subtle jab received zero acknowledgement from the CNN crew or the reporter on the line.

Drew continued with the interview, which lasted for twenty minutes. It seemed to go well. All the questions were purely topical, but I could never be sure how it would be edited before air.

On the ride home, Sagnik and I went back and forth about how it went. I used the full breadth of the three empty lanes on Constitution Avenue to avoid the potholes, neglected since the tourists no longer frequented the Mall and a federal stimulus was paying workers to stay home. I lamented that all of us were stuck in our respective ideological ruts, unable to touch the grass growing above our earthen entrenchments. As an Asian-Indian immigrant, Sagnik agreed that in America, above the infighting there was so much more.

It was a feeling of powerlessness that I experienced when Shelby and I acknowledged that we may be mere pawns when we published footage of the vicious Proud Boys beatdown outside CHAZ. I was caught in the center of yet another instance of what was being framed as political violence and it seemed there was little I could do to prevent the system from slicing the full picture into two distinctly different, binary tales. I was just as helpless as the protesters and rioters who became expendable foot soldiers on the front lines of the 2020 presidential campaign.

⋮⋮

The riots in Kenosha began when Jacob Blake, whose father abandoned him on a doorstep when he was a child, wrestled with and then was shot seven times by cops. Kyle Rittenhouse's dad was an absent drunk. Joseph Rosenbaum, whom Rittenhouse killed first, had a dad who was convicted of murder and, according to court records, his stepdad sexually abused him at a young age, including anal rape and forcing Rosenbaum to watch while he abused another minor. Rosenbaum passed on the same evil to others who were also minors. He was charged with abusing multiple victims under the age of 15, then convicted of sexual assault of a minor in the second degree. Some of those whom he assaulted went to jail for the same crimes. Rosenbaum was released from a mental hospital the morning before he was killed. The bag he threw at Rittenhouse came from that hospital. Anthony Huber, who was the second man killed by Rittenhouse's AR-15, had a father who tried to give him away when he was a kid, then started another family in another state. Huber was convicted of domestic assault for strangling his brother and kicking his sister. An avid skater, the skateboard he used to attack Rittenhouse was also his solace.

Friends gathered for a memorial at Kenosha Skatepark the day after he died.

These cycles of tragedy were rooted in an intergenerational sequence of sadness, all ruinous illustrations of the Information Age's termination of the American Dream. The lowest rung was unhappy with their stations in life because the tracks laid previously would not take them to a better future, and the billionaires were on Instagram bragging about private jets.

In the six months since the pandemic spread to America's shores, the absence of in-person relationships and economic prospects were filled by the most immediate family in a digital world — the political tribe. This impassioned desperation was seen in the faces of the kettled protesters in front of St. John's Church, the rioters using ropes to tear down Jackson and his horse, the budding idealistic yet ultimately violent experiment known as CHAZ, the autonomous zone defending umbrella wielders facing off against the NYPD in front of the replica of the Arch of Constantine, the shielded leaf blowers battling walls of tear gas dealt by federal storm at the Mark O. Hatfield Courthouse in Portland, and the Kenosha activists, arsonists, and anarchists alike.

The notion that one's political identity was the foundation of their being was fed to the lonely hundreds of millions watching at home by an overwrought, atrophied press. The wall-to-wall attention that the shooting in Kenosha gained confirmed a symbiosis between the second and fourth estates.

In nineteenth-century France, the second estate was represented by the nobility, the top one percent. With the rise of cheaply produced mass media, the fourth estate became the journalists, the overseers of the public square of the realm. History proved that when the second and fourth estates get in bed together, as they did during the World Trade Organization protests in 1999, then the third estate, the 99 percent, gets screwed. In twenty-first-century America, the nobility was the wealthy urban and suburban elite. America's fourth estate was still the press, but they were beholden to their corporately endorsed narratives rather than their Constitutionally protected responsibility: keep the nobility in check. This was translated and accelerated now that news was mostly consumed on the internet rather than the TV, through multi-billion-dollar algorithms engineered to keep people engrossed by partisan rage or fear of an ever-spreading virus while in remote purgatory at home.

In this digital news world, with local news sources rapidly dying, massive multinationals swallowed up smaller news companies that told us their versions of the world. It was easy to forget that the people speaking robotically on TV and the staff who supported them work for these big companies because their substantial footing provided a steady, well-paying wage. The radical activists and malcontents out in the streets clung as tightly to their causes as the news generators did their jobs. The only difference was that the activists rebelled against the broken system because they could not attain one of these well-paying jobs, while the newscasters pontificated so their positions could be maintained.

Jobs in middle-class towns like Kenosha, once an automotive capital, had been shipped overseas. The freedom to gas up a car and drive to a job or a dream was beyond the growing have-nots, while the corporate elite with its coastal, outward-looking, internationalist worldview profited more than ever before. The American body tasked with holding truth to power didn't care about the little guy or his small towns anymore, unless it served an agenda that sounded nice in an air-conditioned board room.

I wanted to lash out at these institutions. I was angry watching the life extinguished in front of me being used for ratings and political points.

⁙

Pasted across the news websites I read every morning, the specter of the upcoming trial haunted me even while I was at work. The Fortune 500 advertisers and politicians shamelessly pandered to BLM, an objectively corrupt nonprofit that trickled only a small fraction of their tens of millions in donations to the grassroots groups I saw demonstrating on the streets.

When the CNN package aired on an episode of *The Situation Room with Wolf Blitzer*, I was relieved that it stuck to my observations. Because it was not a live broadcast, Griffin and his team edited the interview down to five minutes. It turned out Sagnik's safety recording was not necessary because the package did a thorough job of summarizing how I came to meet Rittenhouse, and, without additional editorialization, what he said during our interview. It even included my description of Rosenbaum pursuing Rittenhouse and then lunging for his gun in the parking lot, despite the fact that that ran counter to the narrative that most of CNN's hosts were describing for the previous week; namely that the demonstrators were "mostly peaceful," and Rittenhouse had not been chased down by the deceased as the conservative outlets had claimed.

During the CNN interview, my exact words were, "I think there has been a lot of confusion as to whether or not Rosenbaum was pursuing Rittenhouse. I did see him running after Rittenhouse, Rittenhouse running away from Rosenbaum. And I did see Rosenbaum reach for the front portion of Rittenhouse's rifle. I was extremely close to them at the time, and I know what I saw with my eyes."

At this point in the interview, I used my arms to demonstrate how Rittenhouse had the gun aimed toward the ground, dodged around the advance, then fired. "He lunged for the gun, and Rittenhouse had the gun in this position. He dodged around the lunge, and that's when he releveled the weapon and fired."

The package covered the aftermath of the shooting in vivid detail, using my account interwoven with clips by Drew Hernandez, Ford Fischer, and Brendan Gutenschwager. With a little bit of finesse and a proper application of professional pressure, CNN diverged from the corporate talking points, unearthing a nascent bridge I had not seen before the coverage surrounding the riots landed me in the mud.

⋮ ⋮ ⋮

The Gilded Age once separated the rich and the poor more than any other time in the country's history. But Irish immigrants like my McGinniss ancestors, who arrived during the Potato Famine of the 1840s, were given stable, good-paying government jobs as firemen and cops on Long Island. My grandfather was born in 1897, the youngest of eleven and the first one in the family to attend college over the bridge in Manhattan at Columbia School of Journalism.

The difference between America and the collapsed empires of the past: America has a Constitution, and within that Constitution is enshrined the freedom of the press. Unlike countries under the postcolonial order that America's ruling class inherited, our country was not founded by a treaty in which it was carved out cynically on a map. It was started by forebearers who crossed land and ocean to build anew.

While Boss Tweed built up incredibly corrupt wealth, a fresh wave of unwashed off the boats was enfranchised by Tweed and provided a living wage. The cartoonist Thomas Nast, though Tweed outweighed him by at least 150 pounds, took down the hulking Boss through the Gilded Age version of an internet meme.

From that shift came a middle class that filled the great gulf that the new American power of industry gouged between those who provided capital and those who labored below. The color printing press, originally reserved for the powerful publishers, eventually gave alternative papers and tabloids a voice. Unrestful periods like the counterculture movement of the 1960s inspired a course correction. The alternatives filled their front pages with news of the riots of the late 1960s, when the institutional papers of record were too corporately minded to care.

In 1947, in an article in the *Chicago Daily Tribune* headlined, "KENOSHA: RARE BLEND OF GRACE AND INDUSTRY/City Looks Ahead, but with a Glance Back," the author, Rita Fitzpatrick, declared a bright future for Kenosha: "But here on the high ground overlooking a sweep of Lake Michigan shoreline is a compact city that has blended its background with its future, and might well typify the American story." It went on to identify the storied history of humble men that made Kenosha into the promising city of its day: "Its pioneer tales are of simple, sturdy settlers who came west by wagon train, and cart, by horse and schooner, to clear a shore and carve a forest into a city." This lofty perspective was now but a sad memory, stacked in the classic stone Kenosha library just up from the shore.

From the wreckage of two World Wars rose a new middle class, one with an optimism typified in Rita Fitzpatrick's article and one that my parents rebelled against and, with the Stonewall riots and the Summer of Love, marked their generation's moment to chart a new course. They inherited the system their protests once proclaimed broken, and their generation still runs it today. My parents' mistakes, our country's mistakes, all in the past. In spite of their progress, the burdens of racism, bigotry, condescension, and hate remained a scarred anchor, dragging America down and drowning its aspirations in resentful despair. In 2020, demonstrators and rioters were once again marching in the streets, an inflection point or perhaps the final primal scream of a teetering empire just before its fall.

The first night in Kenosha.

Protesters confronting the police line.

Cops expanding the police line.

Armored Personnel Carriers, aka Bearcats, were brought out to bolster the police line.

The crowd retreated into the park.

The crowd inching closer to the police line.

Reinforcements arrived from a march to bolster the crowd in front of the Kenosha Courthouse.

Fireworks exploding in the police line.

Cops responding with volleys of pepper balls, flash bangs and tear gas.

Police preparing an offensive.

Protesters/rioters forced back by tear gas and pepper balls.

A garbage truck set alight amidst the pandemonium.

Fireworks launched from behind umbrellas and repurposed road signs.

A premature fireworks explosion inside the umbrella gang.

Examining a rock that came up short of its target—along the trolley tracks in no-man's-land.

Recording from no-man's-land.

A flaming broom sweeping trash in front of the police line, with "BE WATER, SPREAD FIRE" graffiti in the background.

Fireworks illuminating the umbrella gang's last stand.

"Trash dragon."

From left to right: Bearcat, Stella Hotel, burning cars, church.

Bearcat in front of the burning furniture store.

An elevated angle of burning cars in the Car Source 1 parking lot—
moments before the attempted mugging.

The volunteer fire brigade used buckets and a power washer to put out
fires at the Car Source 2.

The National Guard finally showed up for the final broadcast of the night.

Construction crews erecting non-scalable fencing in front of the courthouse.

Fencing completed in front of the Kenosha County Courthouse.

Community-led cleanup.

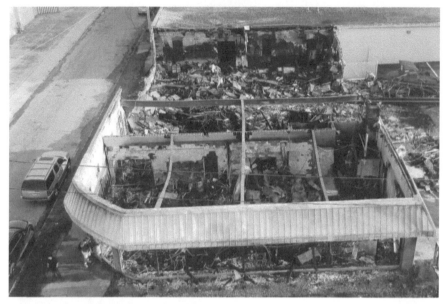

Aftermath at the B&L Furniture store.

Damage from above.

Damage from above, continued.

The Car Source 1 parking lot, burned to a crisp.

RIOT DIET

From bottom to top—burned cars, church, Kenosha waterfront, Lake Michigan.

Attempted burning of the flag right before pepper balls foiled the plot.

The umbrella gang in front of non-scalable fence.

The umbrella gang backing up behind trolley tracks while using a
dumpster for protection.

Fireworks exploding in front of the Bearcat as cops came out in front of the fence for an offensive.

Umbrellas vs. Bearcat.

Filming the scene wearing my BLM shirt. *Photo by E. Mackey @emackeycreates.*

Stealing a peek as cops emerged from behind the fence. *Photo by E. Mackey @emackeycreates.*

Retreating with my hands in the air. *Photo by E. Mackey @emackeycreates.*

Surveying the expanse of the police line. *Photo by E. Mackey @emackeycreates.*

Less than an hour before I used the BLM shirt to stem the bleeding. *Photo by E. Mackey @emackeycreates.*

The longest police line I ever saw.

Police mounting an offensive to push protesters/rioters out of the park.

The baby-faced rifleman explaining his mission in front of the Car Source 2.

Following Baby Face and Biceps Guy away from the Car Source 2.

Yellow Pants confronting Baby Face minutes before the shooting.

The photo I took of the ground outside Car Source 3—instead of hitting video Record moments before the shooting.

Moments before appearing on *Tucker Carlson Tonight,* wearing my dad's blue polo shirt.

Man dressed as pig-cop, writing me a ticket for "NO GOOD REASON."

RNC fireworks over the Washington Monument.

Ripping a bogey in front of the police line.

Moments before the cop smashed the window of the BLM Snack Van.

A cop about to pull BLM Snack Van driver from the vehicle.

"Hey Phillip, how was your first peppy spray?"

"For the news, man!"

My appearance on Fox News' *Tucker Carlson Tonight,* reframed by CNN. *Screenshot from CNN Newsroom and Fox News Tucker Carlson Tonight.*

Correcting the record on CNN. *Screenshot from CNN Situation Room with Wolf Blitzer.*

At the beach where my dad saved a young man's neck 20 years earlier.
Photo by Alex.

EPILOGUE.

September 6, 2020: DC to Long Island

I pack up my bags at my house in DC, and get ready to join my family in New York, back to the beach where my dad once saved that young man's neck on a hot August day. Labor Day initiated the end of summer, but also the best month for surf. The water remained warm, and the hurricanes send waves from their far away torrent of wind and rain. The swells generated are more harmonic and organized than any local storm could create; they arrive in pristine weather, groomed by the miles traveled, a memory of entropy turned to glorious waves. With the change of the seasons the days would grow shorter, the ocean frigid, but the heat from the summer would yield a harvest that could sustain life through the cold.

Dad succeeded where I failed, I think to myself as I turn over the old but sturdy six-cylinder engine. It may not start the first time, but it has never failed ignition on the second try. The pistons begin vacillating, a testament that some machines stand the test of time.

I purchased the car in the summer of 2018 because one of the last cognizant sentences my dad uttered was, "I have two regrets in life—selling that M3, and not letting you play goalie."

I scoured the country for the exact model my dad once had, a stick shift E46 BMW, black exterior with a gray, brushed chrome interior, manufactured between the years 2001 and 2006. This was the last good model because in 2007 the Bavarian Motor Works switched to a glitchy, computer-controlled V8 engine that was oversized and too complex for easy repair.

I was especially interested in driving that model because my dad sold the car right before I got my license, and I never got a chance to drive it proficiently on my own. I only had a learner's permit at the time, so I was nervous just to keep from stalling with my dad watching closely in the passenger seat, performing a far less competent version of when I saw him drive. He would get back behind the wheel and I would admire him shifting succinctly and calmly. Then we'd pull into a wet parking garage or a sandy lot by the beach. With a twinkle in his blue eyes, my dad would burn rubber in first, second, and third gears. Fifty-something years old, fishtailing the little coupe at over fifty miles per hour like a kid in a go-cart.

After a year of searching after his death in 2017, I finally found my car at a dealership only a few miles from my house in DC. The only difference between that M3 and my dad's was that mine was blue and with a retractable roof, while his was black with a hard top. I even got some pads and started practicing hockey goalie, driving the old car to play.

While my goalie skills still had me defending the net as well as Swiss cheese, after a few years owning the vehicle, it became a mechanical extension of myself. The familiar interior was like a time capsule that harbored a safe atmosphere because its smell and sound brought back a time when someone dependable was driving the car. It had the same smell, the same sounds. When I put the ragtop down and pop the clutch, I listen to the tires squeal. The back end breaks free, the smell of rising rubber smoke hits my nose. His spirit is with me behind the wheel.

As with the death of my dad, I face a choice. I either learn from the tragedy or let it drag me into infectious pain. My dad was faced with the same choice after my grandfather died when he and his twin brother were twenty years old. My Dad decided to become a doctor after that, to fix broken people and give a stable life to his future family. His twin never had a family, and succumbed to substance abuse that killed him before his time.

I resented my dad for being a hard-ass when I was a trouble-making adolescent and young adult. After he passed, I realized it was his sternness that guided us. His flaw…the unhealable scar of his dad dying early, his mom selling the house he grew up in at the wrong time, then squandering what money they had. By the time he was a senior in college he had no bed to sleep on in the condo his mom bought. His twin and younger brother fell into the drug scene, which strengthened his motivation to protect his three boys.

The last time I started the convertible on my way to the CNN appearance, I thought that our generation was doomed, that the Boomers ran our future into the ground, just as my dad's twin brother was irreparably maimed by a muscle car that flipped over and landed on his arm. But then, during a moment of strife after Kenosha, as in past moments of American unrest, I saw the potential for a new road.

We are ensconced in a fog, where time is viewed in 15-second clips and 4-year elections. As with the printing press, the technology of the internet was quickly consolidated under huge companies that controlled distribution, only granting exposure to the stories they deemed worthy of clicks. But with time people will find alternatives, as they had during the paradigm shifts of the past. The torrent of disunion only made the beacon of good faith burn more brightly through the dark clouds of the storm.

But this is not the pages of history, a slide deck for a fancy tech company, or a sexy headline that would get clicks on the site, this is my real life. Unlike those who watched the shooting then put down their phones, there is a part of me that will never forget. My voluntary recollection of the event—as when speaking to police about the position of the shooter's gun, the lunge for the front portion by the pursuer, the gunshots in rapid succession—can easily be brought forth as if taking a book off a shelf and quoting a passage, growing into more of a memorization than a lived experience with each time I read.

I now know my eye is not a mere camera that records pixels of the images I see in my brain.

There's an impression there too, the feeling I had while witnessing what happens when lawlessness and doom take hold. It's this involuntary remembrance that mauls me when I am not ready, entirely independent from my pictorial memory sitting quietly collecting dust on a shelf. I take the book down and tell the story when people ask about it. I feel nothing at all. But when I hear a garbage disposal or the gargle of an emptying toilet, it fires up the part of my brain, and of the Kenosha story, that cannot be quieted no matter what the history of that day will say. All those who were at the deadly center of the tragedy share the DNA of a series of disasters that spanned from ogre father to son, only to be overcome if we can rise out of the nightmare and see the existence of a revenant dream.

On my way out of town, I stop at a McDonald's. I hear the last remnants of a soda being drained through a straw and it comes flooding back, not the images or the pictures in my mind, but the sensation of watching defiled hopes disappearing into the pit. All the evil things Rosenbaum did grab hold of every fiber of my being. Perhaps in these instances I recall my dad's vibrant blue eyes as some kind of defense mechanism, as if my dad's death is shielding me from the wickedness of those who confront the shade and see nothing but remorse.

I have successfully compartmentalized my understanding of Rosenbaum, filed away neatly in the unfeeling part of my mind. What I learned about his despicable past after the shooting is cataloged there too. But the experience of watching his life extinguished is alive and always nearby. It stalks me like a stray dog in the dirty streets of my subconscious, biting my pleasant thoughts when I hear an angry man howl in the street or smell sulfur when fireworks go off nearby. These recollections obey no orders or laws.

I plead with the thinking part of my brain. *I never knew the man and only saw him for a few minutes, why me? I barely know him, get away from me you mangy fucking mutt!* I think I've kicked it away because it runs back into the dark alleys. No matter how much I rationalize why Kenosha happened, the mutt won't go away. Here I am sitting in the McDonald's waiting and I'm fighting tears because I can't get the regretful eyes and blood-gurgling breaths out of my brain.

I realize that with tragedy you have no choice in the matter because it's untamed and has the primal instincts to know when the time is right to strike. I guess my dad didn't make a choice to move on. The terrible imprint of living through his family thrown into disorder hardwired in him an unflinching instinct to keep his kids protected from the reckless abandon that consumed him and his brothers after his father's death, a trauma which sent his twin brother and two of his younger brother's three sons down a seductive numbing of the mind that took their lives. He lived with the grief and simply tried his best to ensure his own family would not endure the same fate.

There's no place to put this mangy dog, no leash I can summon to control it. So, I wipe my tears in the McDonald's and realize that they're calling my order for two McDoubles with extra McD sauce.

I'm not hungry anymore because I'm thinking of what the cow sounded like when it was killed, of how the cow once lived in a hellish McDonald's slaughterhouse and probably died on some dirty patch of concrete with fear in its eyes, consumed by doom just like the evil man I saw die. The abundantly cheap burger and the ample fake sauce are only so cheap and tasty because of that cow's dread. I want to move on, but I can only summon tears.

I leave the McDonald's, and I ask myself why I can't just heal and forget. Now I'm crying in the parking lot and I'm mad I can't stop. I'm mad at myself for being too weak to man up. I'm mad at all the clean-cut newscasters who stirred up tumult then moved on without so much as a yawn. I keep telling myself it was just a few minutes of your life, get over it. I hear the comments on Twitter, telling me I'm a pussy or that I should end up like the dead pedo if I feel any remorse.

I feel too much remorse; it is almost too much to stand. My mind steers to that man's sad childhood, of whoever his dad killed, what terrible things his stepdad made him endure, the abuse he then passed on to other kids, some of whom committed the same horrific and unspeakable crimes. My brain is a boat without a rudder heading straight for the rocks. I feel as helpless as I did that night, and in my panic I can't breathe.

I'm stuck with Rittenhouse.

When I walk outside, his puppy eyes longingly stare me down. This is a different stray that's not mangy or angry, it's fluffy and sad, because his first owner never gave him a secure home. He bit the man who failed to properly train him and now he's sitting in a pound waiting to get put down. Those puppy eyes won't stop looking at me. He's quietly whimpering because in an instant he was cast into the unforgiving world. He is grown up in size and weight, but his whiskers are too faint to see. This dog knows what death looks like. Judgment day is nearby. and it will determine his fate. I know those puppy eyes are deceiving because they can aim swift destruction—and they did. I give up blaming this dog, not because it is worthy of forgiveness but because it was too naive before it was too late. I don't know where to put this dog either. I try to leave it outside because it's not mine.

I didn't kill those men—he did! It's his fault! I tell myself this because I don't want to see his sadness in my mind. *You stupid fucking kid! This isn't* Call of Duty. *This is real life, and there are bad mother fuckers out here!* If I had told him that when we first met, maybe we wouldn't be here. Maybe it's my fault. I've given up trying to reason with these visions, so I just accept there's no right answer and I carry that instead. I know logic is of no use to box up this tragedy and put a ribbon on it so I can tell everyone I've shelved it, that these are the good guys and the bad guys, it's neat and OK.

I don't know where to put these damn dogs, so I just let them follow me to my car.

I throw away the McDonald's because the miserable cow deserves at least some kind of burial.

Even if it's in a landfill, it would be better than being eaten by the stomach acid that digests the ground-up animal inside me, or the dogs. I get back in the car.

The dogs jump in the back.

When I hit the three-lane highway I know where there are no cops and I can go fast. The engine swallows up my wandering thoughts. First, then second, then third, gear, an ascending bawl as the old engine heats and climbs up the gears. The sound of the fuel exploding under the hood is soothing, proof that mankind can bottle up the fury and bend it to our will; that some chaos can be tamed and turned into pure motion down the road.

With the top down, there's plenty of room for all of our baggage beneath the bright blue sky. I'm gliding across the wide-open road from fifth to sixth gear at over a hundred miles per hour. The sordid experiences blur into one solid abstraction, like the lines on the road. In that moment, there's such a broad, open landscape in front of me I no longer find my eyes looking back. But I am speeding so I steal a glance at the left side view mirror to look for cops who might be pacing my speed.

I see only the mangy dog, his tongue out and his crooked, fucked-up teeth glistening in the light.

Then I look out the right-side view. The puppy has his head out of the car in the wind, the eyes scanning the huge open space, not with terror, but with glee.

On my way to the coast, I'm glad that I have the expanse of American pavement laid before me—some of it battered and old, but other stretches freshly paved by a new generation. I go faster. I can't even hear the engine anymore. I don't need to draw breath because there is so much air. I can't feel the burn or the pain, only the heat of the sun and the sound of the cool wind.

A PREVIEW OF RIOT DIET II

PROLOGUE

January 6, 2020, 2:10 PM EST: United States Capitol West Plaza, Washington, DC

A man wearing a MAGA hat looked more like a Capitol Hill staffer than a rioter, except that he was using his suit jacket as a protective mask for his eyes and mouth while blindly blasting a bunch of police officers with a can of mace. I had just shown up to the ol' "Insurrection" as half the country called it. The other half called it a "false flag" or a "police-sponsored tour of the Capitol." When I arrived at the western plaza the two groups were already clashing and all I could ask myself was, *why am I better prepared than that cop?* A maskless officer turned away and doubled over hacking and crying. Walking past him casually, I shook my head. He was still clutching the metal barrier bearing a small white sign, "PROPERTY OF U.S. CAPITOL POLICE."

Not for long.

I proceeded from stage left through the spicy mace curtain like a breeze. By this time, it was January 6, and this deep into the post-election chaos, I knew the routine at yet another "Stop the Steal" street fight: hoodie over a bullet proof vest, bulletproof backpack, ballistic helmet, and gas mask. I held my skateboard in my left hand as a potential shield, though its primary purpose was to glide through traffic in a rush to capture what was sure to be bad. In my right hand I carried my phone, slowly turning my torso with a steady arm to show both sides of the battle on the west side of the Capitol. *Is this legal? Is that guy carrying a baseball bat? Where are the rest of the cops?* I was very confused, but my job was simple, bundle up behind a mask and some Kevlar and turn the camera to capture what the people needed to see.

I was plodding along; the mission had to remain simple. But after I entered the pit—the valley of ashes between the Trump supporters who wanted to change the official results of the election and the cops who were enforcing the certification of electoral college votes for the next President of the United States—my mission evolved: Avoid getting whacked and don't let go of the phone. During nine months of covering America's unrest, I had learned how munitions and the spice tend to scramble one's ability to think. What followed the spice and the brain scramble was nearly always unthinkable.

A 5-foot upside-down American flag hung from a 10-foot pole rooted in the hands of a man with plastic reinforced gloves on the MAGA horde's leading edge. The flag was hanging down on the other side of the "blue line." An officer emerged from behind the inverted stars and stripes wearing his plastic visor flipped up and a light blue cloth gaiter, which did nothing to protect him from the pepper spray. But he struck me as a man who would not get phased by mace or much of anything else. He stood 6'3" with a torso the size of an oil barrel. He was carrying two large cans of mace, and discharged one of them across the bedlam in an even thicker cascade, sidearm winging it like a paper boy might casually toss a newspaper at a door while riding along.

The MAGA dude in the suit, unfazed, shouted, "You fucking traitor! You fucking traitor!"

The next officer on the line was one of the fortunate minority with a gas mask and full riot gear; he donned more pads than I do at a men's league hockey game. He held onto a temporary metal police barrier and his plexiglass shield simultaneously.

A guy wearing blue jeans and a black Carhart jacket hugged the thick brass banister that guided four long, flat marble stairs below the Capitol Police's last line of defense. He had his own 3-foot flag stationed vertically and rolled around its pole, as if holstered temporarily while he utilized the metal railing's mooring for better stability. He kicked the riot shield, knocking the officer backwards.

What a bunch of sorry bastards we are, I thought. I saw in Drop Kick Carhart Guy the rest of the country—probably stacked to his middle-aged man titties in debt, addicted to sugar food, with payments on an over-priced truck, nowhere left to turn but rolling up his flag and kicking the plastic shield of a cop. And that poor copper probably didn't think he'd be overrun by thousands of pepper-spray-drunk Trumpers when he woke up and had his cup of coffee that morning, that's for sure. America drank coffee over tea, the buzz from tea being too mild and the taste too soft. Especially at this time, people were ready to get jacked up. *POTUS-tweet. News man mad because Orange Man bad.* So history goes. I can unequivo-cally confirm that America rocks harder than anywhere else.

I was watching the whole thing from behind the two portholes of the scratched-up tempered glass on my Desert Storm–era M40 gas mask. I was just bumbling along; my hands burned a bit but that was it.

Covered from head to toe in pepper spray, I used the interior of my 50% polyester hoodie to clear the lens of my phone from the pepper blur. I was only 20 feet from the half-completed inauguration tower I knew would give me a better angle of the fight. But before I could make it, I had to cross a bedlam the likes of which I have never seen.

Right in front of me was Ray Epps, who would become the Q Shaman of the right, the real bad guy behind the sacrifice ritual that January 6 turned out to be. Another cloud of something spicy went off and wafted from the inauguration tower down the line. Could be a smoke grenade, could be hard tear gas. Hard to tell with the mask on. I was masked up on a nice stroll. *Are you human? I am a meat popsicle* I thought, mimicking Bruce Willis' deadpan delivery from the futuristic apocalypse film *The Fifth Element.*

An officer discharged more pepper spray as I walked through the veil of smoke. Mother Nature was not kind to the officers of the law on this afternoon of January 6. With a steady, cold breeze from the northwest, the clouds of both the smoke and the spray wafted toward the defend-ers of the U.S. Capitol's western front, rather than the hundreds stacked up to thousands who were watching their brothers and sisters in their political tribe in an all-out battle against the Metro and Capitol Police. Another gap for me to continue my mosey along the line.

A metal barrier was missing from the section directly underneath the inauguration tower. I assumed it was forcibly removed then dragged down the four stairs into the mob. A man wearing a tricorn hat like minutemen at the Battle of Lexington and Concord was holding onto the adjacent barrier that was swung 45 degrees toward the stairs. Rendered blind, he might have remained steadfast, had one of the Metro officers not smashed his hand with a telescopic baton. Ouch. Drop. The Revolutionary War Hat Man covered his eyes and clutched the hand that had probably just been broken. He promptly abandoned his post, turning from the police line then retreating into the crowd. I stepped around the metal fence and continued my stroll.

Ray Epps ran down the stairs to avoid the spicy skirmish located between the two of us. Four Metro Police officers were beneath me at various levels of the stairs. I assume they ventured beyond the police line to wrestle back the missing barrier, but it was nowhere in sight. They turned their attention instead to a man wearing blue jeans lying on the ground. He must have had something to do with the barrier theft, or perhaps something worse, because two of the officers were stomping and beating him with their billy clubs. The Flag Man took one of his reinforced gloves and offered one to the man on the ground. When the cops started shoving the Flag Man, the guy lying on the marble got back up and escaped into the crowd. Flag Man fought back swinging the pole down onto one of the cops' helmets. The officer pushed the flag away with his club. The cop gave up on the battle when his partner tapped him on the back and pulled him back up the stairs. They were seriously surrounded and had no chance of detaining anyone in this environment. I followed behind them, utilizing the opening from their unsuccessful counteroffensive to finally reach my destination at the base of the tower.

Closer to the tower there were more Capitol officers with gas masks. They clutched the edge of the barrier with one hand and swung their batons wildly with the other. As I raised my left hand to stop recording, I realized that I still carried my skateboard. It might be more difficult to scale the tower with my board, so I stashed it at the base of the tower and started my climb. With both arms wrapped around the metal scaffold, I received a call from my mom. In the race to get to the Capitol I had forgotten it was her 69th birthday.

How did I end up in the middle of another riot? Why were the "Back the Blue" types brawling with the cops? What follows is a compilation of memories from sight, sound, smell, and touch, combined with direct quotes and details pulled from videos I recorded with a phone held just beneath eye level, so I simultaneously witnessed everything I recorded. I occasionally share mainstream media's mostly clueless interpretations of what I experienced firsthand. The inner dialogue is there too. Pardon me for the unsavory things my brain is about to share with you.

After what happened in Kenosha, I had an inkling that I must remember the important stuff, for the sake of someone who might want a perspective from someone who was there—when the red-hot MAGA rubber met the road of Joe Biden's establishment coalition, which was pot-holed but steadfast only on opposition to Trump and abstract campaign statements like "Build Back Better." While simultaneously accusing Trump for being reductive with things like "Build the Wall," the Biden camp was sitting behind literal walls and armed guards. That's not to say this was a problem of Democrats; the reader knows that Republicans ignored a porous immigration system for decades because illegals meant low wages and high profits for the corporate interests that be. In order to tell this story of the political right descending into the same street violence that I saw during the BLM protests, I gotta go to the beginning for me and for the country.

For me, my interest in politics began when George Bush was president, the second in a family dynasty that invaded Iraq two times. I didn't blame George Bush, he was just the dummy who numbly repeated the sins of his father, a father whose success was thanks to royal investments from Saudi Arabia. I was in my adolescence on that clement fall morning with the sun shining brightly. It ended with a waning moon that was growing darker over a world I thought was stable, but was actually feebler and eviler than my young American mind could surmise.

For our country, the story began with the Inauguration of America's most beloved Founding Father, in the same city where my youthful buoyancy collapsed.

ACKNOWLEDGEMENTS

It was a long road writing this book, especially given the last real thing I penned was a philosophy paper titled, "The Role Morality of Bartending" in 2012. I am a video guy and I can't write *good*. But thanks to the army of family, friends, former coworkers, and new friends, I finished a few books (Book II is on its way) in a mere three years! Thank you to my brothers, their significant others, my mom, and my dad up above. I was feeling around in the dark for a year until my cousin Bobby put me in touch with Anthony Swofford, aka the *Jarhead*. Without Swoff, I would never have had the courage to say *F you* to the big boys, start a publishing company, and let this Pigeon fly. Thank you to the other Jarheads who gave me the stubborn courage required to swim against the empty vessels bouncing on the surface of our discourse's angry sea: Geoff Ingersoll, Craig Grossi, Chad Robichaux, and Smedley Butler for teaching me that *War is a Racket*. I will throw in a thank you for an Air Force guy known as *Dragon*. Thank you to my editorial team: Anthony Swofford, my book boss K.D. Sullivan, Devin Murphy, and Ginni Smith and speed-reader Uncle Al. Major props to my art gang: Rodger Roundy, Sagnik Basu, Maria Johnson, Gigi, Anders. Thank you to my unofficial legal team: the Dans, Karl the Kat, Bela. Thank you to my official legal team: Brendan and Charles Glasser. Thank you to all the *Daily Caller* goofballs for having my back when the poo-poo hit the fan: Shelby, Jorge, Neil, Chad, Vince Coglianese, Megan, Hank, Annabel, Bastasch, Sydney, Caruso, Jon Brown, Thomas for letting me use the printer, Adele, Vince Shkreli, Kaylee, Sean Moody, riot Mary Poppins Grae Stafford, and the rest of the ViD SqUAd. Thanks to E. for taking those epic photos in Kenosha, the other E. for having my back on the riot trail, and the rest of the Riot Squad: Julio, @bgonthescene (Brendan Gutenschwager), Drew, Kalen, and the young intern Phillip for taking the peppy spray like a man. Thanks to all my friends who listened to me incessantly talk about this book at every wedding for three years: *The Bondies* (you know who you are), and I'm sorry for hijacking Gopher's wedding reception trying to get revenge on Murph. Thanks to my DC family: Harp, Rosie, Roach, Utah, Yoga Mike, Stan the Man, Pete B. Sr. and Jr., Dave D., Al, the GTown hockey boys who kept me young, and all the men's league bros on the Narcs who didn't kick me off the team despite wearing number 420 and being a useless player beyond blocking some shots. Thanks to my Hawaii bro, Bodhi. Thank you to Keanu and Swayze for demonstrating the duality of the American mind in the greatest movie of all time, *Point Break*, which provided the pseudonyms for this book. Thanks to the media folks: Ralph; Leo; 'Zo, formerly of Nebraska Ave.; Doug Goodstein; and David Padrusch, who gave me the break I needed when I was a freelancing, bartending bum wearing dusty khaki pants that had been cut at the knees; Paige Williams for telling the truth when it mattered most; Tuck; Emily Lynn; Matt Dornic; and Drew Griffin for setting the record straight on CNN, Rest In Peace. Thank you to Brad and my wife Isabela for saving me, to Bobby for being my first editor aside from my mom, and to the rest of the Graceway family (more on that in Book II).

REFERENCES
(in order of appearance)

Chapter 1

Thomas, Lowell. *Old Gimlet Eye: The Adventures of Smedley D Butler.* Farrar & Rinehart, 1933.

Krone, Seamus C. "Gimlet Eye Butler: America's Greatest Marine." *Stag* magazine VOL. 11. NO. 12., December 1960.

"Smedley D. Butler, A Register of His Papers" in the Archives Branch, Marine Corps University, 2011.

Chapter 2

Joesting, Edward. *KAUAI: The Separate Kingdom.* Kauai Museum, 1988.

Sides, Hampton. *The Wide Wide Sea: Imperial Ambition, First Contact and the Fateful Final Voyage of Captain James Cook.* Doubleday, 2024.

Freeman, Phillip. *St. Patrick of Ireland: A Biography.* Simon & Schuster, 2005.

Chapter 3

Meacham, John. *American Lion: Andrew Jackson in the White House.* Random House, 2008.

Brown, David S. *The First Populist: The Defiant Life of Andrew Jackson.* Simon & Schuster, 2022.

Library of Congress, Manuscript Division. *Index to the Andrew Jackson papers*. Washington, D.C.: Library of Congress, 1967. Pdf. Retrieved from the Library of Congress, <www.loc.gov/item/67060014/>.

Chapter 4
Beurge, David M. *Chief Seattle and the Town That Took His Name.* Sasquatch Books, 2021.

Kazin, Michael. *A Godly Hero: The Life of William Jennings Bryan.* Anchor, 2007.

Bryan, William Jennings. *The Memoirs of William Jennings Bryan.* United Publishers of America, 1925.

Bagley, Clarence B. *History of Seattle Volume 1.* Loschberg, Germany: Jazzybee Verlagm, 2017. Originally printed 1916.

Crain, Esther. *The Gilded Age in New York, 1870–1910.* Black Dog & Leventhal, 2016.

Best, Carmen. *Black in Blue: Lessons on Leadership, Breaking Barriers, and Racial Reconciliation.* Harper Collins Leadership, 2021.

Thomas, Janet. *The Battle in Seattle: The Story Behind and Beyond the WTO Demonstrations.* Fulcrum Publishing, 2000.

Chapter 5
Ackerman, Kenneth D. *Boss Tweed: The Rise and Fall of the Corrupt Pol Who Conceived the Soul of Modern New York.* Da Capo Press, 2005.

Adler, John, and Draper Hill. *Doomed by Cartoon: How Cartoonist Thomas Nast and* The New York Times *Brought down Boss Tweed and His Ring of Thieves.* Morgan James Publishing, 2008.

Mendelbaum, Seymour J. *Boss Tweed's New York (New Dimensions in History: Historical Cities)*. Ivan R. Dee, 1990.

Goodnow, Frank Johnson. *The Tweed ring in New York city*. London and New York: Macmillan & co, 1888. Pdf. https://www.loc.gov/item/17003665/.

Breen, Mathew P. *Thirty years of New York politics up-to-date*. New York: The author, 1889. Pdf. https://www.loc.gov/item/99004163/.

Carter, David. Stonewall: *The Riots That Sparked the Gay Revolution*. New York: St. Martin's Press, 2010.

Chapter 6
Abbott, Carl. *Portland in Three Centuries: The Place and the People*. Oregon State University Press, 2011.

Chandler, JD. *Hidden History of Portland, Oregon*. The History Press, 2013.

Haneckow, Dan. *Portland Then and Now*. Pavilion Books, 2017.

Ballestrem, Val C. *Lost Portland, Oregon*. The History Press, 2018.

Bottenberg, Ray. *Bridges of Portland*. Arcadia Publishing Library Editions, 2007.

Spencer, Judith. *The Yellow Journalism: The Press and America's Emergence as a World Power (Medill Visions of the American Press)*. Northwestern University Press, 2007.

Chapter 7
The History of Racine and Kenosha Counties, Wisconsin. Chicago, IL: Western Historical Company, 1879.

Neuenschwander, John A. *Kenosha County in the Twentieth Century: A Topical History*. Kenosha County Bicentennial Commission, 1976.

Doyle, John F., and Diane Doyle. *Kenosha on the Go (Images of Rail: Wisconsin)*. Arcadia Publishing, 2008.

Foster, Patrick. *Kenosha's Jeffery & Rambler Automobiles (Images of America)*. Arcadia Publishing, 2018.

Bader-Stein, and Lois Roepke. *Kenosha, 1835–1983: A Pictorial History*. Walsworth Pub Co., 1986.

ABOUT THE AUTHOR

Richie McGinniss is a former video director, semi-nonprofessional small wave surfer, and men's league hockey scrapper. He graduated from Georgetown University without honors, majoring in Middle Eastern History and minoring in Arabic and Philosophy. He started his career in media with an internship at Al-Jazeera Arabic, at MSNBC/NBC News DC as a production assistant, then a freelance videographer and bartender—emphasis on the latter—before landing a job as a video editor for Conservative Radio Host Mark Levin's new all-online show *LevinTV*.

McGinniss took a huge pay cut to take a new job running the ragtag video operation at an antiestablishment news website, *Daily Caller* (though the "respectable" media referred to the outlet as a tabloid or blog). As Paige Williams of *The New Yorker* wrote on McGinniss' role at *Daily Caller*, "he took the job because it offered him the opportunity to run his own video unit and because he believed that 'the special interests of corporate America' have 'led our media to forget about the common, individual American.'"

When the pandemic and subsequent civil unrest hit the shores of the U.S., McGinniss led a team of reporters through lawless zones across the country: DC, Seattle's "CHAZ," Portland, Kenosha, Minneapolis, Wauwatosa, the southern border, and Philadelphia, then back to DC for the 2020 election, Stop the Steal I, II, and III. His lifetime of surfing around the world and scrumming it in the corner on the ice came in handy when he embedded with and interviewed protesters/rioters of all creeds, all while enduring police beatings. Covering riots in Kenosha, Wisconsin, McGinniss witnessed Kyle Rittenhouse kill Joseph Rosenbaum, then testified as a key witness (and named victim) in the trial. Also recording the Capitol riot on January 6th, McGinniss has a firsthand understanding of how news events can be cannibalized and refashioned by the media. After 16 years he is still stuck in Washington, DC.

Made in United States
Troutdale, OR
11/07/2024

24525902R00266